BOMBS BURSTING IN AIR

BOMBS BURSTING IN AIR

MUSIC AND THE STATE

Edited by **Mat Callahan**

University Press of Mississippi / Jackson

The University Press of Mississippi is the scholarly publishing agency of
the Mississippi Institutions of Higher Learning: Alcorn State University,
Delta State University, Jackson State University, Mississippi State University,
Mississippi University for Women, Mississippi Valley State University,
University of Mississippi, and University of Southern Mississippi.

www.upress.state.ms.us

The University Press of Mississippi is a member
of the Association of University Presses.

Any discriminatory or derogatory language or hate speech regarding race,
ethnicity, religion, sex, gender, class, national origin, age, or disability
that has been retained or appears in elided form is in no way an endorsement
of the use of such language outside a scholarly context.

Copyright © 2025 by Mat Callahan
All rights reserved
Manufactured in the United States of America

∞

Publisher: University Press of Mississippi, Jackson, USA
Authorised GPSR Safety Representative: Easy Access System Europe -
Mustamäe tee 50, 10621 Tallinn, Estonia, *gpsr.requests@easproject.com*

Library of Congress Cataloging-in-Publication Data

Names: Callahan, Mathew, 1951– editor
Title: Bombs bursting in air : music and the state / edited by Mat
Callahan.
Description: Jackson : University Press of Mississippi, 2025. | Includes
bibliographical references and index.
Identifiers: LCCN 2025040555 (print) | LCCN 2025040556 (ebook) | ISBN
9781496859198 hardback | ISBN 9781496859204 trade paperback | ISBN
9781496859211 epub | ISBN 9781496859228 epub | ISBN 9781496859235 pdf |
ISBN 9781496859303 pdf
Subjects: LCSH: Music—United States—History and criticism | Popular
music—United States—History and criticism | Patriotic music—United
States—History and criticism | Nationalism in music | African
Americans—Music—History and criticism | American Federation of
Musicians—History
Classification: LCC ML200 .B65 2025 (print) | LCC ML200 (ebook) | DDC
780.973—dc23/eng/20250916
LC record available at https://lccn.loc.gov/2025040555
LC ebook record available at https://lccn.loc.gov/2025040556

British Library Cataloging-in-Publication Data available

CONTENTS

Preface. An Ancient Question..................................vii

Introduction. How Many Arms Has the State?..........................3
    Mat Callahan

Chapter 1. A Sonic Palimpsest: Replacement
as a Method of Suppression..35
    Mat Callahan

Chapter 2. "The Roads to Perdition": Lawrence Gellert
and Black Songs of Protest in the Cultural Front and Cold War..........61
    Steven Garabedian

Chapter 3. Curating Music: What Is Perpetuated and Why................97
    Franz Andres Morrissey

Chapter 4. *The Etude* Magazine and
Cultivating the American Musical Canon............................117
    Elissa Stroman

Chapter 5. Making a Racket: Inventing the Modern Music Business........141
    Jim Rogers

Chapter 6. The American Federation of Musicians: Becoming Invisible......167
    Dick Weissman

Chapter 7. All That Jazz: CIA, Voice of America,
and Jazz Diplomacy in the Early Cold War Years, 1955–1965.............194
    James E. Dillard

Chapter 8. Music as Torture / Music as Weapon 217
  Suzanne G. Cusick

Chapter 9. Maintaining a Racket: How the Contemporary
Music Business Keeps On Keepin' On 233
  Jim Rogers

Chapter 10. "The Way We Put an End to War": Song and War 265
  Franz Andres Morrissey and Britta Sweers

Chapter 11. "It Don't Make Sense": Willie Dixon,
the Blues, War, and Peace 300
  Steven Garabedian

Chapter 12. Compared to What? Representing
and Misrepresenting American Music 322
  Mat Callahan

Summary Reflections. On Responsibility, Academia,
and Asking Questions 344
  Britta Sweers

About the Contributors 361

Index 365

PREFACE
An Ancient Question

Bombs Bursting in Air will explore the role of music in the history of the United States. Contributions from historians, musicians, and musicologists will exhume music that has been forgotten or deliberately buried while drawing comparison with what has been promoted as "American Music" by the academy, the music industry, and journalism as well as uses made of this music by the US government. This study, however, is conducted within a broader context.

The relationship between music and the state has been a subject of controversy for at least 2,500 years. The oft-quoted passage from Plato's *Republic* that "the musical modes are never changed without changes in the most basic of the City's laws" not only underscores the importance of music in general but warns of music's ability to affect how society is governed. The state must therefore employ music to serve its ends while at the same time guarding against the lawlessness music is capable of introducing. While the present volume is primarily focused on American music and the American state, the relationship between the two can best be understood as contradictory or conflicted in much the way Plato described. This is evident in the concerns expressed by critics, educators, religious leaders, and politicians to the "Jazz Problem" in the first decades of the twentieth century. Specific references to Plato's statement began appearing with some frequency in the 1960s, for example in the work of poet Allen Ginsberg, in a song by a rock band, the Fugs, and in the writing of music critic Ralph J. Gleason. Ginsberg wrote an essay titled "When the Mode of the Music Changes, the Walls of the City Shake" (1961); the Fugs released a song, "When the Mode of Music Changes" (1968); and Gleason used the same Plato reference in an essay in *The American Scholar* in 1967.

In hindsight, this is not surprising given the controversy that erupted with the appearance of rock 'n' roll along with the teenager, juvenile delinquency, rebels without causes, and blackboard jungles. Though in most respects—especially its overt racism—the rock 'n' roll controversy resembled the outrage expressed earlier regarding jazz, it seemed in the 1960s that Plato's prediction was even more pertinent. Though the word *state* was not often used, for reasons peculiar to the United States, it was replaced by others such as "the Establishment," "the Powers That Be," or most ubiquitously, "the System." Nomenclature notwithstanding, the basic fact is that music was fomenting social unrest that threatened the established order. Interestingly, the same reference to Plato was made by historian Michael Denning in a recent book, *Noise Uprising: The Audiopolitics of a World Musical Revolution* (2015). Plato was again referenced, albeit using another quote from the *Republic*, in another recent book, *Dangerous Melodies* by Jonathan Rosenberg (2020). And even more recently, Plato's statement provided the epigraph opening Maria Cristina Fava's *Art Music Activism* (2024). The subject, it seems, cannot be avoided.

It can, however, be questioned. In the case of jazz and rock 'n' roll, the sudden emergence and widespread popularity of two "genres" of music were debated furiously. Yet, notwithstanding some hysterical attempts at suppression, the ultimate result was that jazz and rock 'n' roll were absorbed into the melting pot of American music and ultimately used to propagandize for the American state. Moreover, we have statements from leading theorists of music and its political purposes that indicate that Plato was wrong. For example,

> No one had any idea what would be the nature of revolutionary music, you see, and it took me a long time after this to realize that there's no such thing as revolutionary music. Music doesn't take any cognizance of the dichotomy between what is revolutionary and what is not revolutionary. To change musical technique is not revolutionary, outside of music. I considered myself a musical revolutionist simply by reversing old technical devices, such as the preparation of consonance. Instead of preparing a dissonance and resolving a dissonance, I turned it upside down, and I prepared a consonance. My first species of counterpoint was all dissonance. Well, that was musically revolutionary, but it had no significance socially. (Seeger quoted in David Dunaway, "Charles Seeger and Carl Sands: The Composers' Collective Years," *Ethnomusicology* 24, no. 2 [May 1980]: 165. Interview with Seeger took place in April 1976)

One might take this argument a step further and postulate that what aroused the ire of authorities were the texts of songs and uses to which songs were put, for example, in rallies, strikes, and other sites of conflict rather than the music accompanying those texts. This is often how critics and historians have evaluated the social role of music referring almost exclusively to the titles and lyrics of songs or to the stated intentions of musicians and composers and not the music itself. From Joe Hill to Ella May Wiggins, from Paul Robeson to Harry Belafonte, from Nina Simone to John Lennon, it wasn't the music, it was the words and the political associations of the musicians that brought down the repressive apparatus of the state. It might be argued that music, especially instrumental music, has only stirred controversy in particular cases where new styles emerged that for fairly obvious reasons challenged social mores such as those pertaining to sex, miscegenation (race-mixing), alcohol or drug use, and dancing. These controversies were prevalent in the case of jazz and rock 'n' roll and later in the case of rap or hip hop. And in all these instances there was suppression, banning and burning of recordings, arrest and imprisonment of musicians for violating laws governing lewd and lascivious conduct and other antisocial behavior.

None of this resolves the larger issue, however, and for two reasons. First, because even if Charles Seeger was correct and there are no musical modes that, in and of themselves, can threaten a modern state (as opposed to Plato's Athens), there remains the fundamental fact that music is an activity and not a product. Making music, a participatory process involving communities of ordinary people not confined to professionals, let alone stars, is by its nature a social gathering that can, under certain circumstances, pose a threat to the powers that be.

Conversely, there is the role music plays in the maintenance of the state which has a twofold character. On the one hand, it is a recognition by the authorities that music is a necessary component of society the state cannot do without. On the other hand, when the state's interests form the criteria for what serves best and what does not, it follows that certain characteristics—musically and functionally—will preponderate and these will, moreover, be known to all, as in the case of national anthems, patriotic songs, and soundtracks for propaganda films or advertisement for military recruiting.

Taken together, we can see how the state seizes upon and promotes music that it needs while marginalizing or suppressing that which it opposes. This includes the lyrics, of course, but much more, it exalts and rewards aesthetics and practices that uphold the state's claims while marginalizing and punishing aesthetics and practices that do not. The threat that was posed by music can therefore be understood not by a narrow, formal criteria of particular modes, scales, rhythms, or compositions but by the apprehension of music-making practices, the functions music performs in service of other social ends, and the extent to which these practices and functions criticize or challenge the authority of the state and all its apparatuses, including the academy, the music industry, and journalism. Here it is important to explore the error Charles Seeger admits he made as well as those made by others in a similar vein.

To begin with, a class distinction has to be made between intellectuals and working people. It is self-evident that most theorists of music come from the intelligentsia while a vast array of music arises from the working classes. It is not surprising that there would be a discrepancy between the practice of researching and theorizing about music and the practice of making music itself. Research, writing, and theorizing require resources that the great majority of people have little or no access to. At the same time, the essential tools of music reside in the human body and are available to everyone; indeed, they are used by vast numbers of otherwise uneducated people in the activity called music-making.

This class distinction has a direct bearing on politics, as in who decides and directs society, not because "everything is political" but because music and music-making forever elude the clutches of power, politics, authority, and the state. Music-making can, and often does, provide a form of social organization and coordinated effort that is the envy of the state. Examples abound: community choruses, summer music camps, fiddlers' conventions, and myriad other gatherings where music-making is the collective activity that activates collectivity.

In this process, music's ability to convey morals, aesthetics and history is ever present. Woven into the fabric of the melodies, rhythms, and techniques employed is an enriching experience that is both timeless and immediate. The only way the state can compete with this aspect of music-making is to co-opt or suppress, to appropriate or regulate, and, ultimately, to exalt celebrity while enclosing the commons that music-making creates.

This broad framework should facilitate a more comprehensive appraisal of the musical and historical record. Foregrounding the relationship between music and state overcomes the limits set by genre or style, indeed, by any particular formal or cultural characteristics of music, focusing instead on the universality within the appearance of things. The attention paid to American music and the American state should not, in any case, be viewed as nationalistic or "exceptionalist." Instead, this study aims to put the music of one country into a conversation, a dialog of mutual appreciation and respect, with the countries and peoples of the world.

BOMBS BURSTING IN AIR

INTRODUCTION
How Many Arms Has the State?

Mat Callahan

> Music is almost as dangerous as gunpowder; and, it may be, requires looking after as much as the press or the mint.
> —Jeremy Collier, *A Short View of the Immorality and Profaneness of the English Stage* (1688)

My generation had a special relationship to music. The demographic bulge known as the "Baby Boom" elevated music to preeminence among the arts, making it, to paraphrase Shelley, "the unacknowledged legislator of the world." Long seen as a *herald* of change,[1] music now became an *instrument* of change, not only singing the praises of a new and better world, but acting as a means of bringing that world into being. As Tom Johnston of the Doobie Brothers and writer of their hit "Listen to the Music" put it in an interview many years later:

> It was all based around this somewhat Utopian view of the world. The idea was that music would lift man up to a higher plane, and that world leaders, if they were able to sit down on some big grassy knoll where the sun was shining and hear music—such as the type I was playing—would figure out that everybody had more in common than they had not in common, and it was certainly not worth getting in such a bad state of affairs about. Everybody in the world would therefore benefit from this point of view. Just basically that music would make everything better. And of course I've since kind of realized it doesn't work that way.[2]

Latter-day mea culpa notwithstanding, Johnston's view was repeated often, from diverse perspectives, constituting a consensus, at least among the young. From Albert Ayler calling music "the healing force of the universe" to Fela Kuti calling music "the weapon of the future" to Joni Mitchell singing of "Woodstock Nation" with its "half a million strong" engaged in "song and celebration," it was understood by everyone that music was the voice to which a generation not only listened but through which it spoke. Its purpose, furthermore, was to change the world.

The slogans and the fanfare were supported by the fact that music demonstrated its transformative power in concrete, experiential terms. The festival came to characterize social gathering galvanized by music's oracular presence. But this new kind of festival bore scant resemblance to the folk or jazz festival of the preceding period wherein audiences came to listen to outstanding examples of a particular style or genre. Now the festival appeared in its ancient, precapitalist form. Contrary to the conventional concert at which a seated audience listens more or less reverently to a presentation by extraordinary individuals, the ancient festival only comes about through the active participation of the community in a public performance *of* itself *for* itself. This performance was encouraged and supported by musicians but, ultimately, *festival* meant the audience was the show. Participants came together to celebrate themselves as a community and not to worship at the feet of celebrities. As producer David Rubinson put it: "It wasn't the headliners who drew people to the Fillmore, it was the experience."[3] Indeed, music, for a brief period—approximately 1965 to 1975—was viewed as music: a universal expression of humanity, not as a certain type or style, be it classical, jazz, folk, or rock.

Breaking the grip of genres, fads, and hierarchies of high- and lowbrow posed a challenge to the ways music had been codified, segregated, ranked, and marketed at least since the advent of the modern music industry in the late nineteenth century. Exalting music and musicians as oracles of truth threatened the academics, critics, and salesmen who acted as guardians of moral values and arbiters of taste. But this embrace of music went further still as it directly challenged the state as the state is usually understood: the police, courts, and government agencies who regulate the public performance of music. And, yes, music is strictly regulated in the land of the free.

Not only are there noise ordinances and limitations on amplification but there are age restrictions, curfews, and licenses required for dancing, sale of alcohol, public gathering, and so forth. Prior to the 1960s, rock 'n' roll[4] was available to the teenager[5] only in recorded form (radio, television, jukeboxes, and records) or in closely monitored concerts at high schools, state fairs, sock-hops, and in packaged shows where a dozen or more acts would perform their hits for fifteen to thirty minutes at arenas used for sporting events, industrial trade shows, or cattle auctions. Dancing was carefully chaperoned to prevent lewd and lascivious display and to maintain racial segregation.[6] (Nightclubs were legally restricted to adults while coffeehouses were most often situated near college campuses and catered to students and faculty—not teenagers; thus the musical fare tended to be jazz in nightclubs, folk in coffeehouses.) The challenge therefore posed by "dance-concerts" at the Fillmore Auditorium, the Avalon Ballroom, and free concerts in the park had greater impact than mere "dance crazes" such as the Twist or the Jerk, which had been key to the marketing of rock 'n' roll. The "dance-concert" and free outdoor concert formats effectively circumvented all the legal limits imposed by the state to maintain control over the public performance of music.

At the time, however, few participants, if any, referred to the state by that name, preferring instead to designate their adversary as "the system." The system was an all-encompassing term including the government, of course, but also diverse institutions be they religious, educational, commercial, or artistic. Authority, in general, was being challenged because it had obviously made a mess of things and had to be swept away. Conventional political struggle continued, mounted first by what remained of the labor movement of the prewar, pre-McCarthyite period, carried forward by the civil rights movement and then by the burgeoning antiwar movement. Marches, boycotts (such as the United Farmworkers grape boycott), sit-ins to desegregate lunch counters, and teach-ins to mobilize students, directly appealed to and involved youth. As conflict intensified, influence broadened beyond membership in groups such as the Student Nonviolent Coordinating Committee (SNCC), Students for a Democratic Society (SDS), or the Free Speech Movement (FSM). By the mid-1960s the appellation most often used by participants and observers was simply "the movement."

This widespread opposition, as much an attitude as a defined program, would eventually be shared by millions of young people unaffiliated with any organization or preexisting social formation, and would be identified by Theodore Roszak in a seminal book, *The Making of a Counter Culture* (1969). In his highly influential study—which gave us the word *counterculture*—Roszak explicitly describes the phenomenon as "a major lever of radical social change"[7] and not, as has often been portrayed, a gaggle of middle-class brats, pampered by permissive, liberal parents, descending one summer on San Francisco.

Along with "the system" and "the movement," two other terms were in such common use as to be emblematic of an era: "consciousness" and "liberation." Consciousness, either expanding or raising it, became the touchtone of daily life, a quest or journey upon which all were bound, while liberation was the goal toward which the movement was directed. The differences between politics—including revolutionary politics—and "dropping out," between the New Left and the counterculture, might be blurry or antagonistic, but there was nonetheless a shared antipathy with the oppressive forces painfully visible in the jungles of Vietnam or the streets and schools of the United States. As comprehensive and sweeping as these terms were, participants often used them indiscriminately to designate affiliation, with the "freaks," for example, or with Black and Third World liberation, as opposed to a theoretical or programmatic position. Few had a nuanced view of the mechanisms by which the system operated. Indeed, few saw the interconnections, the mutual interdependence, of key institutions with which they had regular contact, in particular the academy, the music industry, and journalism. Even though there was deep-seated mistrust of all three institutions, and even though there was a growing awareness on the part of millions that the system was the enemy that had to be done away with, it was nonetheless unclear how the state was connected with educational, commercial, and news institutions.[8]

Many, for example, assumed that commercial pop and authentic folk came from different sources and these sources were in conflict. Furthermore, Bob Dylan, the Beatles, and Aretha Franklin were all on major labels, so that couldn't be all bad, could it? When Columbia Records launched a notorious ad campaign under the heading "The Man Can't Bust Our Music," it was widely ridiculed, but that did not lead to a boycott of Columbia or major labels. Indeed, when Marty Balin of the Jefferson Airplane was signing with RCA Victor, he realized he was "working for the enemy,"[9] but that didn't stop him from signing. The ambivalence is typical of the era and its many unresolved contradictions.

Upon reflection, however, I think it likely that many of my generation would now recognize that at least some of those unresolved contradictions can be explained by what connects the academy, the music business, and journalism and that these connections are mutually reinforcing rather than antagonistic. Though none of us used the term, an "unholy trinity" aptly describes this cluster of authorities against which we were rebelling.

THE ACADEMY

For example, the academy, as in folklore studies or musicology, was represented by the proselytizing of American folk music in the postwar period. The folk music revival included legendary figures like Guthrie, Robeson, and Seeger, the newly famous like Baez and Dylan, as well as the soon to be electrified like the Chambers Brothers and Mother McCree's Uptown Jug Champions (who evolved into the Grateful Dead). "American Folk Music" (note the capitalized "F") was promoted by a host of scholars, among whom were Alan Lomax and Charles Seeger, dedicated to the preservation of music that arose prior to the urbanization and industrialization of America. Far beyond the borders of the United States, *folk music* came to mean American Folk Music, so closely was it identified with Appalachia and the antebellum South (the reasons for this will be explored in subsequent chapters).

The folk music revival was furthermore aligned with the civil rights movement and thus established a relationship between music and politics that both prefigured and laid the basis for a more general alignment of music with revolution in the decades to follow. This alignment was not an accident. The Cold War, McCarthyism, and the House Un-American Activities Committee made music a target of repression. Ironically, the crushing of the Communist Party USA occurred at the same time the Weavers were topping the charts with "Good Night Irene." The Weavers would be blackballed and their careers destroyed, but not before the folk revival was well underway. This was due in part to the work of the aforementioned Alan Lomax and Charles Seeger, who were not only highly qualified folklorists and musicologists but communists. What they saw was not "folk music" in the abstract but proletarian music in the concrete. They not only sought to preserve in accordance with standards set by their forebears in the song-collecting field (such as John Lomax, Alan's conservative father) but to popularize the music of working-class America in contradistinction to that of bourgeois America. This episode is well-documented in Richard and Joanne Reuss's book *American Folk Music and Left Wing Politics, 1927–1957* (2000). The Reusses' effort cuts through Red Scare propaganda to contextualize and explain what was, in fact, a major trend in popular American music.

Nonetheless, in spite of this duality of preservation and social change in the folk music revival, the conservatism inherent in a practice codified by the likes of Francis Child, Cecil Sharp, and William Wells Newell was decisive in making anathema not only commercial "pop" songs, but the rhythm and amplitude of drums and electric guitars. It posited a pristine purity that never existed and cannot exist, especially in a country such as the United States. Yet such abstract criteria dominated the curation of vernacular music and the construction of a canon.[10]

The legendary apostasy of Bob Dylan, while largely misrepresented in subsequent years, is nevertheless symptomatic of the resulting controversy and disillusionment of a generation. This not only led to the rejection of academic dogma as to what constituted "folk" music but it encouraged the development of new blends and combinations that were living examples of what breaking certain rules could produce. By the time Beatlemania exploded, the crisis was already terminal. The bonds were broken and, though order would later be restored, it was nonetheless a momentous victory for music, musicians, and the public at large.

THE MUSIC INDUSTRY

Confrontation with the music industry was simultaneous and equally effective. The breakdown of stylistic categories, the elimination of time limits for songs (set originally by shellac 78s and later by radio formats), the integration not only of bands but of music itself, in hybrid forms that could not be segregated as white or Black or Latin, all took place in defiance of the authority of producers and A&R men,[11] their corporate employers, and indeed, the very standards and mores set by an outmoded business model. Lawrence Welk and Mitch Miller were cast into the dustbin of history and a musical renaissance ensued. Not surprisingly, it was a group formerly aligned with both the folk music revival and the civil rights movement that made the breakthrough. The Chambers Brothers with their song "Time Has Come Today" (1966) exemplified all the foregoing: their song was six minutes and five seconds long, and it was rejected by Columbia Records because it was deemed a "white" song and thus could not be performed by a Black group although it posed a vibrant alternative to "We Shall Overcome" with that song's plaintive conclusion, "someday."

For a few short years, the industry was thrown into turmoil. Control of music production in both live and recorded form was wrested from the grip of established promoters and producers, agents and broadcasters. To a large extent, musicians and other artists (especially poster artists) seized those means and charted a different course. Famous festivals such as Monterey Pop (1967) and Woodstock (1969) highlight the ensuing conflict. Contrary to their rosy, anodyne portrayal in the decades that followed, the most significant festivals were a battlefield of clashing interests and outlooks—especially between key artists (such as the bands from San Francisco) and corporate executives and concert promoters. A detailed account is beyond the scope of this introduction but suffice it to say that relations between musicians and the music industry became increasingly antagonistic. Producer David Rubinson summarized the prevalent attitude among musicians: "It was a crusade—not only to change the world but to change the grownups. Change the way they looked at things, change the results of how they looked at things—it had to change, it was not sustainable."[12]

In an apparent paradox, the music industry was enjoying record profits. More records and concert tickets were being sold than ever before in history.[13] Indeed, these figures were often referred to as a "victory" since it proved that "The Kids Are Alright" and the parents didn't get it. The paradox is explained, however, when one considers that the stakes were higher than those narrowly defined by business. Parallel with what happened with "folk" and the doctrinaire criteria applied by academic experts, there was a wholesale rejection of music as entertainment, as a disposable commodity little different from soda pop. So ubiquitous was this attitude that commentators took to quoting Plato: "The musical modes are never changed without changes in the most important of a City's laws."[14] In short, against a backdrop of massive opposition to the Vietnam War and in support of Black and Third World liberation, music was viewed as a threat to the established order.

Subsequent histories have often missed this by focusing exclusively on the lyrics to songs and the intentions of musicians. This obscures the more significant fact that music itself forced the confrontation with authority because it asserted its significance as more than mere accompaniment. While music certainly does accompany poetry, dancing, or theatrical presentation, it is not confined to that role. Fundamentally, music is a socially binding agent capable of mobilizing diverse populations. Music, moreover, does not need an "industry" to do this. It does not need words to explain it or "stars" to draw attention to it. If proof is needed, it is given by the immense popularity enjoyed by jazz at the very moment industry hype was claiming this was a "rock revolution." To limit our attention to rock is to miss the main event.

JOURNALISM

As for journalism, there were several streams that flowed together in ways that challenged corporate media, its music critics, and its standards of judgment. First, there was the vast proliferation of alternative or underground newspapers, which was a result of a mass rejection of mainstream newspapers, radio, and television. The grip on the popular imagination was shaken. Young people ridiculed the posturing and pontificating of public figures who were obviously lying while implementing policies of war and oppression at home and abroad. The underground press, furthermore, duly acknowledged the importance of music in changing the world. This is evident in the regular reference to benefit concerts or, alternatively, to the repression directed at musicians by the police.[15]

Second, there was the birth of free-form radio which, of course, depended upon music programming to attract listeners but did so in ways that violated every norm established by governing authorities and the music industry. This included deejays playing what they wanted to, not what station managers told them to. Playlists featured sequences such as Sun Ra followed by Ravi Shankar, followed by Country Joe and the Fish, followed by Terry Riley, followed by Sly and the Family Stone. Not only did this celebrate a view of music radically at odds with prevailing norms, it challenged the legitimacy of those institutions that had established such norms. Criteria used to distinguish high from low in art and music were challenged. But so was crass commercialism. Instead, beauty was celebrated as a quality of human being, neither a dead butterfly to be examined under glass nor a treacly treat to be consumed and disposed of. Rigid definitions of "correct" interpretation or "authentic" music were rejected and replaced by the participatory aspects of music making—an activity and not a product. Simultaneously, the carefully guarded boundaries erected to specify and separate consumers as, for example, rural farmers, urban Blacks, middle-class white women, and above all, the newly invented category of "teenager," were cast aside and in their place was put an embrace of sharing. Sharing the gifts of creativity and reciprocity itself: this is what music presented and represented in daily life.[16]

Needless to say, this couldn't last. Such a naive and altruistic view of music would eventually crash upon the rocks of a reality it had tried to change. The system reestablished its dominance and has, as a result, written its own history of the period. It is now customary to view with either outright disdain or condescending paternalism the folly of a generation and its childish (or dangerous) utopian fantasies. In an epitaph to the sixties written while the body was still warm, *Rolling Stone's Illustrated History of Rock and Roll* (1976) began:

> At the outset, rock 'n' roll was a *succés de scandale*, an outrage to an older generation's aesthetic and sexual tastes. With the Beatles, it became fashionable to value rock, not simply as an affront, but also as a calculated political gesture, protesting the rigidities of the prevailing culture. In both eras, rebellion (whether repudiated or admired) was the byword. Today, on the other hand, rock is first and foremost a member in good standing of the American entertainment industry, welcome in Las Vegas and Hollywood, on the screen and over the air, in homes and theaters, despite the glum warnings of Reverend Boykin. Rock gossip sells newspapers; rock concerts pack stadiums; rock records dominate the radio. No one much worries about artistic respectability anymore, and the question of political commitment has died a quiet death.[17]

While this statement contains more wishful thinking than fact or analysis, the elements of a set are all present: the cult of adolescence and sexuality (biological as opposed to sociological categories such as classes, nations, or conquest of political power), rebellion as "cultural" or "political gesture" (as opposed to revolution, the overthrow of governments), transgression as narcissistic consumerism (as opposed to collective acts of defiance), the invincible might of the "entertainment industry" (as opposed to the remarkable fact that an alternative had in fact existed only a short time before), and the sighing, wistful resignation at the "quiet death" of "political commitment." This is the epitaph Jann Wenner always wanted to write (although Jim Miller actually wrote it). Wenner's self-congratulatory "I told you so" summarizes the "party line," as it were, that has been enshrined in institutions like the Rock and Roll Hall of Fame and "rock history" courses ever since. Yet, it is not true, and when compared to the clarion call made by William Blake almost two hundred years earlier (and quoted by Theodor Roszak in *The Making of a Counter Culture*), we can compare not only fact and fiction, but the visionary and the blind. William Blake:

Art Degraded, Imagination Denied: War Governed the Nations
Rouse up, O Young Men of the New Age! Set your foreheads against the ignorant hirelings! For we have hirelings in the Camp, the Court, and the University, who would, if they could, for ever depress mental, and prolong corporeal war.[18]

The fact remains that the revolutions of the sixties did change the world in remarkable and irreversible ways. On the one hand, these revolutions were defeated. Acknowledging that defeat is crucial to understanding both the events themselves as well as their consequences, felt to this day. On the other hand, especially in terms of music, revolution exposed the fraudulence of claims made by capitalism and its mouthpieces and, most importantly, left an indelible record: the most vital music was made, to a large extent, in defiance of the authorities and in rivalry with the state.

MUSIC'S RIVALRY WITH THE STATE

This last point needs elaboration. Kenyan novelist and revolutionary Ngũgĩ Wa Thiong'o theorized the rivalry between art and the state, particularly as it manifested in Africa in the decades following decolonization. Ngũgĩ eloquently characterized this rivalry, writing:

the struggle between arts and the state can best be seen in performance in general and in the battle over performance space in particular. Performance is representation of being, the coming to be, and the ceasing to be of processes in nature, human society and thought. If before the emergence of the state the domain of culture embodied the desirable and the undesirable in the realm of values, this was expressed through performance. The community learnt and passed on its moral codes and aesthetic judgments through narratives, dances, theater, rituals, music, games and sports. With the emergence of the state, the artist and the state became not only rivals in articulating the laws, moral or formal, that regulate life in society, but also rivals in determining the manner and circumstances of their delivery.[19]

Ngũgĩ's insight explains both how music could become such a social force in a revolutionary period and the motives, indeed the necessity, for the state to reassert its control over music production and distribution as a crucial part of reasserting control over society as a whole. This bears upon the role of the aforementioned "unholy trinity" since the academy, the music industry, and journalism are arms of the state. There is a pretense of independence. We are led to believe that in liberal democracies such as the United States, there is limited government, freedom of speech and assembly, guaranteed rights, and so forth. But this pretense conceals the intimate relations between the regents of universities, the boards of directors of industrial and commercial firms and the owners and editors of news outlets. It is self-inflicted blindness to ignore the interdependence of the state, as government, and these mutually reinforcing institutions which merely reflect a division of labor, not of interest, much less of rivalry or opposition of the sort Ngũgĩ describes (and will be explored further, below). Indeed, as subsequent chapters will show, it was once stated openly that the purpose of these institutions was patriotic, to serve the state, to uphold America as a new kind of country and to extol its virtues as a beacon for all the world's oppressed (witness the Statue of Liberty).[20]

FROM CIVIL WAR TO CIVIL RIGHTS

It is now evident, from the remove of half a century, that the storms of the sixties were the culmination of a much longer sequence. The civil rights movement, the women's movement, and to a largely unacknowledged extent the labor movement all trace their origins to the abolitionist movement, the Civil War, and Reconstruction. The struggle of formerly enslaved people and women for their rights as citizens accompanied a great upsurge in the struggle of labor against capital, threatening to transform society at its economic and political roots. This could not be endured with equanimity by the ruling elites of the victorious Union. It had to be stopped.

The reactionary wave that followed the defeat of Reconstruction was brilliantly summarized by W. E. B. Du Bois in his 1935 classic, *Black Reconstruction*:

> God wept; but that mattered little to an unbelieving age; what mattered most was that the world wept and still is weeping and blind with tears and blood. For there began to rise in America in 1876 a new capitalism and a new enslavement of labor. Home labor in cultured lands, appeased and misled by a ballot whose power the dictatorship of vast capital strictly curtailed, was bribed by high wage and political office to unite in an exploitation of white, yellow, brown and black labor, in lesser lands and "breeds without the law." Especially workers of the New World, folks who were American and for whom America was, became ashamed of their destiny. Sons of ditch-diggers aspired to be spawn of bastard kings and thieving aristocrats rather than of rough-handed children of dirt and toil. The immense profit from this new exploitation and world-wide commerce enabled a guild of millionaires to engage the greatest engineers, the wisest men of science, as well as pay high wage to the more intelligent labor and at the same time to have left enough surplus to make more thorough the dictatorship of capital over the state and over the popular vote, not only in Europe and America but in Asia and Africa.
>
> The world wept because within the exploiting group of New World masters, greed and jealousy became so fierce that they fought for trade and markets and materials and slaves all over the world until at last in 1914 the world flamed in war. The fantastic structure fell, leaving grotesque Profits and Poverty, Plenty and Starvation, Empire and Democracy, staring at each other across World Depression. And the rebuilding, whether it comes now or a century later, will and must go back to the basic principles of Reconstruction in the United States during 1867–1876—Land, Light and Leading for slaves black, brown, yellow and white, under a dictatorship of the proletariat.[21]

These words are prophetic. They are also vehemently contested. "The basic principles of Reconstruction in the United States in 1867–1876" would reassert themselves in the 1930s and again in the 1960s and, each time, would meet a similar fate. Great advances were followed by the Restoration of Imperial Command. Fundamentally, this was due to the superior force commanded by the state, which cannot be discounted even as it is resisted.

At the same time, it must be acknowledged that these struggles always had both reformist and revolutionary components. All along there were those who wanted the United States to live up to the promise of its founding documents, including those amendments added as a result of the Civil War (13th, 14th and 15th Amendments). All along there were those who saw that it was capitalism and its state that had to be overthrown if a more just social order was ever to be established. This tension among the people was exploited by many means but it was the special role of the "unholy trinity" to, on the one hand, exalt the populace as sovereign in a democratic republic, and on the other hand to divide the populace into sections that could be pitted against one another. At first, white, property-owning males, *were* the populace—or the only ones who counted—and in its formative years, the "unholy trinity" reflected that, devoting almost all its attention to the concerns, musical and otherwise, of white, propertied males. This gave way, in subsequent waves, to greater and greater inclusion, culminating in women's suffrage (1920) and the Voting Rights Act of 1965.

Corresponding to these political developments were, not surprisingly, changes in the collection of folk songs, the marketing of music, and the valorization of the process in the press. Indeed, every large-scale social movement has been met not only by police, courts, and legislation but by redefinition of the "folk" and the "authentic" along with marketing strategies directed at hitherto ignored populations. In the chapters that follow, examples of this pattern will be given. The point here is to note the relation of necessity that existed from the founding of the republic. On the one hand the folksong collector used the rubric of precapitalist utopias, Rousseauian visions of equality, and simplicity in harmony with nature, which needed to be preserved from the steam engines of capitalism. On the other hand, the music industry used the latest novelties, technical and musical, to transform a restless, amorphous mass into a market. In both cases the fundamental selling points or organizing principles were that it was popular and it was American and that the discerning consumer would accept no substitute.[22]

This, in turn, was what I came face to face with in researching three musico-historical projects, *James Connolly's Songs of Freedom*, *Working Class Heroes*, and *Songs of Slavery and Emancipation*. In each case, the record had been significantly altered to exclude facts, events, organizations, and individuals that played a crucial role in the shaping of history. In the case of Connolly, it was the discovery, not only of a songbook, *Songs of Freedom*, but the fact that that songbook had lain, virtually unseen, in the Dublin National Library for a hundred years. This, despite the fact that Connolly was an important historical figure, a national hero in Ireland to this day, and that a quote from that very songbook was widely circulated:

> No revolutionary movement is complete without its poetical expression. If such a movement has caught hold of the imagination of the masses, they will seek a vent in song for the aspirations, the fears and hopes, the loves and hatreds engendered by the struggle. Until the movement is marked by the joyous, defiant, singing of revolutionary songs, it lacks one of the distinctive marks of a popular revolutionary movement, it is the dogma of a few, and not the faith of the multitude.[23]

Indeed, I had often read that quote as it was, and still is, painted on the wall of the Starry Plough, an Irish nightclub in Berkeley, California.

But who knew that *Songs of Freedom* was published in New York and that Connolly's effort was explicitly directed at the American working class? Who knew that this songbook was actually used in rallies and demonstrations of workers, then waging the battles that had brought the world May Day and would soon thereafter bring us International Women's Day? Who knew or even suspected that the music Connolly chose to accompany his lyrics was not "traditional," according to folkloric criteria? Connolly chose tunes or airs that suited the spirit of the text but, above all, were already popular among workers. There were traditional melodies such as "Clare's Dragoons" and "The Boys of Wexford" but there were also "pop" hits like "Love's Young Dream" and "The Holy City" along with revolutionary anthems from France (The Marseillaise) and Germany (Auf Socialisten).

The contrast is stark. While Connolly proudly and publicly declared his purpose, the song collectors and song-pluggers concealed theirs. One announced the goal of human freedom, yet to be achieved, the other donned the cloak of a human freedom said to have already been achieved. One saw music as a means to inspire resistance to oppression; the other saw music as a means to inspire obedience to authority. One saw music as providing nourishment for everyone, the other saw music as a means to acquiring prestige and wealth for a few. In short, *Songs of Freedom* blew a large hole in the claims of both the academic collector and the purveyor of musical product.

In the case of *Working Class Heroes*, it was again the reviewing of a songbook, composed in 1941 but only published in 1967, that led to similar conclusions. *Hard Hitting Songs for Hard-Hit People* was the work of Alan Lomax, Woody Guthrie, and Pete Seeger with an introduction by Nobel Laureate John Steinbeck. How could a book containing 196 songs written mainly by workers engaged in historically important struggles be consigned to oblivion? How could one ignore the fact that the lyrics were uniformly militant and that their composers were not "outside agitators" but native to the communities and the class they represented? How, furthermore, could heroic figures like Ella May Wiggins, Sarah Ogan Gunning, and John Handcox be erased from history by song collectors, folklorists, and musicologists at precisely the moment when the Coen brothers' film *Oh, Brother Where Art Thou?* was popularizing the same period, region, and much of the same music? How could this glaring misrepresentation be reconciled with the purported objectivity and impartiality of the press that was covering the film and its enthusiastically received soundtrack? Was it that the "experts" didn't know? Hadn't done their homework? The authors of the songbook—Lomax, Guthrie, and Seeger—were world famous. Seeger had recently died, bringing further acclaim to his life and work. It is impossible to believe that mere ignorance was responsible for the neglect of such an important document.

On the contrary, here, in all its turpitude, was the work of the "unholy trinity" as an arm of the state. Here in all its glory was the musical, lyrical and human rebuttal.

Then, even before finishing *Working Class Heroes*, another line of inquiry opened up.

> Arise! Arise! shake off your chains
> Your cause is just, so Heaven ordains
> to you shall Freedom be proclaimed.

These words leapt off the page of a pamphlet I discovered in an antiquarian bookstore. They were purported to have been composed by slaves preparing an insurrection in South Carolina in 1813. The pamphlet was called *Negro Slave Revolts in the United States 1526–1860* and was published in 1939. It was written by Herbert Aptheker. Aptheker reported that more than two hundred documented slave revolts occurred in the territory of the United States between the years 1526 and 1860. Many more were likely to have occurred but were either not recorded or were deliberately hushed up. The evidence was compelling, but so was the fact that the pamphlet had been publicly available for almost one hundred years. Yet it is still commonly asserted that the slaves did not rebel.[24]

At the moment of discovery, however, it was the song that had the most striking effect. It was immediately apparent that this lyric was extraordinary in that it so little resembles what we've been accustomed to expect from the

Negro spiritual. Even though there are many majestic songs like "Go Down, Moses," "Deep River," "Many Thousands Gone," and "Steal Away" that express the longing for freedom, this overtly political, indeed revolutionary, text called out for explanation and substantiation. If those were found, then there were very likely other similar songs to be discovered and reclaimed. And so the search began. It took five years of digging to locate enough songs to present the evidence: along with the burial of the historical record, there was the concomitant erasure of the musical one. *Songs of Slavery and Emancipation* was published to bring to light not only the songs but the mechanisms used to conceal them so long.

Time and again, I was confronted by the size and scope of this deception. Time and again, I sought proof of the contrary—that either diligent scholars had previously brought this material to light, or it had already been proven to be false. But every new detail, every new piece of evidence supported the conclusion. There was simply no way to ignore the music, on the one hand, and the systematic suppression on the other. And all of this in a liberal democracy that claims to uphold principles of academic rigor, fairness in business, and the pursuit of truth in journalism.

While subsequent chapters will provide the evidence in greater detail, one exemplary work will illustrate the scope of the problem and its relevance to music. This is an essay, also published in 1939, called "The Social Implications of the Negro Spiritual" by one John Lovell Jr.[25] Lovell cites Aptheker's pamphlet (proving it was in circulation at the time) and boldly claims that even such valiant champions of Black humanity as Alain Locke and W. E. B. Du Bois had missed the essential point: not only did the slaves rebel but their rebellion was encouraged, commemorated, and disseminated in songs. There were, no doubt, "sorrow songs" as Du Bois had eloquently reported. But they were not the only ones and furthermore did not characterize the Negro spiritual. Indeed, the entire legacy of the Negro spiritual had to be reappraised from a completely different perspective than that which had prevailed since the defeat of Reconstruction, the passage of Jim Crow laws, and the reenslavement of Black labor.

Lovell argued, "Approaching the heart of the spiritual we must recognize three fixed stars." First was the quest for freedom obsessively repeated in song after song. Second was the quest for justice, which infused even the most religious text with political import. Finally was the characteristic of prophecy: A great conflagration was coming that would bring an end to slavery. This prophecy was realized with the outbreak of the Civil War.[26] Not widely known but nonetheless a fact, that conflict was seized upon by 200,000 former slaves who joined the armed forces of the Union and an additional 200,000 who flocked to serve behind the Union lines as spies, cooks, laborers, and nurses.

The course of history was shaped by such events and their musical expression. The facts are inescapable and the songs speak for themselves. But this presents a greater task yet to be fulfilled: the critical examination of all the material available and the excavation of more that is certain to lie beneath a century's debris.

It also raises the question of how the relationship between music and the state has unfolded in the decades subsequent to those recounted above. How have all these controversies and conflicts affected current affairs and to what extent do they confirm or refute Ngũgĩ Wa Thiong'o's thesis regarding art's rivalry with the state? One recent example sheds light on these questions.

THE AMBASSADOR'S SPEECH

It was in 2020 that I happened to be on a program, "Playing for Progressive Change," which featured, among other guests, Cynthia Schneider, former US ambassador to the Netherlands. Just prior to the ambassador's appearance, my partner and I performed "There Is Mean Things Happenin' in This Land," a song composed in the 1930s by John Handcox, a Black sharecropper and leader of the Southern Tenant Farmers Union. Handcox was widely known as both a union organizer and songwriter, which led to his being recorded by Charles Seeger and Sidney Robertson at the Library of Congress in 1937. Shortly thereafter, Handcox's activities made him a target of plantation owners in his native Arkansas, and, threatened with lynching, he fled the state and disappeared for the next forty years. We sang this song for its historical and contemporary relevance, having no idea of what the ambassador who followed us was going to say.

The ambassador's speech was brief and informal but nonetheless illuminating for what it revealed about US foreign policy and American music.[27] The ambassador began with a description of "soft power" and its deployment, referring to the theories of Joseph Nye of Harvard University as guiding principles. By way of example, she cited the use the State Department had made of jazz:

> Many people know about the jazz diplomats who traveled during the Cold War period, many of whom were African American. Louis Armstrong, Dizzy Gillespie, traveling around the world playing their music, which everyone loved, and they not only performed in fancy halls, but they would insist on jamming

with local musicians. And if there wasn't already a provision for it, they insisted on giving a public free concert. So, they not only brought their music, they brought very core concepts of democracy. And another core concept of democracy is dissent and criticism of authority. So, think of it, you have in the 1950s, '60s, '70s, '80s, jazz musicians traveling at the time of the peak of the Jim Crow era. So, they are welcomed as heroes wherever they go, but in the US they often couldn't go in the front door of a theater where they were performing because they were African American. Now their job wasn't to give a speaking tour on segregation. But if they were ever asked about their life in the US, they spoke very openly about it. And their audiences, and we have this documented, were so impressed by this, they said, "We can see this isn't just a slogan the US says, Freedom of Speech, they actually allow it." And here we have these people who are funded by the US government. and they're criticizing the US government. And they're not getting put in jail the way we would here. They're getting put on an airplane to go somewhere else and do the same thing. So, this must be real.[28]

Leaving aside for a moment the fact that many musicians were blacklisted, harassed, and even imprisoned by the US government precisely because they spoke out against injustice, what the ambassador said deserves scrutiny not only for its inherent content but because it clearly reveals a strategy employed by the US State Department. To begin, let's explore the content.

The ambassador openly acknowledges the segregation and discrimination of the Jim Crow era in order to prove that we have freedom of speech. Since the musicians "spoke openly about it," the government that "allowed" them to speak is somehow cleansed of its culpability in perpetuating the injustices they suffered and are speaking about. Thus, the right to speak—outside the country—exonerates the denial of rights within the country. From this pretzel logic (thanks Steely Dan) the ambassador descends into deeper quagmires of contradiction implying that somehow the history of the United States is rendered innocuous or immaterial by the fact that we are allowed to talk about it. We are, today, a model of what other countries should aspire to become.

It doesn't matter that it took a Civil War to abolish slavery or that it was one hundred years later that the Voting Rights Act of 1965 was passed or that the US government was proven complicit in the murder of Dr. Martin Luther King Jr., not to mention countless other opponents of government policy.[29] It doesn't matter that there remain, to this day, political prisoners in the United States. These are people incarcerated for their political beliefs and activities, albeit under the guise of dubious criminal charges. Mumia Abu-Jamal and Leonard Peltier are two of the best known. And these are the ones who survived. There are dozens of others, Fred Hampton, Mark Clark, and George Jackson being the most famous, who were murdered by the FBI, local police, or prison authorities. The list is so long, in fact, that it would fill pages. Yet, even if we stay strictly within the limits of the ambassador's statement and only talk about music and musicians, the facts undermine her claims.

In 1950 world-renowned musician Paul Robeson applied to renew his passport in order to travel internationally. The government refused his application and an eight-year court battle ensued, which only ended when the Supreme Court ruled in another case, *Kent v. Dulles*, that forbidding travel was an infringement of a citizen's rights. This was far from an isolated case, especially when it concerned overseas travel sponsored by the State Department. According to Lt. Col. (USAF, Ret.) James E. Dillard:

> "Modern jazz" to these black artists connoted mobility and freedom but also meant a return to the roots of the African diaspora's intricate rhythms and sounds. Moreover, the leftist political ideologies of a few entertainers made them persona non grata with VOA tours abroad. For example, Mary Lou Williams, a talented jazz composer and pianist who had joined the Gillespie Band for a performance of the *Zodiac Suite* at the 1957 Newport Jazz Festival, was denied a visa to join a State Department tour. Many Washington officials regarded her as too "unstable," citing her "religious fanaticism." Dancer and choreographer Katherine Dunham repeatedly was rejected for State Department tours partly in response to her avant garde ballet *Southland*, which critiqued the South's history of African American lynchings.[30]

These policies were not confined to foreign travel but were directed more broadly in a blatant attack on freedom of association as well as expression. Summarizing the effects of the postwar witch hunt, known as the McCarthy era, on the thriving music scene of the prewar Popular Front, historian Michael Denning concludes:

> The demise of Café Society in the anti-Communist cultural war also crushed the dream of a cabaret blues, an interracial union of Brechtian political theater and African American music. Billie Holiday was imprisoned and denied a cabaret card; Benjamin Davis was hounded from the New York City Council to prison; Paul Robeson was persecuted; and a host of musicians—Ellington, White, Lena Horne, and Hazel Scott, among them—were publicly humiliated, forced to distance themselves from Davis and Robeson. By 1955, all that remained was Louis Armstrong's hit version of "Mack the Knife," the Brecht-Weill song that Marc

Blitzstein had adapted, and even that was occasionally banned and boycotted because of Blitzstein's communist affiliations. Nevertheless, out of the ruins of Café Society, the cabaret blues of Billie Holiday and Josh White continue to disrupt the pastoral scene of the American Century.[31]

This raises another aspect of what the ambassador calls "soft power" and how that technique uses music. Not only does soft power rely on American music to make its case but it makes dubious claims about that music in the process. As the ambassador elaborates:

> What I could do was to remind people what was American about jazz. And the idea that this music that involved risk-taking, that involves an individual going out and the group joining in in a harmony, but really all about taking risks and the individual standing out and being joined by the group and improvisation, and how American those characteristics were. So when my Dutch guests would go to the Jazz Festival and listen, maybe just a little thing would go on in their minds saying "huh, this is something American" and hopefully it would be positive associations.[32]

Risk management is what bankers do. The ambassador is importing terminology and concepts appropriate to the *Wall Street Journal* or *Financial Times* and applying them to musical practices. Would it not be more appropriate to speak of improvisation as adventurous, experimental, and creative, *dependent*, in fact, upon the interaction of a soloist with the group as opposed to the "individual standing out"? The emphases the ambassador places are driven by free market ideology and have little to do with a process which is above all collective and social. Besides, improvisation is not a unique feature of jazz and the "risk taking" she describes is commonly found in many other musics of the world. It is far from "something American."

THAT WAS THEN, THIS IS NOW

At this point in her speech the ambassador shifts focus. She states that in the twenty years since she was serving in the Netherlands changes have occurred.

> Now there are places in the world today where music is still tremendously important for communicating ideas and messages. I happen to be working in one of them, Mali. . . . So now . . . it's not a moment for us to send American

musicians around, or certainly not to Mali, they have the greatest musicians in the world, the role of the US and Italy and many European countries is to leverage those local voices. To use our skills in production, distribution, marketing, to enable those local voices to maximize their reach to their publics because their messages are the messages people need to hear.[33]

What messages? Clearly, it's what the ambassador stated at the outset: "Soft power—in the context of diplomacy, a term invented by Joseph Nye of Harvard University, but what it means is the power of attraction and influence that comes from being a model. From being a person or a country or an entity that stands for something and acts in a way that people admire. And it's talked about in juxtaposition to hard power, which is trade sanctions or military might."

Given the fact that the United States uses hard power extensively and does so with impunity, it is worth asking why soft power is necessary. Here we get to the crux, not only of the ambassador's stated objective, but to the relation between music and the state, more specifically, the ways music is represented by the state in order to better serve the state's agenda. In contrast we might recall how one leading thinker viewed the issue in 1963. When poet and playwright LeRoi Jones (aka Amiri Baraka) published *Blues People*, it was widely read, its influence so extensive that its message could not be missed by those concerned with America's image worldwide. Jones concluded his study with this remark:

> It is no secret that the West, and most particularly the American system, is in the position now of having to defend its values and ideas against totally hostile systems. The American Negro is being asked to defend the American system as energetically as the American white man. There is no doubt that the middle-class Negro is helping and will continue to help in that defense. But there is perhaps a question mark in the minds of the many poor blacks (which is one explanation for the attraction of such groups as the Black Muslims) and also now in the minds of many young Negro intellectuals. What is it that they are being asked to save? It is a good question, and America had better come up with an answer.[34]

The fact that in 2020 a former US ambassador uses American music, in particular jazz, to prove her point demonstrates the significance of American music and its representation in world affairs. But that she also refers to a *past* period and says things have *changed*, that Mali doesn't need American music to make its own, raises a new question: is American music passé? Is it now more effective to promote "local voices" who in their own vernacular promote the messages the US State Department wants to hear?

As the US State Department carries out policy in a world that is increasingly challenging American hegemony, it would appear that the role American music plays in that strategy is less a matter of musicological properties and more a matter of success as defined by capitalism. Now it is more important to emphasize methods of marketing local musics to make them more profitable and profit-oriented than it is to argue that local musicians emulate American music. No doubt certain styles such as jazz, rock, pop, and hip hop continue to exert an influence worldwide. But it is the American way of doing business that is being promoted and that message no longer needs the gloss or pretension that imitating America's music is the best means to achieve desirable ends. Instead, it is American "values," private property and possessive individualism, which are the aim and these are better served if they wear local garb.

WE ARE THE WORLD?

It is worth pausing to note one other feature that might be overlooked given its apparent banality: the American music the ambassador is referring to is only an element of what should be included when speaking of the music made within the territorial United States. While that might seem obvious and uncontroversial, it is nonetheless the fact that the ambassador can confidently assume that most of her listeners, indeed most people in the world, share a limited and circumscribed view of what American music actually consists of. As mentioned above, jazz and other African American–derived forms are widely known, as are various other genres from country to folk to Broadway musicals. No doubt there is great admiration for the many fine musicians, composers, and compositions emanating from the United States. As well there should be, since so much fine music has been produced.

What is less obvious and is indeed controversial is why this selection is not complete and why it has been made in the first place. Why is a vast array of music excluded from these coordinates and why has certain music—from whole genres to specific musicians—been written out of the description? The purpose here is not to demean or discredit any music simply because it has been co-opted by the state. It is, on the contrary, to situate that music in its larger musical and historical context and to fully explore the controversies and conflicts that surround its making. This will result in bringing to light the music and music-making practices that have been effectively buried, especially those that were a part and product of the struggles of the oppressed and exploited.

MUSIC VS. THE STATE: REPRISE

Ngũgĩ Wa Thiong'o published *Penpoints, Gunpoints, and Dreams* in 1998. Its subtitle is "Towards a Critical Theory of the Arts and the State in Africa." Ngũgĩ argues that art (embracing all the arts from literature to music, from dance to theater, and from sculpture to painting) is simultaneously used by the state and inimical to it. Art is both propagated and policed as indispensable servant and formidable threat. The latter characteristic is not confined to explicitly political art or that which is openly dedicated to overthrowing a regime. Art is a rival of the state at a more fundamental level. "It would seem to me," writes Ngũgĩ,

> ... that the state, when functioning to its logical conclusion as the state, and art functioning as art are antagonistic. They are continuously at war. The state in a class society is an instrument of control in the hands of whatever is the dominant social force. Art, on the other hand, in its beginning was always an ally of the human search for freedom from hostile nature and nurture. But this conflict inherent in the two may not always be visible because the state does not always act with a sledge-hammer against all artistic creations and representations.[35]

Ngũgĩ documents not only many contemporary examples of this sometimes-veiled, sometimes-open antagonism, but also the long trajectory, over thousands of years, wherein art presented an intractable problem the state was compelled to face. In a profound reading of Plato and Aristotle, among other ancients, Ngũgĩ inveighs against common interpretations that have failed to grasp the full import of such thinking:

> Art is more powerful when working as an ally of the powerless than it is when allied to repression. For its essential nature is freedom, while that of the state is the restriction and regulation of freedom. And yet it is this very power that makes the state want to co-opt art into its service.... And for all their disparaging tone and comments about poets, Plato's dialogues contain some of the most pertinent observations on the sources and power of art. To paraphrase what Blake said of Milton and *Paradise Lost*, Plato was on the side of the artistic devil without knowing it.[36]

Though Ngũgĩ focuses his attention on postcolonial Africa, citing specific examples from Kenya, Ghana, and other African countries, there can be little doubt that the theory toward which he is directing us is applicable elsewhere.

Indeed, Ngũgĩ's insights are highly pertinent to the situation in the West, the ostensible model of liberal democratic rule, which purports to have built ironclad defenses against state interference with the arts. For it is precisely in the West, especially the United States, that some of the most stunning examples of the rivalry between art and the state have occurred. The point, however, most often missed by various critics over the last century, is one Ngũgĩ's intervention makes crystal clear: art is insurgent, and no effort made by the state or by commercial interest can ever fully domesticate this force.

The confusion exhibited by Charles Seeger and the Composers' Collective is one example of how this manifests in a period of great ferment. The criticism of bourgeois art was clear enough, but the ignorance of popular art was more than a lack of familiarity with certain forms, it was a failure to grasp what spontaneously arises from the conditions under which people live and, furthermore, that some of what the common people produce is revolutionary. While the effort to produce proletarian music was sincere and did in fact result in music of quality, it could not solve the conundrums resulting from missing the underlying significance of Plato's original insight: music will always pose a threat to the ruling class.

This error was repeated by Adorno and Debord in different ways at different times. In Adorno's case it was the outright rejection of the popular, jazz in particular, as repetitive, dumb, and easily co-opted by commercial interests. In Debord's case it was the overawed obeisance to capitalist spectacle that prevented him from acknowledging a more fundamental truth. What Ngũgĩ argues is that song and story constantly and spontaneously arise from among the popular classes to mock injustice, ridicule misrule, celebrate defiance, and applaud the heroes and heroines who have struggled to elude the clutches of the authorities and aspire to liberty and justice. The evidence of this phenomenon is so abundant it can be considered self-evident. The fact that the struggle continues and has yet to be won is no argument against it; indeed, current conflicts only emphasize the significance of grasping the point.

What has been deliberately obscured can therefore be traced. This process necessitates identifying the agents and institutions who work to suppress the music of resistance. These agents, generally speaking, do not work at the State Department or the Pentagon. They are recruited, as the jazz ambassadors were, at particular times for particular campaigns. Instead, the agents responsible for propagating and policing are found in other institutions such as the academy, the music industry, and the media. The purpose of this book is to bring to light examples and demonstrate how the process they are a part of works.

It is furthermore to call attention to music that has hitherto been forgotten or deliberately erased. There are reservoirs of musical composition, practices, and communities that are not only aesthetically pleasing but are evidence of historical events often misrepresented in "official" or "textbook" accounts. By and large, these events can be characterized as those in which the main protagonists were ordinary people, taking matters into their own hands and seeking, by whatever means were available, to liberate themselves from oppression and exploitation. This book hopes to restore that musical legacy to a place of honor in the music and poetry of the world.

CHAPTER SUMMARY

What follows is a brief breakdown of the chapters contained in this edited collection.

In chapter 1, Mat Callahan sets out the rationale for the current authors undertaking this edited volume. Reflecting on his earlier projects relating to historically significant songs and books (in the United States and Ireland), Callahan recalls specific and unexpected problems that arose to hinder the research-gathering process—namely a lack of awareness, and challenges in obtaining relevant materials. Despite the significance of these works and their authors, the author found that there was little recognition or accessibility in many cases, suggesting that important cultural and historical works have been neglected or forgotten over time. Crucially, Callahan identifies a process of "replacement," where certain musicians, songs, and genres have been suppressed or forgotten, while others have been promoted in their place. This replacement process can be seen as systematic and intentional, driven by criteria that favor the elevation of certain works over others. The chapter ultimately explores how and why certain cultural works were replaced, examining the strategies behind this process and its implications for the understanding and preservation of cultural heritage.

In chapter 2, Steve Garabedian introduces us to politically radical folklorist and musicologist Lawrence Gellert, who collected and documented African American folk songs during the early to mid-twentieth century. Gellert's role as a white collector of African American vernacular music was complex. Unlike many of his peers, he straddled two worlds—participating in the white-dominated tradition of folklore collection, while also critiquing it. Here, Garabedian illustrates how Gellert distanced himself from the typical academic, music industry, and journalistic approaches to folklore, choosing instead to focus on Black protest songs, which were largely overlooked by the mainstream. The emphasis here is on how Gellert's work blurred the distinction between folk and protest songs, challenging both disciplinary boundaries and Cold War–era ideologies. His disputes with the Library of Congress and Folkways Records over authorship and copyright issues, coupled with his enigmatic disappearance, highlight the persistent marginalization of Black vernacular resistance, even as mainstream culture began to adopt aspects of it during the Lomax Consensus and the sixties revival.

Music and songs, Franz Andres Morrissey tells us in chapter 3, are fleeting entities that exist only in the moment of performance and vanish as soon as the performance ends. Here, Andres Morrissey probes several questions, particularly how such performed pieces can be preserved, and more relevantly within the context of this edited collection, why some songs endure, remaining relevant for decades or even centuries, while others fade away without a trace. This phenomenon is especially intriguing in the realm of popular songs categorized as folk music, which is often viewed as an oral tradition passed down through performance. Folk music is also frequently associated with the lower, often illiterate, classes, or seen as addressing their concerns, accompanied by the assumption that these groups, either unaware, careless, or uneducated, cannot be trusted to preserve these cultural treasures. These are just some of the issues Andres Morrissey scrutinizes and unpacks across the chapter.

Chapter 4 sees Elissa Stroman deliver a critical analysis of *The Etude*, a magazine for musicians founded in 1883 by music publisher and philanthropist Theodore Presser, which played a crucial role in reflecting and shaping early twentieth-century gender expectations, musical genres, class, and race. While the magazine catered to genteel music lovers amid a surge in music appreciation, Stroman advances that the significant role women played in its success has been understudied. She deconstructs *The Etude*'s portrayal of femininity from 1883 to 1926, focusing on the musical genres and guidance it provided to amateur female musicians. Moreover, Stroman illustrates how during a time of shifting societal roles for women, the magazine documented how women chose musics that had long-term community impacts. These women often favored European classical works, specific folk traditions, and the burgeoning American art music, distancing themselves from popular trends. This strategy allowed them to gain influence in genteel society without confronting the male-dominated musical establishment. Ultimately, this chapter shows how *The Etude*'s publishing ecosystem promoted these preferred genres, reinforcing cultivated American musical tastes and shaping the cultural canon.

The music industry as we know it may well be global, but its origins can be tracked down to an exact location and time. In chapter 5, Jim Rogers outlines the emergence and swift growth of the popular music publishing industry in the United States (and in particular, its convergence on New York) at the turn of the twentieth century, where a revolutionary new approach to the generation and circulation of musical forms and practices surfaced and took hold. Rogers demonstrates how such developments were deeply intertwined with the broader evolution of capitalism, and resonated with its core dynamics in many ways, such as standardization, mass production, the evolution of corporate structures, and in particular, the formalization of copyright laws that paralleled the capitalist emphasis on property rights. The chapter points to these changes carrying profound implications for musical practices and values, and the role and function of music in modern society. The commercial songwriter was thus born, and the machinery to traffic music on a mass scale was assembled. In essence, a new music order was established. By the dawn of the twentieth century, a new and radical popular music industry was rapidly and firmly taking shape. As Rogers illustrates, this formative period of the modern music business from the 1880s to the 1910s would produce the template from which the contemporary music industry was constructed.

A historic analysis of musicians' rights and working conditions form the focus of chapter 6. Here, Richard Weissman reminds us that like any other job, music making necessitates fair compensation, and the long-standing disputes between musicians and their employers are frequently overlooked or dismissed in scholarly and journalistic accounts. In fact, the concept of music as labor—something that creates value rather than being merely a source of enjoyment—has been largely neglected in scholarly study. This chapter, informed by Weissman's personal experience (as a songwriter, recording artist, and record producer) and independent research, breaks down and interrogates the history of the American Federation of Musicians. The chapter critically examines the relationship of the AFM with the music industry over time, and the significant challenges it has encountered. This history, which stretches back to the late nineteenth century, parallels many of the other events and conflicts explored in this book. Weissman's work here illustrates that this connection is not coincidental but rather a result of the economic and political changes in the United States after the Civil War.

Chapter 7 switches our attention to the "jazz ambassadors"—those jazz musicians sponsored by the US State Department to promote American cultural values around the world during the Cold War era. Here, James Dillard examines how the US government, particularly through the CIA and the

Voice of America, used jazz music and some of its most popular performers to promote American cultural values and counter Soviet influence abroad. The article analyzes the strategic deployment of jazz musicians on international tours, particularly in regions like Eastern Europe, the Middle East, Asia, and Africa, as part of a broader effort to win hearts and minds in the ideological battle between the United States and the Soviet Union. Dillard discusses how jazz, as a symbol of freedom and creativity, was leveraged to project a positive image of American society and to challenge negative perceptions of the United States globally. While these "jazz ambassadors" may often have been unaware of the hidden and often covert political and economic agendas tied to their tours, they were not, as Dillard concludes, completely ignorant of them either. The chapter also points to the complexities and contradictions of this form of cultural diplomacy, given the domestic racial tensions in the United States at the time.

Suzanne Cusick's examination of the systematic use of music as a weapon in post–Cold War America is the focus of chapter 8. This practice first drew widespread attention in 1989, when US troops used loud music to force Panamanian President Manuel Noriega's surrender. Since then, "acoustic bombardment" has become a routine tactic in Iraq, integrated with sensory deprivation and sexual humiliation as a nonlethal method to coerce prisoners—from Abu Ghraib to Guantanamo—into divulging information without violating US law. The concept of music as an instrument of torture offers a disturbing perspective on contemporary American musical culture, prompting reflection on what this usage reveals about US society and its self-perception. It also raises important questions about the implications of the government's use of music in the "war on terror" for both Americans and their adversaries. The chapter delves into the military and cultural logic behind the modern use of music as a tool of torture and warfare. It traces the development of acoustic weapons in the late twentieth century, their deployment during the second battle of Fallujah in 2004, and examines the intersection of late twentieth-century US musical culture with the security community's perception of music as a weapon.

Chapter 9 sees Jim Rogers examining power and wealth in the contemporary global music industry. The core argument of this chapter is that if we focus solely on how technology is perceived to be transforming the music business (as the industry urges us to do), we overlook a subtler but more critical reality. While recent discourse surrounding the potentially damaging and dangerous role of artificial intelligence (AI) in music resonates strongly with earlier debates surrounding peer-to-peer file-sharing in the early years of the century and streaming, Rogers argues that major music labels have strategically shifted their policies and practices to reinforce their long-established dominance. The intervention of the legislative and judicial arms of the state in the form of intellectual property regulation has, among other things, been fundamental to this process. As such, despite the perceived impacts of the "fourth industrial revolution," power in the music business remains as concentrated as it has been for over a century, with wealth more polarized than ever. The "star system" remains relevant, and copyright (and increasingly trademark) laws continue to reinforce these inequalities.

There then follows two chapters that analyze the relationship between music and war. First, in chapter 10, Franz Andres Morrissey and Britta Sweers consider the dual role of songs in times of war, highlighting their use both as a tool for state-driven propaganda and as a medium for antihegemonic expression. Songs and music have historically been employed to instill a sense of belonging and purpose in soldiers, reinforcing the objectives of the state and encouraging patriotism. However, alongside these state-sponsored songs, the chapter highlights the existence of a contrasting tradition of antiwar and antiauthority music. This type of music, often created by frontline soldiers, expressed bitter sarcasm and criticism of the war and those in power. These songs, which circulated widely among troops, frequently parodied popular patriotic tunes, using familiar melodies to spread messages of discontent and protest against the harsh realities of war. Andres Morrissey and Sweers critically interrogate these two musical traditions in the context of conflicts such as the Korean War, Vietnam War, and the Cold War, demonstrating how music has been used both to support and resist wartime ideologies.

Then, drawing inspiration from blues "poet-philosopher" Willie Dixon, chapter 11 sees Steve Garabedian focusing on a much-neglected aspect of African American blues tradition: its role in expressing protest against war and advocating for peace from the 1940s to the 1970s. Dixon, the author of more than five hundred compositions, was also an advocate for peace and social justice. His 1980s song "It Don't Make Sense (You Can't Make Peace)" exemplified what Dixon argued was the deep wisdom of the blues. It is only one among many blues, by multiple artists, illustrating the absurdities and contradictions of modern war from World War II to Vietnam. Although the blues crossed over into mainstream popularity in the 1960s, unfortunately, African American blues songs on war faded from public attention. Ultimately, Garabedian uses this chapter to argue that blues has been underappreciated as part of a global movement for peace.

In chapter 12, Mat Callahan probes the gap between common perceptions of American music and the realities those perceptions overlook or erase. The chapter questions how these perceptions were shaped, by whom, and for what purposes, examining the historical actors and their interests. Callahan critiques the formation of a canon of American music, including the criteria used to include or exclude certain music and musicians. He also considers how geographical, historical, and musicological factors combined to influence both the music that existed and the music that was promoted by various agents, such as the state, private publishers, and scholars. Ultimately, Callahan argues for an approach to music representation that aligns more closely with its actual presentation, serving the broader goals of social justice and human upliftment. He suggests that musicologists and critics should prioritize the perspectives of music makers rather than those of publishers or propagandists, advocating for a more ethical and socially conscious approach to music appreciation and study.

Ultimately, Britta Sweers offers a short reflective chapter, synthesizing and distilling some of the most pertinent arguments arising across the various chapters in this book, and drawing together the key themes that emerge, while evaluating their significance and implications.

NOTES

1. See Jaques Attali, *Noise: The Political Economy of Music* (Minneapolis: University of Minnesota Press, 1985), 4.

2. See interview, Tom Johnston of the Doobie Brothers, https://www.songfacts.com/blog/interviews/tom-johnston-from-the-doobie-brothers.

3. Interview with author.

4. "Rhythm-and-blues, as it developed after the Second World War, was the folk music of urban blacks in the 1940s, when one and a quarter million blacks left the South for the Northern and Western ghettos. They constituted a new market, which was then supplied by independent record labels like Chess Records, founded in Chicago in 1949 by two Polish immigrants connected with the club circuit, and specializing in the so-called 'Chicago Blues' style (Muddy Waters, Howlin' Wolf, Sonny Boy Williamson) and recording, among others, Chuck Berry, who was probably—with Elvis Presley—the major influence on 1950s rock-and-roll. White adolescents began to buy black R&B records in the early 1950s, having discovered this music on local specialized radio stations which multiplied during those years, as the mass of adults transferred its attentions to television. At first sight they seemed to be the habitual tiny and untypical minority which can still be seen on the fringes of black entertainment, like the white visitors to Chicago ghetto blues clubs. Yet, as soon as the music industry became aware of this potential white youth market, it became evident that rock was the opposite of a minority taste. It was music of an entire age-group." Eric Hobsbawm, *Uncommon People* (London: Weidenfeld and Nicholson, 1998), 379.

5. "In the years just prior to World War II, there were no teenagers, no teenage magazines, teenage music, or teenage culture. The word itself had not even been invented." Michael E. Malone and Myron Roberts, *from pop to culture* (New York: Holt, Rinehart and Winston, 1971), 178. "As the teenager became more and more aware that he shared a distinct status as a member of a group set apart from adult society, he began to adopt and adapt artifacts of popular culture as his own. The early adoptions were drawn, in the main, from black culture and took the forms of (among other things) rhythm and blues music and 'jive' talk." George Lewis, *Side-Saddle on the Golden Calf* (Pacific Palisades, CA: Goodyear Publishing, 1972), 225.

6. "Fear went beyond simple integration of black music into mainstream culture with the widespread concern that rock's popularity would lead to interracial sexual relations. Record companies avoided promotional material that portrayed a mixture of races in the same photograph. Network censors forbade television programs to depict interracial mingling on popular dance shows. Alan Freed's television show, Rock 'n' Roll Dance Party, was canceled after a cameraman filmed a white girl dancing with black singer Frankie Lymon (of Frankie Lymon and the Teenagers)." Eric Nuzum, *Parental Advisory: Music Censorship in America* (Perennial, 2001), 105.

7. Theodore Roszak, *The Making of a Counter Culture: Reflections on the Technocratic Society and Its Youthful Opposition* (Anchor Books, 1969), 1.

8. For a fuller discussion, see Mat Callahan, *The Explosion of Deferred Dreams: Musical Renaissance and Social Revolution in San Francisco 1965–1975* (PM Press, 2017).

9. "The Marty Balin Show," *Artists Archives with Barry Flast* (2009).

10. When it is asserted that the only music that is authentically "folk" is that of rural laborers or formerly enslaved field hands, what are we to make of a book such as James Monroe Trotter's *Music and Some Highly Musical People* (1878) that provides biographies of highly accomplished musicians, including former slaves as well as free-born Black people? Are these people to be excluded from "folk" because of their education, their skill, or their renown? What about the poets and musicians who, though enslaved, wrote eloquently about the system against which they were struggling?

11. "A&R" stands for "artists and repertoire" and was a job description widely used in the music industry. It is more or less synonymous with "talent scout" or "artist development." The basic function is the discovery and signing of musical acts, but it may also include choice of material (hence "repertoire") and the grooming of the "look" or public personae of musicians.

12. Interview with author. Further details and documentation can be found in Callahan, *The Explosion of Deferred Dreams*.

13. There are many sources for this data, e.g.: Eric Hobsbawm, *Uncommon People: Resistance, Rebellion and Jazz*, Abacus, 379–80.

14. An example is "Like a Rolling Stone," an article written by music critic Ralph J. Gleason in *American Scholar* Vol. 36, no. 4 (Autumn 1967).

15. See Abe Peck, *Uncovering the '60s: The Life and Times of the Underground Press* (Citadel, 1991).

16. See Susan Krieger, *Hip Capitalism* (Sage Press, 1979).

17. Jim Miller, Introduction, *The Rolling Stone Illustrated History of Rock and Roll* (Rolling Stone Press, 1976), 9.

18. Epigram quoted in Theodore Roszak, *The Making of A Counter Culture: Reflections on the Technocratic Society and Its Youthful Opposition* (Anchor Books, 1969).

19. Ngũgĩ Wa Thiong'o, *Penpoints, Gunpoints, and Dreams: The Performance of Literature and Power in Post-Colonial Africa* (Oxford: Clarendon Lectures in English Literature 1996, Oxford University Press, 1998), 37.

20. This is also about how history is being written now and how the State Department uses music, in particular, to promote its agenda and to "market" America to the world.

It's called "soft power" and is openly applied by ambassadors and other representatives throughout the world. Such strategies demand critical evaluation as much as their historical antecedents do. It is just as important to understand the enduring effects and likely future consequences as it is to uncover the causes or mechanisms that brought them about in first place. See Ambassador's speech below.

21. W. E. B. Du Bois, *Black Reconstruction in America 1860–1880* (New York: Free Press, 1992), 634–35.

22. These strategies are best exemplified by a comparison between the song collecting done by academics (or amateurs like Dorothy Scarborough) and the song collecting done by representatives of the music industry at the same time and in the same places. The peculiar collection assembled by Harry Smith, *The Anthology of American Folk Music*, makes this comparison relevant. Smith's choices were from commercially produced and distributed 78s. Smith considered this made them more authentically folk music since people had to pay for them! Their musical content is diverse in more ways than one. The music is first of all hard to categorize stylistically, and in some cases it is difficult to determine by sound alone the ethnicity of either the performers or the origins of the songs they sing. Yet these were records that sold well. Some "stars" were among them, like Charley Patton and the Carter Family. But that does not explain what these musicians thought or the sources they were drawing on when they made their recordings. Nor does it explain the incongruity evident in the music itself when compared with what we have come to think of as American music—that is, spirituals, blues, and jazz on the one hand, and hillbilly, string band, or old-timey on the other. In fact, the cross-pollination of influences predominates and the inescapable conclusion to be drawn is that, despite rigid segregation—or perhaps in defiance of it—Southern musicians overheard each other, exchanging whatever they liked from church hymns to jigs and reels. And this does not even touch music such as sea-chanties, songs of the Sacred Harp, or New Orleans Opera.

23. James Connolly, *Songs of Freedom* (PM Press, 2013 [1907]).

24. An example is the recently published book *The Half Has Never Been Told* (Basic Books, 2016), in which author Edward Baptiste flatly states on page xx of his introduction: "And there were very few rebellions in the history of slavery in the United States."

25. John Lovell Jr., "The Social Implications of the Negro Spiritual," *Journal of Negro Education* (October 1939): 634–43.

Discovered by this author in Bernard Katz, ed., *The Social Implications of Early Negro Music* (New York: Arno Press and the New York Times, 1969), 127–37.

26. Lovell further asserted in a book published in 1973 that he had counted six thousand songs bearing similar militant content. It became urgent to understand how this evidence could be avoided, if not deliberately buried, by scholars trained in song-collecting, folklore, or musicology. It also became apparent that very few of the scholars I consulted even knew about Lovell's work, let alone could provide information as to the songs in question. Indeed, it was only through the further study of numerous overlooked or discredited song collectors that it became apparent that this was systematic and had roots in a period following the defeat of Reconstruction wherein a narrative was constructed to justify the continued subjugation of nominally emancipated people.

27. "Playing for Positive Progress II reduced—American Roots Folk House," September 24, 2020, https://youtu.be/-osJpFXNmq4.

28. Cynthia Schneider, "Playing for Positive Progress II reduced."

29. "Did You Know? US Gov't Found Guilty in Conspiracy to Assassinate Dr. Martin Luther King, Jr.," NewsOne, January 18, 2021, https://newsone.com/2843790/did-you-know-us-govt-found-guilty-in-conspiracy-to-assassinate-dr-martin-luther-king-jr/.

30. Lt. Col. (USAF Ret.) James E. Dillard, "All That Jazz: CIA, Voice of America, and Jazz Diplomacy in the Early Cold War Years, 1955–1965," *American Intelligence Journal*, vol. 30, no. 2 (2012): 39–50.

31. Michael Denning, *The Cultural Front* (London and New York: Verso 1997), 361.

32. Cynthia Schneider, "Playing for Positive Progress II reduced."

33. Cynthia Schneider, "Playing for Positive Progress II reduced."

34. LeRoi Jones, *Blues People* (New York: William Morrow, 1963), 236.

35. Ngũgĩ Wa Thiong'o, *Penpoints, Gunpoints, and Dreams*, 28.

36. Ngũgĩ Wa Thiong'o, *Penpoints, Gunpoints, and Dreams*, 33–34.

CHAPTER 1

A SONIC PALIMPSEST
Replacement as a Method of Suppression

Mat Callahan

When I began looking for a copy of James Connolly's book *Songs of Freedom*, I assumed I would easily find one online or in a bookstore. Connolly's heroic stature, at least in Ireland, would surely mean that in the run-up to the one-hundredth anniversary of the Easter Rising (2016) there would be renewed interest in this work.

The fiftieth anniversary of the publication of *Hard Hitting Songs for Hard-Hit People* in 2017 would be the occasion, I thought, for commemorative articles and musical events, at least in those outlets and venues devoted to American folk music. I furthermore assumed a general awareness of the book, at least among aficionados of the genre, given the enduring fame of its authors, Alan Lomax, Woody Guthrie, and Pete Seeger. Seeger had only recently died and was celebrated worldwide at the time.

And when I discovered, in a dog-eared pamphlet from 1939, a song purported to be composed by slaves planning an insurrection in South Carolina (ca. 1813), I thought, surely, that research into its origins and implications had long ago been undertaken by folklorists, historians, or musicologists.

In each of these three instances, not only were my assumptions wrong, but obtaining relevant materials proved to be difficult. While here and there I encountered knowledgeable individuals familiar with what I was looking for, in most cases I met with incomprehension or skepticism. Indeed, it took years of work, during the course of which, more came to light than I could present in those publications which were the immediate result, namely, *James Connolly's Songs of Freedom*, *Working Class Heroes*, and *Songs of Slavery and Emancipation*. In each case, the presentation of all that I learned in my research was beyond the scope of the projects themselves. The books and accompanying

CDs focused mainly on the musical, lyrical, and historical evidence and only secondarily on the obstacles that had to be overcome to obtain it.

These obstacles went beyond those one might expect when seeking to uncover lost or forgotten works and form a related but distinct subject: *replacement*. While certain musicians and songs *were* suppressed and whole genres of music were consigned to oblivion, this process was accompanied by another: the replacement of the missing musicians, songs, and genres by others which, generally speaking, fit certain criteria (more on these criteria to follow).

REPLACEMENT

Suppression is most often thought of as the work of the state. Censorship, banning books, imprisoning or executing authors, arresting booksellers and publishers are all functions of government. Earlier, these functions were carried out by the Church, which prior to the revolutions of the eighteenth century, was inseparable from the state. As a result, in Western popular imagination such authoritarian measures bring to mind the Spanish Inquisition, the auto-da-fé, the burning of witches, and so forth. Today, they are usually associated with fascist or communist dictatorships. Liberal democracies such as the United States do not do those sorts of things.

While there is abundant evidence that such suppression did, and does, occur in liberal democracies, it is nonetheless the case that a different method was the main one employed toward similar ends. This method is what I call *replacement*. Instead of banning and burning, imprisoning and executing, instead of any legal or judicial intervention at all, the production and promotion of substitutes—always claiming authenticity—becomes the primary means by which the marginalization or burial of works and practices that conflict with the agenda of ruling elites is accomplished. Speaking only of music, there are specific criteria by which replacement was guided and by which its traces can be clearly seen.

The most basic of these criteria was that works with no known author were to be replaced by those that had one, that is, an author of the work according to copyright law. This law is Article I, Section 8 of the Constitution of the United States. Its full implementation only took place in the early twentieth century with the passage of the Copyright Law of 1909 and a supporting Supreme Court decision of 1917. Nevertheless, the impact of copyright law was felt in the earliest years of the new republic, providing the state sanction necessary for a music industry to develop.[1]

Other criteria were also applied, and these corresponded as much to the content of compositions and the practices of their performance as they did to their ownership via copyright. In short, the songs calling for rebellion, condemning government, or challenging the economic system were unwelcome. Likewise, the customs and practices by which music was composed and performed by the common people had to be made less attractive, if not outright prohibited. These two moves meant the replacement of topical-critical and rebel songs with other types which were more suitable to public order and patriotic mobilization. Meanwhile, community singing, dancing, and music-making was replaced by professionals skilled in musical craft providing dazzling displays of virtuosity to an awed assemblage of passive listeners.

These three basic criteria formed the bedrock of a successful strategy. For approximately two hundred years the American music industry and the American republic have enjoyed ever-increasing dominance in the world as the model was implemented and improved upon to meet the evolving needs of both industry and state. The results are contradictory.

The richness and vitality of musical expression arising out of social conditions in the United States are beyond any doubt. Whether or not they equal or surpass music originating simultaneously in other countries is a separate question. What concerns us here is the music, musicians, and music-making practices that for all intents and purposes were cast aside in the process. First of all, to what extent has this left us bereft of music as an activity in which all can participate? Second, to what extent has this impacted historiography, the way history is constructed and recorded?

This chapter will present examples of what was replaced, drawing first on the three works mentioned above but including others that help provide a more comprehensive picture. It will then focus on how strategies of replacement were developed and deployed.

♪ ♪ ♪

The first and most egregious example is the fate that befell music and poetry composed by slaves, free people of color, and abolitionists from as far back as the seventeenth century and extending up to the Civil War. The book *Songs of Slavery and Emancipation* documents the process that involved not only the suppression or burial of a great body of songs and poetry but the rewriting of history to exclude the centuries-long struggle to end the slave system. The evidence is contained in songs, poems, and other written material of exemplary individuals and groups. Among the earliest examples are the writings of Phillis Wheatley and Olaudah Equiano; among the most recent, the songs of the Hutchinson Family Singers, Henry Clay Work, and Joshua MacCarter Simpson.[2]

Over and above the specific individuals and works there is the more general distortion of the history of the slave system and the struggle to achieve its abolition. The songs, therefore, express more than their specific lyrical and musical content. They are evidence that from beginning to end, slavery was resisted, first of all by the slaves themselves, then by their supporters in the abolitionist movement. When this resistance is more accurately assessed, it reveals the decisive role played by slave revolts and the movement they spawned in the conflict that culminated in the Civil War and the formal or legal abolition of slavery in the United States.

It should be noted that even as I write this, there are many people, scholars included, who do not know that slave revolts in the United States occurred, much less that they played an important role historically. This is an example of replacement since the evidence, especially the pioneering efforts of Herbert Aptheker, has been available for more than a century. While not suppressed in the sense of a legal ban on the publishing of a book, the evidence and analysis has been marginalized by means of large quantities of well-funded books, films, monuments, and commemorations denouncing the failure of Reconstruction, ennobling the Lost Cause of the Confederacy and, above all, recounting the quiet patience of the suffering slaves. This in turn presents an obstacle because it means that many researchers, archivists, and authors, laboring under false premises, are unable to pose the right questions or see what's before their eyes. A classic example, to be more fully explored in another chapter in this book, is the song-collecting of Lawrence Gellert. Gellert's collecting provided slave songs that displayed those characteristics of rebel songs found throughout the world and yet strangely missing in the "canon" of slave songs in the United States.[3]

Moreover, this poses a challenge to certain prevalent notions about American music in general and African American music in particular. Blues, jazz, rhythm and blues/rock 'n' roll, and hip hop/rap are commonly assumed to be rooted in the music made by field hands in the southern United States. That is, simple, unsophisticated rhythms, melodies, and lyrics combine in either grooving, driving dance music or in moody complaint and bitter sarcasm. While jazz is recognized as a highly sophisticated development, it is nevertheless a development from these so-called "authentic" roots: the truer to that root, the more authentic the music, and so forth. Of course this fails to account for, let alone explain, religious music of which a vast store is plainly evident simultaneously. Not only gospel music, which is well known, but the music of the Sacred Harp, Dr. Watts singers, or the Negro spiritual more generally, can claim authenticity and yet do not neatly fit into the categories made by either folklorists or music industry salesmen. The division between Sinful Tunes and Spirituals, discussed by Dena J. Epstein in her seminal book by that name,[4] is a complex sociopolitical and philosophical-theological question and not fundamentally a musicological one, except as it pertains to categories established for the marketing of commodities. All these questions will be explored in greater detail below, but the point here is that while there is some truth in these common assumptions, there is also falsehood. This falsehood, furthermore, reinforces other more pernicious beliefs about "race," about slavery, and, especially, about popular resistance to exploitation and oppression. Ultimately, they prevent an accurate appraisal of history in general and musical history in particular.

Before proceeding, it is important to note the two institutions that have symbolically and practically framed virtually all discussion of American popular music. Harvard University pioneered and policed American folklore from 1888 onward. Tin Pan Alley dominated the popular music industry from about the same time until the tumultuous 1960s undermined its dominance. Harvard was America's brain. Accreditation by Harvard gave first anthropology and later folklore the status of professions. From Francis Child to Franz Boas, benediction by Harvard and the American Folklore Society founded there in 1888 guaranteed national influence and authority.

The music industry began much earlier with the publication of sheet music and the manufacture of instruments. It evolved through the sale of player pianos, Edison discs, and Berliner platters to the advent of Tin Pan Alley, radio broadcasting, and the mass marketing of music (that is, music sold to the plebian masses as opposed to cultivated elites). Long before there was any scholarly interest in folk song, the music business had been selling its wares via broadsides, medicine shows, wild-west shows, and above all, minstrelsy-blackface and related styles (see Harrington and Hart's Irish parodies that parallel blackface).[5] By the time Harvard became interested, their cherished folk were dying off, didn't want to sing the old songs, and in any case were thoroughly contaminated by what came out of New York. This process, however, left in its wake a trace: the evidence of what the actual people of the United States had done and were doing. (It is worth noting how rarely the word *citizen* is employed in these discourses when, in fact, it is citizenship in an ostensibly democratic republic that is purported to be the raison d'être of the entire enterprise.)

Left out of most accounts are Francis Johnson's many compositions and career, the role of slave "musicianers" within the slave system, and publications such as James Monroe Trotter's *Music and Some Highly Musical People* (1878), John Wesley Work's *Folk Song of the American Negro* (1915), and Thomas Talley's *Negro Folk Rhymes/Wise and Otherwise* (1922). Furthermore, the pioneering efforts of Dena J. Epstein and Eileen Southern seem not to have corrected popular misconceptions regarding the long, creative interaction of African American musicians with European and European American music and musicians.[6] While Epstein's work is recognized for having proved beyond doubt the African sources of instruments such as the banjo as well as musical practices and sensibilities derived from African sources, what is often overlooked is that Epstein did not do so by denying or evading the absorption of influences, linguistic, musical, and religious, that enslaved people (and free people of color) had obviously accomplished.[7] This interaction was not only in rural areas where Black and white farm laborers lived in close proximity and shared musical influences (both secular and religious), but included the interaction of dockworkers, sailors, and urban-dwelling African Americans (witness the development of opera in New Orleans).[8] It includes the mastery of musical instruments, compositional techniques and orchestration as well as the absorption and creative transformation of an entire repertoire of Protestant hymnody. Even the development of the Negro spiritual has been less than accurately portrayed in many accounts. Not only have the musical aspects of this development been blurred, but the sociopolitical content of much of the repertoire has been misrepresented. (See Introduction for reference to James Lovell's claims.)[9]

James Monroe Trotter was born in slavery, escaped, and went on to join the Union Army, rising to the rank of second lieutenant, the highest occupied by an African American up to that time. His education and interest in music led him to write a book that was the first comprehensive musical history published in America (1878). As Eileen Southern wrote, Trotter's book was "the first time that anyone, black or white, had attempted to assess a body of American music that cut across genres and styles."[10]

Trotter's scholarship explicitly situates African American music within an appraisal of musical history from antiquity to the present. He does not differentiate style or genre in doing so, only describing those features of music that make it a universal form of human expression. He does so in order to prepare for his principal objective, which he summarized thusly:

> While grouping, as has here been done, the musical celebrities of a single race; while gathering from near and far these many fragments of musical history,

and recording them in one book,—the writer yet earnestly disavows all motives of a distinctively clannish nature. But the haze of complexional prejudice has so much obscured the vision of many persons, that they cannot see (at least, there are many who affect not to see) that musical faculties, and power for their artistic development, are not in the exclusive possession of the fairer-skinned race, but are alike the beneficent gifts of the Creator to all his children. Besides, there are some well-meaning persons who have formed, for lack of the information which is here afforded, erroneous and unfavorable estimates of the art-capabilities of the colored race. In the hope, then, of contributing to the formation of a more just opinion, of inducing a cheerful admission of its existence, and of aiding to establish between both races relations of mutual respect and good feeling; of inspiring the people most concerned (if that be necessary) with a greater pride in their own achievements, and confidence in their own resources, as a basis for other and even greater acquirements, as a landmark, a partial guide, for a future and better chronicler; and, finally, as a sincere tribute to the winning power, the noble beauty, of music, a contemplation of whose own divine harmony should ever serve to promote harmony between man and man,—with these purposes in view, this humble volume is hopefully issued.[11]

Trotter then provides biographical material on dozens of accomplished African American musicians whose work spans the century between the founding of the United States and the end of Reconstruction, when Trotter's book was published. Viewed from our present perspective, Trotter's appraisal raises doubts about the persistent image of African American music consisting exclusively of music made by field hands or rural, uneducated farmers. While there *is* such powerful music and it *is* undoubtedly an important contributor to modern popular music, it is not the sole ingredient nor is it representative of the broad range and sophistication of music made by African Americans, slave or free. Furthermore, this expands our understanding of slavery as a system, since it was never so simple as a mass of workers and a handful of masters. There were, certainly from the early eighteenth century on, many enslaved and free people of color who had mastered the English language and acquired the skills to perform and compose music of high quality, certainly the equivalent of other compositions made during the same period (witness the marches of Francis Johnson and his great popularity as a composer, band leader, and instrumentalist in the early nineteenth century).[12]

Yet even if one were to confine one's interest to music made by the great mass of uneducated and brutally treated field hands, the picture is more complicated than that preserved in legend and lore. In a detailed study, Paul A.

Cimbala shows how the slave system fostered stratification among the slaves themselves and the role that musical skill played in enhancing the status of one who acquired such skill.[13] Musicianship, especially on the fiddle, enabled greater mobility and less backbreaking labor for the individual who acquired it. Greater mobility meant traveling, in some cases widely, beyond the confines of a particular plantation and its strictly policed locale. (The use of slave patrols is well documented and referred to in slave songs, the most famous of which is "Run, N----r, Run.") Less backbreaking labor must be understood as more than simply hard work:

> Slaves were both capital assets and labor. The rules of profit maximization in the slave economy, when there was an active slave trade capable of very rapid replacement of human chattel, led to the frequent application of a *seven years rule*, viewed by the planters as the average life of their slaves, on which their computations of value were based. Slaves were so overworked in Jamaica and other British colonies that their lives were generally consumed in seven years. For the slave-owning capitalist, it was of relatively little significance if the turnover of slaves through premature exhaustion of their working lives and existence took place as long as they were easily replaceable. Furthermore, under slave production, it was possible to work slaves more intensively, superexploiting them, than in the case of wage labor.[14]

Thus, the incentive to become a musicianer was great. Not only as elevated status, it could literally be a matter of life and death. While this clearly motivated individuals to acquire and perfect their skills, these skills corresponded to the requirements of their masters. Slaveowners routinely leased their talented property to provide entertainment on other plantations and in cities and towns, making money in the process. On some occasions they might share a portion with the musicianers they owned. This in turn affected what such musicianers learned to play or composed themselves since not only was the incentive great but it meant meeting the musical demands of his or her employer (though most musicianers were men, there were some women, as well).

Cimbala notes, however, that "Plantation owners also had reasons other than entertainment for desiring slave musicians on their estates. They believed that fiddlers and banjoists were necessary instruments of slave control. By encouraging music and dancing, masters hoped to keep moody slaves happy, lazy slaves productive and idle slaves out of mischief. If planters did not own musicians, they usually hired instrumentalists from their neighbors who did. This in turn allowed the owners of musicians to exploit their chattels in one more way. By hiring out their slaves the owners supplemented their income."[15] Cimbala then cites "the interesting case of a planter who purchased a musician for the specific purpose of slave control. John Thomson's owner bought a fiddler named Martin because he had begun to worry about his slaves' newfound religiosity. He hoped 'that fiddling would bring them back to their former ignorant condition.' According to Thompson, the tactic worked until Martin, a well-liked man who curiously had been purchased for a term of ten years, left the plantation."[16]

Such dubious purposes did not prevent musicianers from performing at ceremonies and frolics (as celebrations were called) attended only by other slaves. Indeed, Cimbala cites the important community function played by skilled instrumentalists not only in accompanying such social activities but in teaching others how to play. Though there may have been no music schools or printed manuals, there was instruction, apprenticeship, and generational transmission that accounts, far better than "natural" causes, for the development of African American music. But musicianers did more than that. "The slave fiddler George assumed one more duty in the quarters that went beyond the drilling of would-be 'musicianers.' On regular occasions he gave singing and dancing lessons to the black children on his Tennessee plantation home and thus acted as a transmitter of musical folk culture to a new generation of Afro-Americans."[17] This helps convey the larger process by which skills were practically acquired and transmitted, thus demystifying the process. Robert Johnson's deal with the Devil may never have been taken seriously by anyone but his fans, but this "legend" subtly supported a racist misconception that somehow Black people were musical either by birth and blood or by some supernatural process instead of having to learn, like all human beings, and doing an outstanding job of it under the most arduous conditions.

This furthermore goes a long way to explaining the interplay between a variety of song styles, including those Africans brought with them to America, those they acquired from church, and those from other sources such as social dances, minuets, quadrilles, waltzes, mazurkas, and so on, and vernacular sources such as Irish or English songs. This point is especially relevant due to the much-admired musical skills of slave musicianers, on the one hand, and the fakery sold by the music business as blackface minstrelsy. While advertisers of blackface always insisted they were providing the "real" thing, authentic Negro music, what they were in fact using was Irish and English melody and song structure with lyrics in quasi-Black dialect.[18] Authenticity was a selling point that, after a hundred years of propagation, had the effect of completely confusing the musical record. While there can be no doubt that Africans and their descendants in the United States preserved and developed musical and lyrical forms originating in Africa, it is equally true that Africans and African Americans, enslaved or nominally free, adopted and adapted music they learned in the Western Hemisphere. These facts challenge one-dimensional notions of slavery as a system that were largely the product of racist bias, either explicitly white supremacist or cloaked as sympathetic curiosity, and that, to a large extent, persisted long after the Civil War. Indeed, they were vigorously revived in the wake of Reconstruction and are responsible for many of the misconceptions we are still grappling with today.

The sources Cimbala quotes are derived largely from the testimony of former slaves who were interviewed extensively in the Federal Writers Project of 1935–1939, wherein 2,300 of their number were interviewed. This research was further enhanced by George Rawick's forty-one-volume *The American Slave: A Composite Autobiography*, which was published in two parts, 1972 and 1977. This source, incidentally, is of incalculable value and has much to tell us about slavery in general and the the music heard, composed, and performed by enslaved people in particular. I scanned all forty-one volumes in my search for revolutionary slave songs and found not only confirmation for a number of such songs but also much more regarding which songs were most often cited over a broad geographical range.

Thomas Talley's work raises other questions that challenge prevailing notions. Talley was a scientist who taught chemistry and biology at Fisk University. He studied at Harvard and was influenced by the seriousness with which folklore was taken there. Talley's personal and lifelong interest in music led him to pursue song collecting in his Tennessee neighborhood, including those he remembered from his childhood there (he was born in 1870). However, Talley differed from other academics in that his first concern was not origin but active use. In short, what did the people actually sing or remember having sung? In addition, Talley had the advantage of being Black, which meant his interlocutors were more at ease than they often were with white song collectors. Finally, though Talley uses certain classificatory labels such as the ballad, his use is idiosyncratic in that he includes within the ballad a wider range of material, thus stretching the definition beyond that of his Harvard colleagues. His method, moreover, was more scientific than the pretensions of the academy. Talley remarks: ". . . about all Folk Rhymes are Nature Ballads." He continues,

> I do not have reference to the thought content, but have reference to what I term Nature Ballads in form. Permit me to explain by analogy just what I would convey by the term Nature Ballad in form.

All Nature is one. Though we arbitrarily divide Nature's objects for study, they are indissolubly bound together and every part carries in some part of its constitution some well defined marks which characterize the other parts with which it has no immediate connection.

After a detailed comparison of animal, vegetable, and mineral components, Talley sums up: "Nature's method, then, of making things seems to be to put in a large enough amount of one thing to brand the article, and then to mix in, in small amounts, enough of other things to lend charm and beauty without taking the article out of its general class."[19]

This analogy illuminates his method, which was intended to both dignify Negro folk rhymes according to prevailing academic criteria and to respectfully differ in a fundamental way. In *Segregating Sounds*, historian Karl Hagstrom Miller calls attention to the origins of some of Talley's selections: "Several selections were related to Tin Pan Alley or minstrel songs that had circulated commercially in the previous decades. Other were songs popular with white singers in the area and were recorded by white hillbilly artist during the 1920s. He [Talley] gave little indication that he knew or cared that this collection contained songs originating with music publishers."[20] None of which in any way undermines the quality of Talley's work. It simply reaffirms his original purpose: to collect what the people sang or remembered singing in the past.

Talley makes other observations; for instance, he claims that the most common instrument used among the formerly enslaved population was the quills, not, as one would expect, the banjo or the fiddle. The quills are pan-pipes, one or more rows of tubes of different lengths, and are one of the world's most widespread instruments. Talley writes:

> Banjos and fiddles (violins) were owned only limitedly by antebellum Negroes. Those who owned them mastered them to such a degree that the memory of their skill will long linger. These instruments are familiar and need no discussion.
>
> Probably the Negro's most primitive instrument, which he could call his very own, was "Quills." It is mentioned in the story, "Brother Fox, Brother Rabbit, and King Deer's Daughter" which I have already quoted at some length. If the reader will notice in this story he will see, after the singing of the first stanza by the rabbit and fox, a description in these words, "Den de quills and de tr'angle, dey come in, an' den Br'er Rabbit pursue on wid de call." Here we have described in the Negro's own way the long form of instrumental music composition which we have hitherto discussed, and "quills" and "tr'angles" are given as the instruments.[21]

Moreover, Talley brings forward songs that might have escaped white song collectors as informants might not have wanted to share them, either for fear of reprisal or for fear of offending. One such example is the song "Promises of Freedom." Talley writes:

> This is that which goes to make Negro Folk Rhymes Nature Ballads in form. They are ballads, but all in the midst of even a Dance Song, by Nature an ordinary ballad, there may be interwoven comedy, tragedy, and nearly every kind of imaginable thing which goes rather with other general forms of poetry than with the ballad. As an example, in the Dance Song, "Promises of Freedom," we have mustered before our eyes the comic drawing of a deceptive ugly old Mistress and then follows the intimation of the tragic death of a poisoned slave owner, and as we are tempted to dance along in thought with the rhymer, we cannot escape getting the subtle impression that this slave had at least some "vague" personal knowledge of how the Master got that poison. It is a common easy-going ballad, but it is tinted with tragedy and comedy. This general principle will be found to run very largely through the highest types of Negro Folk Rhymes. It is the Nature method of construction, and thus we call them Nature Ballads in structure, or form.[22]

Talley's classification of folk rhymes raises other issues as well. While acknowledging that perhaps the only dignity granted the Negro by the dominant society was his apparent religiosity—and Talley was loath to dispute anything that brought dignity to his people—he politely suggests that what the people actually sang was not so easily separated as religious or secular, certainly not in musical terms. This bears on the overly simplistic divide that has long been promoted, for example the spiritual vs. blues or jazz. Popular misconception has followed to the present day and is common in discussions of the origins of rock 'n' roll. It is asserted that music of the church is opposed to the music of the brothel or juke-joint and never the twain shall meet. No doubt, there was great debate within African American communities over the issue and no doubt, there were religious, social, and political principles at stake. Yet, if one considers the music of Sister Rosetta Tharpe, for example, one immediately recognizes that that distinction is not musical but lyrical. Tharpe's guitar playing precedes Chuck Berry's by a generation, her music is rock 'n' roll in all but name, but her lyrics are almost uniformly religious or spiritual. This not only problematizes the division but it harkens back to the usurpation made by blackface minstrelsy with its claims to be authentically "Ethiopian" or Negro music (more on this below). The significance of this point is both musicological and historical. Music cannot be so simply characterized as it has been by academics or advertisers. Definitions have been imposed upon, not extracted from, the musical evidence. They are in any case far too narrow and prejudicial. This in turn distorts the historical record because it presents an image of the slave system and resistance to that system that is, at best, incomplete.

💣 💣 💣

The second example is of a different type. I am referring here to the marginalization or "disappearance" of a variety of popular musical practices and their replacement by music, lyrics, and performers as consumer goods—in short, music as a social activity vs. music as a saleable commodity. The songs and practice of shape-note singing, especially that represented by the songbook *The Sacred Harp* (1844), are particularly noteworthy. Their widespread and enduring popularity among white and Black communities is indisputable. But the practice is also not much known except among practitioners and aficionados. The inherent musical content, that is, songs and performance practices, is significant in and of itself: quintessentially democratic, community-based, music-making, which, one would think, defines the word popular. It is also historically important in at least two ways: first, as evidence of the religio-political views of a group that would play a key role in the founding and future of the United States; second, as evidence of what was more generally replaced by a burgeoning music business and how the advance of capitalism meant the retreat of the music formerly popular among the broadest mass of people.

In the first case, as is well known, the Puritans who settled New England were dissenters who defied the Church of England and the Crown. Their movement ultimately led to the English Revolution, 1640–1660 (usually referred to as the English Civil War), which was ultimately defeated by the restoration of the monarchy. Less known is the fact that these dissenters brought music with them as a central component of their social life, a subject to which we will return. Yet Puritans were not a denomination or sect in and of themselves.[23] Puritans were in fact more varied and politically radical than is usually acknowledged. If one considers the punishments that were routinely meted out to opponents of the Church of England and the Crown—imprisonment, the stocks, hanging, and disemboweling—one begins to glimpse Puritanism as a radical movement (and also why, in defeat, many fled to North America). Not only did the term *Puritan* encapsulate a wide range of radical views, but it was the force behind the founding of the New Model Army, the poetry of John Milton (*Paradise*

Lost), and the proselytizing of John Bunyan (*The Pilgrim's Progress*). Puritanism rallied diverse strains of thinking: Ranters, Seekers, Fifth-Monarchists, and Muggletonians, as well as Levellers and Diggers (the True Levellers).[24] It should not surprise us that among the descendants of these movements were the first abolitionists. Anthony Benezet and Benjamin Lay are two famous examples of Quakers who devoted their lives to abolishing slavery.

The English Revolution also produced a large number of revolutionary songs, some of which entered the repertoire of denominations tracing their origins to the same course of events. Presbyterians, Unitarians, Quakers, Methodists, and Baptists all grew in opposition to the Church of England, and all, to one degree or another, supported the abolition of the monarchy (the beheading of Charles I) and the establishment of the Commonwealth. All were committed to community singing, carrying on and further developing a body of musical literature that predominated in the original Thirteen Colonies. Indeed, this Protestant music predominated among the populace well after the American Revolutionary War. It is evident in many regional styles from New England to Appalachia and throughout the South, involving Black and white congregations, even infusing secular music with its melodic, harmonic, rhythmic, and timbral content to this day.

But there is more obscured by legend and lore than the sources of melodies or lyrics. Contrary to prevailing notions, the Puritans and subsequent Protestant denominations were not antimusic, nor did they frown on joyous celebration of the holy spirit. The first book published in British North America was the *Bay Psalm Book* (1640), one indication of the importance of singing to the community. There was, however, great controversy over *how* to sing, and this may have left a false impression of attitudes toward singing as such. John Wesley, himself a strong advocate of music in worship, warned against diverting from the written text, a warning, no doubt, directed at congregants who got carried away. The issue was made more acute by the camp-meetings which brought the Second Great Awakening far and wide in the early nineteenth century, thereby propagating new forms of community singing.[25] The wild and unruly singing that came to characterize these events was criticized in a book whose lengthy title aptly describes the phenomenon: *Methodist Error; or, Friendly, Christian Advice, To those Methodists, Who indulge in extravagant emotions and bodily exercises.*[26] Such controversy was typical. Music, including common folk tunes, was welcome and encouraged, yet it was always the tendency of uneducated rural folk to sing their own way, ecstatically celebrating deliverance. Eventually, this way would preponderate, forming the basis of much that we call folk or popular music today. This did not, however, limit the proliferation of musical literature. On the contrary, the succeeding century saw the vast expansion of this musical literature.

Of special importance were the more than eight hundred compositions of Isaac Watts. Watts's songs were sung everywhere and still are. The many community and church choirs that continue the tradition of "Dr. Watts" are exemplified by the Dr. Watts Singers of St. John Missionary Baptist Church in Meridian, Mississippi.[27] Outside those communities that carry on this tradition, very few are aware of Dr. Watts's contribution and the extent to which his was a conscious effort to ensure a musical and moral education for the common people.

Yet one more example in this set is the music of the Shakers. This is preserved in recordings and in the recently republished *Millennial Praises: A Shaker Hymnal*, originally published in 1813. One Shaker song, "Simple Gifts," was so well-known it formed the basis of Aaron Copland's orchestral suite, *Appalachian Spring* (1944). But, the tale of another song, "Babylon Is Fallen," displays the web of mutually reinforcing influences even further. This song that originates in the English Revolution was popularized widely and taken up by many denominations including the Shakers, albeit with lyrical modifications. It migrated into the African American church and became part of regular repertoire there. Later, a song by that name was composed by abolitionist Henry Clay Work during the Civil War. Finally, the original song appeared on an album recorded in 1973 by the British group Swan Arcade.[28]

In sum, the legacy of music and music-making of this kind is rich and vital in spite of having been marginalized and effectively superseded by the music industry. It marks the change of definition of the word *popular*. Until quite recently, popular meant arising from the populace. This is the usage common to virtually all discussions of music prior to the twentieth century. Now, however, that definition has been supplanted by one designating popular as that which is consumed by the populace. "Popular" or "pop" music no longer describes or defines the musical activity of the people, instead it only registers their buying habits. This linguistic sleight of hand has far-reaching implications but has been largely accepted without a peep by opinion-makers or influencers (as they're currently known). Nevertheless, exploring it requires historical as well as musicological method. As the excavation of long-buried slave songs shows, resistance to oppression and the building of communities of resistance is an often overlooked but central component of actual popular music-making. Central to such music and music-making practice is collective participation, consciously directed at community building. It is unabashedly devoted to the common good.

♪ ♪ ♪

A third example involves blackface minstrelsy. The blackface phenomenon has been studied and denounced widely in recent years. Books by Eric Lott, Robert Toll, Hans Nathan, and Dale Cockrell are among numerous such studies. It might therefore seem redundant to include this example here except as further, albeit well-known, proof of the racism prevalent in America from its founding. However, what most accounts fail to mention is that at the same time blackface was being promoted, it was being opposed not only by political critics such as Frederick Douglass but by musicians as popular as any blackface performer, if not more so. Yet while many are familiar with Stephen Foster, Christy's Minstrels, Dan Emmet, or Thomas "Big Daddy" Rice, who remembers the Hutchinson Family Singers, Henry Clay Work, Benjamin Hanby, or Joshua MacCarter Simpson? In short, blackface is remembered but its opponents are not; why not?

The Hutchinson Family Singers are the prime example of this opposition to blackface but they were not the only ones (see below). In fact, the literature on this subject is inadequate and incomplete in two different ways. First, because most accounts fail to acknowledge that blackface built the modern music industry, its sales and performance techniques are in use to this day. The industry, furthermore, has never been held accountable. All the "blame" for this musical and theatrical current is placed on the audiences who attended its performance. This characterizes the way entertainment that is morally or politically reprehensible continues to be treated (a recent example being the opprobrium heaped upon gangsta rap). But what's left out of this treatment is both the role that concert promoters, publicists, and publishers played in popularizing the trend and the fact that many other forms of music were as widely popular and influential, some deliberately opposed to slavery as an institution and blackface as slavery's propagandist.

The five hundred songs gathered together by Vicki Lynn Eaklor in her *American Anti-Slavery Songs* (1988) prove this point.[29] These songs were the work of many people, among whom were poets and musicians of national and international reputation, such as James Russell Lowell and George W. Clark. They were both widely popular in the years between 1830 and the Civil War and often directed their efforts explicitly at blackface minstrelsy, co-opting the very tunes used in blackface and transforming them into antislavery weapons. Here, the work of Joshua McCarter Simpson stands out because he clearly stated his method and purpose. In the introduction to the first of three songbooks he published, Simpson wrote: "In offering my first little production to the public, I am well aware that many superstitious, prejudiced, and perhaps many good, conscientious, well-meaning christians [sic] will have serious objections to the 'Airs' to which my poetry is set. My object in my selection of tunes, is to kill the degrading influence of these comic Negro Songs, which are too common among our people, and change the flow of these sweet melodies into more appropriate and useful channels."[30]

As mentioned above, the Hutchinson Family Singers are perhaps the most outstanding example of this phenomenon, given that they were acknowledged as the most popular group in America in contemporary and subsequent accounts (see Gilbert Chase: ". . . no other group was as internationally famous or as controversial as the Hutchinsons." *America's Music*, 163). Their sold-out shows in New York and other cities led to tours in Europe of equal distinction. Among the best accounts of their political and musical career are those of Brian Roberts. In his book *Blackface Nation*, and in an essay for the American Antiquarian Society, Roberts documents the Hutchinsons' political commitments as well as their enormous popularity. He goes on to assert: "The Hutchinsons were abolitionists. They were also extremely popular. To be sure, the content of some of their songs made them unwelcome south of the Potomac River. But they were the favorites of a northern middle class. In fact, a close look at the singers within the context of popular music and the theater in the antebellum Northeast reveals that their success came not despite their beliefs but instead as a direct result of their involvement with increasingly 'radical' reforms." Furthermore, Roberts concludes: "This story argues for a new approach to abolitionism, one that places it not on the 'radical' margins of American politics or society but at the very center of American popular culture."[31]

Yet despite the facts and the conclusions Roberts draws from them, the Hutchinsons are forgotten and, more egregiously, the abolitionist movement has been removed from "the very center of American popular culture" to the margins where no one will notice it. It is important to add that the Hutchinsons were not a fluke or exception. Other abolitionist composers and performers wrote songs that became nationally famous, including a few that do remain in the canon of American song. Benjamin Hanby's "Darling Nelly Gray" is performed to this day (albeit with many performing it unaware of its abolitionist roots). Henry Clay Work's "Marching Through Georgia" is remembered, as well. But forgotten are others of his militant antislavery songs such as "Kingdom's Coming" and "Babylon Is Fallen." And, of course, the most famous and best-loved example is "Amazing Grace." Though widely performed, very few recall its composer and his purpose in writing it (abolitionist John Newton, Anglican clergyman, formerly captain of slave ships).

These are only a few examples, but they are enough to cast doubt upon the "objectivity" or rigorousness of much historical and musicological literature.

Not only have these materials been largely ignored, but an assumption has been made by the authorities in the respective fields that they deserve to be. In other words, the reasons we know little about these people, this music, and the movement to abolish slavery is because, ultimately, it doesn't count.

♦ ♦ ♦

One more example completes this survey: the music of the labor movement. Notwithstanding the noble efforts of Archie Green, Richard Reuss, three generations of the Seeger family, and numerous others, and though there are available collections assembled by Ronald Cohen and Dave Samuelson at Bear Family Records or those of Patrick Huber and Marshall Wyatt at Old Hat Records, no body of musical literature has been more thoroughly expunged from American music than this one.

When one considers that several folk music revivals have occurred, the most recent following the release of the Coen brothers film *O Brother, Where Art Thou?* in 2001, with only passing reference to the labor movement, one begins to glimpse the problem. The aperture opens a bit if one makes a song-by-song comparison of the repertoire in the movie with the repertoire presented in the book *Hard Hitting Songs for Hard-Hit People* (published in 1967 but originally completed in 1941). Everyone loved the movie music without realizing that some of the tunes were slave songs that had been adapted to serve the purposes of striking miners in Kentucky ("The Good Ol' Way" turned into "Come On Friends and Let's Go Down"), others were popular hits that had similarly been transformed ("Man of Constant Sorrow" turned into "Girl of Constant Sorrow") and still others were written by committed members of the Industrial Workers of the World (Harry McClintock's "Big Rock Candy Mountain"). McClintock, who died in San Francisco in 1957, claimed he was the first to sing Joe Hill's most famous song, "The Preacher and the Slave," which deepens the connection between this repertoire and the labor movement. The fact that there are such close associations raises the obvious question: did the people involved in making the selection for a hit soundtrack know? Did they deliberately fail to mention these points of historical interest? I have no way of approaching these celebrities to inquire, but I can do the research myself to show that it can be done and does reveal a pattern of deliberate omission or glossing over that has even greater ramifications. It begins to explain how figures such as Woody Guthrie and Paul Robeson can be commemorated on postage stamps while their lifelong dedication to the cause of the working class is swept under the rug.

The reasons for this and the mechanisms by which it is accomplished become clearer when one relates the musical record to the historical one. Class antagonism in the United States has been systematically obscured by patriotic appeals mixed indissolubly with white supremacist and male chauvinist messaging. Popular music has had to be purged of all references to the confrontation between labor and capital. This is so pervasive it is hardly noticed. Indeed, many folklorists and, certainly, many record company employees, seem blissfully unaware of their unquestioned assumptions regarding the consciousness of the people, let alone the struggles those people have engaged in and led. This is evident in songs mentioned above and presented in my book *Working Class Heroes*. These are far from anomalous and are indeed representative of a much larger number, for example, the songs of Aunt Molly Jackson, Sarah Ogan Gunning, Ella May Wiggins, John Handcox, and Jim Garland. But the list is much longer and includes songs from all corners of America. There could be entire collections assembled of songs of Mexican and Filipino farmworkers organizing in California. Or miners in the West and Southwest. Or textile workers organizing in New England. And so on. In the afterword for the 2012 reissue of *Hard Hitting Songs for Hard-Hit People*, Pete Seeger wrote that it had been a mistake not to include this wider diversity of songs that certainly exist. He further noted that there could/should have been a whole section devoted to the songs of textile workers, who, it will be recalled, were mainly women and children. This reveals another dimension of the problem.

Given present-day preoccupation with gender issues, isn't it peculiar that we are asked to forget how big a role women workers played in the labor movement? This role, too, is represented musically by the forgetting of once popular musical revues such as *Pins and Needles* or the origins of the song "Bread and Roses," along with the numerous other plays and musicals that expressed outrage at capitalism and support for the workers cause (including Blitzstein's *The Cradle Will Rock*, Odets's *Waiting for Lefty*, and Copland's *Into the Streets May First!*).

The evidence is abundant but so is the blindness. This blindness is cloaked in certain terms that are frequently used: "authenticity," "outside agitator," "no commercial potential," and "foreign influence." The quest for the pure "folk" is a cover for downplaying or ignoring altogether the resistance to oppression and exploitation, expressed in songs, of the real, living folk. The marketing of "Old Familiar" and "Novelty Songs," which typifies strategies applied by record companies, promises to "give the people what they want" and is therefore only reflecting—not inculcating—popular consciousness. Thus even the musically diverse and undoubtedly well-intentioned collections such as those at the

Library of Congress or Harry Smith's wonderful *Anthology of American Music* are largely comprised of music performed by people for collectors and those people giving the collectors what those people thought the collectors wanted to hear (not to mention the fact that many of the recorded musicians were professionals with long experience in minstrel shows, medicine shows, and vaudeville). Why do I know that? Because the people and the collectors said so themselves. There are many accounts of collectors bemoaning the fact that when they went hunting for "authentic" folk material they kept running into genuine folk offering the latest commercial ditty they'd picked up off the radio, records, or from other sources.[32] Musicians, furthermore, often testified to the fact that to make a living you had to learn everything: white, Black, country, city, it didn't matter. You learned it all.[33] (On a personal note, as a musician, I find this so obvious I must look askance at the naiveté of the "experts.")

Ralph Peer knew what he was looking for. He wanted music that would sell and he based his search on well-established practices developed in the marketing of blackface minstrelsy, as well as catering to ethnic nostalgia (European immigrants—Polish, German, Swedish, and more). In fact, these practices developed a hundred years prior to Peer's famous Bristol Sessions (1927) but did not take off until after Reconstruction and the concomitant development of recording technology. They were certainly in full effect decades prior to Peer's arrival. Scott Joplin had the first million-selling song with the sheet music of his "Maple Leaf Rag" in 1899. Enrico Caruso sold large numbers of records as early as 1906. Vernon Dalhart was the first million-selling recording artist with "The Wreck of the Old '97" in 1920. Mamie Smith had the breakthrough hit "Crazy Blues" the same year. The bottom line here is that almost any reference to politics, except patriotism or electoral politics, is barred. Almost any pro-union, explicitly working-class (as opposed to individual experience), or revolutionary content is not allowed. Yes, certain workers' songs are among America's favorites. "Sixteen Tons," "Busted," "Workin' Man Blues," and "Working in the Coal Mine" come to mind. But as wonderful as these songs are, they are known mainly as catchy tunes or hard luck stories and are thus amputated from the body of which they are a part.

Another aspect of this is more a matter of the historical record pure and simple, although it is never far from the musical one. The antiunion, antiworker policies of the US government are abundantly evident from the first stirrings of organized labor in the period following Reconstruction. While a recounting of labor history is beyond the scope of this chapter, suffice it to say, massive strikes took place throughout the United States between 1877 and 1947, including all major industries and every part of the country. International Workers

Day grew out of the Haymarket Riot of 1886. International Women's Day drew inspiration from several major strikes of women workers in the United States.

Fear of anarchist and socialist influence, particularly that of recent immigrants like Sacco and Vanzetti, emboldened authorities to build police forces and spread hysteria. These tactics were institutionalized by the formation of the FBI and the launching of periodic "red scares." While communism, especially after the Russian Revolution, was indeed seen as a threat, the ultimate purpose of government attack was to crush the working class. While there was a truce of sorts in the New Deal era and the period leading up to World War II, the attacks resumed in earnest almost immediately after. The AFL-CIO was purged of its most militant unions (more than a million members), the Taft-Hartley Act was passed, and McCarthyism ran rampant across the country. But because this was directed at crushing the working class, music could not be exempt.

The absurd lengths to which this witch hunt would go is well documented in *American Folk Music and Left Wing Politics, 1927–1957.* In his introduction, Richard Reuss recounts a hilarious incident wherein a right-wing civic group demanded a Congressional investigation claiming folk music was a communist plot. And this was in 1963! The charge was so insipid (and the group so obviously right-wing) that a Republican senator, Kenneth Keating, found it politically opportune to read into the *Congressional Record* a satirical rebuttal.[34] Nevertheless, the attacks of the government escalated, as is well documented in the recent book *The Folk Singers and the Bureau* (2021).[35] Careers were ruined, lives destroyed, and American music was cleansed of subversive content. In the broad sweep of musical history, this is perhaps the most ridiculous, although sinister, of effects. By any objective measure, a crucial component of popular music from almost anywhere in the world is its subversive content! Why should that be surprising?

One body of songs proves this beyond reasonable doubt. These can be loosely grouped under the heading "Irish rebel songs" and are so well known as such that they have a Wikipedia entry devoted to them. Representative samplings can be found in numerous collections, songbooks, recordings, and the repertoires of significant performers such as the Clancy Brothers, the Dubliners, and others. One outstanding collection is the commemorative set produced for the fiftieth anniversary of the Easter Rising in 1966. Yet, this body of songs is not unique, indeed, it is representative of all that concerns us here, including the fact that it is not simply "Irish" but displays an intense interaction between the struggle for Irish independence and the cluster of revolutions that filled the last decades of the eighteenth century (American,

French, Haitian, and Irish) and the musical exchange between Ireland and North America that has never ceased. It further illustrates the connection between the struggle for national liberation and the labor movement that parallels the struggle to abolish the slave system and achieve the emancipation of enslaved African Americans. In this broader context, it is important to note the specific contribution of James Connolly, with which this inquiry began.

Connolly's songbook, *Songs of Freedom*, was published in New York in 1907, preceding by several years the publication of the world-renowned songbook of the Industrial Workers of the World (1911). The Wobblies' Little Red Songbook is so well known it needs little exposition here. But Connolly's book is important for several reasons including the fact that it was effectively forgotten for a hundred years and even the most knowledgeable folklorists or collectors fail to mention it. Connolly's introduction makes clear that his effort was directed at the American working class and was a contribution of Irish poets to the socialist literature of the world. Indeed, echoing James Monroe Trotter's insistence that calling attention to Black music and musicians was in no sense "clannish" or intended to promote division among people, Connolly's intention is clearly internationalist in spirit, aimed at elevating all workers, not ranking one nationality over another.

Reference was made in the Introduction to the present volume to the method Connolly and other contributors used in choosing the musical settings for their lyrics. This method is typical. It is the way music of almost any movement for liberation uses music: use whatever melody is appropriate to the spirit of the text and is popular among the intended audience. But it is revealing of something else that has to be mentioned since so much mystification and obfuscation is blown away by this common practice.

In an essay contained in the reissue of Harry Smith's *Anthology of American Folk Music*, entitled "The Old Weird America," Greil Marcus brings forward many interesting facts about musicians and musical traditions with some mention of the occupations and living conditions of these individuals. Marcus furthermore acknowledges the controversies surrounding folk vs. popular music and Smith's categorical rejection of academic purism. However, the overall impression one gets is expressed in the title of the piece itself. Its purpose is to convey an aura or mystique that is ultimately counterproductive. There is no mystery about these people and their music. Furthermore, there is plenty to be learned about America that is occluded by such mystifying. It is neither weird nor impenetrable on any level, musical, historical, or political. Yet this is how marketing has long been successful not only in selling particular commodities, but in selling selling as a norm. As the Clash once sang: "Selling is what selling sells," going on to describe the degradation left in selling's wake. The relevance here goes beyond poetic or literary devices to questions of method and, ultimately, how a reappraisal of American (or any other) music might be made.

NOTES

1. See Suisman, *Selling Sounds*.
2. See Basker, *Amazing Grace*; see also Sinha, *The Slave's Cause*.
3. Garabedian, *A Sound History*.
4. Epstein, Sinful Tunes and Spirituals.
5. See Goldberg, *Tin Pan Alley*.
6. See Southern, *The Music of Black Americans*.
7. Referring to the camp-meetings of the "Second Great Awakening" that were profoundly influential on the populace of the South, Dena Epstein writes: "There is no room for doubt that blacks and whites worshipped and sang together in an atmosphere highly charged with emotion at camp meetings during the first half of the nineteenth century. That the participants were mutually influenced seems inescapable. Songs, parts of songs, and ways of singing must have been exchanged, without the excited folk knowing or caring who started what." Epstein, *Sinful Tunes and Spirituals*, 199.
8. See Hugill, *Shanties from the Seven Seas*; see also Opera Créole, mailto:https://www.operacreole.com/.
9. See Lovell, *Black Song: The Forge and the Flame*.
10. Southern and Wright, *African-American Traditions*, 149.
11. Trotter, *Music and Some Highly Musical People*, 4–5.
12. See "Francis Johnson, 1792–1844," University Archives and Records Center, University of Pennsylvania, https://archives.upenn.edu/exhibits/penn-people/biography/francis-johnson/.
13. Cimbala, "Fortunate Bondsmen: Black 'Musicianers' and Their Role as an Antebellum Southern Plantation Slave Elite."
14. Foster, Holleman, and Clark, "Marx and Slavery."
15. Cimbala, "Fortunate Bondsmen."
16. Cimbala, "Fortunate Bondsmen," 294n10.
17. Cimbala, "Fortunate Bondsmen," 298.
18. Byrd, "Whitewashing Blackface Minstrelsy," 77–86. Byrd writes: "But the concern here is not with fiddle and banjo music, but with the songs—songs that came to capture the American imagination. The musical inspiration for these tunes was not African, but familiar Irish and British folk songs (Tosches 24–25)." The reference is to Nick Tosches, *Where Dead Voices Gather* (Boston: Little, Brown, 2001).
19. Talley, *Negro Folk Rhymes, Wise and Otherwise*, 352–53.
20. Miller, *Segregating Sounds*, 249.
21. Talley, *Negro Folk Rhymes, Wise and Otherwise*, 420–21.
22. Talley, *Negro Folk Rhymes, Wise and Otherwise*, 354.
23. See Hill, *Society and Puritanism in Pre-Revolutionary England*.
24. See Hill, *The World Turned Upside Down*.
25. See Wheeler, "The Music of the Early Nineteenth-Century Camp Meeting."
26. By "A Wesleyan Methodist." The title page adds: "Let all things be done decently and in order, unto edification; for God is not the author of confusion, but of peace."

27. "Playing for Positive Progress II—American Roots Folk House." YouTube, September 24, 2020. https://www.youtube.com/watch?v=BkKDT-9lJiU.
28. "Babylon Is Fallen," Folk and Traditional Song Lyrics, https://www.traditionalmusic.co.uk/folk-song-lyrics/Babylon_is_Fallen(2).htm; "Babylon's Falling," NegroSpirituals.com, https://www.negrospirituals.com/songs/index.htm; Swan Arcade, "Babylon Is Fallen," YouTube, https://www.youtube.com/watch?v=SmDwjDiDXb8.
29. Eaklor, *American Anti-Slavery Songs.*
30. Simpson, *Original Anti-Slavery Songs*, 3.
31. Roberts, *"Slavery Would Have Died of That Music,"* 309–10.
32. ". . . the folklorist Dorothy Scarborough lamented being 'tricked into enthusiasm over the promise of folk-songs only to hear age-worn phonograph records' and 'Broadway echoes' as she attempted to collect songs in the South." Miller, *Segregating Sounds*, 210.
33. Miller quotes musician Samuel Chatmon saying, "You take a fellow that can play anything, he can get a job more or less anywhere." Miller goes on about Chatmon and his fellows in the Mississippi Sheiks: "The men were musical omnivores. Plying their trade in the streets, storefronts, and cafes, they performed blues and ballads, fiddle tunes, coon songs, and the latest Broadway hits." Miller, *Segregating Sounds*, 222.
34. Reuss with Reuss, *American Folk Music and Left-wing Politics: 1927–1957*, in the Introduction.
35. Leonard, *The Folk Singers and the Bureau.*

REFERENCES

A Wesleyan Methodist. *Methodist Error or, Friendly Christian Advice To those Methodists Who indulge in extravagant emotions and bodily exercises.* D. and E. Fenton, 1819.

Aptheker, Herbert. *American Negro Slave Revolts.* International Publishers, 1983; originally published by International Publishers, 1943.

Aptheker, Herbert. *Essays in the History of the American Negro.* International Publishers, 1954.

Aptheker, Herbert. *Negro Slave Revolts in the United States 1526–1860.* International Publishers, 1939.

Baptist, Edward. *The Half That's Never Been Told.* Basic Books, 2014.

Basker, James G. *Amazing Grace: An Anthology of Poems About Slavery 1660–1810.* New Haven, CT: Yale University Press, 2002.

Basker, James. *American Anti-Slavery Writings: Colonial Beginnings to Emancipation.* Library of America, 2012.

Byrd, Joseph. "Whitewashing Blackface Minstrelsy in American College Textbooks." *Popular Music and Society* 32:1 (February 2009).

Chase, Gilbert. *America's Music, from the Pilgrims to the Present.* New York: McGraw-Hill, 1955, 163.

Cimbala, Paul A. "Fortunate Bondsmen: Black 'Musicianers' and Their Role as an Antebellum Southern Plantation Slave Elite." *Southern Studies* 18:3 (Fall 1979).

Du Bois, W. E. B. *Black Folk Then and Now.* Oxford: Oxford University Press, 2007.

Du Bois, W. E. B. *Black Reconstruction in America 1860–1880.* Free Press Edition, 1998; originally published by Harcourt, Brace, 1935.

Du Bois, W. E. B. *John Brown.* Kraus-Thompson Organization, 1973; originally published by George W. Jacobs, 1909.

Du Bois, W. E. B. *The Souls of Black Folk.* Dover Publications, 1994; originally published by A.C. McLurg, 1903.

Eaklor, Vicki Lynn. *American Anti-Slavery Songs*. Greenwood Press, 1988.
Epstein, Dena J. *Sinful Tunes and Spirituals: Black Folk Music to the Civil War*. Urbana: University of Illinois Press, 1981; originally published 1977.
Foster, John Bellamy, Hannah Holleman, and Brett Clark. "Marx and Slavery." *Monthly Review*, July 1, 2020. https://monthlyreview.org/2020/07/01/marx-and-slavery/.
Garabedian, Steven P. *A Sound History: Lawrence Gellert, Black Musical Protest, and White Denial*. Amherst: University of Massachusetts Press, 2020.
Gellert, Lawrence. *Me and My Captain*. Hours Press, 1939.
Gellert, Lawrence. *Negro Songs of Protest*. American Music League, 1936.
Goldberg, Isaac. *Tin Pan Alley: A Chronicle of the American Popular Music Racket*. John Day, 1930.
Greenway, John. *American Folksongs of Protest*. A. S. Barnes, Perpetua edition 1960; originally published by University of Pennsylvania Press, 1953.
Higginson, Thomas Wentworth. *Army Life in a Black Regiment*. Penguin Classics, 1997; originally published by Fields, Osgood, 1870.
Hill, Christopher. *Society and Puritanism in Pre-Revolutionary England*. Schocken Books, 1967.
Hill, Christopher. *The World Turned Upside Down: Radical Ideas During the English Revolution*. Penguin, 1972, 1991.
Hugill, Stan. *Shanties from the Seven Seas*. Mystic Seaport, 1961.
Johnson, James Weldon, and J. Rosamund Johnson. *The Books of American Negro Spirituals*. Da Capo Press, 1969; originally published in two volumes by Viking Press, 1925 and 1926.
Katz, Bernard, ed. *The Social Implications of Early Negro Music in the United States*. Arno Press and the New York Times, 1969.
Krehbiel, Henry Edward. *Afro-American Folksongs: A Study in Racial and National Music*. G. Schirmer, 1914.
Leonard, Aaron J. *The Folk Singers and the Bureau: The FBI, the Folk Artists and the Suppression of the Communist Party, USA—1939–1956*. Repeater Press, 2020.
Lovell, John, Jr. *Black Song: The Forge and the Flame*. New York: Macmillan, 1972.
Miller, Karl Hagstrom. *Segregating Sounds*. Durham, NC: Duke University Press, 2010.
Rawick, George. *The American Slave: A Composite Autobiography*, 41 vols. Greenwood Press, 1941.
Reuss, Richard A., with JoAnne C. Reuss. *American Folk Music and Left-wing Politics: 1927–1957*. Scarecrow Press, 2000.
Roberts, Brian. *Blackface Nation: Race, Reform, and Identity in American Popular Music 1812–1925*. Chicago: University of Chicago Press, 2017.
Roberts, Brian. "Slavery Would Have Died of That Music": *The Hutchinson Family Singers and the Rise of Popular-Culture Abolitionism in Early Antebellum-Era America 1842–1850*. American Antiquarian Society, 2006.
Scarborough, Dorothy. *From a Southern Porch*. New York: G. P. Putnam's Sons, Knickerbocker Press, 1919.
Simpson, Joshua McCarter. *The Emancipation Car, Being an Original Composition of Anti-Slavery Ballads Composed Exclusively for the Underground Railroad*. Zanesville, OH: E.C. Church, 1854; reprinted by Mnemosyne Publishing, 1969.
Simpson, Joshua McCarter. *Original Anti-Slavery Songs*. Zanesville, OH: printed for the author, 1852.
Sinha, Manisha. *The Slave's Cause: A History of Abolition*. New Haven, CT: Yale University Press, 2016.
Southern, Eileen, ed. *Readings in Black American Music*. New York: W.W. Norton, 1971.
Southern, Eileen, and Josephine Wright. *African-American Traditions in Song, Sermon, Tale, and Dance, 1600s–1920*. Greenwood Press, 1990.
Suisman, David. *Selling Sounds*. Cambridge, MA: Harvard University Press, 2009.

Talley, Thomas. *Negro Folk Rhymes, Wise and Otherwise.* New York: Macmillan, 1922.
Trotter, James Monroe. *Music and Some Highly Musical People.* Charles T. Dillingham, 1878.
Wheeler, Anne P. "The Music of the Early Nineteenth-Century Camp Meeting: Song in Service to Evangelistic Revival." *Methodist History* 48:1 (October 2009).

CHAPTER 2

"THE ROADS TO PERDITION"
Lawrence Gellert and Black Songs of Protest in the Cultural Front and Cold War

Steven Garabedian

In liner notes for an album of his documentary field recordings from the 1930s, independent white folklorist Lawrence Gellert wrote, "I presume there are as many ways to become a Negro Folk Song Collector as there are roads to perdition." In his day and ours, Gellert's quip resounds with a healthy dose of irony. Gellert was, after all, outing himself as one of these white collectors of African American vernacular song. At the same time, he was trying to draw a line between himself and said peers. As a radical music collector, Gellert posed a challenge to the instruments of state that resounded in an emergent folklore consensus at mid-century.

This essay surveys Lawrence Gellert's roots in Black vernacular protest and the interracial Cultural Front of the 1930s and 1940s, and his uprooting from folk music consciousness after World War II. Gellert happened upon African American music research when he relocated from New York to North Carolina in the early 1920s. By the 1930s, he was making field recordings and publishing. Gellert garnered some prominence before World War II. He was spotlighted in the left-wing and mainstream press. Black Southerners assessed him a "safe white man" and confided songs, and African American peers such as Langston Hughes, Sterling Brown, Hall Johnson, and Paul Robeson held Gellert in high regard. But, the collector and his collection were never safe in the categories, canons, and professional circles of institutional folklore. As Dick Weissman puts it in his book *Which Side Are You On? An Inside History of the Folk Music Revival in America*, Gellert's person and archive were a "can of worms" that "threatened the credibility of what other collectors had found."[1] In the postwar era, some doubters questioned whether the Gellert archive was authentic Black expression. Were these real songs from the field, or did Gellert "ghost-write" the material? Were they genuine "folk" material from the grassroots or topical songs from a Communist propagandist? By the 1960s, institutional strictures, changed political circumstances, and Gellert's personal iconoclasm impeded awareness of *Negro Songs of Protest*. At age eighty in 1979, Lawrence Gellert disappeared from his New York City apartment never to be heard from again.[2] The Gellert field archive has similarly disappeared, dogged by mystery, and too little heard.

ROOTED IN BLACK PROTEST

Lawrence Gellert was not marginal to vernacular music research in the United States. Rather, he was marginalized. The absenting is all the more striking when one considers Gellert's comings and goings, connections and overlap, with key people, places, and events in the folksong revival crescendos of the 1930s and 1960s. Gellert's name and collecting work were notable in the left-wing folksong revival before World War II, and Gellert hovered in the wings, ever on the verge of stepping back onstage it seems, in his associations and activities in the Greenwich Village scene of his home in New York City in the postwar popular folk revival.

Songs such as this item, encountered by Gellert as "a group sing on a plantation near Hamburg, S.C.," made an impression:

Went to Atlanta
Neber been dere afo'
White folks eat de apple
N----r wait fo' core[3]

Went to Charleston
Neber been dere afo'
White folks sleep on feather bed
N----r on the flo'

Went to Raleigh
Neber been dere afo'
White folks wear de fancy suit
N----r de over-o

Went to Heben
Neber been dere afo'
White folks sit in Lawd's place
Chase n----r down below

The lyrics were among those in a sheaf of handwritten transcriptions and commentary that Gellert sent from the South to his older brother, communist artist Hugo Gellert, in New York. They appeared in his first article, "Negro Songs of Protest," in November 1930, and under the title "Went to Atlanta" in his first book, *Negro Songs of Protest*, in 1936.[4]

"Stand Boys Stand" was also striking:
Stan' boys stan'
No use arunnin
Look up yonder hill
White trash acomin'
Is acomin'

He got knife in one han'
Pistol in de odder
Stan' boys stan'
Brother stan' by brother
Stan' by brother

N----r don' you run 'way
White trash acomin'
Is acomin'
Get dat whackin' stick in yo' han'
Ruckus boun' to happen
Boun' to happen

The text was also among those Gellert mailed in the sheaf to brother Hugo, and it was printed in Gellert's same November 1930 print article. White collector Dorothy Scarborough had included an antecedent version referencing "massa," "oberseer," and slavery in *On the Trail of Negro Folk-Songs*, her songbook from 1925. But, the directness of the Gellert transcription in the era of "Jim Crow" was of a different quality.[5]

A third example, "Sistren an' Brethren," is also noteworthy in its open call to armed self-defense in the face of racial lynching:

Sistren an' Brethren
Stop foolin' wit' pray
When black face is lifted
Lawd turnin' way

Heart filled wit' sadness
Head bowed down wit' woe
In the hour of trouble
Where's a black man to go

We're buryin' a brother
They kill for the crime
Tryin' to keep
What was his all the time

When we's tucked him on under
What you goin' to do
Wait till it come
They arousin' fo' you too

Your head tain' no apple
For danglin' f'om a tree
Your body no carcass
For barbecuein' on a spree

Stand on your feet
Club gripped 'tween your hands
Spill their blood too
Show 'em yours is a man's

The song was included in Gellert's second installment of the "Negro Songs of Protest" article series in January 1931, and it was published as the second item in *Negro Songs of Protest* in 1936.[6] Again, we find a possible precedent, "O-O-Oh, Sistren an' Bred'ren,"[7] in Scarborough's *On the Trail of Negro Folk-Songs*. But, the entry is listed in her book in the chapter "Songs About Animals," and hardly has the import of the Gellert transcription. The version from the Gellert collection, identified under the moniker "Negro Songs of Protest," we need remember, registered with a different meaning. Scholar John Szwed identifies "Sistren an' Brethren" as the first song published about racial lynching in America, and musicologist Nancy Kovaleff Baker has suggested that it may have been one source of inspiration for Abel Meeropol's song "Strange Fruit," recorded by Billie Holiday in 1939.[8]

In the 1930s, Lawrence Gellert contextualized such songs of Black social consciousness and expressive resistance in the conditions of "the Southland" as "it touched the lives of millions of Negroes." He held that the music voiced "on the one hand the peonage, poverty, degradation, savage brutality of the Law and the lynching mob," and on the other, the "crystallization of the new attitude to all that." Gellert wrote: "A hundred songs freshly minted were current[,] stamping upon the racial consciousness the glorified images of men who were waging daily struggle against the oppressors of the race. They were rapidly absorbed into the woof and warp of folk lore patterns.... always the music is fluid and plastic and changeable to accommodate verses which may be added, taken away or substituted for immediate use of a member of the in-group in the folk process of recreating, revising or editorializing."[9] Historian Michael Denning dubs this musical strain a Black "political vernacular," and mentions Gellert as one of its chroniclers.[10] For Gellert, in looking back from the vantage point of the 1960s, "Negro Songs of Protest" were "freedom songs" of the kind in active embrace in civil rights movement culture.[11] In the same period, contemporaries Alan Lomax, Irwin Silber, Pete Seeger, John Steinbeck, and Woody Guthrie might have called them "hard hitting songs for hard-hit people," as compiler Lomax and his collaborators titled their 1967 songbook. Prepared in 1940, the manuscript was sidelined with the coming of World War II, and then languished in the chill of the Cold War. "No publisher would take it then," recalled Lomax, "because post-war America was afraid to look reality in the eye." Lomax stated that "sharp, angry and self-conscious songs of protest have always formed a small but important part of the folk-song tradition." The famed Library of Congress folklorist concluded that he believed such "hard hitting songs for hard-hit people" were "a testament to an unknown America, the folk poets who had become politically active and still kept their gift for song-making."[12]

All of this overlap and continuity came to little lasting recognition for the Gellert archive, though. Sam Charters, for instance, a founder of 1960s blues revival scholarship with personal ties to people and places in common with Gellert, professed to only discovering Gellert's work at the end of his storied career. "I wasn't expecting a collection titled *Negro Songs of Protest*," Charters writes in his career anthology from 2004. The 1936 Gellert songbook took Charters aback. "So, as I held the collection and carefully turned its pages, I found myself asking, 'Can I trust it?' 'What can I say about the songs?'"

Charters had chanced upon the item in a Swann Galleries auction house catalog. The book was from Eleanor Roosevelt's personal library and was signed by Gellert. Charters was intrigued, but remained dubious.[13]

Similarly, Gellert's onetime booster, Bruce Conforth, has registered modern-day ambivalence. In the 1980s, Conforth encountered the Gellert archive as a graduate student at Indiana University, Bloomington. He published his master's thesis on Gellert's life and fieldwork, and produced two LPs compiling Gellert's documentary recordings. At that time, Conforth championed Gellert as an unequaled independent collector of Black expressive protest deserving of "rightful" status alongside famous peers like John and Alan Lomax.[14] In his biography of Gellert in 2013, however, Conforth recasts shadows that had long trailed Gellert. Conforth contends: "Based upon existing material and interviews, it seems clear that 'Negro Songs of Protest' (as a special body of material collected by Gellert) never really existed within the folk music tradition, but were, rather, the creation of the left wing and US Communist Party in order to use as propaganda, with Lawrence as either their unwitting or identity-hunting dupe."[15] Further, the author characterizes Gellert himself as suspect, not just his music archive. Conforth describes Gellert as a slippery personality, a "chameleon," whose life involved "misinformation" and "false pretenses." In the final analysis, Conforth judges Gellert a mixed character with a mixed legacy. Gellert's conventional folksong documentation, Conforth assesses, is authentic and underappreciated, but his most striking Black songs of protest are the product of a "radical in the woodpile," with the "radical finger" pointed "directly to Lawrence Gellert."[16]

I do not hold with these views. Instead, I deem Lawrence Gellert an honest collector of genuine Black musical resistance. Now is not the place for a full delineation, and I urge interested readers to explore a number of sources, including the primary materials at the Archives of Traditional Music (ATM) and Lilly Library at Indiana University Bloomington as well as my own book from 2020.[17] For me, at this stage in Gellert research, the question is not whether the collection is real African American expressive protest. Rather, the question is why and how this real material has been subjected to a real and enduring absenting from institutional folklore.

STATE OF DENIAL

At the beginning of my scholarly path, I had a formidable personal encounter with Gellert denial. In January 2001, as I was advancing my graduate studies as a predoctoral research fellow at the Smithsonian Institution, I received an unsolicited friendly email from Irwin Silber. The former founding editor of *Sing Out!* magazine from 1950 to 1967, Silber was a leading figure in folk music culture in the United States, someone who bridged the worlds of the left-wing folksong movement of the 1930s and 1940s and the commercial "boom" of folk music recording and mass media in the 1950s and 1960s. Silber had reached out to caution me against staking a budding career on the questionable work of an "unstable" individual. He doubted the authenticity of Gellert's archive, suggesting that Gellert might have gone so far as to create original agit-folk propaganda songs and then to have Black field informants sing these compositions into his 1930s portable disc cutter. Silber explained that in the 1930s and 1940s, he had touted Gellert's fieldwork as "groundbreaking," but that as he "got to know more about blues and folk music more broadly" over the ensuing years, he developed reservations about the credibility of the material. Additionally, he cited two other factors: 1) the "precedent for some folklorists to create songs themselves and then pass them off as collected folk songs," mentioning the example of John Jacob Niles, and 2) the overenthusiasms of a Communist movement culture, which "felt it appropriate to create 'class consciousness' where it should have existed but simply could not be found."[18]

Decades before the personal email to me, Silber had been public about these misgivings. "Frankly, as a person familiar with folk music and folklore materials for considerable time, I find it very difficult to accept the material presented by Gellert as folk songs which he really collected," Silber asserted in *Mainstream* magazine in 1963. He posited: "I am strongly of the opinion that these songs of Lawrence Gellert are more likely his or someone else's original creation rather than material, which by any stretch of the imagination, could fall into the domain of folk songs."[19] Several years before my personal encounter with Silber, in the beginning stage of my graduate learning, I was surprised when first reading the influential editor's original denunciation from the thick of the civil rights era folk revival in the 1960s. In 2001, upon receiving his email, I was daunted by his continuing certainty even after so many years, and even after Gellert field recordings had been released to some vindicating approval on several vinyl compilations in the 1970s and 1980s. It was one thing to question the songs when all that was available were lyric transcriptions in print sources, but it was still another to continue to question them when compelling audio of the actual documentary recordings were now in circulation.[20]

"NEGRO SONGS OF PROTEST"

Silber's and Gellert's respective individual histories overlapped in the interracial Cultural Front of the 1930s and 1940s. Both were movement radicals in the Communist-oriented New York epicenter of the left-wing folksong revival. Lawrence Gellert was born in 1898, and had emigrated as a child with his Hungarian-Jewish family from Budapest to New York in 1906.[21] By the Popular Front years of "New Deal" and left-labor convergence in the mid-1930s, Gellert was a known quantity. He had gone south from New York in the winter of 1922, not to hunt for folk music, but simply for recuperation. A struggling journalist and aspiring actor, always feeling the weight of his older brother Hugo's considerable artistic reputation in the "Old Left" bohemia of Greenwich Village, the younger Gellert had "quit everything," as he later recalled, and vacated to Tryon, North Carolina, "to make a new life" for himself. An iconoclast with a romantic flair and apparent underdog sympathies, Gellert quickly established a local reputation. He worked at the local *Polk County News* and acted in the Drama Fortnightly theater company. In 1926, he was recruited by African American residents to arrange a fundraiser for a collapsing Black community church. Gellert staged the "Sing Fest" at the town's white Parish House to financial success, and some considerable town furor. More than a decade later, it was still being remembered in the *Asheville Citizen-Times*: "It was while he was in Tryon that Mr. Gellert became interested in the music of the Southern negro, and many citizens here remember a concert which he organized one winter, in which many of the fine negro voices in the community were heard in their native songs."[22]

Gellert always claimed that he had stumbled into Tryon and folk music with no prior knowledge or interest. The church fundraiser "Sing Fest" in 1926, he related, occasioned a profound awakening. The performance was "all church music," he said, but "that church had never rocked like that." He elaborated, "I was very curious, and I got acquainted with some of the boys, and we had a couple evenings together. Then, I heard something which had nothing to do with church." It was "tremendous protest." In shorthand and eventually on sound recordings, Gellert began collecting the Black vernacular music to which he was afforded a hearing. By 1930, his field transcriptions and accompanying commentary started appearing as a running series in the left-wing *New Masses*, and in 1936 and 1939, respectively, Gellert published his two formal songbooks, *Negro Songs of Protest* and *Me and My Captain: Chain Gang*.[23]

Lawrence Gellert's collecting work struck a responsive chord in the "proletarian" culture surge of the early 1930s. Marxist periodical *New Masses* was

Lawrence Gellert with brother Otto and nephew James, Tryon, North Carolina, 1930s. Courtesy of Penny Gellert Freeman.

"the principal organ of the American cultural left" of the time, relates scholar Barbara Foley.[24] The journal's illustrious editor-in-chief, Michael Gold, unified Gellert's projects under the name "Negro Songs of Protest," and published five such Gellert pieces in the then-monthly between 1930 and 1933.[25] British expatriate radical Nancy Cunard included an eleven-page essay, "Negro Songs of Protest," by Gellert in her mammoth *Negro: An Anthology* in 1934. Cunard held that the "Communist world-order is the solution of the race problem for the Negro," and she featured Gellert's work alongside that of fellow white and Black radicals and literary contemporaries Michael Gold, Theodore Dreiser, Sterling Brown, John Spivak, James Ford, W. E. B. Du Bois, Langston Hughes, Alain Locke, Zora Neale Hurston, Countee Cullen, Walter White, Arna Bontemps, Arthur Schomburg, George Padmore, George S. Schuyler, and E. Franklin Frazier, to name just some of the notable contributors.[26]

Gellert's *Negro Songs of Protest* (1936) featured twenty-four lyric texts and musical arrangements. Noted composers Elie Siegmeister and Wallingford Riegger were involved. Siegmeister provided the arrangements, and Riegger authored the foreword. Brother Hugo did the cover illustration. The songbook, which showcased the material that Gellert had collected and adapted for the purposes of movement singing, was his greatest success in terms of critical reception and visibility. There were Russian and German editions.

Paul Robeson and accompanist Lawrence Brown performing in Moscow, Soviet Union, 1936. Schomburg Center for Research in Black Culture, Photographs and Prints Division, New York Public Library.

The Russian translation was facilitated by Langston Hughes while he was in the Soviet Union in 1933. In Germany, Paul Robeson reportedly once held up Gellert's book at a public event when asked about the background of Black popular music. "This is where it came from," he indicated.[27] Robeson, in fact, released songs from the Gellert archive. "Work All De Summer," from 1937, and "Lay Down Late," from 1938, were recorded in Europe and featured Robeson with his regular accompanist Lawrence Brown. The label credits for these Victor 78 rpm records show "Coll. by L. Gellert" and "Arr. L. Gellert." In both instances, the audio performances match the lyric content and musical notation as printed in Gellert's *Negro Songs of Protest*. As it happens, Robeson and Gellert were the same age, and, as we will see, maintained a years-long association. For both, Black protest and workers' revolution went hand in hand, and the musical realm was a natural front for solidarity and social foment.[28]

This Gellert CV could be expanded and detailed further, but that work has been done elsewhere.[29] The point is that Gellert was center stage for a time in the Cultural Front of the interracial Left. Historian Robin D. G. Kelley has characterized Gellert as "probably the Party's most enthusiastic champion of Black music," and Mark Solomon has echoed the sentiment, writing that Gellert was "the prime collector of Negro music in the CP orbit." In his seminal doctoral research, left-wing folksong revival expert Richard Reuss identified Gellert as singular and pioneering. In the inchoate stage of the 1930s folksong revival,

Reuss wrote, "[R]elatively few urban radicals were exposed directly to Black folk music. Mention of its 'new' revolutionary qualities was confined principally to the discussion surrounding Lawrence Gellert's 'Negro Songs of Protest.'"[30]

GOOD MORNING, REVOLUTION

The path by which Gellert became an active intermediary between white and Black arts and activism is telling. In the "New Negro Renaissance" of the 1920s, young Missouri-born writer Langston Hughes had established himself in Harlem as a leading figure. By the early 1930s, Hughes, like many others, had radicalized to the Left amidst the economic and political crises and mobilizations of the Depression. Hughes composed poems such as "Good Morning, Revolution," "Goodbye, Christ," "Ballads of Lenin," and "A New Song":

> Revolt! Arise!
> The Black
> And White World
> Shall be one!
> The Worker's World!

Such poems signaled the emergence of Hughes, the socialist radical and Black proletarian literature proponent. "Good Morning, Revolution" and "Goodbye, Christ" were published in the Left press in 1932 (*New Masses* and *The Negro Worker*); "Ballads of Lenin" appeared in *Proletarian Literature in the United States: An Anthology* in 1935, and "A New Song" was included as the title item in *A New Song*, a slim pamphlet of Hughes's poetry released in 1938. In these radical endeavors, Hughes found himself alongside Gellert in print and overlapping with Gellert in personal associations. *Proletarian Literature in the United States* included two items in a "Folksongs" section that were attributed to the Gellert collection, and Hughes's 1938 *A New Song* featured an introduction by Michael Gold, the *New Masses* editor who, we will remember, originally labeled Gellert's print dispatches of lyric transcriptions and annotations "Negro Songs of Protest."[31]

Hugo Gellert and Gold were longtime friends, and Hugo was an editor and board member with Gold at *New Masses*. These overlapping relations led to a connection between the younger Gellert and Hughes. It was Hugo who reached out initially. In a handwritten letter, Hugo wrote formally "Dear Langston Hughes," and went on to broach the prospect of Hughes contributing an introduction to a forthcoming publication compiling his brother Lawrence's "Negro Songs of Protest," which "were printed in the *New Masses* on various occasions." Hugo expresses, "I hope you are willing," invites Hughes to "call me tomorrow (Sunday) morning at any time," and ends "Comradely Yours."[32]

Lawrence Gellert and Hughes then began their own direct correspondence and collaboration in an exchange of letters from 1931 and 1932. The first is from Lawrence to Hughes. It provides valuable details from the collector at the outset of his activities. Gellert relates, in typical wry fashion, the origins and nature of his project in Black vernacular song. In a long typed two-page letter, Gellert writes:

> The songs attached I picked at random from the collection. I believe them fairly representative. The music is rough, mostly. No attempt has been made to "operate" them. As a matter of fact the 100 Farrar and Rinehart plan to publish, even the customary piano accompaniments will be omitted. . . .
>
> The protest song, I believe a contemporary product. Undoubtedly the outgrowth of the present industrial crisis. Never above the lowest rung of the economic ladder, the Southern negro is now being crowded off altogether. . . .
>
> Frankly, I'm not much of a musician. When some eighteen months ago I heard the first protest song, I was at sea about some way to jot it down. Then a happy thought occurred to me. I borrowed a portable phonograph. Bought some cheap recording disks [*sic*]. And a huge megaphone. The latter was the bane of many a jaunt on foot through North and South Carolina, Georgia, Florida, Alabama and Mississippi. On more fortunate trips I rode on train or automobile and had but little reason to cuss the five foot megaphone. The collection took the greater part of last year and entire six months of the current one. I visited jails, chain gang encampments, lumber and construction jobs, plantations—in fact every conceivable negro worker haunt. Even whore houses—until I learned only "respectable" whites frequented there.

Gellert ended by asking if Hughes could "possibly have the preface here before the end of next week" and that he would be "awfully obliged." He added that he had "yet to make the financial arrangements" with the proposed publisher, Farrar and Rinehart, but that he did not "mean to get your work for nothing. As soon as I have the stuff in shape, it'll be taken care of, I'm sure."[33]

The details shared in this letter are relevant. Gellert, who would later be accused of tampering or outright fabrication, here comments, long before any real public attention, that the song material is presented untouched and unpolished (no effort made to "opera-te," he puns). He also recounts his philosophy of the music, field collecting process, and geographic range, and he provides a general dating for his work. (Eighteen months prior would put Gellert's start date for Black folksong collecting in 1929. Interestingly, this dating is consistent with the language of an archival document—an unfinished funding proposal drafted by the collector in the 1930s—in the Gellert papers at Indiana University.[34]) For Gellert-interested scholars, it is also striking to hear that the genesis of *Negro Songs of Protest*, ultimately published as a slimmer volume by Communist Party affiliate the American Music League in 1936, can be traced back to a much larger manuscript proposal of one hundred songs with illustrations that was intended for commercial publishing house Farrar and Rinehart (in operation 1929–1946). Despite Gellert's letter remark to Hughes that Farrar and Rinehart was "a pretty good outfit," and that he was sure the financial matters would be "taken care of" satisfactorily, something clearly went amiss with the book project. Gellert later called it one of "those stillborns that never happen."[35]

In the immediate term, however, before the project derailed, the Gellert and Hughes exchange seemed to be progressing, albeit with fits and starts, toward fruition. On January 2, 1931, Hughes wrote to "Mr. Gellert" that the "songs are swell." Both Hughes and Gellert seemed loose about what precisely Hughes was meant to contribute. The language shifted between "introduction," "preface," and "foreword." Hughes, for instance, regretted in his January 2 letter that he had been too busy "to do anything about an introduction," and closed, "I'm hoping I'm not too late to do the foreword for your splendid songs." Gellert updated Hughes a year later, now mentioning a "preface" only (no introduction), in a letter dated January 7, 1932. He wrote that the manuscript had "been at the publisher's several weeks together with three of the four drawings Hugo is doing for the book." He stated, "Naturally, the sooner you can get that preface here the better," wondering if "within the next two weeks" was possible. Gellert explained, "I want to continue my wanderings through the West Indies this time. And would like to be free to go by the first of February. Thanks." Hughes finally sent his draft piece in February from Tougaloo College in Mississippi with a letter dated "On tour, February God knows what, 1932." The writer opened, "I hope this introduction is not too late, and that you will like it." He stressed, "I think the songs are great, and am honored to be chosen to do the foreword," again with a slippage in wording. Hughes recommended that Gellert include "an author's note as to how they were collected, etc.," added "I am glad your brother is doing the drawings," and signed off, "With all good wishes." As it turned out, Gellert did include "an author's note" explaining his methods in the preface to *Negro Songs of Protest* in 1936, but unfortunately, the Farrar and Rinehart project fell apart and Hughes's introductory piece was never published.[36]

Lawrence Gellert clearly prized Hughes's imprimatur, however. In his interviews years later, he mentioned Hughes's preface with pride, and Hughes personally with affection. Certainly, Hughes was approving. In the four-page piece, he was unequivocal in his approbation: "These songs collected by Lawrence Gellert from plantations, chain gangs, lumber camps, and jails are of inestimable value, if they do nothing more than show that not all Negroes are shouting spirituals, cheering endowed football teams, dancing to the blues, or mouthing inter-racial oratory. Some of them are tired of being poor, and picturesque, and hungry. Terribly and bitterly tired."[37] Hughes was hardly the only African American luminary to endorse the collection. As we have already seen, Paul Robeson recorded arrangements attributed to the Gellert archive. Additionally, a Robeson contemporary, baritone William Bowers, was slated to record six items as well from among those printed in *Negro Songs of Protest*. A dust jacket to the *Negro Songs of Protest* songbook announced the ten-inch 78 rpm recordings "under the personal supervision of Lawrence Gellert and Elie Siegmeister." The discs were meant to be on the independent left-wing Timely Records label, but do not seem to have ever been released, if recorded at all.[38]

Intriguingly, the Timely discs were advertised on the dust jacket of *Negro Songs of Protest* as including "music accompaniment by Gabriel Brown, guitar." Brown, a blues singer-guitarist, had first been recorded in Eatonville, Florida, in 1935 by folklorist Zora Neale Hurston when she was collecting with a twenty-year-old Alan Lomax and Mary Elizabeth Barnicle. Gellert crossed paths with Hurston in that period when he was hired to work in the "Negro Unit" of the Federal Theatre Project in New York City. In an oral history interview in 1976 about the Federal Theatre, Gellert spoke emphatically of the encounter. Because Hurston had yet to be rediscovered to general academic and popular acclaim, Gellert's interviewer does not recognize Hurston's name or understand her significance when Gellert makes mention in the conversation. Gellert stresses that Hurston was "very knowing. And, she should have been the head of the Project . . . because she was an organizer. She was a dynamic human being, you know. She could have handled anybody. She's really a fighter." Hurston had been retained in the "Negro Unit" as a drama coach on the Project in 1935, a "helping role" only, and a "serious underutilization," as one Hurston scholar puts it, of Hurston's many talents. Gellert indicated as much from his firsthand experience: "She was a writer. She was a

Zora Neale Hurston, 1937. Prints and Photographs Division. Library of Congress.

better writer than any Negro on our entire project there." But, he laments, "She was permitted to do nothing."[39]

In the years prior, Zora Neale Hurston had complained in private correspondence about Gellert contemporaries, folklorists Howard W. Odum and Guy B. Johnson, both professors at the University of North Carolina at Chapel Hill. Coauthors Odum and Johnson had gained influence in Black folksong studies in the 1920s for their publications *The Negro and His Songs: A Study of Typical Negro Songs in the South* (1925) and *Negro Workaday Songs* (1926). Hurston was unimpressed. To Alain Locke, a dean of the "New Negro Renaissance" of the era, she fired, "They evidently know nothing of how folk-songs grow." To her Columbia University mentor, Franz Boas, she wrote, "I have been following the works of Odum and Johnson closely and find that they could hardly be less exact. They have made six or seven songs out of one song and made one song out of six or seven. . . . Some of it would be funny," she cracked, "if they were not serious scientists! Or are they?" To friend Langston Hughes, she was even more frank, confiding, "It makes me sick to see how these cheap white folks are grabbing our stuff and ruining it. I am almost sick—my one consolation being that they never do it right and so there is still a chance for us."[40]

Gabriel Brown (with guitar) and Rochelle French, Eatonville, Florida, 1935. Hurston-Lomax-Barnicle southern field trip. Photograph by Alan Lomax. Prints and Photographs Division. Library of Congress.

Did Zora Neale Hurston take notice of Lawrence Gellert's collecting work? Might she have felt any differently about it as compared with that of his white peers Odum and Johnson? By the time Hurston and Gellert intersected on the Federal Theatre Project in 1935, Hurston had broken with Langston Hughes, and in the same month that she was hired on the Project (October), Hurston published her own study of Black folklore, *Mules and Men*. In it, she famously cautioned: "Folklore is not as easy to collect as it sounds. The best source is where there are the least outside influences and these people, being usually under-privileged, are the shyest. . . . And the Negro, in spite of his open-faced laughter, his seeming acquiescence, is particularly evasive. . . . The Negro offers a feather-bed resistance. That is, we let the probe enter, but it never comes out. It gets smothered under a lot of laughter and pleasantries."[41] Beyond Gellert's own interview, no archived correspondence or direct documentation links Hurston and Gellert. That the two were placed in the "Negro Unit" together in the interracial arts scene of Depression-era New York in 1935, and that a Hurston folklore informant, singer-guitarist Gabriel Brown, might have come into Gellert's orbit of singers, is a tantalizing *what might have been*. As we can see, though, it is not entirely surprising. Gellert's interactions with and reputation among African American intellectuals and artists amounted to something considerable.

Composer Hall Johnson, 1947. Photography by Carl Van Vechten. Prints and Photographs Division. Library of Congress.

Vocalist William Bowers, to return to personages referenced above for instance, had come to the stage through Hall Johnson, a leader in Black fine arts music. Originally from Georgia, Johnson, a trained musician and composer, had relocated to New York City and founded the highly regarded Hall Johnson Choir. In 1936, the National Urban League magazine, *Opportunity*, published an effusive review by Johnson of Gellert's *Negro Songs of Protest*. Though he acknowledged that it was a "big statement to make about any book and a surprisingly big statement to make about a little book," Johnson enthused, "Here are some fine, genuine Negro songs, collected by a white man and arranged by a white man [composer Elie Siegmeister]" that "should claim and hold the attention of everybody in the world who is at all interested in how the world is getting on." He affirmed, "In my opinion, these two-dozen big little songs, so lovingly collected and so sincerely offered, are well worth singing and hearing for *all* that they contain."[42] Gellert referred to the lengthy review in his interviews in the 1960s ("one of the most beautiful reviews I ever had," he said), and he also proudly highlighted a Hall Johnson Choir stadium performance in New York in 1938 in which one of the items from the *Negro Songs of Protest* book ("Scottsboro") was performed to what Gellert said was a rousing ovation.[43]

William Bowers began his professional career with the Hall Johnson Choir, and the two shared the connection to Gellert. This went beyond simply the intended 78 rpm Timely records meant to accompany the publication of *Negro Songs of Protest*. As a *New York Age* article reported, Bowers gave a recital in part featuring "Negro Songs of Protest" from the Gellert collection at Steinway Hall in New York City in June 1936. The review is glowing in its appraisal of both Bowers's performance and the Gellert material. The piece opens, "In inaugurating what will probably make musical history, the American Music League . . . presented William Bowers, popular young baritone, in a unique presentation of 'songs of protest' culled from the south." It contextualizes Gellert's fieldwork in "the need of a true portrayal of the Negro's attitude toward the inferior position imposed upon him by the traditions of the South," and acclaims Bowers as "an outstanding Negro artist worthy of comparison with Roland Hayes or Paul Robeson." Readers are informed that Bowers had joined the "internationally famous Hall Johnson Choir" after he had relocated from the South, and had "gained immediate recognition." The article further reports that Langston Hughes was in the audience, and had contributed an original composition, the "Ballad of Ozzie Powell."[44]

CULTURAL FRONT AND COLD WAR

As these examples show, Lawrence Gellert was counted in the dynamic interface of the Cultural Left and Black arts in the period. One of the towering figures of African American scholarship, teaching, and creative writing, Sterling Brown of Howard University, in fact, shared a pleasant day sightseeing in Boston with Gellert and Nancy Cunard in 1932. Both Brown and Gellert were included in Cunard's *Negro: An Anthology* two years later, and each was at the opening of his respective trajectory. Gellert described the day fondly in a memorial piece celebrating Cunard's life. He wrote, "I remember Sterling Brown walking with us on Boston Common and writing a poem about the three of us at the cradle of American independence— an English Lady, an Hungarian immigrant's son, and a descendent of slaves." The "three of us strangely met with," Gellert reflected, but "with one and the same objective toward which we were pushing: the full equality of the black race." The association evidently made an impression on Brown, too. Gellert's song archive represented a "very adept self-portraiture," Brown insisted in *Negro Poetry and Drama* in 1937, and "put to shame much of the interpretation of the Negro from without." Sixteen years later, and at a height of Cold

War anticommunism in the United States, Sterling Brown was still referencing Gellert. In "Negro Folk Expression: Spirituals, Seculars, Ballads and Work Songs" in 1953, Brown spotlighted Gellert (along with John and Alan Lomax, and musician Josh White, too) for unlocking a "verboten" tradition of Black expressive resistance rarely heard by outsiders. "Only to collectors who have won their trust . . . and only when the white captain is far enough away, do the prisoners confide these songs."[45]

In his book, *Jim Crow America* in 1947, radical journalist Earl Conrad, chief of the Harlem bureau for the *Chicago Defender* newspaper, self-identified as a "white war correspondent" in the ongoing "racial fight" for social justice in the United States. Conrad valued Lawrence Gellert as a comrade-in-arms. Gellert "is a poetic figure," wrote Conrad, "who has spent twenty years in the South gathering folksongs: he has a thousand of them. He looks like a native Southerner and 'passes' as such when he is there." Indeed, Gellert's "ally" status in the movement culture of antiracism led to some identity confusion on occasion. Arthur B. Spingarn, a fellow white "ally" in the fight and future long-time president of the NAACP, misidentified Gellert in his inclusion of *Negro Songs of Protest* in an annual round-up of "Books by Black Authors" in *The Crisis* in 1936.[46] Similarly, in a *Chicago Defender* article from 1938, Gellert is profiled as a "37 year old Negro composer and author."[47] Though it was not a case of identity confusion and misidentification, Gellert, as noted previously, was published in the illustrious company of major African American thinkers and artists in Nancy Cunard's *Negro: An Anthology* in 1934. Additionally, he worked in the "Negro" units of both the Federal Theatre Project and Federal Writers' Project, intersecting with Zora Neale Hurston, Langston Hughes, Richard Wright, Ralph Ellison, and others. From the early 1930s to the mid-1940s, Gellert's activities were covered with some frequency in the Black press.[48] In 1941, Gellert was one of the few white contributors to *The Negro Caravan: Writing by American Negroes*. In the book, coeditors Sterling Brown, Arthur P. Davis, and Ulysses Lee called out the banality of dominant misrepresentation. They charged that "white authors dealing with the American Negro have interpreted him in a way to justify his exploitation." Cultural distortion, they stated, "has often been a handmaiden to social policy."[49]

One item of coverage in the African American press, the *Chicago Defender* piece from 1938 referenced above, highlights two elements of note. First, the article, "Harlem to See Big Drama," announces a limited-engagement January 1938 run of dancer-choreographer Helen Tamiris's *How Long Brethren?* at the Lafayette Theatre. The award-winning production set material from Gellert's "Negro Songs of Protest" to modern dance. It had already enjoyed acclaim on Broadway the year prior as the longest-running stage success of the WPA Federal Dance Theatre in New York City, and now, the article related, the production was coming to Harlem's Lafayette. Additionally, the piece reports that "Lawrence Gellert, 37 year old Negro composer and author," had been "awarded a grant of $500 from the Rockefeller Foundation." Gellert "has in his collection more than 500 Negro folk-songs," it states, and the prestigious grant would allow him "to complete his research."[50]

The Rockefeller grant was indeed big news. It was reported, for instance, in the African American dailies *The Pittsburgh Courier* and *The New York Age*, and in the "hometown" North Carolina papers the *Statesville Daily* and *Asheville Citizen-Times*. A $500 grant sum in 1937 money would equal some $10,000 today. Gellert was at a height of prominence. He had been profiled positively in the *New York Times* for unearthing a "new genre" of Black songs "dealing with everyday life" when *Negro Songs of Protest* was released, and *Time* magazine credited him with "collecting Negro songs that few white men have ever heard." In *The Pittsburgh Courier* coverage, Gellert was described as "widely-known," and in another news blurb on the grant in the *Brooklyn Daily Eagle*, he was identified as "an authority on Negro folk music." As a friend put it in a letter to Lawrence's brother Hugo, "I hear news from Larry. The latest is pretty good. He has gotten some of that promised 'pay' from the government and is going ahead with collecting his songs. I judge that he is not prosperous [sic] yet, but if he has managed [sic] to land way off in Atlanta with a machine that weighs a ton, I think he deserves some credit."[51]

The climate turned cold, however, for Lawrence Gellert. The Rockefeller Grant was revoked. "I had it for, I think, about eighteen months. I could have been on to this day," he recalled, with wistful exuberance. "But, it was the kind of songs I was getting. I couldn't help them. These were the songs that came up." Word was sent up the chain of authority in the Rockefeller organization: "This guy isn't interested in Negro folk songs; he's interested in revolution," as Gellert summarized it. "That was the end of my grant," he said.[52]

Meanwhile, in the same year of 1937, a young Alan Lomax, son of the celebrated "ballad hunter" John A. Lomax, took a position as the first salaried (albeit nominal) official of the Archive of American Folk-Song at the Library of Congress. When World War II came, Lomax left the Archive to work as an "information specialist" in the Office of War Information (OWI). Alan, in his twenties, was finding his way in the institutions of state power; Lawrence, meanwhile, was paving a path on the outs. Gellert, in his forties, mustered into the army in the Special Services branch in World War II, but he positioned himself for something other than morale boosting and troop entertainment.

Lawrence Gellert in uniform, World War II. Courtesy of Penny Gellert Freeman.

During the War, Gellert visited African American servicemen in their segregated units on Army bases in Georgia, Texas, Mississippi, and Florida. He collected piano blues from a Private Odell E. Hall at the Service Club at Camp Wolters, Texas, yet he also collected frank Black sentiment from informants unnamed for a *New Masses* article titled "Jim Crow in Khaki." Despite the racist abuse and degradation they faced in the war, Gellert wrote, the "Negro soldier did his part in knocking Hitler into a cocked hat." How? "As a Negro top sergeant put it," Gellert ended, "'Boy, I made believe all them Germans was just crackers from Georgia. And didn't we give 'em hell!'"[53]

In the war and afterward, opportunities narrowed for Lawrence Gellert and "Negro Songs of Protest" to maintain a hearing. The collector was already so "sore at the whole folklore racket" in World War II, he said, that he pondered volunteering his aluminum field discs as raw material for the War Department.[54] "I went off in 1941 with the Army," Gellert explained, "and then when I came back, folk music somehow or other flip-flopped. And, I always had trouble because of the title of my songs, 'protest songs.' That's all I was interested in. . . . Nobody would touch it for a while."[55] In an interview in 1968 with Richard Reuss and Izzy Young (likely conducted at Young's celebrated Folklore Center in Greenwich Village), Gellert recollected a telling episode to this point: "Courlander came to me several times. I was pretty friendly with Courlander." Gellert was referring to collector and writer Harold Courlander, who headed the Ethnic Library series of Folkways Records from the late 1940s through the 1950s. Courlander "wanted me to come around" with an "armful" of field discs for release on Folkways, Gellert related. But, Gellert stressed, this "was fifteen years ago [1953]," and it was "the height of the McCarthy period, and I think I frightened him a little bit.... Since then, no one has ever approached me." Even a figure as well-connected as Alan Lomax, we must remember, ended up in the cross-hairs of state anticommunism and Cold War intolerance by the turn of the decade. In 1950, Lomax removed himself to a political self-exile in Europe that would last until 1958.[56]

Black contemporaries Langston Hughes, Paul Robeson, and Sterling Brown, however, appear to have stuck with Gellert and "Negro Songs of Protest." This despite the fact that each, to differing degrees, suffered the squeeze of Cold War suspicion, surveillance, investigation, and persecution in the way of popular and state-sponsored anticommunism, as did Lawrence and brother Hugo. As early as 1934, Hugo, a prominent Party member of longtime record, was listed as "Communist" "painter and cartoonist" in Elizabeth Dillings's *The Red Network: A "Who's Who" and Handbook of Radicalism for Patriots*. For his part, Lawrence's name came up in questioning in a Dies Committee hearing on the Federal Theatre Project in 1938. Eighteen years later, in November 1956, Hugo was called to testify to the House Un-American Activities Committee (HUAC). He appeared with a lawyer and "took the Fifth" as regards incriminating questions; his wife, Livia, and deceased older brother Ernest (a conscientious objector who died mysteriously in military custody in World War I) were mentioned and thus also listed by name in the investigative record. Gellert biographer Bruce Conforth has written that Lawrence was under Federal Bureau of Investigation (FBI) scrutiny for years. Indeed, research expert Aaron Leonard, author of *The Folk Singers and the Bureau: The FBI, the Folk Artists, and the Suppression of the Community Party, USA, 1939–1956*, has identified a New York FBI office file spanning 1947 to 1964 with the subject heading "Lawrence Gellert." For years, the Gellerts faced off against the state and its surrogates in an ongoing "red scare" that stigmatized and criminalized alternative thinking, creativity, and activism on the Left.[57]

For their overt Left radicalism or simple civil rights convictions, Langston Hughes, Sterling Brown, and Paul Robeson also suffered in the chill of American anticommunism. The story of Robeson and the extremes of US state persecution is well known, but Hughes and Brown were targeted, too. For his outspoken partisan poetry, Hughes was placed under FBI suspicion from the 1930s on, ultimately with a file that exceeded five hundred pages. Director J. Edgar Hoover was such a personal antagonist for crusading justice against the "red" poet that he fashioned himself a Hughes literary scholar by dint of his detective work. Hughes was called to testify to HUAC at the height of McCarthyism in 1953. Sterling Brown, a teacher and writer of open progressive sympathies but never a Communist partisan, found himself under periodic government threat for his "suspicious" civil rights leanings and general insistence on Black dignity and self-determination. Brown was interviewed by the FBI in 1941 and reinterviewed in 1953; he did not "give names" or self-incriminate in questioning, and was never called to testify by HUAC. Brown's genius in handling his FBI interviewers have become part of his legend. Without sacrificing his principles, he evaded the net of state and academic repression through charm and acuity. When asked whether he was or had ever been a member of the Communist Party, for instance, Brown recalled answering with metaphor: "Listen son, any Negro who has been to the seventh grade and is against lynching is a Communist. I have been to the eighth grade and am against a hell of a lot more than lynching."[58]

Lawrence Gellert said much the same thing about his African American folk informants. Under southern apartheid and terror, "radicalism" was natural and "Negro Songs of Protest" a given, he stated. Black associates Hughes, Brown, and Robeson seemed to agree and never turned on the Gellert collection. Lawrence Gellert, in turn, remembered them fondly throughout his life. "I lectured at Tuskegee. I lectured at Howard University. I even took a class of Langston Hughes," Gellert related. He continued:

> I'll never forget it. I was walking along the street in Atlanta. Broke. Absolutely broke. And, I stop in front of a bookstore, and who do I see in there? Langston Hughes autographing books, as big as life. I went in. I reminded him, you know, that he had borrowed some rubles from me from my Soviet book when he took it over there. Well, he says, 'Come on. I'll give you money, but you have to work it out.' So, I went with him. I lectured his class, out in Atlanta. Well, they were a bunch of wonderful kids he had there. And, he practically gave me my fare back to New York.[59]

The encounter took place in 1947. Gellert had come south to investigate a notorious quadruple lynching in Monroe, Georgia, for Earl Conrad at the *Chicago Defender*, and was now scheming further with Conrad on ways to ambush segregationist politicians Herman Talmadge or Theodore Bilbo by photo bombing them with a copy of Conrad's new book *Jim Crow America*.[60] For his part, Hughes was teaching as a visiting professor of English and creative writing at Atlanta University. In the bookstore, Hughes may have been signing copies of *Fields of Wonder* (1947), a new volume of poetry that came

Langston Hughes, 1942. Photograph by Jack Delano. Prints and Photographs Division. Library of Congress.

out while he was at the university. Among the documents in the Langston Hughes Papers at Yale University, there is postcard indicating some kind of related transaction between the two. Gellert addressed the card to Hughes at Atlanta University. Gellert wrote, "Dear Langston—No, I haven't forgotten. I've been under the weather some and way behind in my commitments and consequently ditto on funds. I hope to send it to you without too much additional delay." The postcard is dated May 7, 1947.[61]

In 1951, Gellert was still involved with Paul Robeson, too. A Gellert piece shows up in an early issue of Robeson's *Freedom* monthly newspaper. The radical publication, based in Harlem and founded by Robeson and activist-journalist Louis Burnham, persisted from 1951 into 1955 through the extremes of US anticommunism and the determined political persecution of Robeson. The banner headline on the cover of the September 1951 issue in which Gellert appeared read "'Voice of America' Peddles Dixiecrat Lies to Europe." The article called out the government-sponsored "Voice of America" broadcast network for parroting the "Dixiecrat attitude toward the Negro people" and, in effect, justifying "Klan terror," and as well State Department–sponsored "Negro good-will ambassadors" touring the world to "explain US race relations." Gellert's contribution, "A West Point 'Sacred Tradition': Anti-Negro Violence," traced a history of systemic racism at West Point US Military

Paul Robeson, backstage at a Russian war anniversary benefit, Watergate, Washington, DC, 1942. Photograph by Gordon Parks. Prints and Photographs Division. Library of Congress.

Academy.[62] None of this content would sit well with the instruments and agents of Cold War state containment, be they legal-governmental or institutional-academic. As noted previously, Sterling Brown still had positive things to say in print about Gellert as late as 1953, but such compliments from the field of folklore studies largely disappeared from consensus discourse in these years, never to resurface in broad again.[63]

UPROOTED FROM FOLKLORE

As I and others have detailed elsewhere,[64] the disciplinary strictures and institutional conventions of academic and public sector folklore rang in harmony with postwar cultural nationalism in the United States. Disciplinary conservatism in the academic sense fit comfortably with Cold War conservatism in the political sense. Vernacular song that was not old, anonymous, and of communal circulation long and wide was disqualified as "folk," and the formulation "folksongs of protest" was dismissed as oxymoronic. In 1953, John Greenway published *American Folksongs of Protest*, for a prime example. In preparation for the book, Greenway had written Gellert for assistance two years earlier as doctoral student. The volume included some Gellert song texts in a chapter expressly titled "Negro Songs of Protest." Disciplinary specialist Stith Thompson, a leading figure and former president of the American Folklore Society, pilloried the Greenway publication. "Here is a book called American Folksongs which contains not a single example of what a competent folklorist would call by that name," Thompson railed. "Folk songs are songs that are traditional, that are handed down from singer to listener and that are still alive. The songs in this collection . . . are not and never were folk songs."[65]

To Gellert, the problem was the folklorists, not the folklore. "Scholars are shit," he cursed. Granting their terms and conditions, he declared, "I'm not a folklorist. I never claimed to be a folklorist." The goal of the work was political rather than academic. The purpose was to "push the Negro movement, such as it was," he said. "I think if they ["Negro Songs of Protest"] have any value, they'll have a great deal of value to the Negroes themselves. I should really give these to a Negro university." Sterling Brown "expressed a wish for them" at Howard University, Gellert claimed.[66]

Through the late 1940s, 1950s, and early 1960s, Lawrence Gellert remained an active contributor to the Left press, publishing freelance pieces in, for instance, Robeson's *Freedom* newspaper, and in *New Masses*, *Daily Worker*, *Masses and Mainstream*, and *Mainstream*. One late installment of "Negro Songs of Protest" came as late as 1972. However, Gellert contributions in *Sing Out!* ceased after 1953. In the February issue of that year, lyrics and musical notation to "Steel Got To Be Drove" appeared, with attribution to "Lawrence Gellert's fine collection of chain gang and protest songs." And, folk music impresario Izzy Young mentioned Gellert encounters on occasion in his journals and columns from 1960 to 1965. Still, in the dynamic years of "folk boom" popularity and civil rights politics in the sixties, the work of Lawrence Gellert is a relative absence in the flagship folk movement magazine.[67]

Gellert's absenting is even more pronounced in the *Journal of American Folklore*, the official scholarly journal of the American Folklore Society. The Gellert songbook *Negro Songs of Protest* was included in the journal's "Some Recent Publications" roundup in 1936, and Gellert material was cited in articles in the 1940s and in a 1951 article by commanding figure Richard Dorson. But, after that, Lawrence Gellert's name and work do not appear again in the *JAF* for a period of twenty years. When Gellert and "Negro Songs of Protest" did resurface in the journal, it was in a mixed review of Gellert's privately released compilation LP, *Collection of Lawrence Gellert: Negro Songs of Protest*, in 1972. The review was authored by D. K. (Donald Knight) Wilgus, who was in fact president of the American Folklore Society in 1971–1972. "There is no doubt that these are field recordings," held Wilgus, but were they "nonce-creations" by "a militant Black?" he wondered. Neither a vindication nor a pan, Wilgus put in writing the collective reservations of conservative disciplinary mindset. Gellert may genuinely have collected these field recordings, after all, he acknowledged, but the songs were perhaps not genuine folklore.[68]

In the 1960s, acclaimed folk revival historian Richard Reuss conducted approximately nine hours of taped interviews with Gellert over a period of years in New York City. Reuss devoted considerable space to Gellert in his influential 1971 dissertation.[69] Before that, in 1969, he shared his research and conclusions with peers at the American Folklore Society annual meeting in Atlanta. Reuss was the fifth presenter on a "Black Song and Music" panel, which also included blues specialist David Evans. Reuss summarized Gellert's rise and the "wide vogue" for his collection of Black songs of protest in the 1930s, and then related the allegations of fakery, compositing, and fabrication "for political or other reasons" that had surfaced in the ensuing years. In his remarks, Reuss explained that "analysis of the material coupled with considerable interviewing of Gellert and others" had persuaded him of the credibility of the material. He concluded for his academic peers that "while the Gellert songs are hardly what one would ask of a properly trained folklore student or collector, one must take into account the motivations and circumstances under which the songs were gathered." Therefore, he stipulated, the Gellert collection "was understandable in its own light" and, if approached "carefully," could be of "some value to folklorists."[70]

Reuss's co-panelist at the AFS annual meeting in 1969, ethnomusicologist David Evans, published a positive review of Gellert field recordings in the *Journal of American Folklore* in 1973, and folklorist Norm Cohen weighed in the following decade in a *JAF* review in 1986. Cohen stated that "Gellert's field collecting in the South, which resulted in some remarkably candid protest material (the genuineness of which was at one time questioned) has been neglected too long." He concluded, "If ever an album required and deserved extensive documentation, this is it—and not because we still doubt its authenticity."[71] Despite these approving late-stage reappraisals, Gellert's archive of "Negro Songs of Protest" never seemed to fully break through to wide consideration. At best, the collection remained a curious footnote, never a portal for serious academic reinvestigation.

In her incisive intervention, "The Practice of Refusal in Willis Laurence James's Song Collecting," scholar Ellie Armon Azoulay writes about James (1900–1966), an accomplished Black folklorist, musician, and composer, as a defier and disruptor of white-dominated academic discourse. James, like Thomas Talley before him, refused the categories and definitions imposed by

Lawrence Gellert, the year he disappeared, 1979. Courtesy of Penny Gellert Freeman.

an emergent short list of mid-century influencers and canonizers in the dominant strata. In 1939, James began work on a project of Black vernacular song collecting and analysis. Branching out from his base at Spelman College in Atlanta, James conducted southern fieldwork in the region and wrote a manuscript, *Stars in de Elements (A Study of Negro Folk Music)*, that he completed in 1945. Azoulay's research locates James's work within a tradition of Black radical reappropriation, agency, and empowerment in the face of systemic white misrepresentation. She argues that his "criticism highlighted white collector's misconceptions and stereotyping as examples of a range of exploitative practices, while stressing the urgent need for Black-authored scholarship."[72]

Stars in de Elements includes lyric texts, musical notation, and music history and analysis. In James's purview, African American "folk music" is a field of expression deep and wide, from the sacred to the secular, and including work songs and union songs of topical import. Rigid definitions of music as only old and anonymous are artificial and inapplicable to the fluid reality of grassroots Black music-making in everyday life. James wrote that real-time vernacular song-making and song-adaptation are "a strong index" to creative ability. "It also shows what actually happens to the songs of the Negro as they pass through the hands of highly gifted people who are honest in their efforts at self-expression."[73]

Lawrence Gellert's *Negro Songs of Protest* is listed in James's bibliography, and James praises Hall Johnson and Sterling Brown in the manuscript, both of whom, as we have learned, were admirers of Gellert's collecting. In Brown's coedited *Negro Caravan* from 1941, song texts from James are included on the pages adjacent to song texts from Gellert. Brown accompanied Willis Laurence James on a collecting trip during World War II; James wrote that Brown "is closer to the heart of Negro folk music than any Negro poet has ever been before." These three individuals—James, Brown, and Gellert—overlapped, in other words, in a shared interpretive community.[74]

In his fieldwork, Lawrence Gellert worked the same ground as James. Literally, Gellert collected in some of the same years and in the some of the same places (particularly Georgia, South Carolina, and Alabama), and figuratively, Gellert operated with a similar defiance of disciplinary category and convention. Their folk material runs parallel as well. In *Stars in de Elements*, James included common stock lyrics to work songs of the kind that appeared in Gellert's archive: "Ef I had mah weight in line / I'd whip dis cap'm / Twell his clothes start fryin'."[75]

The verse below is illustrative as well of the kind of "Negro Songs of Protest" encountered by Gellert. James printed the following:

Dam de cap'm!
Dam de comp'ny too!
I'm ntachal bawn eas' man
Thoo an' thoo.
White folks don' cuss me!
Done buke me 'round!
I'll take dis here pick
An' tare yo' down!
Cap'm, cap'm, hear me,
Listen to what I say:
Cap'm, cap'm, hear me,
Dis here's my last day.[76]

And, James did not discount topical songs of protest in his analysis of Black folk music:

All I want is Union,
Oh Lawd! Hanh!
Union make me happy,
Oh Lawd! Hanh![77]

As Azoulay points out, "James saw more than music in these songs." Like Gellert, James's folksong research was corrective, humanistic, and justice-minded, not antiquarian or strictly academic. "The testimonial aspects of these songs, as well as the resentment expressed in them," Azoulay determines, "are most likely the reasons why the songs were neglected by the early white collectors."[78] Unfortunately, that neglect persisted long past the early stages of Black folksong collecting. James's "practice of refusal" was, in effect, refused. Though extensive and accomplished, *Stars in de Elements (A Study of Negro Folk Music)* remained unpublished until 1995.

Lawrence Gellert and "Negro Songs of Protest" were, we might say, refused as well. But, we need add, African American contemporaries never refused the work or renounced their appraisals. "Look, I was a revolutionary.... I got sort of on fire with the condition of the Negroes, and I really concentrated on that," Gellert emphasized. "I've pointed it a certain way; I used it as a weapon."[79] In part, because of these social convictions and outspoken political commitments, the "undisciplined" qualities of Gellert's stances, associations, and collecting work were in themselves weaponized by the agents and accomplices (witting and unwitting) of the disciplinary state of folklore to defame a rich archive of Black vernacular music as not "folk" and maybe even not real.

In the end, the uprooting and refusal of Lawrence Gellert is about more than Gellert, and this work of scholarly recovery is about more than character rehabilitation. After all, the question of Black vernacular protest has long been settled in US arts and history. Additionally, it is well to say, Gellert need not be mythologized as a paragon or white savior figure. The marginalization and erasure of Gellert is about the marginalization and erasure of interracial radicalism in the postwar "American Century"; it's about the systems of privilege—white and male and class-based—which prevail into our age. The denial of Gellert's work and of the reality of "Negro Songs of Protest" is about the denial of systemic injustice in the United States, and a denial of the radical movements for change and alternatives for progress in the US past. As Gellert was uprooted and refused, so went his contemporaries of color and women of significance, too. Music and knowledge in the American state was left all the poorer.

NOTES

1. Dick Weissman, *Which Side Are You On? An Inside History of the Folk Music Revival* (New York: Continuum, 2005), 26.

2. Jerry Schmetterer, "80-Yr.-Olds Are Sought by Cops, Kin," *Daily News*, November 4, 1979, 84. Family and friends never had closure as regards the tragic disappearance. Gellert did leave a "last note" found by nephew James Gellert. Though the content is reflective of a pained and

disordered mind, the note cannot necessarily be deemed conclusive of suicide, and no body was ever recovered. I found a copy of the note among the materials in the Hugo Gellert Papers, TAM 150, Box 2 of 2, Folder 6, "Gellert, Jim," 1979, Tamiment Library, New York University.

3. Readers will note the dialect transcription and inclusion of the "N"-word. Though jarring now, such language was a standard of the time, albeit one, even then, fraught and contested. In Gellert's rendering, it was meant to convey truth rather than to exoticize or dehumanize. Similarly, in 1935, Zora Neale Hurston published *Mules and Men*, which conveyed the language and rhythm of African Americans in southern Black dialect. Hurston was committed to dialect transcription as a "way to produce a written text that maintains the orality of the spoken word." See Hurston, *Mules and Men* (1935; New York: Harper Perennial, 1990) and, for the quotation referenced here, Hurston's *Barracoon: The Story of the Last "Black Cargo"* (New York: Amistad, 2018), xxii.

4. Series 1 "Biographical Material," Box 1, Folder 4: "Lawrence Gellert Collected Folksong Lyrics and Notes, circa 1930–1939." Hugo Gellert Papers, 1916–1986, Archives of American Art, Smithsonian Institution; Lawrence Gellert, "Negro Songs of Protest," *New Masses* (November 1930): 10; Lawrence Gellert, *Negro Songs of Protest* (New York: American Music League, 1936), 9.

5. Series 1 "Biographical Material," Box 1, Folder 4: "Lawrence Gellert Collected Folksong Lyrics and Notes, circa 1930–1939"; Hugo Gellert Papers, 1916–1986, Archives of American Art, Smithsonian Institution; Gellert, "Negro Songs of Protest"; Dorothy Scarborough, *On the Trail of Negro Folk-Songs* (Cambridge, MA: Harvard University Press, 1925), 232.

6. Gellert, "Negro Songs of Protest," *New Masses* (January 1931): 17; Gellert, *Negro Songs of Protest*, 10–11.

7. Scarborough, *On the Trail*, 189.

8. John Szwed, *Billie Holiday: The Musician and the Myth* (New York: Viking, 2015), 157; Nancy Kovaleff Baker, "Abel Meeropol (a.k.a. Lewis Allen): Political Commentator and Social Conscience," *American Music* 20 (Spring 2002): 46. Meeropol traced his direct inspiration to the well-known Lawrence Beitler photo of the double-lynching of Thomas Shipp and Abram Smith in Marion, Indiana, in 1930.

9. "Negro Songs of Protest," Gellert, Lawrence, Drafts/undated, Federal Writers' Project Negro Group Papers, JWJ MSS 40, Box 1, Folder 7, Beinecke Rare Book and Manuscript Library, Yale University.

10. Michael Denning, *The Cultural Front: The Laboring of American Culture in the Twentieth Century* (New York: Verso, 1996), 358, 355–56.

11. Lawrence Gellert, "Negro Songs of Protest," Federal Writers' Project Negro Group Papers, JWJ MSS 40, Box 2, Folder 32, Beinecke Rare Book and Manuscript Library, Yale University.

12. Alan Lomax, Woody Guthrie, and Pete Seeger, eds., *Hard Hitting Songs for Hard-Hit People* (1967; Lincoln: University of Nebraska Press, 1999), 365–66.

13. Samuel Charters, *Walking a Blues Road: A Selection of Blues Writing, 1956–2004* (New York: Marion Boyars, 2004), 136–38.

14. Bruce Conforth, liner notes, *Cap'n You're So Mean: Negro Songs of Protest, Volume 2*, LP, Rounder 4013, 1982.

15. Bruce M. Conforth, *African American Folksong and American Cultural Politics: The Lawrence Gellert Story* (Lanham, MD: Scarecrow Press, 2013), 159.

16. Conforth, *African American Folksong and American Cultural Politics*, xvi, xii, 71–72, 15, 30, 39, 53, 231–34, 141.

17. Steven P. Garabedian, *A Sound History: Lawrence Gellert, Black Musical Protest, and White Denial* (Amherst: University of Massachusetts Press, 2020). See also an open-source web supplement, https://umpressopen.library.umass.edu/projects/a-sound-history. In the 1970s, Lawrence Gellert deposited his field recordings and papers at the Archives of Traditional Music (ATM) and Lilly Library at Indiana University, Bloomington. Additionally, the ATM

holds nearly nine hours of audio interviews that researcher Richard A. Reuss conducted with Gellert between 1966 and 1969.

18. Irwin Silber email message to author, January 3, 2001, and Irwin Silber interview by author, June 13, 2002. In a 1948 piece in *The Atlantic*, Niles addressed the issue. See John Jacob Niles, "My Precarious Life in the Public Domain," *The Atlantic* (December 1948).

19. Irwin Silber, "Dubious," letter to editor, *Mainstream* (July 1963): 61.

20. Blues scholar Paul Garon made this point in 2001 in the revised edition of Garon, *Blues and the Poetic Spirit* (1975; San Francisco: City Lights, 2001), 200.

21. Adolph Greenbaum, "Petition for Naturalization," filed May 20, 1909, Department of Commerce and Labor, Naturalization Service, United States of America. Thanks to researcher and artist James Wechsler for sharing essential Gellert family history. See James M. Wechsler, "Retaining the Accent: Hugo Gellert and the Hungarian Cultural-Political Nexus," *Hungarian Studies Review* 31:1–2 (2004): 77–78.

22. Lawrence Gellert, interview by Richard A. Reuss, March 28, 1968, and August 31, 1966, Archives of Traditional Music, Indiana University, Bloomington. "Former Tryon Man Will Do Research Work," *Asheville Citizen-Times*, January 5, 1938, 8.

23. Lawrence Gellert, interview by Richard A. Reuss, March 28, 1968, and August 31, 1966, Archives of Traditional Music, Indiana University, Bloomington. Lawrence Gellert, *Negro Songs of Protest* (New York: American Music League, 1936), and Gellert, *Me and My Captain: Chain Gang* (New York: Hours Press, 1939).

24. Barbara Foley, *Radical Representations: Politics and Form in U.S. Proletarian Fiction, 1929–1941* (Durham, NC: Duke University Press, 1993), 65.

25. Gellert writings continued to appear past Gold's tenure in *New Masses* in the 1930s and 1940s, and in the successor periodicals *Masses & Mainstream* and *Mainstream* in the 1950s and early 1960s. See Garabedian, *A Sound History*, chapters 1, 2, and 5 et passim.

26. Nancy Cunard, ed., *Negro: An Anthology* (1934; New York: Frederick Ungar Publishing, 1970), xxxi, 226–37. Gellert's piece followed right after Zora Neale Hurston's "Spirituals and Neo-Spirituals" in the Music section of the book.

27. Gellert interviews, March 28, 1968, ATM: "I have a clipping—he was in Germany; they asked about the background of jazz, he held up my book—this is where it came from." The Russian edition of *NSP* was *Negrityanskie Pesni Protesta*, trans. G. M. Shneerson (Moscow: Gosudarstvennoe Izdateil'stvo "Iskusstvo," 1938); the German publication was *Protestlieder des Amerikanischen Negroproletariats*, trans. G. M. Shneerson and Ernst Busch (Berlin: Verlag Lied der Ziet, 1949).

28. "Work All De Summer," Victor 25809-B, 78 rpm, 1937; and "Lay Down Late," Victor 26251-B, 78 rpm, 1938. Readers can listen to both items at the Internet Archive: https://archive.org/details/78_1-work-all-de-summer-2-didnt-my-lord-deliver-daniel_paul-robeson-lawrence-brown_gbia0397182b, and https://archive.org/details/78_lay-down-late_paul-robeson-lawrence-brown-l-gellert_gbia0183101b.

29. See Garabedian, *A Sound History*, passim; Garabedian, "Reds, Whites, and the Blues: Lawrence Gellert, 'Negro Songs of Protest,' and the Left-Wing Folk-Song Revival of the 1930s and 1940s," *American Quarterly* 57 (March 2005): 179–206; and, Garabedian, "Forgotten Manuscripts: Lawrence Gellert, Negro Songs of Protest" in *African American Review* 49:4 (Winter 2016): 297–311.

30. Robin D. G. Kelley, "'Afric's Sons with Banner Red,'" in *Race Rebels: Culture, Politics, and the Black Working Class* (New York: Free Press, 1996), 117; Mark Solomon, *The Cry Was Unity: Communists and African Americans, 1917–1936* (Jackson: University Press of Mississippi, 1998), 278; Richard A. Reuss with JoAnne C. Reuss, *American Folk Music and Left-Wing Politics, 1927–1957* (Lanham, MD: Scarecrow Press, 2000), 95. See also Robbie Lieberman, *"My*

Song Is My Weapon": People's Songs, American Communism, and the Politics of Culture, 1930–50 (Urbana: University of Illinois Press, 1989); Michael Denning, *The Cultural Front: The Laboring of American Culture in the Twentieth Century* (New York: Verso, 1996).

31. Faith Berry, ed., *Good Morning Revolution: Uncollected Social Protest Writings by Langston Hughes* (New York: Lawrence Hill, 1973), 2–4, 49–50. "Good Morning, Revolution" appeared in *New Masses* in September 1932, and "Goodbye, Christ" appeared in *The Negro Worker* in November/December 1932. "Ballads of Lenin" in Granville Hicks et al., *Proletarian Literature in the United States* (New York: International Publishers, 1935), 166; Langston Hughes, *A New Song* (New York: International Workers Order, 1938), 20, 24–25. See also, Jonathan Scott, *Socialist Joy in the Writing of Langston Hughes* (Columbia: University of Missouri Press, 2006).

32. Hugo Gellert to Langston Hughes, n.d., Series I: Personal Correspondence, Gellert, Hugo/n.d., Box 67, Folder 1279, Langston Hughes Papers, JWJ MSS 26, Beinecke Rare Book and Manuscript Library, Yale University.

33. Lawrence Gellert to Langston Hughes, n.d., Series I: Personal Correspondence, Gellert, Lawrence/ca. 1931–1947, Box 67, Folder 1280, Langston Hughes Papers, JWJ MSS 22, Beinecke Rare Book and Manuscript Library, Yale University. Gellert later recounted the same South Carolina county jail episode in the annotation with lyric transcription to "Work All the Summer" in his "Negro Songs of Protest" installment in *New Masses* (May 1932): 22.

34. Gellert, "Draft Proposal," Gellert Mss., Lilly Library, Indiana University, Bloomington.

35. Gellert, interview by Richard A. Reuss, March 28, 1968.

36. Hughes to Gellert, January 2, 1931; Gellert to Hughes, January 7, 1932; and, Hughes to Gellert, n.d., 1932. Series I: Personal Correspondence, Gellert, Lawrence/ca. 1931–1947, Box 67, Folder 1280, Langston Hughes Papers, JWJ MSS 22, Beinecke Rare Book and Manuscript Library, Yale University. The unpublished Hughes preface is archived among the Lawrence Gellert Papers, Bancroft Library, University of California, Berkeley, and reproduced in the Gellert materials at Indiana University, Bloomington.

37. Hughes preface, Lawrence Gellert Papers, Bancroft Library, University of California, Berkeley.

38. Dust jacket to Gellert, *Negro Songs of Protest*, shared from the personal collection of Paul and Beth Garon.

39. Valerie Boyd, *Wrapped in Rainbows: The Life of Zora Neale Hurston* (New York: Scribner, 2003); Jennifer L. Freeman Marshall, *Ain't I an Anthropologist: Zora Neale Hurston Beyond the Literary Icon* (Urbana: University of Illinois Press, 2023). See also Zora Neale Hurston, "Three Letters to Alan Lomax," Cultural Equity, https://www.culturalequity.org/alan-lomax/friends/hurston. Quote comes from Carla Kaplan, ed., *Zora Neale Hurston: A Life in Letters* (New York: Anchor Books, 2002), 171. Gellert interview by Lorraine Brown, October 22, 1976, Works Progress Administration Oral Histories Collection, #C0153, Special Collections Research Center, George Mason University, Fairfax, Virginia.

40. Carla Kaplan, ed., *Zora Neale Hurston: A Life in Letters* (New York: Anchor Books, 2003), 119, 151, 172.

41. Zora Neale Hurston, *Mules and Men* (1935; New York: Harper Perennial, 1990), 2–3; Yuval Taylor, *Zora and Langston: A Story of Friendship and Betrayal* (New York: W. W. Norton, 2019).

42. Hall Johnson, "Songs of Protest: A Review," *Opportunity* (August 1936): 241, 243, 244.

43. Lawrence Gellert, interview by Richard A. Reuss, August 31, 1966, March 28, 1968, and September 11, 1969. The Hall Johnson Choir appearance was covered in the press, and Gellert's collection and "Scottsboro" was mentioned: "Negro Folksongs Stadium Feature," *New York Times*, July 6, 1938, 21.

44. "Presents Negro Protest Songs: Noted Young Concert Artist Featured in Recital," *New York Age*, June 27, 1936, 7.

45. Lawrence Gellert, "Remembering Nancy Cunard," in *Nancy Cunard: Brave Poet, Indomitable Rebel, 1896–1965*, ed. Hugh Ford (Philadelphia: Chilton, 1968), 143; Sterling Brown, *Negro Poetry and Drama* (Washington, DC: Associates in Negro Folk Education, 1937), 29; Sterling A. Brown, "Negro Folk Expression: Spirituals, Seculars, Ballads and Work Songs," *Phylon* XIV (1953): 58–59. From that 1932 meeting on, states scholar Lorenzo Thomas, Sterling Brown cited Gellert "in almost every article on the blues he subsequently published." Thomas, "Authenticity and Elevation: Sterling Brown's Theory of the Blues," *African American Review* 31:3 (Autumn 1997): 413.

46. Arthur B. Spingarn, "Books by Negro Authors in 1936," *The Crisis* 44:2 (February 1937): 48.

47. *Chicago Defender*, January 8, 1938, 19.

48. Coverage in the Black press includes "A.N.P. Correspondent Writes For Soviet Books," *Pittsburgh Courier*, December 3, 1932, 10; "Presents Negro Protest Songs," *New York Age*, June 27, 1936, 7; "Harlem to See Big Drama," *Chicago Defender*, January 8, 1938, 19; "WPA To Present Ballet in Harlem," *New York Age*, January 8, 1938, 9; "Lawrence Gellert Plans Negro Opera," *Pittsburgh Courier*, January 8, 1938, 20; "'How Long Brethren' Opens at Lafayette on January 18," *New York Age*, January 15, 1938, 9; "Musical May Hit Broadway," *Pittsburgh Courier*, March 30, 1946, 19.

49. Sterling A. Brown, Arthur P. Davis, and Ulysses Lee, eds., *The Negro Caravan: Writing by American Negroes* (New York: Dryden Press, 1941), 3.

50. "Harlem to See Big Drama," *Chicago Defender*, January 8, 1938, 19; on the *How Long Brethren* dance production, see Susan Manning, "Black Voices, White Bodies: The Performance of Race and Gender in *How Long Brethren*," *American Quarterly* 50 (1998): 24–46.

51. "Lawrence Gellert Plans Negro Opera," *Pittsburgh Courier*, January 8, 1938, 20; "WPA To Present Ballet in Harlem," *New York Age*, January 8, 1938, 9; "Former N.C. Newsman Gets Folk Opera Grant," *Statesville Daily Record*, December 31, 1937, 1; "Former Tryon Man Will Do Research Work," *Asheville Citizen-Times*, January 5, 1938, 8; H. Howard Taubman, "Negro Folksongs: New Genre Dealing with Everyday Life Produced, Particularly in South," *New York Times*, July 5, 1936, X5; "Songs of Protest," *Time*, June 15, 1936, 51; "WPA Composer Honored," *Brooklyn Daily Eagle*, December 31, 1937, 6; Louise Kates to Hugo Gellert, April 11, 1937, Box 1, Folder 29: "Correspondence, 1936–1937," Hugo Gellert Papers, 1916–1986, Archives of American Art, Smithsonian Institution.

52. Lawrence Gellert, interview by Lorraine Brown, October 22, 1976. Works Progress Administration oral histories collection, Collection #C0153, Special Collections and Archives, George Mason University, Fairfax, Virginia; Gellert, interview by Richard A. Reuss, March 28, 1968.

53. John Szwed, *Alan Lomax: The Man Who Recorded the World* (New York: Viking, 2010); Gellert, "Jim Crow in Khaki," *New Masses* (March 19, 1946): 13; and Chris Smith, "Odell Hall," *The Frog Blues & Jazz Annual No.6: The Musicians, The Records and The Music of the 78 Era* (2022): 85–88. Sterling Brown also collected testimony from African American soldiers on base in World War II. This material was published posthumously in John Edgar Tidwell and Mark A. Sanders, eds., *Sterling A. Brown's "A Negro Looks at the South"* (New York: Oxford University Press, 2007).

54. Gellert, interview by Richard A. Reuss, March 28, 1968.

55. Gellert, interview by Richard A. Reuss, August 31, 1966.

56. Gellert, interview by Richard A. Reuss, March 28, 1968; Szwed, *Alan Lomax: The Man Who Recorded the World*.

57. Elizabeth Dilling, *The Red Network: A "Who's Who" and Handbook of Radicalism for Patriots* (self-pub., Elizabeth Dilling, 1934), 283; Committee on Un-American Activities, US House of Representatives, *Investigation of Un-American Propaganda Activities in the United States: Hearings Before A Special Committee on Un-American Activities, House of Representatives, Seventy-Fifth Congress*, 1938, 2799; Committee on Un-American Activities, US House of Representatives, *Supplement to Cumulative Index to Publications of the Committee on*

Un-American Activities 1955 through 1960 (84th, 85th, and 86th Congress), June 1961, 117, 291, https://archive.org/details/supplementtocumu1961unit/page/n3/mode/2up; for Hugo's testimony from November 14, 1956, in Washington, DC, see Committee on Un-American Activities, US House of Representatives, *Communist Political Subversion Part I: Hearings Before the Committee on Un-American Activities, House of Representatives, Eighty-Fourth Congress, Second Session*, 1957, 6229, 6325–6332, https://archive.org/details/1956HUACCommunistPoliticalSubversion/page/6334/mode/1up?q=Gellert. See also Conforth, *African American Folksong*, 155–57; Leonard, *The Folk Singers and the Bureau*; Aaron Leonard, email message to author, October 17, 2019.

58. Gerald Horne, *Paul Robeson: The Artist as Revolutionary* (London: Pluto Press, 2016); William J. Maxwell, *F.B. Eyes: How J. Edgar Hoover's Ghostreaders Framed African American Literature* (Princeton, NJ: Princeton University Press, 2015), 165–69, 234–36, 89–90, 297; Joanne V. Gabbin, *Sterling A. Brown: Building the Black Aesthetic Tradition* (Charlottesville: University Press of Virginia, 1985), 51, 81–82; and see John Edgar Tidwell and Steven C. Tracy, eds., *After Winter: The Art and Life of Sterling A. Brown* (New York: Oxford University Press, 2009); and Tidwell, "The United States vs. Sterling A. Brown," *Folklife Today: American Folklife Center and Veterans History Project* (blog), November 16, 2023, https://blogs.loc.gov/folklife/2023/11/the-united-states-vs-sterling-a-brown-john-edgar-tidwell/. For Maxwell's essential "F.B. Eyes Digital Archive" of primary documents on African Americans, see http://digital.wustl.edu/fbeyes/.

59. Gellert, interview by Richard A. Reuss, August 31, 1966, and March 28, 1968.

60. The Conrad and Gellert schemes are documented in correspondence in the Earl Conrad Collection, Cayuga Community College, Auburn, New York.

61. Arnold Rampersad, *The Life of Langston Hughes: Volume II: 1947–1967: I Dream a World* (New York: Oxford University Press, 1988), 128–31; Gellert to Hughes, May 7, 1947, Series I: Personal Correspondence, Gellert, Lawrence/ca. 1931–1947, Box 67, Folder 1280, Langston Hughes Papers, JWJ MSS 26, Beinecke Rare Book and Manuscript Library, Yale University.

62. Claude Blanchette, "'Voice of America' Peddles Dixiecrat Lies to Europe," and Gellert, "A West Point 'Sacred Tradition': Anti-Negro Violence," *Freedom* (September 1951): 1, 3.

63. Sterling A. Brown, "Negro Folk Expression: Spirituals, Seculars, Ballads and Work Songs," *Phylon* XIV (1953): 58–59.

64. See Garabedian, *A Sound History*; Denning, *The Cultural Front*; Benjamin Filene, *Romancing the Folk: Public Memory and American Roots Music* (Chapel Hill: University of North Carolina Press, 2000); Richard A. Reuss with JoAnne C. Reuss, *American Folk Music and Left-Wing Politics, 1927–1957* (Lanham, MD: Scarecrow Press, 2000); Lieberman, *"My Song Is My Weapon"*; Leonard, *The Folk Singers and the Bureau*; and, Jesse Jarnow, *Wasn't That a Time: The Weavers, The Blacklist, and the Battle for the Soul of America* (New York: Da Capo Press, 2018).

65. John Greenway, *American Folksongs of Protest* (Philadelphia: University of Pennsylvania Press, 1953); Stith Thompson, review of *American Folksongs of Protest*, by John Greenway, *American Historical Review* 59:2 (January 1954): 454.

66. Gellert, interview by Richard A. Reuss, September 11, 1969, and August 31, 1966.

67. Gellert, "Steel Got to Be Drove," *Sing Out!* (February 1953): 3; "Young's Anecdotes" from 1960, Izzy Young to author, 2002; and Young, "Frets and Frails," *Sing Out!* (December–January 1962): 65, and (July 1965): 75. This material is now compiled in Scott Barretta, ed., *The Conscience of the Folk Revival: The Writings of Israel "Izzy" Young* (Lanham, MD: Scarecrow Press, 2012).

68. "Some Recent Publications," *Journal of American Folklore* 49, no. 193 (July–September 1936): 280; Catharine Ann McCollum and Kenneth Wiggins Porter, "Winter Evenings in Iowa, 1873–1880," *Journal of American Folklore* 56, no. 220 (April–June 1943): 102; Russell Ames, "Art in Negro Folksong," *Journal of American Folklore* 56, no. 222 (October–December 1943): 253; J. Mason Brewer, "Afro-American Folklore," *Journal of American Folklore* 60, no.

238 (October–December 1947): 381; Richard M. Dorson, "Folklore in Periodical Literature," *Journal of American Folklore* 64, no. 251 (January–March 1951): 136; and, D. K. Wilgus, "From the Record Review Editor: Afro-American Tradition," *Journal of American Folklore* 85, no. 335 (January–March 1972): 105–6.

69. See Richard A. Reuss, "American Folklore and Left-Wing Politics, 1927–1957" (PhD diss., Indiana University, 1971), and Reuss with JoAnne C. Reuss, *American Folk Music and Left-Wing Politics, 1927–1957* (Lanham, MD: Scarecrow Press, 2000).

70. Richard Reuss, "Lawrence Gellert's 'Negro Songs of Protest.'" Panel program, "Black Song and Music," Friday, November 7, 1:10–3:00 P.M., Columbus Room, American Folklore Society annual meeting, 1969, Atlanta American Motor Hotel, Atlanta, Georgia; Gellert, Lawrence, "Corporate Subject," Folder 1, AFC, Library of Congress.

71. David Evans, "Afro-American Music: Early Commercial and Field Recordings," *Journal of American Folklore* 91, no. 360 (April–June 1978): 737; and Norm Cohen, "The American Folklife Center's Selected Lists of Recordings," *Journal of American Folklore* 99, no. 391 (January–March 1986): 107.

72. Ellie Armon Azoulay, "The Practice of Refusal in Willis Laurence James's Song Collecting," *Comparative American Studies: An International Journal* 18:3 (2021): 357.

73. Willis Laurence James, *Stars in de Elements: A Study of Negro Folk Music* (1945; Durham, NC: Duke University Press, 1995), 153.

74. James, *Stars in de Elements*, 339, 200, 222–23, 235, 213, 238. Azoulay, "The Practice of Refusal," 357. Brown, Davis, and Lee, *The Negro Caravan*. The songs included in *The Negro Caravan* are James, "Roberta Lee" (467), "It Sound Like Thunder" (468), "Hyah Come De Cap'm" (469), and Gellert, "Standin' on De Corner" (470), "Lay Down Late" (470–71), "Me and My Captain" (471). Gellert is highlighted in *The Negro Caravan* alongside the Lomaxes and Josh White for having recently "brought to light many songs of strong social protest . . . not new to the Negro folk, but fairly new in song collections"; in fact, Gellert is credited above the other parties for amassing "the richest yield of such songs" (426).

75. James, *Stars in de Elements*, 72.

76. James, *Stars in de Elements*, 102.

77. James, *Stars in de Elements*, 96.

78. Azoulay, "The Practice of Refusal in Willis Laurence James's Song Collecting," 360.

79. Gellert, interview by Richard A. Reuss, August 31, 1966, and September 11, 1969.

CHAPTER 3

CURATING MUSIC
What Is Perpetuated and Why

Franz Andres Morrissey

PREAMBLE: THE STATE, MUSIC, AND THE "UNHOLY TRINITY"

The topic of this book, Music and the State, developed out of earlier discussions that considered the position of musicians within an existential framework that is defined by three elements we came to regard as an "Unholy Trinity." This trinity, we found, consists of, to begin with, the institutions that administrate knowledge and thus initiate, codify, and, to a considerable extent, control the accepted discourse: *academia* in the widest sense. The second element is represented by *journalism* as the source of information about music, whose verdicts affect musicians and even genres to the point where it can make or break them. The third institution, playing a crucial if not the all-decisive role, is the one that regulates the cash flow, the *music industry*, whose activities are fairly exclusively shaped by the commercial potential of musicians or of a type of music.

This Unholy Trinity, I want to argue, clearly has a solid foundation, the state, in which it is, at times surreptitiously, embedded. The state cherry-picks findings from the wellspring of knowledge and research of academia; it creates the environment in which opinions can be voiced (admittedly not always being able to exclude unwelcome ones), how they can be expressed, and how they are disseminated through journalism; and, finally—as James Carville memorably quipped in 1992, "It's the economy, stupid!"—it relies on a functioning industry, which (not only in the West) firmly relies on the profit motive, on capitalism. In other words, there is a fundamental connection between the Unholy Trinity and the state, with the state both feeding into but also feeding on this Trinity. The connection is not always an entirely overt one, but, as culture and popular music can be described in Joseph Nye's term as "soft power," wielded by state-sponsored institutions or influenced, financed, and supported by governments.[1]

The focus in this chapter is on the impact of the Trinity on music and song curation, in particular in terms of the ideology/ideologies of the curators, which determines what they will consider for curation.

PERFORMANCE AND PERPETUATION

Songs, in fact any piece of music or a recitation, are ephemeral creatures that live in the performance and are gone the moment the performance comes to an end. This raises a number of questions, such as how this performed piece can be perpetuated, and, for our purposes more pertinently, why it is that some songs achieve longevity, remaining current for decades or even centuries, and why others seem to disappear without trace. This is particularly intriguing in the context of the kind of popular song that would be described as folk music, often considered, on the one hand, as an oral genre, transmitted through performance, and, on the other hand, as being associated with lower and allegedly illiterate classes (Auer, Schreier, and Watts 2015) or as addressing their concerns. This comes with the attendant expectation of these illiterate classes being unaware, too careless, or too uneducated to be trusted with the preservation of these treasures (Harker 1985; Watts and Andres Morrissey 2019b, 321). We shall explore this perception in more detail below.

If there is to be any means by which songs can be rescued from oblivion once their performance is over, nonperformative strategies are needed for their perpetuation, and these inevitably require some form of *transmediation*, a translation of a song, at least of its salient elements, into another medium. The simplest form of perpetuation is a transcription of the words; a more demanding one, requiring a level of training and skill not always readily available, is the notation of the tunes.

Concerning song lyrics, there are several potential issues. If performer and collector have vastly different linguistic and cultural backgrounds, as has often been the case with the song hunters of the eighteenth to the twentieth centuries, pronunciations and understanding of the social practices referenced in the song may create problems in accurately rendering the words. Misheard words, often referred to as *mondegreens*, may lead to rather marked misunderstandings, in some cases drastically changing the meaning of a song.

In fact, the actual term mondegreen (Wright, 1954) is a prime example, changing the lyric "they killed the Earl of Murray / *and laid him on the green*" to "... *and Lady Mondegreen,*" an entirely plausible mishearing, given the fact that in fluent (and particularly in sung) pronunciation we often cannot make out word boundaries (a phenomenon known in phonology as *coalescence*). An additional difficulty is that rendering a vernacular performance is complicated by the fact that there is typically no universally accepted grammatical or orthographic norm of that vernacular variant.

There are similar difficulties on the level of musical notation. On the one hand there is the note-for-note representation of transcripts made by the likes of Percy Grainger and (perhaps better known) Béla Bartók, which create considerable difficulties when nonexpert sight-readers are confronted with such notation, in comparison to the relatively basic outlines usually used in most songbooks, which give a singer an idea of the tune, often on the basis of the first verse, with the assumption that the singer will find a way to adjust the tune and phrasing to differences in syllabification in remaining verses. Seeger (1958) makes the distinction between *etic* and *emic* notation, with *etic* referring to the former and emic to the latter type of notation. Emic notation is sometimes also referred to as *prescriptive* because it assumes that a musician or singer adopting the material is sufficiently well-versed in the relevant musical tradition to have an idea of how a song is to be performed. The assumption in the context of *etic* or *descriptive* notation is that it should be reproducible without such cultural knowledge. However, the question remains whether any notation can be so detailed as to really do justice to the performance from which it was taken; as Sachs put it: "No musical script can ever be a faithful mirror of music" (1962, 31).

What this brief discussion shows is that any transmediation requires choices, thereby inevitably excluding some aspects of the performance while emphasizing others. In other words, transmediations could be described as the equivalent of a Vitamin C tablet in relation to the glass of freshly squeezed orange juice that would be the actual performance. The comparison is also apt because orange juice can vary in taste and texture, while Vitamin C tablets are uniform in their flavor.

So far, we have looked at transmediations onto paper, but we also need to consider actual recordings, be they merely audio, or as has become much more frequent particularly in the last fifty years, as videos. Although there are ethnographic field recordings that would appear to be fairly spontaneous—even if they are rarely completely unrehearsed—audio and video recordings are usually the result of careful editing. Many studio recordings, audio and video, are so thoroughly edited that they do not reflect one actual performance, whereas live recordings result from a choice of several instantiations, a series of takes, with the most flawless one chosen for the final product. For this phenomenon Watts and Andres Morrissey (2019) have used the image of insects caught in amber: such insects may well represent quite exceptional specimens, preserved in a precious medium and considered to be representative while countless other individuals have obviously perished without trace. But in actual fact, these preserved specimens may be untypical of the species, or it is also possible that the process of being encapsulated in amber may have had an impact on the appearance of the encapsulated insect. To put it simply, the preserved specimen may be unrepresentative.

In the same way, a folk song, perpetuated by the efforts of a collector, a sound engineer, and/or a director, may well not be a pertinent example of the cultural practice it is meant to represent. However, the main difference between the processes of preservation in amber and preservation in transmediation is that the former is a matter of chance, the latter the result of deliberate choice. In other words, this choice represents a form of *curation* of songs that are chosen for perpetuation, which raises the question as to the nature of this choice. The answer, a little fluid at this point, seems to be the intention of the curator(s), something that will differ between individual curators, but it will also need to chime with the sociocultural interests and politics at the time of curation. In other words, it has to match or at least meet the perceptions of the social and mental representations associated with the material, the collectors, and the intended audience and thus conforms to van Dijk's definition of *ideology*.[2]

In the following I shall explore the curation of songs associated with the lower classes, either as their own productions or as compositions to highlight their conditions by sympathetic parties outside these classes from a historical perspective, in order to illustrate the interplay between ideology and the selection of materials as well as the elements focused on in the transmediation processes.

THE UNHOLY TRINITY FROM A HISTORICAL PERSPECTIVE

The fact that song perpetuation, and thus curation, is to be discussed from such a perspective takes as a starting point the examination of practices in the Old World. It also means that we need to situate the Unholy Trinity within that historical context.[3] It has to be said, however, that, whereas in other chapters addressing this phenomenon, each element of the Trinity is likely to be represented by distinct institutions, groups, and individuals, in the early stages of song curation it was often one individual, usually the compiler of a collection, the *antiquarian*, who represents all three.

We clearly have an equivalent of the *music industry* in the increasingly lively market for song collections aimed at the emerging middle classes of the late eighteenth and early nineteenth centuries, fueled by an interest in the adaptations of popular songs in parlor music. The work of the *academy*, which would define the selection criteria for curation of the material, corresponds to the antiquarians, whose interest in their material was based on their—often very personal—perspective as to what this material was meant to represent and the manner in which this was to be the case.

In this context, it is perhaps worthwhile pointing out, the antiquarians rarely went out to collect material themselves but relied on the contributions of different informants. These could be middle-class and were often referred to by their names and their professional titles (henceforth referred to as collectors), while lower-class performers and singers usually remained unnamed and were typically defined by their occupations (a ploughman, a housemaid, a wet nurse, and so on). Their performances were usually recorded, often by the collectors, and sent to the antiquarians in this transmediated format, either reduced to the lyrics or as songs with their tunes. It is here that we regularly encounter explicit qualitative judgment of the material, focused on the quality of the lyrics collected, specifically their level of perceived textual corruption, allegedly reflecting, explicitly or implicitly, the inability of the common people, from whom the material originated, to preserve their own cultural treasures.

To summarize, the perspective of this actor in the combined Trinity, the antiquarian, was usually characterized by at least one, but often all three assumptions (Watts and Andres Morrissey 2019a):

- firstly, as pointed out above, that the lower classes, from whom the material originated, were either uninterested in or incapable of preserving their own (low) cultural heritage;
- secondly, that without the efforts of the antiquarians (and their middle-class collectors) these songs were inevitably going to disappear, manifest in an often explicit "last-ditch" discourse, clearly related to the first point;
- and lastly, that usually there was (already) a degree of corruption in the material, which required emendations to restore it to the lost perfection of the material it was assumed to have in a long bygone Golden Age (cf. Watts and Andres Morrissey 2019a, 163 ff.).

This last point, the need for editing, can be linked to the equivalent of *music journalism* in its role as an arbiter of taste for the public. Although during the period in question there would not have been music journalism as we know it, largely because there were few if any publications for this genre, the function of the arbiters of taste is clearly in evidence in the prefaces and forewords of the collections.

However, for the arbiters of taste there are two aspects of judgmental motivation for exclusion: social and historical references on the one hand, usually only implicitly evident in the absence of such material; and concerns about sensitivities and propriety on the other, which not too rarely are explicitly stated in prefaces and introductions.

In terms of overt, topical social criticism, something that has a history in the genre now, but even did so at the time (Ganev 2009), this would not have found a place in most collections, clearly because the antiquarians and their target audience were middle or at times even upper class and therefore unlikely to embrace material that could foment unrest or be critical of their own politics. Historical comment, on the other hand, was a staple in at least some of the collections (Scott 1802–1803).

As far as the second aspect is concerned, there was very explicit reference to propriety of the material in terms of references to eroticism. Ritson (1783), for instance, writes an introductory remark: "Throughout the whole of the first volume, the utmost care, the most scrupulous anxiety has been shewn to exclude every composition, however celebrated, or however excellent, of which the slightest expression, or the most distant allusion could have tinged the cheek of Delicacy, or offended the purity of the chastest ear."

This is part of an attitude illustrated in the English verb *to bowdlerise*, derived from Thomas Bowdler, who, as the 1819 advert puts it, expunged from Shakespeare "those words . . . which cannot with propriety be read in a Family." Clearly, if even Shakespeare was not exempt from being edited to meet the needs for propriety, the culture of the lower classes was fair game for amendments to ensure that no inappropriate references to sexuality or vulgarity would be in line for potential curation.

Therefore, if we combine the considerations presented so far, we find that ideally, for a song to be curated three criteria would have to be met: Firstly, it had to have *commercial appeal*, which would include the possibility that it could be performed in a lay setting, for instance, a middle-class parlor. Secondly, it had to be in line with an antiquarian's thematic focus, the *selection rationale*, based on their ideology; and, lastly, it had to correspond to whatever was considered *in good taste* in the relevant social context. It is the selection rationale and the ideology on which it is based that I want to focus on in more detail in the following section, related to the commercial appeal and the notion of good taste. I shall also undertake to show that the same criteria, in adapted form, continued to apply in the twentieth century.

SELECTION RATIONALES AND IDEOLOGIES

However, before we discuss a number of examples of song curation, mainly of the nineteenth century, we need to revisit the notion of ideology because it has a strong impact on song collections. Extrapolating from van Dijk's definitions (1998, 2001, 2003) we can say that ideology is based on shared beliefs, shared perceptions, shared goals, and shared practices. In order to ensure the purity of material for potential curation, in particular the shared perceptions and practices, such material needs to be subjected to scrutiny, ranging on a cline from conceivable adoption via critical examination of acceptability, possibly with amendments in an adaptation, to rejection or even active eradication. These considerations will apply, to varying degrees, to a number of examples I would posit as being representative, presented in this section. It needs to be emphasized that any such discussion will remain sketchy for reasons of space, and selective, yet intended to illustrate some of the more archetypal antiquarian practices. My aim is to present a spectrum of these practices from the point of view of their underlying ideologies.

As publishing songs has a considerably long history, it makes sense to focus on instances that paint a characteristic picture of the early stages of song perpetuation and the resulting curation of songs deemed worthy of preservation. However, we also need to be aware of the fact that in the nineteenth century there were two distinct tiers of publications. On the one hand, is the material we will mainly focus on, the commercially attractive market of historical song material for middle-class parlor music, deemed traditional and authentic.[4] On the other hand is song material, written or at least edited by hacks, that was for sale in the streets, often in the form of ballad sheets, so-called broadsides sold by itinerant peddlers (who often also sang the songs while selling them), or in relatively cheap chapbooks. This was facilitated by the increase in printing activity in the eighteenth century and more prominently so in the (early) nineteenth century (cf. Ganev 2009). Sadly, we will largely have to ignore these latter song materials for reasons of space except in the context of them either being considered worthy—or not, as was frequently the case (Palmer 1996)—for inclusion in the collections aimed at the middle-class market and their greater market potential.

One of the early collections, which today is still quoted as a source and an influence, is Thomas D'Urfey's *Wit and Mirth, or Pills to Purge Melancholy* (1698–1720). In some ways it is typical of this genre of publication in the sense that it was aimed at an expanding market for such books, which is illustrated by the continuity of its publication and the fact that it eventually comprised six volumes. It is also typical in the sense that it included material that dated back, some to the Elizabethan and Restoration periods—in other words, that part of its merit was the preservation of "ancient" songs and lyrics,[5] supplemented by material composed around the period of its publication. The description of its content on the title page illustrates these points clearly: "Songs Compleat, / Pleasant and Divertive; / SET TO M U S I C K / By Dr. John Blow, Mr. Henry Purcell, / and other Excellent Masters of the Town. / Ending with some Orations, made and spoken by me several times upon the Publick Stage in the Theater. Together with some Copies of Verses, Prologues, and Epilogues, as well for my own Plays as those of other Poets, being all Humerous and Comical." It is, however, less typical of other examples to be discussed below in two ways: firstly, there is an explicit emphasis on entertainment, which included some openly lewd material. Secondly, it does not make claims to contain what we might call "folk" songs,[6] which are the focus of later publications.

Less explicit in terms of including their own material or their editing in respective collections are two Scots, Robert Burns (1759–1796) and Sir Walter Scott (1771–1832). Both are mainly remembered in literary history as writers and poets, but both played an important role in the curation of songs, in particular how they were transmediated. Burns, a perpetually poverty-stricken poet, found employment with two Scottish music publishers and antiquarians, George Thomson (1757–1851), who ensured Burns's cooperation for his *A select collection of original Scottish airs* in four volumes, and James Johnson (ca. 1750–1811) (details in Andres Morrissey 2021). Burns met the latter in the spring of 1787. Johnson originally edited, printed, and sold *The Scots Musical Museum* in six volumes of one hundred songs each, in the period between 1787–1803, but Burns in effect took over as main editor from the second volume onward, emending and adding text from oral tradition, from pamphlets, chapbooks, and earlier collections in addition to writing lyrics for a number of melodies that up to then had no words. The collection also includes Burns's own songs, most famously "Auld Lang Syne," "My Love Is Like a Red, Red Rose," and "A Man's a Man for A' That," which subsequently became part of the Scottish folk song canon. All in all it is assumed that about 40 percent of the songs are in some way attributable or actually written by him. Two quotes are interesting in this context: on his lyrical contributions, Margaret Smith's assessment that "[e]ditorial working to establish the Burns canon have not yet settled which songs Burns partly or indeed completely rewrote, which he edited, and which he merely collected and transmitted" (quoted in Pittock n.d.); and in relation to Burns's musical influence on curating music, Bronson, editor of *The Traditional Tunes of Child Ballads: With their Texts according to the Extant Records of Great Britain and America*, states that "Burns[,] who had an ear for a good tune, ballad words or no, ... was fortunately not musician enough to sophisticate those [songs that] he learned ..." (Bronson 1959–1972, "Introduction" vol., xxi). Burns was aware of his role in the preservation of Scottish song, as he wrote in a letter to Johnson praising Johnson's curation undertaking (which he knew to be largely his own): "Your Work is a great one.... I will venture to prophesy, that to future ages your Publication will be the text book and standard of Scottish Song and Music" (quoted in University of South Carolina 1996, 20). It is important from a point of view of selection and curation ideology that Burns very clearly included the tunes of the songs, but also that he felt he was making a contribution to a national (Scottish) undertaking.

Whereas Burns's interest, apart from the nationalist aspect, was also focused on ideals of social equality coming out of France at the time, Scott, a member of the gentry, was rather more focused on older Scottish history—and, it would seem, of promoting his own writing. His *Minstrelsy of the Scottish Border* (Scott 1802), although originally focusing on ballads about the skirmishes on the border between England and Scotland in mediaeval times, eventually also included several so-called romantic ballads, classic texts we will return to below. Unlike Burns, who was a singer and songwriter as well as a collector, Scott was focused on the historical and the literary, particularly the ballad, but he too had strong patriotic tendencies. In his curation, there is an obvious focus on documenting the history of the Borders on the one hand, but in doing so there is also the intention to draw attention to the Scottish literary soul manifesting itself in these poems, for such these songs were considered to be (Edinburgh University Library n.d.). This had two consequences: firstly, although there was no actual generally acknowledged, definitive poetics of the ballad, there were clear ideas as to their form, their composition prominently being in quatrains with alternating lines of four and three stressed syllables, the so-called *ballad meter* (also used in Coleridge's "The Rime of the Ancient Mariner"). There is an account, possibly apocryphal, that in his efforts to ensure the texts of the ballads being "correct" in their literary form, Scott rewrote "Clerk Saunders" in ballad meter; "Clerk Saunders" is in the so-called *long meter*, a somewhat less common ballad format, with all four lines having four stressed syllables. The effect was that it was no longer singable with its tune in <3/4> measure.[7] Even if this account is difficult to substantiate, it fits into the image of Scott notoriously tinkering with his material to fit in with his ideology, both historical and more importantly in terms of *Scottish* folk literature. In fact, Child, on whom more below, in a comment ascertains that "Scott's variations [of ballads in Child's collection], the contrary not being alleged, must be supposed to be his own" ([1882–1898] 1965, II 423).[8] Furthermore, music as an element of the ballads was not relevant, given the focus on history and the literary value of (folk) balladry as poetry of the national spirit, in keeping with the practice of other nineteenth-century antiquarians and literary scholars (cf. Reed 1991, 8), which in the case of this approach to curation meant that tunes dropped from sight.

Nowhere is this focus on the literary value of song curation more in evidence than in what must be considered the most seminal collection of ballads to this day, Francis James Child's (1825–1896) *The English and Scottish Popular Ballads* ([1882–1898] 1965). Although Child himself never published a poetics of the folk or popular ballad, his selections and how he ordered the songs make a clear statement about his views in this respect. For the philologist Child, these lyrics represented a form of archaic literature, going back in their most ancient form to an idealized, classless society, a rather dubious interpretation at odds with history but a useful strategy to explain why in the "romantic" ballads there was such a focus on protagonists from the gentry (Sweers and Andres Morrissey 2019). Thus, one selection criterion clearly was material that related to these tales of heroism and chivalry, with another an implied origin in the rural population; urban life was largely ignored as was material that referred to social conflict of the industrial age as well as broadside ballads that were not print versions of evidently more ancient texts. Palmer (1996) quotes a telling passage from a letter of Child's to Svend Gruntvig, a Danish scholar: "The immense collections of Broadside ballads, the Roxburghe and Pepys, of which but a small part has been printed, doubtless contain some ballads which we should at once declare to possess the popular character, and yet on the whole they were veritable dung-hills, in which, only after a great deal of sickening grubbing, one finds a very moderate jewel" (157).

The focus on the literary is obvious in the highly detailed listing for each ballad text in as many of its variants as Child was able to round up from his informants, neatly assigned to various categories. "A" texts represented the most valued versions, with less highly regarded material and finally sometimes rather spurious fragments grouped under letters further along in the alphabet. With this meticulous attention to textual variants and the literary emphasis on the collection, it is not surprising that music was not considered worthy of attention. It was not until the second half of the twentieth century that musicologist Bronson addressed this aspect comprehensively and with equal attention to as many variants in the Old and the New World as he was able to print. His introduction to the first volume tellingly begins: "*Question:* When is a ballad not a ballad? *Answer:* When it has no tune" (Bronson 1959–1972, ix, italics in the original). Like Scott's, Child's focus in transmediation was purely on the lyrical, and likewise his undertaking was one of exploring the literary soul, in his case of a broader take on Anglo-Saxon culture in a nostalgic, romantic idealization of a preindustrial but largely fictitious past.

At the turn of the century and into the Edwardian age, we come across the so-called *song hunters*, similarly driven by a focus on their own culture, in this case an explicitly nationalistic one. Sabine Baring-Gould, Cecil Sharp, his often underrated assistant Maud Karpeles, Ralph Vaughan Williams, and Percy Grainger, to name but a few,[9] saw their work as collectors of folk song as a way to preserve something that was quintessentially British or, in fact, distinctly English.[10] The emphatic inclusion of music (with all the issues of transmediation referred to above) in their collections and publications can be seen as a reaction against Oskar Schmitz's famous dictum that England was "Das Land ohne Musik" (the land without music) (Serotsky 2005). The interest in folk song was driven by two aspects, first that the true musical soul of the nation (mostly, it can be argued, of England) was to be found in its folk song tunes (Cole 2019, 22ff). Second was that these songs were collected in rural environments and collectors consistently ignored urban material (Gammon 1980). The ideal informant was what could be called a NORF, a nonmobile old rural folksinger (Watts and Andres Morrissey 2019b, 156n7).[11] Like with folk song collectors in general there was a discursive emphasis on *loss*, in this context not just of the songs, but also of the entire class, meaning the peasantry (Knevett and Gammon 2016). In view of this double loss, the focus on rural music is as unsurprising as it is exclusive of a broader perspective on folk music as "music of the people."

However, there is also a highly insidious aspect to this focus on the "British," in particular in the context of Cecil Sharp's decision to track British song and balladry to and in the New World. "Mining for Songs," the opening track of the CD *Cecil Sharp Project*, contains the very telling lyrics (Pearson 2011), briefly discussed in the following. It opens with Sharp's aims, "I search for song in America / like strangers pan for gold" before making the point that there is a curation rationale that involves "sift[ing] and sort[ing], . . . leav[ing] aside" while other items "[he]'ll gently hold." The song describes Sharp's method, collecting songs by going "[f]rom house to house, from door to door, / Bring them to life, sing them once more." The notion of appropriation is clearly referred to in the last line of the chorus, which goes "I'll write them down, make them my own." Perhaps the most telling notion in the selection rationale, however, is that Sharp's intention to "sift and sort, or leave aside" in order to find ". . . souls of England underground, / whose voices echo still."

The persistent myth of the Appalachians being the new homeland of a homogenous white population with a direct link back to the Old World is thematized in Rhiannon Giddens's keynote speech to the 2017 IBMA Convention with an emphasis on the role of Sharp and Karpeles: "With Maud Karpeles [Sharp] spent three years in the Appalachian mountains, recording families and making much of what he found there—but only [from] the white folks. [. . .] They just plain didn't like black people. [. . .] Sharp says: 'We tramped—a very hard and warm walk, mainly uphill. When we reached the cove we found it peopled entirely by negroes!! All our trouble and spent energy for naught.' Except of course, he didn't say negroes" (Giddens 2017). A more explicit illustration of how ideology affects curation would be hard to find.

A further example of what could be regarded as ideology affecting song curation can be found in the songs of World War I. It makes sense to look at this issue from a point of hegemonic vs. antihegemonic songs, the former represented by music hall material, which has been fairly broadly accessible in the form of sheet music from then to today. Where there may be mild criticism of the politics of the day, especially once the war proved to be much more protracted and bloody than originally assumed and politically stated, these songs do not present a threat to establishment views, neither historically of their days nor today. This is in some contrast to the clearly antihegemonic songs written by the soldiers (Macdonald 1984, 203) and distributed, often in the form of carbon-copied pamphlets in the trenches and soldiers' bars (Andres Morrissey 2020). What helped their rapid distribution and adoption was the fact they used popularly known tunes (in this case hymns and music hall song choruses), a traditional and tested strategy to spread protest music as well as an incentive for the public to buy broadsides (many of which have a note under the title "sung to the tune of . . .").[12] These songs were originally curated during the war but clearly not meant for general circulation as the songs remained largely an in-group form of music. This is partly due to the lewdness of some of the songs; Macdonald describes a tour of veterans and their wives to the old battlefields of Arras and Ypres and recounts that ". . .

they began to sing [. . .] one irreverent ditty after another. The tunes were familiar. The words were not—and many of the fruiter choruses trailed off [. . .] as the tolerant smiles of their wives became a trifle fixed" (Macdonald 1990, 1–2). Nettleingham, a collector of songs during the war, echoes this aspect when he writes, "It is a great pity that a large number of the wittiest—albeit, of a coarse kind—the gayest—as regards tune—and most frequently sung—therefore popular—creations are so untranslatable as to render them unprintable for general consumption, but . . . it seems probable that they will remain unwritten heirlooms for an indefinite period, and in peace-time will be handed down through the generations by drummer-boy to drummer-boy" (1917, 11). Another reason for their minimal curation, the disturbing nature of the material, is highlighted in the foreword, the "Dedication," of McGill's *Soldier Songs*, compiled during the war. He asserts that "[n]one will outlast the turmoil in which they originated; having weathered the leaden storms of war, their vibrant strains will be choked and smothered in atmospheres of Peace. 'These 'ere songs are no good in England,' my friend Rifleman Bill Teake remarks. 'They 'ave too much guts in them'" (McGill 1917, 14). What we find here is that there is something amounting to self-censorship, which was also in evidence in later compilations, where crude material was largely excised and swear words were severely tuned down (for instance to *bally*, an expletive which never have passed a true squaddie's lips). Most of the later collections of World War I soldiers' songs (cf. Palmer 1990a; Arthur 2001; Pegler 2014),[13] are sanitized to varying degrees. However, as so much time has elapsed and most of the material that had hitherto mainly been in nostalgic circulation in reminiscences and recordings passed on in the veterans' families, the (self-imposed) restrictions on the content of the material—if perhaps not the language—has made way for what could now be seen as historical interest. Nevertheless, it is rather unusual to find in a printed version of the frequently anthologized song "The Old Battalion" a verse like "If you want to find Joe Driscoll, I know where he is . . . / On the firestep with half his head blown away" before Palmer decided to include it (1990a, 119).

The selection rationale here is clearly informed by what the general public can tolerate, erring, it would seem, on the side of caution. And it is not until a safe amount of time has elapsed, relativizing the often caustic criticism of the powers that be and placing them in the context of historical interest, that these songs have at last been deemed worthy of curation.

The last examples in this admittedly selective account represent an interesting contrast to the Edwardian (and, of course, earlier Victorian) focus on rural song material of the peasantry with its longing for a pre-industrial arcadia. During and immediately after World War II there was a renewed interest in music 'of the people' in Britain, in fact as a kind of national undertaking to overcome class differences, championed, amongst others, by the BBC; this was coupled with a greater awareness of and interest in American musical practices (Watts and Andres Morrissey, 2019a, 158 ff.). The American folk scene in the twentieth century as perceived in the popular domain differed very markedly from the predominant nationalist conservativism of the Edwardian curation focus.

There was a clear left-wing orientation in the American folk movement, concerned not so much with songs *of* but with songs *for* the people, beginning with song compilers like Joe Hill, who wrote several of the songs for the Wobblies' songbook *I.W.W. Songs to fan the flames of discontent* (1909), later with Pete Seeger, Woody Guthrie, the Weavers, etc., which was later followed by the Civil Rights movement and was still very much in evidence in the 1992 reprint *Sing Out*, where Dave van Ronk is quoted in the preface as describing the collection as 'an Aladdin's cave with something for everyone except perhaps tone-deaf *Republicans*' (Silber, et al., 1992, 2, emphasis mine). The British folk scene, clearly influenced by American antecedents, followed the same trajectory of social criticism and unsurprisingly had a great deal of overlap with left-wing associations, be it the Campaign for Nuclear Disarmament, communist groups, etc. (cf. Bean, 2014). In this light we need to consider (in folk music curation terms, at least) the new interest in urban material and songs exemplified by two prominent figures, in fact, figureheads Ewan McColl and A. L. Lloyd. Industrial confrontation, songs about mining disasters, social upheaval through strikes and lockouts were revisited and collected, Lloyd and McColl curating material in recordings, radio broadcasts as well as in print collections (Lloyd's *Come All You Bold Miners* ([1952] 1978, to mention just one example). In particular, McColl supplemented his vast stock of traditional material—which was by no means limited to industrial and urban songs—with highly popular self-penned works, much of it explicitly focused on social comments. Most of the material put out was very clearly informed by left-wing social criticism, a tradition that lasts to today, obviously alongside less overtly political material. In fact, political awareness and antihegemonic discourse, in many cases ventriloquizing[14] the working class underdog, is a hallmark of the song curation in the twentieth and also in the twenty-first century. British folk musician John Tams is famously quoted in Bean, stating: "I've never been to a Tory folk club yet" (2014, 376). It not only reflects the political and social stance of the folk scene in Britain, but also the underlying selection criteria for at least a sizeable part of curated song both in print and in recordings, audio as well as video.

It is appropriate at this juncture to address a seeming contrast to the cases discussed earlier as the folk 'scene' in the twentieth century stands in some contrast to earlier, more bourgeois attitudes and ideologies. Here the ideology is quite clearly antihegemonic, but the main difference is that for the most part, commercial considerations take a back seat or for some folkies are actually irrelevant. Like the antihegemonic songs of World War I, much of the material alluded to was never meant for mass distribution, and many publishers and record companies were in this for the counterculture or the criticism of the powers-that-be. A telling example of this is that it took over twenty years for *Hard-hitting Songs for Hard-Hit People* finally to be published (in 1967), significantly at a time when activist music and song material was no longer much of a fringe phenomenon.

One final consideration needs to be added. Political awareness that informs positioning and resulting decisions about what is worth curating also accounts for the fact that certain songs in the course of time fall out of favor. This may be because they reflect attitudes that would now appear to be racist, e.g., the term *darkie* in some Stephen C. Foster songs, the reference to the tight-fisted "jewman money lender" in Dominic Behan's "Waxies Dargle"; the misogynistic story lines in many traditional songs, including "I Wish I was Single Again" or the stark male abuse in "Prince Heathen" (Child 104), but also songs, of course in more mainstream songs like "Hey Joe," "I've Got Woman," "Run for Your Life," etc.; or discredited political views, e.g., "The Night They Drove Old Dixie Down," but perhaps more overtly political, Ewan MacColl's "Ballad of Stalin." Similarly, American material of the late fifties in praise of the Western position in the Korean War, particularly songs extolling the efficacy of the Bomb, have been all but forgotten (cf. Andres Morrissey and Sweers, this book) and certainly would, except perhaps as an ironic antiwar statement, neither be included in the repertoire of present-day British folk acts, nor represent likely inclusions in Americana performers' set lists.

CONCLUSION

What I hope to have demonstrated is that transmediation and thus the perpetuation of songs, as well as the curation process of what is deemed worthy of being recorded, is first of all a highly selective process. It can be riddled with errors in the form of linguistic and cultural misunderstandings deriving from the often traditionally disparate backgrounds of collectors/antiquarians and informants. It is likely to exclude elements that the latter may not want to share and others that the former consider of less immediate interest, most notably, as we have seen, melodies or the subtleties of musical variation between various verses of a song (cf. Seeger's concept of emic and etic notation), or it may reflect what the collector/antiquarian, at times rather spuriously or arbitrarily, deems the proper form of the material, leading to swathes of emendations and 'improvements.' And, lastly, of course, in the context of what this book addresses, it reflects the ideology of the collectors/antiquarians who see their work as a mission to curate with the intention to separate wheat from whatever it is they consider their chaff. The result, particularly as far as ideology is concerned, could be described as the 'submersion' of elements, songs or entire genres that do not fit the discursive socio-political understanding or practices of the antiquarians and/or their imagined target audience. Callahan's work *Songs of Slavery and Emancipation* (2022) is a very stark reminder of how the hegemonic discourse can submerge songs of slave revolts because the notion does not fit the traditional historiography of passive African Americans having to wait for the Whites to free them from the bondage of slavery. However, the work is also a testimony that songs can be extremely resilient to submersion, surfacing in unexpected contexts, which is also reflected in the recent find in a local library of the 'Chartist Hymns' (Sanders, 2012 and Calderdale Council, n.d.), in this case, again sadly, without tunes; these hymns clearly advocate an anticapitalist stance, condemning wage slavery and exploitation as a sin in the eyes of God, a very strongly antihegemonistic position in the contemporary nineteenth-century politics. Significantly, no other copies of these hymns have been found elsewhere so far, let alone in visible circulation.

This chapter has focused mainly on what we would now describe as folk music. Particularly in the understanding of the last seven to eight decades, in contrast to the eighteenth- and nineteenth-century antiquarian marketing, publication in print or as recordings has arguably limited financial appeal and is therefore a welcome repository for the inclusion of or even an active focus on material and topics seen as unfit for mainstream curation, e.g., in Tin Pan Alley style music publishing. As Frith (2008) puts it: "'Folk' . . . did not describe musical production but musical values, and these values were derived from a critique of commercialism: the description of folk creation (active, collective, honest) was, in fact, an idealised response to the experience of mass consumption (fragmented, passive, alienating)" (160). This is what has allowed so much twentieth century folk song and material curated in the same period to reflect egalitarian and antihegemonic values and has the ability to counteract the forces of submersion. Nevertheless, curation still depends on the underlying ideologies. That these are subject to change and to cultural values is illustrated by the fact that in Germany and Switzerland folk songs have so frequently been co-opted by the nationalist right (with a relatively brief interruption by the local folk movement in the late sixties and in the seventies), whereas in the British Isles they firmly reflect leftist values. In short: in curation ideologies matter.

NOTES

1. For an overview and definitions, see Clarke (2020).
2. In fact, van Dijk (2003) sees ideology "as the basis of the social representations of groups . . . , where the notion of social representation is . . . any kind of *socially shared mental* representation" (32, emphasis mine).
3. The following discussion is based on Harker's (1985) perspective of the way in which collecting has shaped the resulting collections, that is, the curation of the songs they contain.
4. It needs to be emphasized that both of these terms refer to socially and historically fluid concepts (for a more detailed discussion, cf. Claviez et al., particularly Hagmann and Andres Morrissey 2020).
5. It is noteworthy that an integral part of the discourse concerning collection of what we would now call folk songs is the *age* of the material (cf. Bishop Percy's *Relics of Ancient English Poetry*, emphasis mine), with a yen for a Lost Other, an—obviously fictitious—Golden Age (see above). This is also a recurring theme in Cecil Sharp's perspective on the nature of folk song ([1907] 1972, 157 ff.), in other words, of what he would consider worth curating in order, in accordance with the prevailing "last-ditch effort" discourse to prevent it from disappearing.
6. In fact, the term *folk song*, influenced by Herder's notion of *Volkslied*, is not normally used in antiquarian collections until much later, with terms such as *vernacular* or *traditional* song being preferred.
7. Songs in ballad meter tend to have "regular" measures (4/4 and 6/8) whereas long meter ballads are typically in 3/4.
8. For a detailed discussion, cf. Zug (1969).
9. Although Australian-born and later adopting American citizenship, Grainger was motivated by a strong passion for the British folk revival and is the composer of many settings for English traditional songs.
10. An anonymous reviewer remarked of Sharp's *A Book of British Songs for Home and School*, "although this collection of school songs is designated 'British,' no fewer than sixty-six of the seventy-eight ditties contained herein are English" (quoted in Cole 2019, 22).
11. This is an analogy to the term NORM (nonmobile old rural male) as the ideal informant in traditional dialectology. Sharp in the Introduction to *English Folk Song, some conclusions* explicitly points out, "I have spent every available moment of my leisure in *country lanes, fields and villages* in the quest of folk singers . . ." ([107] 1972, xxi, emphasis mine).
12. For a thorough account on tunes of broadsides, see Simpson (1966).
13. It needs to be mentioned that Joan Littlewood in her revue *Oh What a Lovely War* made use of WWI material around the fiftieth anniversary, in 1963, with both hegemonic (ironically) and antihegemonic songs to emphasize the horrors of that war.
14. MacKinnon convincingly characterizes the British folk scene as follows: "it is a specific sub-section of the middle class which is heavily over-represented in folk music, those in service occupations which are largely in the public sector, jobs such as teaching and social work" (1993, 130). The term *ventriloquizing* in this context is therefore apt.

WORKS CITED

Andres Morrissey, F. (2020). "Plucky Tommies, Angelic Nurses and the Others: Identity Constructions in hegemonic and antihegemonic discourse of First World War songs." In J. Andres, B. Rozema, and A. Schröder, eds., *(Dis-)Harmony: Amplifiying Voices in Polyphone Cultural Productions*, 9–33. Bielefeld: Aisthesis.

Andres Morrissey, F. (2021, October 22). Farewell Lecture "And Warldly Cares and Warldly Men Can a' Gang Tapsalterio." University of Bern.

Arthur, M. (2001). *When This Bloody War Is Over: Soldiers' Songs of the First World War.* London: Judy Piatkus.

Auer, A., Schreier, D., and Watts, R. J. (2015). *Letter Writing and Language Change.* Cambridge: Cambridge Universtity Press.

Bean, J. (2014). *Singing from the Floor: A History of British Folk Clubs.* London: Faber and Faber.

Bronson, B. H. (1959–1972). *The Traditional Tunes of Child Ballads: With Their Texts According to the Extant Records of Great Britain and America.* East Windsor, NJ: Princeton University Press.

Calderdale Council. (n.d.). *National Chartist Hymn Book (Collection of 16 Chartist hymns).* Retrieved September 4, 2022, from From Weaver to Web: Online Visual Archive of Calderdale History. https://www.calderdale.gov.uk/wtw/search/controlservlet?PageId=Detail&DocId=102253.

Callahan, M. (2022). *Songs of Slavery and Emancipation.* Jackson: University Press of Mississippi.

Child, F. J. ([1882–1898] 1965). *The English and Scottish Popular Ballads.* (F. J. Child, ed.) Boston and New York: Houghton, Mifflin.

Clarke, D. (2020). "Cultural Diplomacy." *Oxford Research Encyclopedia of International Studies.*

Claviez, T., Imesch, K., and Sweers, B., eds. (2020). *Critique of Authenticity.* Delaware and Malaga: Vernon.

Cole, R. (2019). "On the Politics of Folk Song Theory in Edwardian England." *Ethnomusicology* 63(1): 19–42.

Edinburgh University Library. (n.d.). *Minstrelsy of the Scottish Border* (P. Barnaby, ed.). Retrieved January 21, 2023, from The Walter Scott Digital Archive: http://www.walterscott.lib.ed.ac.uk/works/poetry/minstrelsy.html.

Frith, S. (2008, November 10). "'The magic that can set you free': the ideology of folk and the myth of the rock community." *Popular Music* 1 (1981): 159–68. Retrieved January 29, 2022, from https://doi.org/10.1017/S0261143000000970.

Gammon, V. (1980). "Folk Song Collecting in Sussex and Surrey, 1843–1914." *History Workshop* 10 (Autumn): 61–89.

Ganev, R. (2009). *Songs of Protest, Songs of Love: Popular ballads in eighteenth-century Britain.* Manchester and New York: Manchester University Press.

Giddens, R. (2017). "Rhiannon Giddens' Landmark Keynote Address to The 2017 IBMA Convention Is Still Relevant Today." Retrieved October 7, 2022, from Northern California Bluegrass Society: https://ncbs.info/2020/06/04/rhiannon-giddens-keynote-.address-to-the-2017-ibma-convention-is-still-relevant-today/.

Lomax, A., Guthrie, W., and Seeger, P. (1967). *Hard Hitting Songs for Hard-Hit People.* New York: Oak Publications.

Hagmann, L., and Andres Morrissey, F. (2020). "Multiple Authenticities of Folk Songs." In Claviez et al., *Critique of Authenticity*, 183–260.

Harker, D. (1985). *Fakesong: The Manufacture of British "Folksong" 1799 to the Present Day.* Milton Keynes and Philadelphia: Open University.

Knevett, A., and Gammon, V. (2016). "English folk song collectors and the idea of the peasant." *Folk Music Journal* 11(1): 44–66.
Lloyd, A. L. ([1952] 1978). *Come All Ye Bold Miners: Ballads and Songs of the Coalfields*. London: Lawrence and Wishart.
Macdonald, L. (1984). *Somme*. London: Macmillan.
Macdonald, L. (1990). Foreword. In R. Palmer, *"What a Lovely War": British soldier's songs from the Boer war to the present day*, 1–5. London: Michael Joseph.
MacKinnon, N. (1993). *The British Folk Scene: Musical Performance and Social Identity*. Buckingham: Open University Press.
McGill, P. (1917). *Soldier Songs*. New York: Dutton. Retrieved April 8, 2015, from https://archive.org/details/soldiersongsoomacggoog.
Montgomerie, W. (1956, April). "Sir Walter Scott as Ballad Editor." *Review of English Studies* 7(26): 158–63. Retrieved from https://www.jstor.org/stable/511839.
Nettleingham, F. T. (1917). *Tommy's Tunes: A comprehensive collection of soldiers' songs, marching melodies, rude rhymes, and popular parodies*. London: E. Macdonald. http://www.horntip.com/html/books_&_MSS/1910s/1917_tommys_tunes_2nd_edition_(HC)/1917_tommys_tunes_2nd_edition.pdf.
Palmer, R. (1988). Introduction. In *The Sound of History: Songs and social comment*, 1–29. Oxford: Oxford University Press.
Palmer, R. (1990a). *"What a Lovely War!" British Soldiers' Songs from the Boer War to the Present Day*. London: Michael Joseph.
Palmer, R. (1990b). Introduction. In R. Palmer, *"What a Lovely War!" British Soldiers' Songs from the Boer War to the Present Day*, 7–18. London: Michael Joseph.
Palmer, R. (1996). "'Veritable Dunghills': Professor Child and the broadside." *Folk Music Journal* 7(2): 155–66.
Pearson, N. (2011). *Cecil Sharp Project*. Retrieved December 18, 2022. http://www.cecilsharp-project.com/.
Pegler, M. (2014). *Soldiers' Songs and Slang of the Great War*. Oxford: Osprey.
Pittock, M. (n.d.). *Editing Robert Burns for the 21st Century*. Retrieved January 15, 2023. https://burnsc21.glasgow.ac.uk/.
Pittock, M., ed. (n.d.). *Oxford Edition of the Works of Robert Burns. II-III. Songs for The Scots Musical Museum*. https://burnsc21.glasgow.ac.uk/songs-for-the-scots-musical-museum/.
Reed, J. ([1980] 2013). *Sir Walter Scott: Landscape and locality*. London and New York: Bloomsbury Academic Collections.
Reed, J. (1991). *The Border Ballads*. Stocksfield: Spredden Press.
Ritson, J. (1783). *A Select Collection of English Songs*. London: J. Johnson.
Sachs, C. (1962). *The Wellspring of Music*. The Hague: Nijhoff.
Sanders, M. (2012). "'God is our guide! our cause is just!' The National Chartist Hymn Book and Victorian Hymnody." *Victorian Studies* 54(4): 679–705.
Scott, W. (1802). *Minstrelsy of the Scottish Border: Consisting of Historical and Romantic Ballads, Collected in the Southern Counties of Scotland; With a Few of Modern Date, Founded Upon Local Tradition*. London and Edinburgh: James Ballantyne (Printer).
Scott, W. (1802–03). *Minstrelsy of the Scottish Border: Consisting of Historical and Romantic Ballads, Collected in the Southern Counties of Scotland; With a Few of Modern Date, Founded Upon Local Tradition*. Edinburgh: Ballantyne.
Seeger, C. (1958). "Prescriptive and descriptive music-writing." *Musical Quarterly* 44(2): 1845–95.
Seeger, P., and Reiser, B. (1986). *Carry It On! A history in song and picture of the working men and women of America*. Poole: Blandford Press.

Serotsky, P. (2005, May 7). "Das Land Ohne Musik?" Retrieved January 14, 2023, from Musicweb International: http://www.musicweb-international.com/Programme_Notes/daslandohnemusik_conc.htm.

Sharp, C. J. ([107] 1972). *English Folk Song, some conclusions.* Wakefield: EP Publishing.

Silber, I., Nelson, P., Raim, E., Seeger, P., Silverman, J., and Traum, H. (1992). *The Collected Reprints from Sing Out! The Folk Song Magazine, Vols. 7–12, 1964-1973.* Bethlehem, PA: Sing Out Corporation.

Simpson, C. M. (1966). *The British Broadside Ballad and Its Music.* New Brunswick, NJ: Rutgers University Press.

Street, J., Hague, S., and Savigny, H. (2007). Playing to the Crowd: The Role of Music and Musicians in Political Participation. *British Journal of Politics and International Relations*, 1–17. doi:10.1111/j.1467-856x.2007.00299.x.

Sweers, B., and Andres Morrissey, F. (2019, March 18). "Lecture: Community Building through Anti-hegemonic Performances." *Singing Social Friction.* Bern: University of Bern.

University of South Carolina. (1996). University of South Carolina Libraries—Robert Burns: 1759-1796. University of South Carolina Scholar Commons, 3.

van Dijk, T. A. (1998). *Ideology: A multidisciplinary approach.* London: Sage.

van Dijk, T. A. (2001). "Discourse, Ideology and Context." *Folia Linguistica: Acta Societatis Linguisticae Europaeae*, 11–40.

van Dijk, T. A. (2003). "Political Discourse and Ideology." *Anàlisi del discurs polític.* Barcelona: Universitat Pompeu Fabra, IULA, 15–34.

Watson, A. (2006). "Self-deception and Survival: Mental Coping Strategies on the Western Front, 1914–18." *Journal of Contemporary History* 41(2): 247–68. doi:10.1177/0022009406062063.

Watts, R. J., and Andres Morrissey, F. (2019a). *Language, the Singer and the Song: The sociolinguistics of folk song performance.* Cambridge: Cambridge University Press.

Watts, R. J., and Andres Morrissey, F. (2019b). "The Song: Text and entextualisation in performance." In *Language, the Singer and the Song: The sociolinguistics of folk song performance.* Cambridge: Cambridge University Press.

Wright, S. (1954, November). "Who killed Lady Mondegreen?" *Harper's*, 48–51.

Zug, C. G. (1969). "Sir Walter Scott and the Ballad Forgery." *Studies in Scottish Literature* 8 (I): 52–64. https://scholarcommons.sc.edu/ssl/vol8/iss1/4.

CHAPTER 4

THE ETUDE MAGAZINE AND CULTIVATING THE AMERICAN MUSICAL CANON

Elissa Stroman

In these days advance is the watchword, progress is the motto, and no enterprise may come to a standstill and expect to hold its own. THE ETUDE now, as heretofore, aims to be the best and the standard journal for musicians and the music-loving public in this country, a journal that shall disseminate the truths of the art of music in its purest and best phases, that can go into any home to add to liberal culture and to increase the appreciation of music as a factor in a refined, social life, that shall stand for all that is high and lofty in aspiration and earnest, thoughtful, and sincere in expression. . . . it is the intention of the editor and publisher to place before the American public of music teachers and amateurs a journal that shall make the art a vital force in their daily lives.[1]

This chapter will investigate Theodore Presser's *Etude* magazine between its founding in 1883 and his death in 1926. I argue that in this period, *The Etude* was at the center of classical musical culture and became an arbiter of taste, providing metacommentaries on the importance of magazine study for the promotion and elevation of American musical culture. First, I will address the origins and expansion of *The Etude*, situating it within other music periodicals and cultural ideologies of the age, and discuss Presser's immense success growing his Philadelphia publishing company. I will analyze what readers were told regarding music selections, genres, and styles, arguing that readers were told to herald certain works and composers while removing what was

"Music Inspiring America," *Etude* Vol. 42, no. 11 (November 1924).

deemed too ephemeral or "trashy," meaning popular music. I will also address authors' suggestions for the improvement of amateur musicians' tastes, their valorizing women as culture bearers, and directions for creating an authentic American musical style.

Because *The Etude* was a genteel music appreciation publication, I situate the magazine within previous scholarship by Julia Chybowski, Gavin James Campbell, and Lawrence Levine. Due to the scope and scale of this chapter, my textual analysis of this music periodical recognizes that print publications involve a great number of individuals to make this singular product, but of necessity cannot cover every perspective, article, or viewpoint expressed in *The Etude*.[2] My hope is that by introducing these broader themes, more scholars will seek out this incredibly rich resource to uncover more perspectives and insights into Gilded Age American musical culture.

The 1880s and 1890s saw the birth of the modern consumer culture.[3] The Industrial Revolution precipitated an outpouring of goods, the rise of the mail-order catalog, and increased advertising and marketing opportunities. For the first time in American history, "nation-scale businesses" connected the entire country with their products.[4] Companies were emboldened by lower mail rates, better postal routes, cheaper overhead costs for producing magazines,[5] and printing advancements that made it easier to circulate print products.[6] Compound these advances with a strong editorial voice, and single individuals had an opportunity to shape an entire subculture's discourses.[7]

PRESSER AND THE GROWTH OF *THE ETUDE*

Theodore Presser was a powerful force due to his intersection of being an academic, turned publisher, who also was a critic. In 1923, on the fortieth anniversary of the publication, Henry T. Finck suggested that Presser's influence on musical America of the period was second only to Theodore Thomas.[8] Born in Pittsburgh, Pennsylvania, in 1848, by eighteen he was a manager of a sheet music business without having any formal music training. In 1868 he studied formally and by 1876 was the head of the music department at Ohio Wesleyan, which is where he founded the Music Teachers' National Association.[9] He later studied at the New England Conservatory and the Leipzig Conservatory before returning to the United States in 1880 to teach at the Hollins Institute in Virginia. The story goes that "he felt the limitations of his sphere and still longed for a life of larger usefulness," desiring to create a "journal that should stand for the best . . . a journal that should be so practical, so necessary and yet so attractive that any musician would be at a loss without it."[10] In Lynchburg, Virginia, with $250 to his name, he started *The Etude* in October 1883. His frugality and practicality became a common narrative, with the magazine's motto "he who combines the useful with the agreeable bears away the prize," and his hunch about the need for this publication hit a nerve. Slowly the magazine began gaining subscribers, and eight months after its founding, the magazine and subsequent music publishing company were moved to Philadelphia where they have remained ever since, despite *The Etude* ceasing publication in 1957.[11]

Initially, many articles lacked author attribution, and there are some intimations that Presser himself was authoring the vast majority of the content in the early issues.[12] It is apparent early on that *The Etude* was focused on a circumscribed audience and prescriptive purpose: "The mission of *The Etude* is to promulgate musical education; to inspire the disheartened toiling teacher; *to point out to the ambitious amateur the true path to pursue to reach the highest artistic goal*; to discuss new ideas in the art of teaching as they are presented to us; to liberalize, broaden, and strengthen our readers' ideas of music, to warn against any false doctrine of charlatanism and imposition; to avoid favoritism, prejudice, and controversy, and, above all, to keep alive an earnest striving for the highest and best in art"[13] [emphasis mine]. With a focus on teachers and students of the piano, and, broadly, amateur music lovers, as Douglas Bomberger explains, initially the readership was not meant to be advanced instrumentalists nor novice beginners but the "vast population of music teachers of modest accomplishment and earnest desire to improve."[14] Each month *The Etude* featured articles on music education and commentaries on musical culture in general, with sheet music selections from Presser publishers.[15]

As the years progressed, the magazine grew in length, due in part to more music selections, more advertisements, but also much more written content. The initial scope of just piano studies was expanded, with "departments" (monthly columns) that addressed voice, organ, violin, women, and children's pedagogical topics specifically. Especially after 1900, printing advances like lithography and halftone reproductions allowed for images and graphics, helping to better illustrate musical exercises, as well as selling various products and enabling *The Etude*'s famous cover images to thrive.[16] Though its scope and content changed over time, especially as the magazine brought on new writers and editors and merged with other publications,[17] the original mission—to educate Americans on the "highest" or "best" music—remained. In the early 1890s, *The Etude* reached approximately 20,000 mail subscribers. By 1908, there were over 135,000 subscribers, and in 1917 their peak readership was 250,000 home subscribers.[18]

In his quest to provide Americans with this music, Presser also expanded business operations. According to the fortieth anniversary write-up of the Presser publishing history, the "Presser catalogue" started organically after Presser realized his subscribers wanted more copies of the music he was publishing monthly in the magazine.[19] By 1908 the publishing company had one hundred thirty employees and boasted selling two million pieces of sheet music per year. Their catalog five years later had over ten thousand pieces of music for sale, which doubled by 1923. Presser Publishers simultaneously sold music education tools: books, graded method books, flashcards, games, and so on, which inextricably tied their company to music appreciation trends in this period and the goal of providing music that was not "of the so-called popular character," but works that would be a "permanent addition to the world's supply of good music."[20] The Presser "brand" became a symbiotic duality: each month's *Etude* featured columns both for editorial notes and publisher's notes, the latter speaking to new publications and music appreciation products newly for sale in the rapidly expanding Presser publishing house, while simultaneously addressing the burgeoning American musical culture Presser himself strove to improve.

The Etude spoke of the importance for music journals to disseminate this knowledge via a "mutual goodwill and an unselfish desire to help others," because "a musical journal is an exchange . . . where one teacher can exchange with others those ideas which his own experience."[21] So Presser initially enlisted prominent tastemakers of the age to help spread this gospel. From its earliest issues, writers argued that music study was a civic duty, a social responsibility, and a moral calling. *The Etude* put it succinctly: "to entertain is good, but to educate and consequently to elevate is better."[22] The right repertoire must be selected, the correct techniques should be taught, and *The Etude* was the clarion call that would make any reader a leader in their community. Regular writers in the magazine in this period are music critics and tastemakers who were prominent in their age: Henry T. Finck, W. S. B. Mathews, James Huneker, William Sherwood, J. S. Van Cleve, and William Baltzell (the editor for a short time prior to James Francis Cooke taking over in 1907). But make no mistake, Presser was the leader of the publication and publishing house, and even after stepping away as editor in 1896, his editorial input remained. The magazine boasted his daily presence in the office, as evidenced by an October 1923 image of Presser at his desk, and all writers and subsequent editors in this period followed in his footsteps and adhered to his philosophies.

The middle class suddenly had an opportunity for social mobility, but the rapidly changing American landscape, caused by three big forces—immigration, industrialization, and urbanization—caused anxious writers of the period to reassess their worlds, leading them to try to protect, preserve, and civilize society. Much like Progressive Era reformers, cultural tastemakers like Presser sought to enact quasi-social controls over people who they felt were weak, in order to protect homes and families.[23] The language in *The Etude* is similar: some musics were not appropriate and others who were stronger could help lead the weak to better music.[24] Further, *The Etude*'s writers sought to separate and remove the ugliness and tediousness of modern daily

MR. THEODORE PRESSER
Mr. Presser has been at his office daily and "all day" with a few intermissions and vacations during forty years.

"Mr. Theodore Presser," *Etude* Vol. 41, no. 10 (October 1923), 658.

life from culture.[25] As Gavin James Campbell explains: "In their writings and speeches, music reformers expressed views shared by a host of other white, middle-class, socially concerned Americans. In particular, they articulated their growing fear that the nation was morally and socially adrift."[26]

The Etude espoused aspirational work that fed directly into the American dream mythology. Hard work would make you a better person and provide upward mobility.[27] Cultural products like music—especially that with character or "integrity, balance, and restraint" became a sacred thing to aspire to, with an emphasis placed on educated voices of the upper classes of English and European (especially German) heritage.[28] Paul DiMaggio has defined such work as "high culture"; in "opposition to popular culture, it is a process by which urban elites forged an institutional system embodying their ideas about the high arts."[29] In his article DiMaggio speaks to voices of this period who valorized "knowledge and familiarity with styles and genres that are socially valued and that confer prestige upon those who have mastered them" by placing "strong and clearly defined boundaries between art and entertainment," especially popular culture that might be considered sacrilegious.[30]

This ideological bent and aspirational focus puts *The Etude* in a separate class from publications like trade journals like *The Musical Courier* (running similarly 1880–1940). Presser did not seek to address the concerns of professional trade musicians but instead focused on classical music lovers who wanted to study, elevate their skills and taste, and be inspired by exemplar composers and virtuosos. *The Etude* lacked announcements of upcoming tour dates or concert events, though there were sometimes very short write-ups before or after.[31] From its inception, *Etude* writers explained that the magazine's "pages are not open to the useless gossip about music people. . . . Our purpose is to conduct a magazine, not a newspaper given up to current topics. *The Etude* has enduring value."[32] Similar publications that were philosophically aligned with the aims of *The Etude* include W. S. B. Mathew's short-lived *Music* (published in Chicago and running from 1891–1902), or H. W. Hatch Music Company's (later Oliver Ditson's) *The Musician* (1896–1948), but neither *Music* nor *Musician* saw circulation numbers like Presser achieved.

Articles in this period were written as an altruistic push to grow and better American musical culture, to reach the outermost regions of the United States and expose them to classical music. But Presser also had a business to run, and many months of *The Etude* include metacommentary on the usefulness of these publications. Each issue had sections describing clubbing rates, with readers encouraged and incentivized to have their friends and students subscribe.[33] Arguing that the content was timeless, readers were encouraged to save issues, to bind an entire year into a leather-bound volume, or create personalized indexes or scrapbooks with their favorite articles.[34] Writers suggested that having a quality musical library (filled with materials like those sold in *The Etude*) in the home was an indicator of culture and status and encouraged its readers to consume more music appreciation products.[35]

Presser and his writers saw the opportunity, the potential usefulness, and the impact the magazine could have in American culture. "Village students" and readers in remote or rural areas of the country sought out these resources because they might not have access to quality teachers. John H. Gutterson wrote on "The Value of a Musical Magazine to a Young Teacher," remarking that he could not "afford to be without the living, breathing magazine that comes to [him] almost like the counsel of a beloved and honored teacher."[36] The *Etude* became their teacher and was an equalizing, democratic self-education publication. Fannie Bloomfield Zeisler observed that "such a journal, going into homes of musical people all over the country is bound to do a great deal of good, especially in the smaller towns where advantages are few and far between."[37] While Bloomfield Zeisler wrote that in 1913, twenty-two years earlier, *Etude* authors were already asserting that, "it is a remarkable fact that in a town where *The Etude* is taken its readers are the progressive and growing teachers of that community, the ones that have the best pupils and the most of them ... never before was the influence of this magazine so great as now."[38]

Presser had a distinct marketing approach, articulated later by James Huneker: "*The Etude* has a subscription list that must make envious even Mr. Bok.... [Presser] knew that the daughter of the plumber, the daughter of the policeman, hankered after music, and he deliberately built a machine to cater to their needs. The curious part of it is that he really improved their taste."[39] In the first few decades of the twentieth century, America gained a middle-class consumer culture that had an increasing need for things, and as more women emerged into the public sphere, they also became a powerful class of consumers. This is the same era of *Ladies Home Journal* (whose headquarters were also located in downtown Philadelphia) and *Good Housekeeping*.[40] In my previous research, I delineate how the magazine catered to its female readers and created a generation of women writers and tastemakers who contributed to the magazine to further their musical endeavors and to share their knowledge with others, which will be discussed further in the next section.[41]

Presser's *Etude* was successful because it filled a niche in music education at the precise moment when such print publications were thriving in Gilded Age American society, but writers would argue within its pages that *The Etude* was successful because of their musical choices. "Ask Theodore Presser why the business each month grows larger, and he will answer: 'Because we deal in no fads. We publish only music which is of a solid character. It will be as good ten years hence as it is to-day. It is as fresh now as it was ten years ago. It is a staple.' ... the secret of the success of Theodore Presser. He began, not by publishing *The Etude* to cater to the jazz of 1882, but to promote good music that doesn't change."[42] As Julia Chybowski explains in her dissertation, "To view music appreciation as ideology is to understand it not only as a cultural movement and a sacralization process, but also a set of beliefs and discursive patterns that have become ingrained in American culture as 'common sense.'"[43] The magazine articulated a hierarchy of music and sacralized certain styles and genres, that they argued was obvious to anyone with taste and education. Thus, it is necessary to unpack *The Etude*'s musical hierarchization to assess what musics were included and excluded from what was defined as "good."

CANON FORMATION AND CLUBWOMEN

Chybowksi states regarding American classical musical culture of the period: "Whether playing the role of musical missionaries, social reformers, scientists, artists, patrons, critics, elitists, or populists, one belief unified the diverse motivations for public music education. The cause of music appreciation hinged on the idea that Americans did not naturally have musical taste for classical music, and, by definition, classical music required education in order to be appreciated. Thus, music appreciation's primary aim became the maintenance of hierarchical distinction between classical music and its usually implicit, sometimes explicit opposite—popular music."[44] In May 1886, *The Etude* implored that "the taste of the public must be gradually improved," and thus this evolutionary scale was created: "classical" and its elegance was the reverse of "popular" trends that were basic or rudimentary. The job of the teacher was to "do all that is possible to show where lies the road to musical truth, and never stop to listen to 'popular taste' talks. If you do, you are lost."[45] Writers argued that with more education and focused studies (not being distracted by modern genres or trends of the age), readers would elevate their taste and cultivate their skills. This canonization—a process in which musics are included or excluded, suggested or discouraged for teachers and performers[46]—was compounded with a similar methodology seen in music appreciation literature of hagiography: writers elevating the biographies of certain famous composers to "help distinguish classical music from popular and teach moral lessons" and sacralizing specific musical works as being "spiritually pure and transcendent."[47] We see this specifically with European male figures like Mozart, Liszt, Beethoven, and Chopin.[48]

Writers openly articulated this musical hierarchy: "symphonies and sonatas are the highest form of musical composition";[49] simpler salon works with broader appeal were acceptable but other musics were discouraged. Sometimes popular songs of the age were singled out and quickly admonished: "After the Ball" was considered one of many "cheap ballads" while the "Maiden's Prayer" was described as "saccharine trash."[50] In 1900 *The Etude* defined popular music broadly (listing for inclusion: mother songs, waltzes, coon songs, and the "rag-time epidemic"): "under this heading are included all compositions that are intended to appeal to and please the masses—pieces of a light character, of no great depth, in which the rhythm is well marked and the melody easily remembered."[51]

In the early years of *The Etude*, ragtime was especially chastised: "this cheap-style popular music is simply no more nor less than an expression of the emotionality of a cheap or ignorant personality.... Of course, we have no objection to a well-written piece of popular-style music in its place, but its place is a microscopic one at best.... Music need not be specifically wicked to be utterly worthless and trashy."[52] Though never overtly stated, many of these critiques featured racist undertones, with popular music often called trash, impure, or vulgar.[53] Arthur Weld called it a "plague of trashy music," that was akin to "an epidemic of cholera," and so the musicians of America must "go out in battle against this musical vulgarity" and "the fight for noble standards and pure ideals in music."[54] Similarly, an article entitled "Musical Impurity" spoke of the "the counters of the music stores are loaded with this virulent poison which, in the form of a malarious epidemic, is finding its way into the homes and brains of the youth to such an extent as to arouse one's suspicions of their sanity."[55]

Specifically, women were conscripted to help elevate music education. At this point it is crucial to speak briefly on the discussions (and later impact) of clubwomen on *The Etude* and American musical culture, because it provides a case study into how *Etude* writers felt musical tastes would improve in America. In 1920, Fern Blanco observed: "club women are now giving their attention to music more than ever before. This augurs well for the future of this art in America, for when two million alert feminine minds are suddenly focused on a subject, that subject is so illuminated that few thoughtful persons can fail to notice."[56] *Etude* articles spoke on how to begin a small-town music club, first educating its members and then providing specially designed programming that could help their communities.

Initially, *Etude* authors were concerned about the seriousness of women, and more generally, amateur musicians' practice. Ada B. Douglass commented: "In the wake of this great wave of musical enthusiasm has come a train of dilettantes who organize musical clubs without serious aim or serious work.... Shades of the great departed! Could Beethoven, Mozart, Schumann, and all that noble army know the play that is done under the shadow of their names, wouldn't they and St. Cecilia herself die a second death?"[57] *The Etude* encouraged readers to pursue a noble, pure love of music, unburdened and unsullied by making money (aside from teachers who educated their students), which was an easier pursuit for the affluent white women who comprised the majority of music club membership in this period. With the rise of a middle class that had time to spare, women were able to devote much time and energy to their music studies. But amateurism, regardless of gender, was always more desirable as writers argued that "in these amateurs that lies the musical hope of the country."[58]

The misconception frequently is that amateurism might imply a lack of skill, when in actuality, *Etude* amateurs were often more diligent with their pursuit of musical knowledge. Women specifically took canonization and hierarchization very seriously: their club programs became rooted in cultivated traditions. Club programming suggestions were given that began with a solid foundation in music history, with works from composers of the baroque through romantic eras. For example, this three-year program[59] from a club in Indiana was heralded by Cora Stanton Brown in April 1895: the first year focused on the "Classical Period," with composers Palestrina, Scarlatti, Bach, Haydn, Handel, Mozart, Clementi, and Beethoven. The second year was the "Transition Era": Schubert, von Weber, Field, Hummel, Mendelssohn, Gounoud, and Thalberg (among others). Of note that year were lectures on "The Ancient and Modern Ballad," as well as "Ancient and Modern Dance Forms of Composition." In the final year, the club studied the "Modern Romantic Period," with composers Schumann, Chopin, von Bülow, Brahms, Saint-Saëns, Tschaikowsky [sic], Grieg, Gottschalk, and others. One exemplar Chopin musical program was also given, starting with a lecture and then alternating song and piano solo and duo works.

This repertoire emphasizes a chronological and figure-based evolutionary style of music history, starting with simpler forms earlier in history and evolving to more modern works, suggesting that classical music was growing and reaching a pinnacle of sophistication. A few years later, each month in the "Woman's Work in Music" department (which ran from 1897–1903 and was edited by Fanny Morris Smith and Emilie Frances Bauer) further suggested similar biographical sketches and chronologies, and women were provided lists of similar suitable composers. If veering into other genres, European countries' folk traditions were selected, and after 1900 it was not uncommon to see programs highlighting women composers or increasingly programs of American classical music and musicians (more on that in a moment).[60] Still obviously absent, however, were more popular genres of music.

Club women eager to dismiss the perceived superficiality of their study added further rigor to their club settings. Obviously, musical selection was key, but also clubs began meeting more frequently, quizzing members, and requiring active participation. It was only after their intense inner study within club meetings that women began to branch out and educate their communities[61] In a speech to the Music Teachers National Association, reprinted in *The Etude*, Mrs. Charles S. Vigil stated that as long as women continued to elevate their clubs with "high, earnest character," then America's musical development would be "largely due to the faithful army of amateurs who by unceasing toil have tried to cultivate a true appreciation of great music and musicians."[62] Small amateur ladies' societies became women's music organizations, enacting the work of what was called "municipal housekeeping" in the Progressive Era.[63] And for women of *The Etude*, their housekeeping job was to sweep away trashy music in their communities whenever possible.

While earlier articles might suggest work for women to be done within the domestic club sphere, "by the 1920s, when feminized moral work with music is discussed in publications with a presumed female readership, like the *Etude*, authors drew less of a distinction between domestic-realm and public work."[64] Blanco's aforementioned article addressed the need for women to help elevate the musical tastes of the general American populace, saying that "primitive peoples" were "susceptible to the power of music," and thus should be exposed to public concerts and other educational opportunities.[65] General audiences who were fans of popular music or not trained in music were also seen as childlike: "the popular song is to the public what the picture-story book is to the child: not literature, certainly, but the one means by which a child . . . may cultivate a desire for the genuine in literature."[66] Because those individuals' musical tastes seemingly were not as elevated as *Etude* readers, articles spoke to methods for meeting the public where they were and leading them to better musical selections.[67] From 1898:

> the great thing to avoid in such work is that the natural desire for popularity shall lower the standard, and the programme shall be leveled to meet the wishes of the untutored ears that hunger for 'tunes.' . . . One can not expect the average untutored listener to be jerked from 'All Coons Look Alike to Me' into the exalted atmosphere of a Beethoven symphony, without a pause between stations, and arrive in other than at breathless condition, somewhat stunned, in fact. . . . But one must ever keep his eye on a pure, high standard, and insist upon intelligent conception.[68]

According to Nellie Cove, ways to "redeem the unmusical public" included selecting moral and "clean" works to help develop tastes, playing selections multiple times (especially for private audiences), and performing works with more suggestive titles or simpler works with clearer melodies.[69] She suggested an approach that would not "ignore popular music, but classify it properly" and ensure that "above all, make them learn that classic music means the best, the grandest, and loveliest of all the music we possess."[70]

The Etude began documenting the work of women's clubs and their repertoire choices regularly in the late 1880s, and only a few decades later, Arthur

Anonymous illustrator, Clubwomen banner, *Etude* Vol. 40, no. 3 (March 1922): 153. This header banner appeared above an article discussing the "important work" of music clubs. The black-and-white illustration features a literal torchbearer, a Greco-Roman feminine figure who points a group of manufacturers, editors, conductors, violinists, singers, managers, teachers, and parents toward "the best in music in the home, school, theatre, concert hall, musical records, printed music, musical journals" and a temple on a hill.

Foote argued that music clubs were changing American music: "what many of us regard as the most powerful factor of all in musical cultivation—the Women's Clubs (especially in the West)—is a product of this fruitful period. It is difficult to overestimate the sound and far-reaching influence that these clubs have had; they make for musical *intelligence*, not only by their concerts, but through the comprehensive study given to the history, development and technical instruction of music" [emphasis in original].[71] Indeed, clubwomen were seen as the leaders who would carry America into a new golden age of musical culture. One illustration from March 1922 draws clubwomen as literal torchbearers (similar to the Statue of Liberty), leading editors, musicians, teachers, and parents up a hill toward the best in music, illustrated as a Parthenon-like temple. Underneath this banner is "What is the most important work to which the music clubs of America may devote their efforts?: A Nationwide Symposium" that includes short comments from leaders in American musical culture, many of which encourage clubwomen to petition Congress or other government entities for a national conservatory, more student scholarships, or various music education programs. In twenty short years, thanks to the work of clubwomen who adopted and cultivated *The Etude*'s American canon, the perception of clubwomen shifted from disparaging amateurs to cultural forces who could potentially influence governmental policy.[72]

This discussion of elevating America's musical tastes (and creation of American music programs) begs the question of how American music was defined by *The Etude* in this period. In fact writers in the magazine further tried to shape these musical genres by making suggestions for improving "American music" overall. Like others of their age, their desire to create a distinct American musical tradition akin to the European classical tradition did not adopt the popular musics that were omnipresent in American culture.

Writers romanticized America's musical past with Stephen Foster, while simultaneously dismissing the increasing ubiquity of music in their modern age, especially the musics embraced by nonelite audiences.[73]

However, writers did encourage music from some nonwhite sources, albeit filtered through white European-trained individuals. Composers like Arthur Farwell and Edward MacDowell, whose Indianist works became paragons of the new American soundscape, were highlighted in issues that valorized the music of Native Americans.[74] Similarly, folk tunes collected by Alice Fletcher and Frances Densmore were called "our vast natural musical wealth."[75] "Negro melodies" or "plantation songs" were considered important source material as well, though that music was rarely seen in club programs of the period.[76] While such folk traditions were valorized, more popular genres and Tin Pan Alley tunes remained separate from these discussions of defining American music.

In 1929, in a speech given to the Anglo-American Conference on Music and reprinted in *The Etude*, editor Cooke outlines American influences on music around the world. He says that America has built upon a foundation of European traditions and folk tunes and praised the technologies and figures that America had produced, like the parlor organ, the phonograph, Isadora Duncan, and John Philip Sousa. But then he argues the "jazz barrage" was "born in a brothel, gradually emerged into semi-respectability by way of the ballroom floor. Attributed to negro composers, it is really far more the scum of the melting-pot of America, a conglomeration of the rhythms and melodies of peoples of all lands fighting for existence in the new world."[77] Enforcing the aforementioned classical canon's hierarchy, Cooke cites Gershwin as a composer who "[fought] his way from the lowest rungs of the musical ladder to the piano concerto."[78] Though the magazine would become more accepting of what once was strictly dismissed and disparaged, it is apparent that the long-held hierarchies and preconceived prejudices would never go away entirely in this period.

CHANGES

Over time *The Etude* writers began incorporating middlebrow or what they thought were higher quality popular music into their practice. Guidance on how to deal with less desirable musics and choosing more wisely appeared throughout the magazine, in every department, for every instrument throughout this period, as ways to "redeem the unmusical public," as Theodore Thomas called it.[79] For example, the Junior Column of February 1919 gave recommendations for a student who was confronted by a friend who wanted to play ragtime with them: play "the best of the songs," "refuse to play any that have vulgar words," use it as a chance to study the theory of it (rhythm, base, accents), and then "the necessary evil of ragtime need not be so evil."[80]

Overall, while popular music arrived, the thematic and philosophical focus of *The Etude* remained on aspirational and inspirational European and American classical music. The music Presser settled into has been called "middlebrow" by some scholars.[81] By August 1905, popular music was still not beloved, but writers stressed finding "well-written" "good music, on the technical side."[82] Likely there was a financial component to this compromise: Presser and his successors had both the magazine and a printing company to run. While the musical selections of the 1890s were quintessential late nineteenth-century pedagogically centered piano works (Chopin and Beethoven and small parlor works for varying levels of technique), the mid-1900s featured advertisements for marches and two-steps, for cakewalks and ragtimes from other publishers. By 1906, the monthly Presser musical selections in the center of *The Etude* even include a plantation lullaby and a pickaninny dance. Popular music crept in under the guise of more educational classical forms. Writers still disparage more popular genres, arguing they are too ephemeral, but at the very least try to justify their existence at the moment or elevate tunes when possible.[83]

The problem inherently undergirding *The Etude* is that this musical hierarchy and canonization is aspirational, unattainable, and largely out of touch with the general American populace—the magazine reached for the best, seeking musics that would have the greatest cultural value for the most people—but that's a limited cross-section really of actual Americans and their listening habits. By the 1920s, the problems of popular music encroaching into this canon never ended, nor did *Etude* writers stop striving to cultivate tastes. Many of the technologies that once worried *Etude* writers (the bicycle, the phonograph, the player piano, the motion picture, and the radio were all critiqued in these pages) were adopted.

And it is notable that during World War I, as Americans' lives were turned upside down, heightened patriotic and nationalistic themes entered discussions of elevating musical culture and keeping music education a central focus but with fewer mentions of the canon that had previously been codified.[84] In May 1918, Presser called music and *The Etude* "a national need in wartime," stating that "a well filled powder magazine was never more important to an army than is this magazine to the musician at this time."[85] For the next few months, Presser proselytized the effects of music in the home and in American communities but without any hierarchies. The September 1918 cover shifted the importance of music education to wartime themes: "music will help win the war: the music-lovers of America proudly point to the immense accomplishments of the art in this hour of national crisis by: stimulating patriotism, maintaining good cheer, arousing recruiting, raising war millions, inspiring fighters, entertaining 'our men,' comforting the wounded, music in our homes keeps courage in our hearts."[86] The writings of the many contributors to *The Etude* in this period—some of whom were enlisted in World War I—and their thoughts on music's impact on the war effort are outside the scope of this chapter but deserve further study.[87]

Writers continued to argue for more music educational opportunities, epitomized in campaigns like editor Cooke's "Golden Hour" that called for more music in public schools.[88] And after Presser's death in October 1925, the magazine diversified its topics even further to appeal to broader audiences and consequently lost its intellectual focus. The genteel nineteenth-century ideologies appeared woefully outdated in the Roaring Twenties, epitomized in covers like August 1924's "The Jazz Problem" and infamous cover from August 1926 of the "Jazzomanic and her victim" that pitted an old guard musician against the younger generation. Music teachers continued to subscribe to the magazine, since *The Etude* became a cultural statement: having it in one's home meant that "the family held high social and cultural aspirations."[89] But educational resources were so multiplicitous by the mid-twentieth century that the magazine became superfluous. Readership continued to decline, with the magazine finally ending in 1957.[90]

The magazine's success and impact on American musical culture were articulated in the thirtieth anniversary issue: "If asked to name the most important factor in the development of music in America during the last thirty years, that is, the factor that has contributed in greatest measure to the dissemination of musical knowledge, I am sure that music teachers throughout the length and breadth of our land would unanimously name *The Etude* and its founder. *The Etude* has accomplished a greater work than can be adequately estimated."[91] In her research on the music appreciation movement, Chybowski suggests that one of its longest-lasting impacts is this hierarchy itself: music appreciation "taught students of various ages to distinguish between classical and popular music as a matter of social importance and integral to the invention of American cultural identity."[92] American music still has these high/low distinctions, this canon Presser purported, because he made it so engrained in American musical culture that today people still say that certain musics are better for you and make you smarter.[93]

"The Jazz Problem," *Etude* Vol. 42, no. 8 (August 1924).

Print artifacts like magazines provide us a portal into the past. We see readers, authors, critics, publishers, and performers meet within these pages to discuss the ideas of their age.[94] We are over a century removed at this point but can still see that discourse Presser established unfold month by month. While in the twenty-first century scholars have rightfully argued that *The Etude* "presented an unwaveringly conservative voice" that "warned its readers that an idealized way of life, exemplified by a narrowly defined type of musical education, was under continual threat from nefarious forces," it is important to acknowledge and articulate Presser's successes and limitations.[95] Exclusionary to be sure, but influential. *The Etude* created generations of amateur musicians who proselytized the edifying effects of the cultivated canon, while shying away from so-called degenerate musics, couched under the guise of creating a great American musical tradition. In a reprinted article in 1893 and 1895, music journals were called "a mirror of the times and a pointer of the way."[96] Undoubtedly *The Etude* pointed a way they felt was best for American musicians in this period. But a mirror of the times? Writers definitely mirrored the genteel ideologies of their age. But based on their narrow approvals and dismissal of anything nonclassical, it's obvious they wanted to do more than mirror, they wanted to alter and improve that reflection.

NOTES

1. "[untitled editorial notes]," *Etude* Vol. 17, no. 1 (January 1899): 3.
2. Here I am echoing Carl F. Kaestle and Janice A. Radway's *Print in Motion*, which addresses the complicated nature of looking at periodical resources. They explain terminology further: "We approach the history of print culture from the point of view of the practices and intentions of multiple actors who involved themselves in the production and use of print, the sites at which they took place, and the multiple effects of these activities. We are especially interested in the production, use, control, and limitation of print. By 'production,' we mean all those activities involved in generating print products from writing and editing to printing and publishing. We try to avoid privileging one aspect of the larger process over another. We use the abstract term 'use' to refer to the many ways people turned to print culture to accomplish particular ends. Writers and readers were both 'users' of print culture in that they sought to employ magazines, books, and newspapers to accomplish particular ends—that is, to address others, to learn, to constitute a sense of the self, or to express their beliefs. Thus the notion of 'use' covers everything from writing to reading, bookselling to library work, advertising to home decoration and display." Carl F. Kaestle and Janice A. Radway, *A History of the Book in America: Volume 4: Print in Motion: The Expansion of Publishing and Reading in the United States, 1880–1940* (Chapel Hill: University of North Carolina Press, 2009), 19.
3. Adrienne Fried Block discusses how industrialization created new ways for women to consume music and be a more integral part of musical culture. See Adrienne Fried Block, "Matinee Mania, or the Regendering of Nineteenth-Century Audiences in New York City," *Nineteenth-Century Music* Vol. 31, no. 3 (Spring 2008): 193–216.
4. Kaestle and Radway, *Print in Motion*, 7.
5. John Tebbel and Mary Ellen Zuckerman, *The Magazine in America 1741–1990* (New York: Oxford University Press, 1991), 66–67.
6. Kaestle and Radway, *Print in Motion*, 8.
7. Tebbel and Zuckerman, *The Magazine in America*, 70. See also: "The printed word became the sine qua non of influence and organization. In a culture of print, the printed word acted as both an instrument and an expression of change, whether directed toward more orderliness or toward new assertions. As the nation expanded geographically and consolidated economically,

print became a key handmaid of nationalization and professionalization." Kaestle and Radway, *Print in Motion*, 8.

8. "Fortieth Anniversary Prophecies and Greetings," *Etude* Vol. 41, no. 10 (October 1923): 661. For more on Theodore Presser's early life, see E. Douglas Bomberger, "Theodore Presser Before *The Etude* Part I," *American Music Teacher* (February/March 2017): 22–27. E. Douglas Bomberger, "Theodore Presser Before *The Etude* Part II," *American Music Teacher* (April/May 2017): 24–30. E. Douglas Bomberger, "Theodore Presser Before *The Etude* Part III," *American Music Teacher* (June/July 2017): 20–24.

9. The activities of the Music Teachers National Association, an organization still in existence today, was heavily featured in *The Etude* with frequent write-ups about their annual meetings. While outside the scope of this chapter, its influence on music education and its continued connections with the magazine (including editor James Frances Cooke's involvement in the 1920s), is something that should be explored further.

10. "Thirty Year Jubilee of The Etude," *Etude* Vol. 31, no. 1 (January 1913): 66.

11. Technically the company now resides in the greater Philadelphia area in Malvern. They were also previously located in King of Prussia.

12. "Theodore Presser: A short Anniversary Biography," *Etude* Vol. 41, no. 10 (October 1923): 658. James Frances Cooke, "Theodore Presser (1848–1925): A Centennial Biography Part Four," *Etude* Vol. 66, no. 10 (October 1948): 587, 614.

13. "[untitled editorial notes]," *Etude* Vol. 3, no. 8 (August 1885): 163.

14. Bomberger, "Presser before The Etude, Part III," 21.

15. This sheet music was placed in the middle of the stapled magazine, making it easier for readers to remove pages for performance purposes without damaging the rest of the publication.

16. Kaestle and Radway, *Print in Motion*, 12–13. For more on *Etude* cover imagery, see William Keith Heimann, "'The True, Unutterable Great Sin . . .': Heteronormative Discourse In The Etude Music Magazine," in *Belonging, Detachment and the Representation of Musical Identities in Visual Culture*, edited by Antonio Baldassarre and Arabella Teniswood-Harvey (Hollitzer Verlag, 2023), 631–62. https://doi.org/10.2307/jj.5211766.30.

17. For example, *The Etude* merged with the publication *The Musical World* in 1895.

18. "Our Fortieth Anniversary: Four Decades in the History of Theo. Presser Company," *Etude* Vol. 41, no. 10 (October 1923): 653.

19. "Theodore Presser: A Short Anniversary Biography," *Etude* Vol. 41, no. 10 (October 1923): 658.

20. "Our Fortieth Anniversary: Four Decades in the History of Theo. Presser Company," *Etude* Vol. 41, no. 10 (October 1923): 653.

21. "[untitled editorial notes]," *Etude* Vol. 16, no. 4 (April 1898): 99.

22. W. F. Gates, "How to enjoy good music," *Etude* Vol. 12, no. 8 (August 1894): 175.

23. Some "advocated the censorship of popular culture as integral to improving urban society." Julia J. Chybowski, *Developing American Taste: A Cultural History of the Early Twentieth-Century Music Appreciation Movement* (PhD diss., University of Wisconsin-Madison, 2008), 44–45.

24. For more, see Chybowski, *Developing American Taste*, 101ff.

25. This echoes the ideologies of gentility, an admittedly complicated term. Joan Shelley Rubin described gentility as separating culture from modern "daily affairs" with this pervasive ideology throughout the publishing houses of the turn of the twentieth century. Joan Shelley Rubin, "The Genteel Tradition at Large," *Raritan* Vol. 25, no. 3 (Winter 2006): 70–91. For more on this, see, for example: Gavin James Campbell, "Classical Music and the Politics of Gender in America, 1900–1925," *American Music* Vol. 21, no. 4 (Winter 2003): 446–73; Lawrence Levine,

Highbrow/Lowbrow: The Emergence of Cultural Hierarchy in America (Cambridge, MA: Harvard University Press, 1988).

26. The quote continues: "Though themselves beneficiaries of growing corporate capitalism, they understood that modern industrialism hindered as many as it helped. The prosperity and optimism that characterized their own lives had little currency among those whose labor made it all possible." Gavin James Campbell, "'A Higher Mission than Merely to Please the Ear': Music and Social Reform in America,1900–1925," *Musical Quarterly* Vol. 84, No. 2 (Summer 2000): 261.

27. See, for example, an illustration by William S. Nortenheim that showed with hard work and courage through practice, you could get out of a rut of carelessness and laziness and reach the pinnacle of musical success. "Are You Getting into a Rut?" *Etude* Vol. 36, no. 3 (March 1918): 153. See also William Keith Heimann, who talks about this: "The new middle class craved social ascension along with its accumulation of wealth." William Keith Heimann, "This is War! Musical Images Used As Propaganda In *The Etude Music Magazine*," *Music in Art* Vol. 41, No. 1–2 (Spring–Fall 2016): 141. For more information on this image and similar types of imagery from magazines of the period, see also William Keith Heimann, "The Road to Success: 'The Long Glorious Grind,'" *Music in Art* Vol. 43, no. 1–2 (2018): 87–99.

28. Joan Shelley Rubin, *Making of Middlebrow Culture* (Chapel Hill: University of North Carolina Press, 1992), chapter 1. ProQuest Ebook Central, http://ebookcentral.proquest.com/lib/ttu/detail.action?docID=837906; Kaestle and Radway, *Print in Motion*, 476. See also Levine, *Highbrow/Lowbrow*.

29. Paul Dimaggio, "Cultural Entrepreneurship in nineteenth-century Boston: the creation of an organizational base for high culture in America," *Media Culture and Society* 4 (1982): 33.

30. Dimaggio, "Cultural Entrepreneurship," 35. See also Paul Dimaggio, "Cultural Entrepreneurship in nineteenth-century Boston, part II: the classification and framing of American art," *Media Culture and Society* 4 (1982): 303

31. In the 1890s, "Musical Items" provided short sentences of general music news: concert tour rumors and reports, notable performances, new compositions, new technologies, and general health and wellness of prominent musical figures. This section provides insights into classical music talk of the age but admittedly is always very brief. (As a scholar of Cecile Chaminade, I was able to see that for many years it was speculated she would tour America before she finally did in 1908.)

32. "Publisher's Notes," *Etude* Vol. 6, no. 10 (October 1888): 151. In 1923, they echo this once again: *The Etude* "is distinctly not a musical newspaper, but a musical educational magazine giving inspiration and advice upon study." "Our Fortieth Anniversary," *Etude* Vol. 41, no. 10 (October 1923): 653.

33. Clubbing rates bundled magazine subscriptions together at a discounted rate. Similarly, the "premium list" was given to those who procured more Etude subscribers. See, for example, December 1897's issue with a list of books that would be sent for free for one to three more subscribers (page 338) or a gramophone for fifteen new subscribers (page 310).

34. Edward Hardy, "Getting The Most Out Of A Musical Magazine," *Etude* Vol. 35, no. 6 (June 1917): 384; "Editorial Notes," *Etude* Vol. 14, no. 7 (July 1896): 158.

35. "The Musical Library In The Home As An Indicator Of Musical Culture," *Etude* Vol. 13, no. 6 (June 1895): 137.

36. John H. Gutterson, "The Value of a Musical Magazine to a Young Teacher," *Etude* Vol. 22, no. 7 (July 1904): 278.

37. "Etude Jubilee Greetings," *Etude* Vol. 31, no. 1 (January 1913): 22.

38. "Publisher's Notes," *Etude* Vol. 9, no. 3 (March 1891): 47.

39. James Gibbons Huneker, *Steeplejack* (New York: Charles Scribner's Sons, 1920), 202.

40. From 1885 to 1910, *Ladies Home Journal, McCall's, Delineator, Woman's Home Companion, Good Housekeeping*, and *Pictorial Review* were all established. See Kathy L. Peiss, "American Women and the Making of Modern Consumer Culture," *Journal for MultiMedia History* Vol. 1, no. 1 (Fall 1998), https://www.albany.edu/jmmh/vol1no1/peiss-text.html (accessed September 20, 2022).

41. For more on this generally, see Elissa Stroman, "The Etude Magazine and the Archetyping of American Musical Women, 1886–1926" (master's thesis, Texas Tech University, August 2010); Elissa Stroman, *Prescribing, Inscribing, and Negotiating Gilded Age Musical Femininity* (PhD dissertation, Texas Tech University, 2016).

42. "Our Fortieth Anniversary," *Etude* Vol. 41, no. 10 (October 1923): 656.

43. Chybowski, *Developing American Taste*, 27. "The music appreciation movement formed as Victorian codes of social behavior declined and some segments of American society felt unease with modernization, stereotyped as urban, mechanized, fast-paced, and morally dissolute. Its advocates employed the language of morality to express their reservations about social change and came to associate immorality with their definitions of popular music.... In legitimizing their moral cause, building their case for reform, and providing instruction, music appreciation proponents defined classical music also in moral terms and prescribed its uplifting function for American society. This chapter explores how music appreciation became an integral force in America's sacralization of culture, a process with nineteenth-century roots that continued well into the twentieth century." Chybowski, *Developing American Taste*, 74.

44. Chybowski, *Developing American Taste*, 230.

45. A. Bidez (?), "Popular Music," *Etude* Vol. 4, no. 5 (May 1886): 113.

46. Anne Shreffler speaks of canonization in three parts: maintaining existing older works, adding new works, and then the process where distinct repertoires break off and become their own "parallel" canon. The canon is the ideology behind it, and we know a work is included in the canon by the number of performances (or mentions in magazines, for example) and its "staying power." Anne C. Shreffler, "Musical Canonization and Decanonization in the Twentieth Century," original English version. Published in German translation as "Musikalische Kanonisierung und Dekanonisierung im 20. Jahrhundert" (translated by Fabian Kolb). in: *Der Kanon der Musik: Theorie und Geschichte*. Ein Handbuch, hrsg. von Klaus Pietschmann und Melanie Wald (Munich: Edition text + kritik, 2013), 6.

47. Chybowski, *Developing American Taste*, 128, 133–37.

48. Entire issues were devoted to these great men of the cultivated tradition. See for example: December 1901 was Mozart, May 1902 was Liszt, and January 1905 featured Chopin.

49. Fanny Morris Smith, "What are Musical Clubs For?" Woman's Work in Music, *Etude* Vol. 17, no. 10 (October 1899): 324.

50. W. F. Gates, "How to enjoy good music," *Etude* Vol. 12, no. 8 (August 1894): 175. Later in the article, Gates adds "next week try to hear a little bit better concert than last week. To-day try to play a better piece than yesterday. To-morrow listen to some better music than you did to-day. Persist in climbing.... This is the sum total of the whole matter, to continually try to gras a little more and a little better." And if you do that, "soon we begin to wonder how we could have ever enjoyed such shallow music, how we could have neglected so many musical opportunities."

51. R. M. Stults, "Something about the popular music of to-day," *Etude* Vol. 18, no. 3 (March 1900): 97.

52. The quote continues, speaking on the moral superiority of hard work, "It is only too bad if it be simply a natural sort of time-waster. Time wasting is the twin-sister of idleness—one of the greatest of sins—and out of these two grow all crime and its attendant suffering in the world." E. F. Beal, "A Criticism of Popular Music," *Etude* Vol. 23, no. 8 (August 1905): 316.

53. This obviously echoes the rhetoric surrounding immigrant and nonwhite populations of the time.

54. Arthur Weld, "The Invasion of Vulgarity in Music," *Etude* Vol. 17, no. 2 (February 1899): 52.

55. "Musical Impurity," *Etude* Vol. 18, no. 1 (January 1900): 16.

56. Fern Blanco, "Americanization, Women's Clubs and Music," *Etude* Vol. 38, no. 8 (August 1920): 524.

57. Ada B Douglass, "A Plea for More Serious Work Among So-Called Musical Clubs," *Etude* Vol. 16, no. 2 (February 1898): 36.

58. W. Francis Gates, "Music as Profession vs. Musical Dilettantism," *Etude* Vol. 16, no. 4 (April 1898): 119.

59. Cora Stanton Brown, "The Amateur Musical Society," *Etude* Vol. 13, no. 4 (April 1895): 154–55.

60. The monthly column "Woman's Work in Music" included programs of study. See for example March 1898, August 1899, October 1899, or November 1899 (which includes books to keep on hand).

61. "What the Club Has Done for Music in America," Woman's Work in Music, edited Emilie Frances Bauer *Etude* Vol. 20, no. 12 (December 1902): 464.

62. "The Woman's Club a Factor in General Music Culture," Woman's Work in Music, *Etude* Vol. 16, no. 5 (May 1898): 132.

63. "Women had taken prominent positions in cultural censorship efforts and the temperance movement, as well as labor organization and other progressive era reforms. Yet, even as gender roles were changing as industrialized society adapted to modernization, permitting women to take on increasingly public roles, and securing voting rights for white women in 1920, the message was still strong among music reformers that feminine duty necessitated wives and mothers using music for creating a "warm, bright, cheerful" home that would prevent husbands and children from turning to bad habits presented by the city outside. Music reformers, like their colleagues working in other arenas of moral reform, turned their attention to domestic living conditions of the urban poor as the cause of moral and social problems." Chybowski, *Developing American Taste*, 46.

64. As Chybowski notes, "Blanco certainly did not believe that all music elevates. It would be the job of women's clubs to guide and censor musical taste, just as others focused on literary and artistic taste as important social and moral issues." Chybowski, *Developing American Taste*, 47.

65. Blanco, "Americanization, Women's Clubs and Music," 524.

66. "The average man comes into the world without the gift of either strong musical or literary instincts." "The Curse of the Unclean," *Etude* Vol. 19, no. 4 (April 1901): 147.

67. "A community moves so slowly.... It takes tremendous enthusiasm to give to it force enough to withstand, and still more to overcome, the impact against the dead-weight of public impassivity." "Woman's Work in Music," *Etude* Vol. 17, no. 2 (February 1899): 36.

68. Mrs. L. E. Chittenden, "Possibilities of Programme Making in Small Cities," Woman's Work in Music, *Etude* Vol. 16, no. 2 (February 1898): 36.

69. Nellie Cove, "Unpopularity of Classic Music," *Etude* Vol. 22, no. 11 (November 1904): 446.

70. Cove, "Unpopularity of Classic Music," 446.

71. "Then and Now: Thirty Years of Advance in Musical America," *Etude* Vol. 31, no. 1 (January 1913): 19.

72. "What is the most important work to which the music clubs of America may devote their efforts?: A Nationwide Symposium," *Etude* Vol. 40, no. 3 (March 1922): 153.

73. T. Rogers Lyons, "Why Popular Songs Don't Last," *Etude* Vol. 40, no. 6 (June 1922): 378.

74. See the October 1920 cover image entitled "The Appeal to the Great Spirit," an illustration of a statue featuring a Native American on horseback looking toward the sky with his arms stretched out.

75. "Our Vast Natural Musical Wealth," *Etude* Vol. 38, no. 10 (October 1920): 653. For more on this see Jeanne Adair Hansen, *James Francis Cooke's Editorial Motifs In The Etude Music Magazine, 1907-1957* (PhD dissertation, Kent State University, 2017), 146ff.

76. Constantin von Sternberg, "What is American Music?," *Etude* Vol. 22, no. 5 (May 1904): 190; Hansen, *James Francis Cooke*, 153ff. "Negro" folk music was suggested in one 1922 club program, in a longer set of programs for "Folk Music and Folk Type Music." Mrs. F. S. Wardwell, "How to Work Up Programs and Special Study Courses for Music Clubs," *Etude* Vol. 40, no. 3 (March 1922): 198. I will be addressing the racial component of women's music club programming and repertoire more in my upcoming book, Elissa Stroman, *"Rivets in a Bond Linking Musical Clubwomen": Music Magazines and the Early Formation of Gilded Age American Women's Music Organizations.*

77. He goes on to say that "The Negro deserves far more credit for the evolution of spirituals than he does for 'jazz.'" James Frances Cooke, "Musical Idealism in the United States," *Etude* Vol. 47, no. 9 (September 1929): 652.

78. Cooke, "Musical Idealism in the United States."

79. Nellie Cove, "Unpopularity of Classic Music," *Etude* Vol. 22, no. 11 (November 1904): 446. "Theodore Thomas says popular music is familiar music. The great cause for the unpopularity of the best music is that it is not known and is not understood."

80. "Junior Etude," *Etude* Vol. 37, no. 2 (February 1919): 120.

81. Marian Wilson Kimber, "American Women's Concerts and the Idea of a Middlebrow Canon" (conference presentation), The Idea of the Canon in the 21st Century, Smith College, Northampton, Massachusetts, September 2018. Christopher Chowrimootoo and Kate Guthrie (Convenors), John Howland, Andrew Flory, Chris McDonald, Heather Wiebe, Richard Taruskin, "Colloquy: Musicology and the Middlebrow," *Journal of the American Musicological Society* Vol. 73, no. 2 (1 June 2020): 327–95.

82. E. F. Beal, "A Criticism of Popular Music," *Etude* Vol. 23, no. 8 (August 1905): 316.

83. For example, in 1922, T. Rogers Lyons poses the question of "why popular songs don't last" and outlines the "cycles" of popular trends of the early twentieth century: waltz ballads, war songs, music with Native American and Chinese motifs, ragtime, and "then having fallen as low as possible, both lyrically and musically, the 'Hit Publishers' evolved 'Jazz.'" T. Rogers Lyons, "Why Popular Songs Don't Last," *Etude* Vol 40, no. 6 (June 1922): 378.

84. An example of this heightened language: the July 1918 cover describes the liberty bell (located mere blocks from Presser's headquarters) as "humanity's musical emblem."

85. "Musical Munitions," *Etude* Vol. 36, no. 5 (May 1918): 295.

86. Cover, *Etude* Vol. 36, no. 9 (September 1918).

87. For example, a June 1918 article mentions that the work of *Etude* writers was being repurposed by the US government's Department of Public Information to emphasize the essential nature of music not only for soldiers but for those on the home front. "Let's Have More Music Than Ever: The United States Government Recognizes a Great Need," *Etude* Vol. 36, no. 6 (June 1918): 371–72. For more on iconography of the period, Keith Heimann has discussed the magazine's history of propagandist imagery. See William Keith Heimann, "'This is War!': Musical Images Used as Propaganda in *The Etude Music Magazine*," *Music in Art* Vol. 41, no. 1–2 (Spring/Fall 2016): 141–61.

88. Cooke felt that children were not morally developed at home or church and needed one hour of music education in public schools. This idea first appeared in *The Etude* in March 1921, was on the cover of the April 1921 issue, and was mentioned many more times throughout the 1920s and into the 1930s. Hansen, *James Francis Cooke*, 124–29.

89. Heimann, "This is War!," 142.

90. For more on the later history of *The Etude*, see Travis Suttle Rivers, "The Etude Magazine: Mirror of the Genteel Tradition in American Music" (PhD dissertation, University of Iowa, 1974).

91. Mrs. Hermann Kotzschmar, "To Etude Readers Everywhere," *Etude* Vol. 31, no. 1 (January 1913): 8.

92. Chybowski, *Developing American Taste*, 243.

93. Chybowski, *Developing American Taste*, 250ff.

94. Kaestle and Radway, *Print in Motion*, 44.

95. Heimann, "This is War!" 142.

96. This quote appeared in a small article printed at least twice, with a source listed as "Echo," and also is printed in Oliver Ditson's *Musical Record* publication. "Take a Music Journal," *Etude* Vol. 13, no. 8 (August 1895): 178.

CHAPTER 5

MAKING A RACKET
Inventing the Modern Music Business

Jim Rogers

IN THE BEGINNING...

"Argument is almost superfluous," declared British philosopher and biologist, Herbert Spencer in 1890, as the evidence shows that "the *origin* of music as the developed language of emotion seems to be no longer an inference, but simply a description of fact" (Spencer 1890, 468). Yet, despite the certainty of Spencer's assertion, numerous subsequent accounts from anthropology, ethnomusicology, psychology, and other fields offer little consensus on precisely where, when and how music first came about. The origins of the instruments human beings invented to create music have some clearer pointers. Wallin et al. posit that "musical instruments are at least as old as anatomically modern humans, if not much older" (2000, 10). In a separate essay in the same volume, Turk and Kunej (2000) tell us of the discovery of a flute made from bones that is believed to be 43,000 years old. De Souza (2014) provides an overview of recent archaeological discoveries in Germany that confirm compelling evidence for the existence of musical practices some 30,000 years before the evolution of writing and the wheel. Elsewhere, Clottes (1999) describes a much more recent 15,000-year-old wall engraving in Ariège, France, that illustrates a harp made from a hunting bow. Point being: music, musical instruments, and music making have been with us humans for a long time. Music is a fundamental aspect of human evolution. As Jay Schulkin and Greta Raglan conclude in their study of the convergence of neuroscience and music, "We probably sang before we spoke in syntactically guided sentences" (2014, 1).

However, the music *industry* is a much, much more recent phenomenon. Again, we may debate its origins. In 1476, when German printer Ulrich Han published *Missale Romanum*, the earliest printed book containing a printed music score (Bernstein 2023)? Or 1637, when Ferrari and Manelli opened the first public opera house in Venice (Thorborn 2003)? However, Simon Napier-Bell, the prominent British music manager of acts like the Yardbirds and Wham! is quite specific: the music business started in 1710, and it started in Britain (Napier-Bell 2022). That year marked the enactment of the Statute of Anne, widely accepted as the world's first copyright act. Consequently, the law granted publishers of books a monopoly on the reproduction of their texts for a period of fourteen years, and for twenty-one years for works already in circulation (see, for example, Goldstein 2003; Rose 1993, for critique of the origins and formation of copyright law). As music could be written, it too was granted the same legal protection. That, Napier-Bell maintains, is where and when the music business began.

Eighteenth-century European (particularly Anglo-Saxon and French) migration to America saw philosophical, political, and cultural ideas cross the Atlantic (see Goldstein 2003). The idea of copyright as a regulatory mechanism devised with the "professed" ideals of generating incentives for creativity and innovation in the interests of the public good was emphatically adopted by the United States (Goldstein 2003). A "Copyright Clause" was agreed at the US Constitutional Convention of 1787, which led to the Copyright Act of 1790, which was closely modelled on the Statute of Anne (see, for example, Kretschmer and Kawohl 2004; Vaidhyanathan 2001). And that, Simon Napier-Bell concludes, is where the music business began in America. And, he emphasizes, while Britain "started things off... it was America that kicked the music business into high gear and a multi-million-dollar industry" (Napier-Bell 2022, 1). However, another full century would pass before the wheels would be set in motion to accomplish that objective.

In 2024, the global music industries are in rude health. Copyright is the lifeblood of the music industries, and the global value of overall music copyrights (recording and publishing) was estimated at a record high of $41.5 billion in 2022 (Page cited in *Billboard* 2023). Additionally, the value of the global live concert industry exceeded $28 billion in 2023 (Gotting 2023), with the same source predicting that it would approach $32 billion by 2025. Notwithstanding the promises and potentials that arose with digital innovations for bypassing the traditional industry intermediaries and rendering established oligopolies in the record industry redundant, that sector remains as concentrated today as at any point in its history, with similar centering of power reflected in music publishing and the concert industries, where a small number of large corporate interests dominate these respective landscapes. Music now flows around the world, and popular music in its many facets exists as a global phenomenon. Musics from all corners of the world can reach and colonize other corners of the world. And the industrial machinery that enables and shapes this operates on a global scale. However, if we are to more thoroughly grasp the order of things in the present, we need to critically engage with the past. Earlier scholars (such as Suisman 2012; Garofalo 1999) direct us to observe a set of processes situated in a specific time and place that represent a "commercial revolution" in music culture, and lay the foundations of the modern music business. The music industry as we know it may well be global, but its origins can be tracked down to an exact location. We can trace the emergence and swift development of the popular music publishing business to the United States (and in particular, its convergence on New York) at the turn of the twentieth century, where a revolutionary new approach to the generation and circulation of musical forms and practices surfaced and took hold. As we shall see below, the evolution of this music publishing business was deeply intertwined with the broader expansion of capitalism, reflecting its key dynamics in several ways. These developments would carry profound implications for musical practices and values, and the role and function of music in modern society. Besides, such developments would lead to a clear delineation between music maker and music user, with the materialization of a consumer market for music. The concept of "participation" in music was redefined, and reshaped further with the subsequent evolution of the phonographic recording industry. The commercial songwriter was born, and the machinery to traffic music on a mass scale was assembled. In essence, a new music order was established. By the dawn of the twentieth century a new and radical popular music industry was rapidly and firmly taking shape. It is that formative period of the modern music business that is our core interest here.

THE "INVENTION" OF THE POPULAR SONG, AND THE MACHINERY FOR SELLING IT

The evolution of the music industries can be divided into three distinct periods, each characterized by the dominance of a different *type* of organization (Garofalo 1999): initially, music publishing companies, when sheet music was the primary medium for selling songs and music; subsequently, record companies, which, by the middle decades of the twentieth century had risen to prominence as phonographic recording evolved as the principal mode for distributing music; and ultimately, the era of the transnational entertainment corporation, where music constitutes one aspect of a broader range of media forms distributed by global conglomerates, and music revenues derive from an increasing range of sources (traditional and new media), and not fundamentally linked to one specific technological medium. As media technologies have evolved, the form and nature of music organizations have accordingly evolved to exploit their potential. However, it is notable that much scholarly work on the music industry focuses largely (and in many cases, even exclusively) on just one of those areas—the recording industry, to the neglect of publishing and other domains (Garofalo 1999; Williamson and Cloonan 2007). Perhaps this can be explained by the fact that phonographic recording has for many decades been the largest and most dominant core music industry sector (although the live concert industry has grown to challenge this dominance in recent years). However, it was Tin Pan Alley, and the US music publishing business at the tail end of the nineteenth century, that "anticipated many of the practices of the music business in later years . . . [and] therefore provides the clearest model for how business would be conducted" in the future (Garofalo 1999, 321). Here, we witnessed the birth of formulaic pop, and the formulation of the blueprint for the commodification of music for decades to come—in effect, the creation of the modern music industry. Suisman summarizes such developments as thus:

> In the decades following the U.S. Civil War, a new musical product transformed American musical culture. . . . This product was the popular song. . . . "Popular" song did exist before this time, but . . . [as] "an outgrowth from the life of the people," as one survey of American music from 1890 put it. In the 1890s, however, popular song was redefined as a new kind of aural commodity. . . . [P]opular song became the cornerstone of a broad new musical culture, initiating changes not just in the music people made and heard, but also in the way music was woven into the fabric of people's lives. Popular song was a consumer commodity for the ear. (2012, 18)

Over time, this "consumer commodity for the ear" became ubiquitous, occupying every available space and place in our social world, but also permeating our private spaces (see, for example, Kassabian 2002). However, there is the realization, David Suisman tells us, that wherever music finds us, or we find it, the music *industry* is present in that moment, too. The music we experience in our lives is almost always directly related to the "commercial economy of the music industry," and while music "may still have cultural and aesthetic value . . . neither governs its commercial production" (2012, 8–9). To more completely grasp the nature and form of the contemporary music business, and how its products colonize our environment (and profit from this), Suisman provides us with some valuable instruction from the past. Informed by a range of contributions (Appadurai 1986; Hart 1992; Taylor 2007) that offer distinct conceptualizations of "commodification," he argues that a specific set of processes unfolded across the decades either side of the turn of the twentieth century that effectively established the modern music business. These developments heralded the advent of a "new musical culture" and had "worldwide ramifications" (Suisman 2012, 9). The manner in which commercial music took shape at this point would effectively serve as the template for how the music industry would continue to evolve across the decades ahead, in fact right up to the present. Moreover, while the occurrences he describes were "multinational and transnational," they were processes in which America took the lead. The bulk of the remainder of this chapter is devoted to describing and unpacking these developments.

A NEW CLASS OF MUSIC PROFESSIONAL

Music publishing had hitherto largely focused on classical and traditional music targeted at middle-class patrons. However, the later decades of the nineteenth century saw this entire realm redefined and reconstructed by an entrepreneurial class who were "market-savvy businessmen" and who recognized the potential scope of profit from selling popular songs to a mushrooming mass, urban audience (Paas 2020, 77–78). Across the final two decades of that century, the overall population of America's major cities grew by approximately fifteen million (Library of Congress n.d.). Overall, the urbanization rate in the United States swelled sixfold between 1830 and 1930 (Boustan et al. 2013). Mass society was thus evolving at a rapid rate alongside sweeping industrialization, and with the concomitant emergence of "leisure time," the environment was ripe for the commercialization of culture (see Sullivan 2013). To put it crudely, mass society meant a mass audience for mass cultural products. The popular music song would form one of those cultural products, designed to exploit this emerging cultural market.

The new players in songwriting and publishing chiefly comprised a group of Jewish immigrants (such as Witmark and Sons; Shapiro and Bernstein; Joseph Stern; Harry von Tilzer, and others) who had arrived in the United States from Europe across recent decades, or first-generation immigrants (see, for example, Karp 2018 on Jewish concentration in the early popular music business in the United States). Across the 1880s and 1890s alone, it is estimated that more than half a million Eastern European Jews entered America (Library of Congress n.d.), with many experiencing religious, social, and economic discrimination (Higham 1957). Even for those who arrived with education and experience, opportunities remained limited. However, as a "relatively" new and novel development, the entertainment business "had vacancy signs all over it ... and the quickest way in was through songwriting or music publishing" (Napier-Bell 2022, 3). In many cases, these music entrepreneurs came not from a musical background, but rather, from a host of commercial contexts. For example, Joseph Stern, Leo Feist, Harry von Tilzer, and Edward Marks all entered the world of music as salesmen from the clothes trade and applied distinct commercial logic to artistic endeavor (Napier-Bell 2022). As such, popular songs and music publishing were designed around, and reflect, the principles of late nineteenth-century capitalist expansion: the pursuit of profit, establishing a division of labor, the market mechanism, and the concept of private property rights. The evolving business practices of the day thus fashioned popular music, and from these formative years of the popular music publishing industry, music came to be produced, marketed, distributed, and consumed like other goods and products.

But moreover, as a commodity, music was distinctive in that it was "heard"—an "aural" experience. As such, "sound" was "the commodity that the music industry trafficked in," and exploitation of the "aural environment" formed the key principle upon which the modern music industry was founded (Suisman 2012, 11). To illustrate the point, Suisman draws upon Isaac Goldberg's (1930) account of the development of the music business at the turn of the twentieth century in which Goldberg advances: "What you sing and whistle, then is ... the result of a huge plot, involving thousands of dollars and thousands of organized agents to make you hear, remember and purchase. The efforts of [song promoters] assail our ears wherever we go, because it is the business of this gentry to fill the air with music" (Goldberg, cited in Suisman 2012, 11). Colonizing the aural environment, populating it with tunes, becomes the core strategy for driving profit.

THE CENTRALITY OF THE DOMESTIC ENVIRONMENT AND POPULARITY OF THE PIANO

The proliferation of the piano offered a fertile environment for this new songwriting and publishing business to evolve. By the turn of the twentieth century, the piano had become one of the most accessible commodities in American society. The production and sale of this instrument was booming, with manufacture centered in major cities like New York, Chicago, and Boston. In the 1860s, some estimates suggest that 25,000 pianos per year were sold across the country (Carson 1965). In the decades that followed, this accelerated to a point where the overall number of pianos owned in the United States increased fivefold between 1890 and 1900 (Carson 1965). What's more, the range of pianos on the market expanded to accommodate the broadest possible spectrum of society. Beyond being a symbol of middle-class affluence, it was a musical instrument that now crossed class boundaries. All socioeconomic contexts, and all types of domestic settings were catered to. Broadway composer Harry Ruby once wrote of his upbringing in 1900s New York: "All the families around us were poor, but they had pianos. . . . You could buy one for a hundred dollars and pay it off on time payments. They'd hoist it up to the apartment on a rope" (cited in Napier-Bell 2022, 7). The shift from Victorian values to consumer culture meant that "[I]n this enlightened age, the piano trade proudly offered the means with which to make music accessible to all" (Roell 1989), and the subsequent emergence of the pianola expanded its reach. As such, the technologies necessary for playing the musical "products" generated by the burgeoning popular music publishing industry were already in countless American homes. Such developments led musicologist and music critic Louis C. Elson to conclude in his 1904 *History of American Music*: "[T]here is probably no country in the world where piano playing is so widespread as in the United States" (cited in Roell 1989).

Furthermore, Carson (1965) tells us that by the late 1880s, seven out of ten children in public schools in the United States were learning to read music. So, America was a society characterized by greater levels of musical literacy, and ownership of or accessibility to the means of playing and listening to music and songs designed for the domestic setting. Conditions were thus ripe for music to become a household consumer product.

MANUFACTURING SONGS FOR THE MASS MARKET

The new publishing industry produced pop music in a range of forms (some of which are outlined below) for voice and piano. Pre-1880, the concept of the professional "composer" and "lyricist" of popular music and song was largely unheard of (Jasen 2003). While earlier/existing forms of "popular" music and songs (folk music, children's music, religious music, and so on) had been printed and published, the idea of a professional songwriter, specifically employed to compose to order did not exist. However, the rise of consumer culture would witness the concomitant evolution of a new class of composer—the popular songwriter.

The form and structure of the "popular song" changed radically to meet industry requirements. Theme, imagery, and sectional song structure all became standardized in Tin Pan Alley (Rafferty 2017). These compositions were distinguished by their simplicity (almost anyone could learn to play them), their accessibility to audiences across the socioeconomic sweep, and their capacity to function as "earworms" (once you heard it, or heard it often enough, you couldn't help singing it). The emphasis was on simple melodies—easy to remember, easy to sing, and easy to play. The chorus, based around a catchy hook, became the cornerstone of the song, with its frequent repetition across the song a standard feature. Equally, the language used "was simple and effective . . . never rising to levels of great artistry but never sinking to . . . convoluted awkwardness" (Cohen 1970).

The application of clear and simple song structures became common practice in writing material. In many respects, what is accepted today as conventional in terms of structure, was established as the norm during this period: verse-chorus form, popular from earlier in the nineteenth century, was ultimately supplanted by thirty-two-bar (AABA) form—two clear sections of melody, where A repeats (often with variations), and B effectively forms a bridge. This would become synonymous with the works of Gershwin, Porter, Kern, and be sustained as an industry standard for decades (Pessen 1985; Rafferty 2017). AABA structure would pervade virtually all forms of popular music across the twentieth century and beyond. It is to be found laced throughout the works of Lieber and Stroller (Covach 2016), and dominating the output of Lennon and McCartney, appearing in some 120 Beatles songs, more than half of that band's recorded music catalogue (Covach 2010). More than half a century after the Beatles broke up, it would continue to top the international charts through acts like Lady Gaga, Olivia Rodrigo, and countless others. AABA remains a staple structure across contemporary pop music genres.

Mathieu (2014) provides a succinct synopsis of Charles Hamm's comparative analysis of sixteen hit songs from the 1890s–1900s:

> Hamm uses a comparison of these songs to make large-scale assertions about form, content, style, and function about these songs: songs feature verses and choruses of equal length with the main melodic content in the chorus; the chorus was intended for a solo voice, not a quartet of mixed voices; songs are most

often in <3/4> time; harmonically, they are built from very simple tonal structures anchored in three basic chords, frequently using a V/V to prepare the dominant in the final cadence; and the narratives of these songs are often either sweet and carefree or decidedly sombre. (Mathieu 2014, 9–10)

Tin Pan Alley drew upon the breadth and depth of existing music forms to feed the "factories" that produced this material. The "sobbing ballad . . . the nascent Coon song . . . the livelier ditty of the black" form "part of a universal pattern" that feed the engines of Tin Pan Alley, where the composer "megaphones his infinite . . . variations upon the eternal themes" (Goldberg 1930, 88–89).

Effectively, in Tin Pan Alley, we were witnessing the creation of musical "types" or genres for marketing purposes. Charles K. Harris, the "king of the tearjerker" (who published more than three hundred songs, including the multi-million-selling "After the Ball") identifies ten specific "writer, publisher and trade" classifications for popular song (ranging from coon songs, to comic songs, to march songs, to a range of ballad types) which act as guides to how songwriters ply their trade (Harris 1906, 12–13). Elsewhere, Daniel Goldmark (2015) acquaints us with a slightly later typology of Tin Pan Alley genres published by Edward Michael Wickes (1916), a successful songwriter whose compositions formed part of the popular music landscape of early twentieth-century America. This classification of popular song comprises two broad, and somewhat crude, categories. First, we have the "ballad" song class (incorporating high-class, semi-high-class, Irish ballads, march ballads, rustic ballads, mother songs, descriptive ballads, and more); then novelty songs (encompassing juvenile songs, flirting songs, comic and Irish-comic songs, suggestive songs, special songs, philosophical songs, ragtime and stage songs). And the aforementioned thirty-two-bar AABA standardization could be perceived right across the gamut of the Alley's song categories, and as such, "a cross genre formula . . . [that] was a stable and coherent structure that served many different audience needs" (Rafferty 2017, 66).

The most significant and enduring (and profitable) song type produced in Tin Pan Alley was the kind of song that endeavored to illicit an emotional response from the public—namely the "sentimental ballad" (Shepherd 1982). We don't primarily relate to music on a rational level, but rather on the level of feeling. It seeks to generate feelings within us. This, Suisman asserts, is fundamental to how it *sells*. It's what hooks us in and makes us desire it so that we part with our money to have it. Music is, as such, "invested with power" (Suisman 2012, 11). In essence, it is the manipulation of our emotions in the interests of creating profit for its "owners." And while, as indicated above, Tin Pan Alley output encompassed different genres, it was "sentimental balladry [that] dominated the stages of the minstrel show, variety, burlesque, and musical comedy" (Ewen 1947, 181). Such songs were churned out at an extraordinary rate by the personnel in the song factories located on West 28th Street between Broadway and Sixth Avenue. Harry Von Tilzer produced a remarkable 3,000 songs—but while this was distinctive in terms of the overall quantity, it was not exceptional in terms of the speed he could write them (Shepherd 1982). Speed was of the essence. These professional songwriters and publishers: "... were in business to write songs much in the same way that Coca-Cola were in business to produce their soft drink. The faster the songs or the Coke could be produced, the more money there was to be made. So, if you were a songwriter, you had to write fast" (Shepherd 1982, 6). Moreover, professional songwriters were expected to produce the goods, anytime, to order: "'It may sound immodest' said Irving Caesar [lyricist of such hits as "Tea for Two" and "Swannee"], 'I wrote songs *any* time, on a bet . . . to be able to write a song at any time of day or night, that's what a pro had to be able to do'" (Shepherd 1982, 6).

Wickes's songwriting "manual" (2016) outlines and compares the qualities and specificities of different song types, and purports to offer in-depth insights into the art of contemporary songwriting. Goldmark details the proliferation of such guides for writing songs, written and sold by already successful songwriters, that offer formulae for the construction of songs in such categories as the above. Such publications were designed as "inspirational" and "aspirational" literature, targeted a consumer market. Goldmark's ultimate analysis of a range of such songwriting manuals and guides from the period is revealing, and reflects the systematized, standardized, set processes for manufacturing the contemporary popular song: "Despite the dissimilarities from manual to manual, the books, taken as a unit, show a profoundly uniform approach to the creation and marketing of songs, almost to the point of regulation, a quality that flies directly in the face of originality" (Goldmark 2015, 19). To emphasize the point, Goldmark proceeds to quote Herbert Taylor, author of just such a manual from 1899: "Do not seek to be original. The good things are those that have been tried. Imitation: that's the word" (Goldmark 2015, 19).

This "redefined" popular song, should thus be considered as "a distinct historical creation" (Hanáček 2010), as its emergence represents a (the?) "moment" when songs became "products" for peddling, with sheet music publishers developing local and nationwide infrastructure for promoting and distributing this new commodity (and vaudeville and traveling minstrel shows and circus troupes as key aspects of this strategy). So, a new mass product for mass consumption. What's more, the abundance of "how to write a song" booklets and guides provided many of the industry's main players with another potentially lucrative revenue stream, offering a pot of gold and rainbow scenario to ordinary "consumers."

Notably, some commentators advance that it would be simplistic and erroneous, however, to assume the songs emanating from these commercial enterprises to be "aesthetically vacant products of a hegemonic culture industry" (Mathieu 2014, viii). Rather, the songs within the new and blossoming popular arena evolved "out of diverse practices including but not limited to composing, collaborating, arranging, performing, recording, listening, and consuming music" (Mathieu 2014). In addition, interpretation and performance of the initial sheet music by theatre or comedy performers was not necessarily uniform, and could lead to a song being "dramatically altered" before its ultimate dissemination to a mass audience (Mathieu 2014, 10).

Also, in this new commercial environment, song titles assumed an unprecedented level of significance (Goldmark 2015; Subotnik 2008; Suisman 2012). Titles were now carefully crafted to engage the broadest audience possible. The title was a fundamental aspect of marketing the song, and was likely to find itself sitting center stage in the chorus, and repeated frequently. A catchy or intriguing title could increase sales and audience interest.

The formulaic structures, and musical and lyrical standards associated with the commercial pop songs of the day contrast starkly with the song collections garnered by musicologists and folklorists such as John Lomax, Francis James Child, and others at the turn of the twentieth century (Miller 2010; Suisman 2012). Their respective work documents countless folksongs that were, in effect "the antithesis of Tin Pan Alley productions: long, complicated, difficult to sing, and lacking choruses" (Suisman 2012, 50).

For some commentators (such as Stanley 2022) the melding of artistic expression and commercial viability that characterized American popular music publishing around the turn of the twentieth century would manifest itself most plainly and bluntly in those hit songs deriving from works that were initially written for corporate advertising campaigns. For example, Harry von Tilzer's "Down at the Old Bull and Bush" (popularized by Australian singer and actress Florrie Forde) had originally been composed as an advert for Budweiser beer. Similarly, "Meet Me in St. Louis" was penned by Sterling and Mills to promote the 1904 St. Louis World's Fair.

HOW TO SELL A SONG

In his 1926 autobiography, Charles K. Harris stresses that a song "must be sung, played, hummed, and drummed into the ears of the public, not in one city alone, but in every city, town, and village, before it ever becomes popular" (cited in Middleton and Manuel 2001). But how was that to be achieved?

The new music order saw a whole new class of music makers. The fledging music business drew upon the creative talents of the songwriters and composers it fed off of, but generating commercial music for the marketplace now involved a host of actors, many of whom were far removed from the creative process. Suisman summarizes it thus: "The radical reorganisation of musical culture in the United States was driven . . . by a new commercial class of music makers, including in one form or another, entrepreneurs, inventors, manufacturers, publishers, sales agents, advertisers, critics, retailers, educators and law makers. . . . Together, they harnessed musicians' creative talents and transformed music . . . into a versatile and valuable commodity" (2012, 15).

Here, it is worthwhile to briefly summarize the process Isaac Goldberg (1930) describes in some detail regarding preparing the song for publication, and promoting the "product" in the marketplace. He points to the firm establishment of a division of labor within publishing houses, fundamental to ensuring a regular and stable supply of new songs for the marketplace. Within this, the production process was broken down into a series of specialized duties or occupations, with each individual task performed by different sets of individuals. Songwriting became a professional occupation, based in its own workplace. In essence, we were witnessing the imposition of core principles of modern industrial organization on the cultural sphere in the interests of increased productivity and efficiency. Writers (who composed songs on demand), arrangers (often viewed as a lesser form of "creative," but seen as technically proficient), musicians and performers (for "demonstrations"), pluggers and marketing staff (to sell the songs to the ears of the public), legal staff (who handled contracts and copyright registration), and additional administrative staff. So, the evolution of an "organization" assembled to manufacture a commodity. In practice, these were "song factories" (see Keightley 2015).

Goldberg guides us through the process of getting a song to its target consumers: Once a publisher decided to accept a song from a composer, a contract was drawn up, which laid out that in return for a "consideration of, let us say, four per cent, he or they relinquish all claim to right, title or interest" (Goldberg 1930, 198). As publishing houses became established, they employed staff writers—"in-house" employees to generate the raw material for packaging and distribution. A professional arranger would then be engaged to rearrange the accompaniment as "best for general piano purposes," and this subsequently became the version of the song for printing. A few thousand "professional copies" were initially produced for distributing to singers and performers on the stage. Beyond this, additional copies were disseminated to "the trade,"—those shops across the country that sold sheet music. To boot, publishers often entered agreements with "retailers" whereby if they consented to take a small number of copies of *new* songs from the publisher each month, they could get these at a discount, thus incentivizing them to sell new songs, as these copies potentially generated greater profits for the retailer. "If," Goldberg tells us, "after a few months, the song was showing signs of the public's interest in it" and "singers occasionally mention it as going well with their audiences" (Goldberg 1930, 199), the next promotional push came in the form of advertising on the margins of the publisher's existing big-selling works. And if all of this demonstrated promise and potential, then large-scale advertising in the newspapers would follow.

A fundamental aspect of getting the song to a broader audience's ears came in the form of "booming," where a legion of canvassers for the song were planted in music halls across the country to stimulate interest among the concert going public. Some would distribute handbills containing the printed lyrics; others would be paid to "take up the chorus with the singer ... and applaud uproariously" (Goldberg 1930, 200). Pluggers were crucial to the implementation of this strategy. It was pluggers who ensured that the air got filled with music, and the "output" from the songwriting factories reached the ears of its ultimate consumers. Perhaps ironically, Goldberg effectively demonizes these characters. A plugger, he tells us, is a "high-pressure salesman who sold not the song, but the idea of the song ... [and] pursued the performer like an evil spirit," before delivering "his prey to the offices of his employers" (Goldberg 1930, 202).

MAKING MUSIC PAY: PERFORMING RIGHTS AND THE 1909 COPYRIGHT ACT

Songs could be sold, and hit songs could generate considerable profits. Charles K. Harris's "After the Ball" was the biggest-selling sheet music song of the early Tin Pan Alley era. Published by Edward B. Marks, it was the music business's first million-selling "hit," and proceeded to sell five million copies (Guion 2011). Harry Von Tilzer's "My Old New Hampshire Home" and "I'd

Leave My Happy Home for You" also sold in the millions, helping to make millionaires out of Von Tilzer and these songs' "ultimate" publishers, Maurice Shapiro and Louis Bernstein. Von Tilzer would proceed to found his own publishing company and amass a vast fortune across his career. Bernstein, a real estate developer, and Shapiro would become two of the most successful music publishers of the era, with interests in a number of publishing companies that would have long-lasting legacies. However, if examples such as these (and there were many) exemplified the possibilities and potentials for wealth creation from sheet music sales, there were many, many more examples to illustrate how fortunes could be lost. There were far more "misses" than "hits" on the "Alley," and the reality was that most songs had a finite period in terms of sales, even those that sold in large quantities and generated considerable revenue. So, the question was how to make hits pay after their sales declined. To address this problem, the new pop music publishing industry took inspiration from earlier developments in Europe.

A defining moment in the process of shaping music copyright can be traced to the Café Concert des Ambassadeurs, a one-time Parisienne café just off the Champs-Elysées. In a much-documented story dating from 1848 (Attali 1985; Frith 2004; Laing 2002, 2004, among many others), three French composers—Ernest Bourget, Victor Parizot, and Paul Henrion—were angered to discover that a guitar quartet employed by the café, were using their material for the purposes of entertaining guests. The composers first refused to pay for their food unless the proprietor of the café compensated them for the use of their music. They subsequently demanded separate reimbursement from the guitar quartet. The failure of the various parties to reach any agreement in the matter resulted in Bourget, backed by his two friends, instigating legal proceedings. The subsequent court ruling in favor of the composers confirmed the existence of a "performing right" for creators of musical works, and led to the establishment of provisions for compensating them whenever their work was used in the "public domain."

A new relationship between music "owners" and music "users" had emerged. Laing (2002) also points to the 1848 Paris court ruling forging a parity between the composers of serious and popular musics. Such equality was resented by the bourgeoisie as an attack on its exclusive privileges to engage in financial dealings in music (Attali 1985). This specific ruling in Paris resulted in the formation of La Société des Auteurs, Compositeurs et Editeurs de Musique (SACEM), a performing rights society with the objective of collecting royalties on behalf of composers when their material was performed (Wallis and Malm 1984; Wallis 2004). Similar societies emerged across Europe throughout the latter decades of the nineteenth century. Like SACEM, these societies were (and still are) based on the principle of "collective management"—a business practice that has stayed at the core of the music industry for a century and a half (Laing 2004). Such a practice means that royalty collection societies, internationally networked and acting as a hub connecting composers with users, can effectively license music rights to users and in doing so, simplify the process of obtaining usage rights and returning resulting royalties to rights owners.

Such developments would form the basis of subsequent developments across the Atlantic. The earliest US copyright bill to explicitly recognize music was the Copyright Act of 1831. This statute extended copyright protection to musical compositions for the first time. However, the 1909 Copyright Act contained amendments and modifications with more far-reaching implications for music. By far the largest and most influential interest group involved in drafting the bill was the music publishing sector. Its most prominent players gave "hundreds of hours of congressional testimony" and provided more witnesses at congressional hearing than all other fields of interest combined (Suisman 2012, 159). As such, they drove the process, and their combined testimonies stressed the primary objective of any resulting copyright bill should be to protect the business of music publishers (Loren 2014).

Their key concerns related to the unauthorized copying and distribution of sheet music, measures to address copyright infringement, and provisions to accommodate music licensing and enforcement of copyrights. The issue around licensing was perhaps the most important item on their agenda. While existing copyright law catered for musical notation and lyrics in printed form, it did not address the issue of music as an aural experience. While copying remained an issue for them, the publishers' main preoccupation was with the use of their works in commercial contexts, most significantly in the field of phonographic recording (including piano rolls and records) which had surged to a value of more than $10 million in the United States by 1904 (Suisman 2012). Consequently, one of the most significant changes emanating from the 1909 Act related to the establishment of compulsory licenses for the use of copyrighted musical works. In particular, the compulsory mechanical licensing system which facilitated third parties to produce recordings of copyrighted music works, without the consent of the copyright owner, conditional upon the payment of a statutory royalty to the rights holder, and adherence to other specific regulatory requirements. This emanated specifically from the use of cylinders, piano rolls, and phonographic records—music that was mechanically reproduced. Mechanical copyright was thus established, and such arrangements would form the basis of future compulsory licensing rights systems, and would influence the evolution of copyright law around music right into the twenty-first century.

Into the bargain, the 1909 Act increased the power of the rights holder by granting them the *exclusive* right to copy, which effectively laid the foundations for future developments in performance rights, and delivered provisions related to ownership of copyrights for songs and music composed by the publishers' staff writers, or on commission (see, for example, Patterson and Lindberg 1991).

In essence, the 1909 Act gave songwriters and music publishers exclusive rights to duplicate, distribute, and perform their works. As such, they now exercised legal control over where their music and songs appeared and were performed. The Act established a formal set of protections for sheet music publishers that enabled them to legally secure copyrights to songs and compositions. It also introduced a number of other revisions to existing copyright law, most notably, extending the term of copyright to twenty-eight years, with the ability of the rights holder to renew this, potentially extending the duration to fifty-six years. And there were other more minor provisions, such as the requirement of authors to insert a copyright notice on copies of their works; prerequisites pertaining to the registration of works; the recognition of fair use in specific contexts such as education, research, journalistic commentary, and criticism; and a provision for noncopyrighted works, or those whose copyright had expired, to enter the "public domain." But perhaps the most radical change brought about by the 1909 Act happened by accident rather than design (Vaidhyanathan 2001). The concept of "works made for hire" effectively formed the basis for what would evolve as corporate copyright, and this too would have implications for the developing popular music business. Now, in instances where works were created by employees of an organization, the employer (that is, the organization, which could include music publishing houses) could now legally claim authorship of these works. In essence, the 1909 Act provided the legal framework that enabled the publishers of popular music to establish control over the rights to songs written and produced by their staff writers and arrangers. The courts would now recognize them as legal authors of works under their control.

Furthermore, as Matt Jackson points out: "[L]iability is a crucial area of copyright law because the incentives provided by copyright are only meaningful if the author's rights can be enforced through the imposition of liability . . . [and] the 1909 Copyright Act imposed strict liability on all infringers.

This... increased the potential liability of intermediaries in the communication chain" (Jackson 2002, 369).

As political scientist Blayne Haggart concludes, the 1909 Copyright Act was effectively hammered out "amongst interest groups . . . with Congress approving the resulting legislation" (2017, 224). As such, those music publishers (and later, phonographic recording labels) that were growing to dominate the landscape, received the endorsement of the state. In actuality, the "problem" of how to make music and hit songs pay beyond their initial sale had been resolved. The groundwork was now laid for new business models to evolve in a context where music was ceasing to be not just a product to be sold, but also a service to be licensed.

Accordingly, the 1909 Act paved the way for the establishment of the American Society for Creators, Authors and Publishers (ASCAP) some five years later.

ENFORCING THE LAW: THE FORMATION OF ASCAP

With a robust music copyright law now in place, publishers required an effective means of monitoring and licensing performances of the works they controlled.

ASCAP was thus founded by a group of prominent music publishers and songwriters (including Victor Herbert, Irving Berlin, and John Philip Sousa) with the objective of administering music performing rights licenses in public venues such as restaurants, bars, and theatres. In essence, ASCAP and subsequent royalty collection societies were formed to operate as enforcement agents, sanctioned by the state to collect payment from music "users" on behalf of their membership.

The formation of ASCAP resembled the careful construction of a gravy train for the privileged elite at the top of the music publishing and songwriters pecking order to ride. As such, ASCAP was "rooted in New York's Tin Pan Alley and Broadway tradition, where it was conceived" (Cusic 1995), with the leading publishers and composers in these domains reigning supreme. Membership was at the discretion of the board (Cusic 1995), and the organization incorporated a highly stratified structure, where any publisher's or composer's "rank" within the society (and by extension, earning power, and decision-making power regarding the organization's policies and operations) was determined by the size of the catalogue's they controlled and managed, the scale of sales they achieved, and so on (Suisman 2012).

ASCAP's power structure revolved very much around its founding members, with emphasis placed on income stability for these members. As they enjoyed voting power, the organization's board was enduring and self-serving. Subsequently, in terms of royalty payments, ASCAP members experienced either a feast or famine (Tinberg 1954). In fact, as the organization expanded across the years ahead, within its own quarters, there was "a stream of protests that privileged insiders and unproductive writers were being unjustly permitted to skim off the cream of ASCAP revenue" (Tinberg 1954, 317). "Membership in ASCAP . . . was skewed toward the more 'literate' writers of show tunes and semi-serious works such as Richard Rodgers and Lorenz Hart, Cole Porter, George Gershwin, and Irving Berlin. Writers of more vernacular forms, such as the blues and country music, were excluded from ASCAP. As proprietors of the compositions of their members, these organizations exercised considerable power in shaping public taste" (Garofalo 1999, 323).

ASCAP fundamentally differed from earlier royalty collection societies in Europe, such as SACEM, in that it operated a blanket licensing arrangement with its customers/"users," with the pool of royalties amassed from customer subscriptions subsequently allocated to its membership in accordance with their seniority in the organization.

With copyright law now in place, ASCAP worked to establish legal precedence by way of a series of test cases through the courts (see, for example, Hugunin 1979; Loren 2014). The most noted of these saw Victor Herbert instigate proceedings against the Shanley Company, a restaurant and cabaret in New York, for playing songs from his repertoire without his permission and with no compensation. The US Supreme Court ultimately ruled that Herbert's music was used for the purposes of generating profit for the restaurant, and as these works were protected by copyright law, Shanley's unauthorized use of this music constituted copyright infringement. The legal precedence for performing rights had now been confirmed and Herbert's victory paved the way for ASCAP to start collecting royalty payments in the years ahead.

Here, it is important to recognize the spectrum of opportunity that was opening up for music rights holders to exploit. The popular music publishing industry effectively took form in the context of the world's "first multimedia revolution"—a period in history where a number of radical media technologies successfully diffused across the social world (Preston 2001). Between 1880 and 1920, society witnessed the emergence of motion pictures, phonographic recording, and radio as key mass communication forms. These had transformed from incorporeal sets of ideas to the application of these ideas into corporeal, real technologies, that successfully and widely diffused because, for the first time, we had the evolution of social formations that necessitated them (see Winston 1998 on how social conditions produce and shape "inventions"). The world was evolving as an increasingly urban space, with a mass society utilizing mass media technologies to consume mass cultural products. With the advent of these new mass media forms, the spaces and places for promoting songs and music expanded. Moreover, with performing rights now enshrined in law, all of these spaces and places potentially existed as sites of direct revenue for music publishers and composers.

In this context, subsequent actions were initiated by ASCAP members against radio stations (see, for example, Barnouw 1966; J. C. W. 1941). Again, the charge was that broadcasters were using copyrighted music and songs for their own commercial gain while failing to pay publishers and composers for the privilege. Furthermore, ASCAP contended that the repetition of songs on radio ultimately limited their economic value by driving down direct sales, thus threatening the welfare of songwriters and publishers "with the result that the composer has been forced to look elsewhere for additional revenues" (J. C. W. 1941, 378). Precedent in this domain was set when Witmark and Son succeeded in a case brought against WOR in New Jersey (Weinberg 2000).

In the wake of these decisions, licensing agreements were brokered with vaudeville and movie theatres (Suisman 2012). Thus, in a short few years, performing rights had been established as a new and potentially enduring source of revenue for the music publishing industry. It was the prime movers behind ASCAP that made songwriting a profitable profession through establishing a legal basis for "licensing" music to virtually every opening in our environment that music can "aurally" colonize (Cusic 1995).

The scale of what was now achievable for those at the top of the pecking order was starkly illustrated by Irving Berlin. As a songwriter and partner in the Waterson, Berlin and Synder Inc. publishing house, his royalties in 1912 exceeded $100,000. However, a decade later, they had mushroomed to approximately $4 million (Pessen 1985). His hit "Cheek to Cheek" yielded $250,000 in the initial year of its publication alone. Popular music was now big, big business.

For many, the concept of performing rights would quickly come to be recognized and accepted as fundamental to the preservation of music and music makers in contemporary society. For some, ASCAP and its sister organizations would come to be viewed as playing a significant role in supporting the democratic principles of fairness and equality. Writing around at the outbreak of World War II in 1939, Irving Propper, a prominent music copyright lawyer and champion of performing rights, stresses:

> ... [t]he American people's inalienable right to enjoy the work of American genius. Our gifted composers are giving us some of the finest music in the world today, and there should be no question that the users of it for profit should pay for the privilege of using it.... The future of American music under the copyright law, and due to ASCAP, looks brighter than it has ever looked. More and more of our gifted young men and women are turning to composition ... [because] their rights are adequately protected.... [Resultantly], American music is being played all over the world and held in high regard in the foreign countries. (Propper 1939, 239–40)

To challenge copyright law and to challenge ASCAP, for Propper, is to pose a grave threat to artistic endeavor and freedom of expression. Society is dynamic, continually shifting over time, and music and song are fundamental to civilization documenting its own history and evolution. Legal protection, he insists, is prerequisite to ensuring the composer can carry out his work. Furthermore, Propper positions ASCAP as a rampart designed to protect American "democracy" from the horrors of dictatorships and totalitarianism prevalent in Europe at the time, where "[music] is taken over by the State and used as a medium for governmental propaganda" (Propper 1939, 246). Copyright and ASCAP are thus advanced as synonymous with freedom and democracy: "Let America hold out like a strong bright light against the cultural darkness of Europe.... Don't let it happen here! ASCAP is a great bulwark against the invasion of personal rights by certain factions. Taking away these rights without compensation is the very essence of any 'ism,' except Americanism.... Let foreign composers know that the United States is a haven for the oppressed.... Our democracy protects human rights in both person and property" (Propper 1939, 246). It's a "you're with us or against us" scenario that Propper presents to his audience. Failure to support and comply with copyright law approximates Nazism. Propper holds up ASCAP as a beacon of light for those artists confronting persecution in different corners of the world. In essence, ASCAP came to be celebrated as a metaphor for an egalitarian society.

THE ALIGNMENT OF ELITES—CONCENTRATED POWER AND CONCENTRATED WEALTH

In effect, performing rights organizations represent an extension of music publishing (Napier-Bell 2022). ASCAP effectively saw the most successful songwriters align with the most successful publishers. M. Witmark and Sons, which was established in 1885, was one of the first big players to emerge in Tin Pan Alley publishing, and boasted George M. Cohan (of "Yankee Doodle Dandy" and "Give My Regards to Broadway" fame) and Victor Herbert among their "collaborators." Jerome H. Remick and Co. was founded the same year, and published works by Harry Von Tilzer. T. B. Harms had been formed in 1875, and also published works by Von Tilzer and others such as Jerome Kern. Founded at the turn of the century, Shapiro, Bernstein and Co. quickly grew to become one of the most successful music publishing firms of the Tin Pan Alley era. Harry H. Williams (whose "In the Shade of the Old Apple Tree" became an early twentieth-century standard), and household names like Irving Berlin and later George Gershwin and Cole Porter produced works that fed their extensive catalogue. Leo Feist Inc. was formed in 1906, and grew to prominence by publishing hits by Cohan, Von Tilzer, Berlin, and Walter Donaldson, among others. And as illustrated by many of those examples, at different moments in time, the most high-profile songwriters found outlets for their material in more than one of the leading publishing houses. Likewise, other notable tunesmiths like Paul Dresser (who penned "On the Banks of the Wabash, Far Away," one of the biggest-selling hits at the turn of the century) collaborated with Witmark and Sons, Shapiro, Bernstein and Co., and also Howley, Haviland and Co. over the course of his career. Equally, Harms, Witmark, and Remick all published the songs of Jerome Kern.

In what would become an established trend in music publishing (and broader music industries per se), alliances formed between the sector's most dominant actors, with mergers and takeovers bringing about a situation where a smaller number of large (and expanding) organizations controlled more of the territory. By the turn of the twentieth century, Tin Pan Alley comprised some forty-five different publishing houses, with a multitude of companies emerging in large cities across the country; however, less than two decades later, just seven publishers had grown to account for more than 80 percent of the music publishing market in America (Paas 2020). As such, the business of popular music came to experience a high degree of market concentration at an early stage of its development, and this would remain a consistent feature of its evolution across time. For example, T. B. Harms and Co. merged with Francis, Day and Hunter in 1908, which in turn was taken over by Warner Bros. in 1929, the same year it acquired the Remick Music Corporation and Witmark (Spring, 2013). Max Dreyfus had bought into Harms at the turn of the century and, with his brother Louis, went on to obtain Chappell Music in the 1920s, arguably the most prominent music publisher in Britain, with established interests in the United States (Leve 2016). Moreover, Shapiro,

Bernstein and Co. would later partner with Decca Records (now part of the Universal Music Group) and Columbia Pictures (now part of Sony).

As the above Warner Bros. example illustrates, the convergence of the popular music business with the film industry was well under way by the late 1920s (see, for example, Spring 2008, 2013; Shepherd 1982). As Hollywood transitioned from silent to sound, the demand for music and songs in movies made it more economically rational to acquire the entities that controlled the rights and generated the "product." Metro-Goldwyn-Mayer (MGM), Warner Bros., Fox, and the Radio Corporation of America (RCA, and its subsidiary, RKO Pictures) each invested heavily in the music publishing sector to a point where, by 1935, those four corporations accounted for "more than half" the music and songs that ASCAP licensed (Suisman 2012, 263).

We were witnessing the evolution of the entertainment corporation with film, music and broadcast media all merging together under the same corporate roof.

CONCLUSION

Overall, the political and economic context of the late nineteenth century provided fertile ground for the growth of Tin Pan Alley. Its success was driven by factors such as urbanization, immigration, changes in copyright laws, the rise of consumer culture, and economic prosperity, all of which contributed to the flourishing of the music publishing industry in New York City. Within this environment, Tin Pan Alley delivered to us the professional songwriter, composing works for the mass market, designing these works to be as accessible as possible to the broadest swath of "consumers" that constituted that market. As all of this unfolded, we witnessed a shift in the conceptualization of "popular" music from music of the people to music for the people. The new music industry did not simply monetize music cultures that already existed, rather, it manufactured music. It was not simply a case of taking music and selling it. Rather, popular songs were the product of an industrialization process, the output that emerged from the song factory for distribution to the masses. The principles that governed manufacturing and marketing in the rag trade now governed the production, marketing, and distribution of music. America now manufactured music, just like it manufactured those buttons (Napier-Bell 2022) or Coca-Cola (Shepherd 1982).

The newly established music business changed how we experienced music; how, when, and where we heard music; and what music we heard. In exercising control over what music was promoted and disseminated, and what wasn't, the music regime now had the power to marginalize "musical production that was not oriented towards the market" and as such, render it "less legitimate" (Suisman 2012, 14).

The philosophies and principles that drove Tin Pan Alley would be successfully exported around the globe, and would continue to inform how the music publishing industry, and also the recording industry, developed and evolved over time. Rules and conventions around songwriting that were established during this period have proved durable, and are reflected in many of the dominant forms of popular music that have emerged across the twentieth century, and right up to the present. Equally, in terms of the fundamentals of how the music business operates, the activities may have evolved, the field of intermediaries used to market and promote music may have become more complex and sophisticated, and the channels for distribution may be more plentiful and pervasive, but in crucial respects, the key principles remain the same. The music publishing and phonographic recording sectors primarily derive their revenues from colonizing the broadest possible spectrum of spaces and places with the repertoires they own and control, with copyright law fundamental to how this successfully functions.

Writing in 1949, music historian Arnold Shaw reflects upon the evolution of the American popular song business as an international phenomenon, with Tin Pan Alley having effectively "shifted its location" to multiple sites, encompassing the East Coast, Midwest, and West Coast of America, to London and other centers on the European continent, and beyond. American popular music now reigned supreme.

BIBLIOGRAPHY

Attali, J. (1985). *Noise: The Political Economy of Music*. Manchester: Manchester University Press.
Barnouw, E. (1966). *A Tower in Babel: A History of Broadcasting in the United States*. New York: Oxford University Press.
Bernstein, J. A. (2023). *Printing Music in Renaissance Rome*. Oxford: Oxford University Press.
Brown, S., B. Merker, and N. L. Wallin (2000). "An Introduction on Evolutionary Musicology." In *The Origins of Music*. Cambridge, MA: MIT Press.
Carson, G. (1965). "The Piano in the Parlour." *Heritage*, Vol. 17, no. 1. https://www.americanheritage.com/piano-parlor.
Clottes, J. (1999). "The Sorcier: A More Recent Tracing." *PAST*, No. 31 (Newsletter of the Prehistoric Society, Institute of Archaeology, University College London). http://www.ucl.ac.uk/prehistoric/past/past31.html.
Cohen, N. (1970). "Tin Pan Alley's Contribution to Folk Music." *Western Folklore* Vol. 29, No. 1 (January): 9–20.

Covach, J. (2006). "From 'Craft' to 'Art': Form and Structure in the Music of the Beatles." In K. Womack and T. F. Davis (eds.), *Reading the Beatles: Cultural Studies, Literary Criticism, and the Fab Four*, 37–53. New York: State University of New York Press.

Covach, J. (2010). "Leiber and Stoller, the Coasters, and the 'Dramatic AABA' Form." In M. Spicer and J. Covach (eds.), *Sounding Out Pop: Essays in Popular Music*. University of Michigan Press.

Cusic, D. (1995). "The Emergence of the Country Music Business: 1945–1955." *Studies in Popular Culture* Vol. 17, No. 2 (April): 17–29.

De Souza, J. (2014). "Voice and Instrument at the Origins of Music." *Current Musicology* No. 97: 21–36.

Ewen, D. (1947). *Songs of America: A Cavalcade of Popular Songs*. Chicago: Ziff-Davis Publishing.

Frith, S. (2004), "Music and the Media." in S. Frith and L. Marshall (eds.), *Music and Copyright*, 2nd ed., 171–88. Edinburgh: Edinburgh University Press.

Garofalo, R. (1999). "From Music Publishing to MP3: Music and Industry in the Twentieth Century." *American Music* Vol. 17, No. 3 (Autumn, 1999): 318–54.

Goldmark, D. (2007). "Creating Desire on Tin Pan Alley." *Musical Quarterly* Vol. 90, Issue 2: 197–229.

Goldmark, D. (2015). "Making Songs Pay: Tin Pan Alley's Formula for Success." *Musical Quarterly* Vol. 98, No. 1/2: 3–28.

Goldstein, P. (2003). *Copyright's Highway: From Gutenberg to the Celestial Jukebox*, rev. ed. Stanford, CA: Stanford University Press.

Goodman, R. I. (1960). "Music Copyright Associations and the Antitrust Laws." *Indiana Law Journal* Vol. 25, No. 2: 168–84.

Gotting, M. C. (2023). "Live music industry revenue worldwide from 2014 to 2025." *Statista*, Tuesday 12th December. https://www.statista.com/statistics/1096424/live-music-industry-revenue-worldwide/.

Guion, D. (2011). "After the Ball, by Charles K. Harris." *Musicology for Everyone*. https://music.allpurposeguru.com/2011/04/after-the-ball-by-charles-k-harris/#google_vignette.

Haggart, B. (2017). "What is Intellectual Property?" in M. Callahan and J. Rogers (eds.), *A Critical Guide to Intellectual Property*. London: Bloomsbury Academic.

Harris, C. K. (1906). *How to Write a Popular Song*. Chicago: Charles K. Harris.

Higham, J. (1957). "Social discrimination against Jews in America, 1830–1930." *Publications of the American Jewish Historical Society*, vol. xlvii: 1–33.

Hugunin, M. (1979). "ASCAP, BMI and the Democratization of American Popular Music." *Popular Music and Society* Vol. 7, Issue 1: 8–17.

Hymer, S. (1979). *The Multinational Corporation*. Cambridge: Cambridge University Press.

Jackson, M. (2002). "One step forward, two steps back: an historical analysis of copyright liability." *Cardozo Arts and Entertainment Law Journal* Vol. 20 (2): 367–416.

J. C. W. (1941). "The Performing Rights in a Musical Composition." *Virginia Law Review* Vol. 27, No. 3 (January 1941): 378–90.

Kassabian, A. (2002). "Ubiquitous Listening." In D. Hesmondhalgh and K. Negus (eds.), *Popular Music Studies*. Oxford and New York: Oxford University Press.

Karp, J. (2018). "The Roots of Jewish Concentration in the American Popular Music Business." In H. R. Diner (ed.), *Doing Business in America: A Jewish History*, 133–43. West Lafayette, IN: Purdue University Press.

Keightley, K. (2015). "Grinding Out Hits at the Song Factory." In A. Bennett and S. Waksman (eds.), *The Sage Handbook of Popular Music*. London: Sage Publications.

Kretschmer, K., and F. Kawohl. (2004). "The History and Philosophy of Copyright." In S. Frith and L. Marshall (eds.), *Music and Copyright*, 2nd ed, 21–53. Edinburgh: Edinburgh University Press.

Laing, D. (2002). "Copyright as a Component of the Music Industry." In M. Talbot (ed.), *The Business of Music*, 171–94. Liverpool: Liverpool University Press.

Laing, D. (2004). "Copyright, Politics and the International Music Industry." In S. Frith, and L. Marshall (eds.), *Music and Copyright*. 2nd ed., 70–85. Edinburgh: Edinburgh University Press.

Leve, J. (2016). *American Music Theater*. Oxford: Oxford University Press.

Library of Congress. (n.d.). *A People at Risk*. https://www.loc.gov/classroom-materials/immigration/polish-russian/a-people-at-risk/#:~:text=All%20in%20all%2C%20between%201880,all%20over%20Europe%20and%20Asia.

Library of Congress. (n.d.). *City Life in the Late nineteenth Century*. https://www.loc.gov/classroom-materials/united-states-history-primary-source-timeline/rise-of-industrial-america-1876-1900/city-life-in-late-nineteenth-century/#:~:text=Between%201880%20and%201900%2C%20cities,the%20two%20decades%20before%201900.

Loren, L. P. (2014). "The dual narratives in the landscape of music copyright." *Houston Law Review* Vol. 52 (2): 537–82.

Miller, K. H. (2010). *Segregating Sound: Inventing Folk and Pop Music in the Age of Jim Crow*. Durham, NC: Duke University Press.

Napier-Bell, S. (2015). *Ta-Ra-Ra-Boom-De-Ay: The Dodgy Business of Popular Music*. London: Unbound.

Napier-Bell, S. (2022). *The Business: A History of Popular Music from Sheet Music to Streaming*. London: Unbound.

Paas, J. R. (2020). "Popular Music: Tin Pan Alley as National Barometer." In *A History of American Literature and Culture of the First World War*, 76–93. Cambridge: Cambridge University Press.

Patterson, L. R., and S. W. Lindberg (1991). *The Nature of Copyright: A Law of Users Rights*. Athens: University of Georgia Press.

Peoples, G. (2023). "Global Value of Music Copyright Climbed to $41.5B in 2022" *Billboard*, November 6. https://www.billboard.com/pro/music-copyright-global-value-2022-will-page-report/.

Pessen, E. (1985). "The Great Songwriters of Tin Pan Alley's Golden Age: A Social, Occupational and Aesthetic Inquiry." *American Music* Vol. 3: 180–97.

Roell, C. H. (1989). *The Piano in America, 1890–1940*. Chapel Hill: University of North Carolina Press.

Rafferty, K. F. (2017). "'The Normal Order of Things': Propriety, Standardisation and the Making of Tin Pan Alley." Thesis, Newcastle University, 2017.

Rose, M. (1993). *Authors and Owners: The Invention of Copyright*. Cambridge, MA, and London: Harvard University Press.

Schulkin, G., and J. Raglan (2014). "The evolution of music and human social capability." *Frontiers of Neuroscience* Vol. 8 (September): 1–13.

Shaw, A. (1949). "The Vocabulary of Tin-Pan Alley Explained." *Notes*, Second Series, Vol. 7, No. 1 (December): 33–53.

Spender, H. (1890). "The Origin of Music." *Mind* Vol. 15, No. 60 (October): 449–68.

Spring, K. (2013). *Saying It with Songs: Popular Music and the Coming of Sound to Hollywood Cinema*. Oxford: Oxford University Press.

Stanley, B. (2022). *Let's Do It: The Birth of Pop*. London: Faber and Faber.

Sullivan, J. L. (2013). *Media Audiences: Effects, Users, Institutions and Power*. Los Angeles: Sage.

Thompson, E. (1995). "Machines, Music, and the Quest for Fidelity: Marketing the Edison Phonograph in America, 1877–1925." *Musical Quarterly* Vol. 79, No. 1 (Spring): 131–71.

Thorborn, S. (2003). "What News on the Rialto? Fundraising and Publicity for Operas in Seventeenth-Century Venice." *Canadian University Music Review* Vol. 23, No. 1–2: 166–200.

Tinberg, S. (1954). "The Antitrust Aspects of Merchandising Modern Music: The ASCAP Consent Judgment of 1950." *Law and Contemporary Problems* Vol. 19, No. 2 (Spring): 294–322.

Turk, I., and D. Kunej. (2000). "New Perspectives on the Beginnings of Music: Archaeological and Musicological Analysis of a Middle Palaeolithic Bone Flute." In Wallin et al. (eds.), *The Origins of Music*. Cambridge, MA: MIT Press.

Vaidhyanathan, S. (2001). *Copyrights and Copywrongs: The Rise of Intellectual Property and How it Threatens Creativity*. New York and London: New York University Press.

Wallis, R., and K. Malm. (1984). *Big Sounds from Small Peoples: The Music Industry in Small Countries*. London: Constable.

Wallis, R. (2004). "Copyright and the Composer." In S. Frith and L. Marshall (eds.), *Music and Copyright*, 103–22. Edinburgh: Edinburgh University Press.

Weinberg, H. R. (2000). "From Sheet Music to MP3 Files: A Brief Perspective on Napster." *Kentucky Law Journal* Vol. 89, no. 3.

Wickes, E. M. (2010/1916). *Writing the Popular Song*. Whitefish, MT: Kessinger Publishing.

Winston, B. (1998). *Media, Technology and Society: A History from the Telegraph to the Internet*. London: Routledge.

CHAPTER 6

THE AMERICAN FEDERATION OF MUSICIANS
Becoming Invisible

Dick Weissman

As I was writing this chapter, two songs kept coming to mind. 'Why Am I Treated So Bad?,'" written by Wesley Westbrooks, is a gospel song about white kids throwing stones at Black kids walking to an integrated school. "What's the Matter with the Mill?" was written and recorded by Memphis Minnie Douglas. It is a metaphor on an entirely different subject, but the lines:

> I want you to bear this in mind
> If you're going to the mill, you're just losing time
> What's the matter with the mill?
> It done broke down

resonate with many aspects of the American Federation of Musicians.

AMERICAN UNION HISTORY

During the mid-nineteenth century, various attempts were made to organize craft workers. These organizations were generally regarded as guilds, or groups of skilled craft workers in specific trades. These early guilds go back as far as 1829 and were local organizations that made no attempt to organize outside their own locales.[1]

Although there were attempts to organize specific groups on a national basis, it was not until the 1880s that the Knights of Labor and the more conservative American Federation of Labor began to enroll workers in unified organizations. By the twentieth century, the AFL dominated the union movement, but in 1905 the far more radical IWW (Industrial Workers of the World) organized mill workers, apple pickers and other groups that the AFL had no interest in recruiting. The IWW made no attempts to organize musicians, but some of its leaders, notably Joe Hill, were also musicians and songwriters.

In 1935 leaders of the United Mine Workers seceded from the AFL and formed the CIO (Congress of Industrial Organizations). Unlike the AFL, from the outset the CIO set out to organize unskilled workers in such industries as steel, auto, meatpacking, and textiles. By 1954 the CIO and AFL, both weakened by antilabor congressional actions, united as a single entity.[2] Although various attempts to organize local musicians go back to the mid-nineteenth century, the American Federation of Musicians began in 1896, and was quickly granted a charter by the AFL.

THE AFM, TECHNOLOGY, AND THE DISAPPEARING JOB MARKET

Over the years the union has repeatedly suffered from technological advances that displaced its members. In the early twentieth century, player pianos, jukeboxes, and the introduction of "talking" movies all affected live music. Musicians and even orchestras had been employed to create music for silent movies. Twenty-two thousand of them were uprooted when silent movies were replaced by the use of recorded sound.

James Petrillo was the president of the AFM from 1940 to 1958. Petrillo opposed the broadcasting of records, maintaining that they limited the jobs for musicians who played live. Under his "guidance," there were two strikes against record companies during the 1940s. The strikes were settled by the creation of a union bonus fund, called the Music Performance Trust Fund (MPTF). This fund entailed a small contribution for each record sold. The proceeds were used to sponsor free concerts at hospitals, nursing homes, and schools.[3]

MPTF turned out to be a good organizing tool for the union. The money was spread out to the five hundred locals of the union, and especially in the smaller ones playing less than a handful of gigs paid more than the equivalent of annual dues. The musicians who played on the recordings did not initially benefit from the fund, but lawsuits and negotiations eventually resulted in a split of MPTF's income, with half the money going to the fund and the other half funneled back to the musicians who actually played on the records. In Professor Michael James Roberts's book about the AFM, he maintains that the creation of the MPTF was a near-revolutionary act that returned money to the laborers who actually produced the product. The problem that I see with this notion is that, in fact, the MPTF fund did not initially return money to those who produced the product. As a result of agitation by recording musicians, these funds were split between the MPTF and the Special Payments Fund. This money represented a minor segment of employers' profits. Furthermore, when record sales declined, the funding for both groups diminished. Although the current union recording contract negotiated by former AFM president Ray Hair does include payments to the fund for streaming, the declining sales of CDs negatively affect the money that the fund receives from record companies.[4]

An article by Joey La Neve De Francesco in the March 2022 issue of *Jacobin* comes down hard on wealthy studio musicians for receiving income that was originally intended to support free performances of live music. He seems not to understand that all musicians who played on records receive income from the Special Payments Fund, not just the "fat cats" who did tons of sessions.

REPRESENTATION OF DIFFERENT MUSICAL CATEGORIES IN THE AFM, AND HOW THIS ORGANIZATIONAL SYSTEM EVOLVED

The AFM represents different constituencies, who over time have achieved representation in the structure of the union. Symphony musicians are represented by two groups. The larger, full-time orchestras are represented by ICSOM (the International Conference of Symphony and Opera Musicians) and the smaller regional orchestras belong to ROPA (the Regional Orchestra Players Association). Recording musicians who play on commercials, records, and films are represented by the RMA (Recording Musicians Association). A Theater Musicians Association (TMA), organized in 1997, is an AFM group that represents musicians who play in theatres. Although many union members are freelance musicians who work for numerous employers, there is no similar union organization that represents them. The AFM includes a Canadian branch, one of the last American unions to do so. There is a vice president from Canada, who attends meetings of the AFM executive board.

ICSOM

The International Conference of Symphony and Opera Musicians (ICSOM) owes its existence not to the AFM itself but to a group of Chicago Symphony musicians who felt that they were being underrepresented in the union's symphonic negotiations. They compiled a written survey of musicians from twenty-six different orchestras. This led to a meeting of symphonic musicians in Chicago in May 1962.

Symphony musicians had a number of issues that they wanted the AFM to address. They wanted to be able to ratify contracts for their own orchestras, rather than for the union to dictate the terms of such agreements. Other issues included establishing a pension fund and pushing the union to set up a symphonic division within the union to better represent their needs. Initially, the AFM was concerned that symphony musicians would secede and form their own union, as the studio musicians in Los Angeles did in 1950 with the Musicians Guild. This never occurred, and the AFM established a symphonic division as part of its organizational structure in 1969. ICSOM has its own newsletter, and its leaders attend regional and national AFM conventions. In looking at the origin and history of ICSOM, what seems to be most significant is that the organization was originally established despite the active opposition of the AFM leadership.[5]

RECORDING MUSICIANS ASSOCIATION (RMA)

The Recording Musicians Association represents musicians who play on recording sessions. It began in New York in 1969. As was the case with symphonic musicians, recording musicians felt that their interests were not being adequately represented by the AFM, in terms of both getting their input on wage negotiations and in ratifying the contracts made with employers in the record, film, and advertising businesses. For example, in the early seventies I was attending a pre-negotiation for the new contract for musicians who played on records. The AFM leaders read their proposal, which called for wage increases. The RMA was actually opposed to raising wages during that particular negotiation, because they felt that the record business was not doing well. Amidst an atmosphere of anger and frustration, it turned out that the AFM had never bothered to ask the RMA what issues they wanted to deal with at the negotiation. Gradually, the RMA became more of a partner than an opponent of the AFM, and it gained formal acceptance by the AFM in 1982.[6]

Other recognized subgroups of musicians within the AFM are the Organization of Canadian Symphony Musicians (OCSM), recognized in 1969, and the Regional Orchestra Players Association (ROPA), attaining this status in 1984. The Canadian group, ROPA, and the Theatre Musicians were recognized without the conflicts and controversies that marked the founding of ICSOM and the RMA.

MOVIN' ON UP; GROWTH OF THE UNION UNTIL THE MID-1970s

During the 1960s the Ford Foundation dispersed millions of dollars in a successful effort to professionalize symphony orchestras. The goal was to create fifty-two-week schedules for symphonic musicians, and also to establish endowments for these orchestras. In order to receive this money, orchestras were required to raise matching funds. The financial support of the Ford Foundation led to the successful creation of major symphonies as we know them today. Symphonies are highly unionized and the only non-AFM symphonies of any size are the Seattle Symphony and the New World Symphony in Miami. The Seattle Symphony has its own guild, formed after symphony members disaffiliated from the AFM in 1988, over a number of issues. This included the members' objection to paying steep work dues (4 percent of their salaries), and the possibility that exiting the AFM might bring opportunities to record for nonunion labels and film scores for nonunion film work. The Symphony did make some recordings for the nonunion Delos Records, but it remains for an intrepid graduate student to research what film scores or TV work that nonunion affiliation actually brought in on a long-term basis.

The New World Symphony is basically a training orchestra for players in the early part of their careers, so its lack of union affiliations is in a different category from the story of the Seattle Symphony.

There are over 1,200 symphony orchestras in the United States, but many of them entail part-time jobs with short seasons, as well as community symphonies, which contain a mixture of professional, semiprofessional, and amateur players. Community symphonies are often found in relatively small metropolitan areas. For example, in Colorado, Denver has a full-time AFM orchestra, while Fort Collins and Greeley have community symphonies.

ON BROADWAY

Broadway is possibly the most organized segment of the entertainment industry. Current wages are above $2,000 a week, with additional payments for playing multiple instruments, appearing on stage, and appearing on stage in costume. Off-Broadway shows represent a different picture: the larger theaters do have agreements with the AFM, but the smaller ones do not. Off-off-Broadway shows take place in smaller theaters and are not unionized. In most major cities, typically there is one unionized theater that features touring Broadway shows, but other local theaters are often not unionized.[7]

BONUS FUNDS

A variety of bonus funds, mostly union-sponsored, pay bonuses to musicians based on new uses or reuses. Commercials pay residuals for every thirteen weeks of uses. Film musicians get extra payments when films go to television, and musicians who play on TV shows get paid for reruns and foreign market uses. The AFM/AFTRA Intellectual Property Fund covers a variety of uses, including foreign ones, and I previously discussed the Special Payments Fund, which goes to musicians who play on recordings. Sound Exchange pays worldwide digital royalties but is not a union-administered fund. All of these funds can provide significant income for the busiest session players. The payment for each of these funds uses different criteria. For example, the Special Payments Fund pays bonuses based on the sale of all recordings, but the Films Fund pays musicians who played on a specific film.[8]

DECLINE AND FALL AND MUSICAL STYLES

Popular music styles change with some regularity. When a new style comes into vogue, the reaction of working musicians, especially older ones, is to question the musical validity of the style. In some cases, this is certainly an honest reaction, but in many cases, it reflects the fear of older musicians that they will be displaced by their inability or unwillingness to play the new music. In the early part of the twentieth century, that was the initial reaction to ragtime. As is often the case, over time ragtime was integrated into popular music, and it became referenced in all sorts of popular songs. A similar but more complex series of events occurred when jazz appeared on the musical scene. There are various quotes from music magazines that denounce jazz as the music of barbarians. A number of the early jazz bands only included African American musicians, and this undoubtedly was part of the initial white middle-class rejection of the idiom.

In its early incarnation, jazz involved extensive improvisation, as opposed to most American popular music styles. The latter often emphasized sight-reading skills. In this way, jazz was certainly a threat to the popular music musician who played at saloons or clubs. During the 1920s, Dixieland or New Orleans–style jazz became transformed into the swing idiom. Paul Whiteman was an important early purveyor of this style. It involved written musical arrangements and larger-sized bands, and many of the important swing figures, like Whiteman, Benny Goodman, or Artie Shaw, were white. Not all swing bands were white, however. There were Black territory bands like Jimmy Lunceford's or Jay McShann's, while bands of national stature like Count Basie and Duke Ellington toured widely. Many of the white pop singers of the 1940s and 1950s began their careers singing with swing bands. Artie Shaw and Benny Goodman were among the earliest white swing bands that included Black musicians or singers. A little later in this chapter, I will discuss the fact that the AFM was mostly not integrated, and separate Black locals existed alongside white ones.[9]

By the mid-1940s, jazz musicians started experimenting with more innovative and creative musical styles. This provoked the same sort of reaction from older musicians that jazz and ragtime had produced in earlier years. Although the majority of bebop musicians were Black, it was not unusual for older Black musicians to join their white colleagues in denouncing the new music. Because bebop was more technically difficult to play than earlier jazz styles, once again the older musicians tended to both dislike this music and to be afraid of it. Over time, these musical wounds were healed. Older Black players started to adapt to bebop, and an increasing number of the younger white jazz musicians also began to play it.

The AFM consists of both full- and part-time working musicians, although the number of part-timers had always exceeded the full-time group. Anything that represented a threat to musicians' ability to be employed has generally been regarded in a negative light by the AFM leadership. Because active union members often participate in the development and use of this technology, such as the use of synthesizers, this opposition is sometimes difficult to resolve.

CONGRESS TURNS ON LABOR

During the presidency of Franklin Delano Roosevelt, Congress passed the Wagner Act, a piece of legislation that opened the way for unions to organize the labor force. By the end of World War II, America had turned more conservative, and Congress passed two measures that seriously affected the AFM.

In 1947 the Taft-Hartley Act extended the rights of employees to refrain from participating in union activities. It also defined limitations on unions, eliminated secondary boycotts (boycotts undertaken against neutral employers who did business with another employer). It also set the stage for state legislation to establish "the right to work." The most critical part of the bill for the AFM eliminated the ability of musicians to negotiate directly with the purchaser of talent. This created havoc among casual musicians, where today's bandleader may be tomorrow's side musician. Bandleaders could no longer collect dues and turn them over to a union local. Essentially, this turned musicians who worked casual gigs into independent contractors.

In 1959 the Landrum-Griffin Act was passed. It further restricted boycotts and picketing and imposed codes of conduct on unions that were designed to limit unfair union practices.[10] The union challenged many of these provisions in the courts, and finally reached an agreement with the National Labor Relations Board (NLRB) in 1978. In 1982 the US Court of Appeals ruled that orchestra leaders and not hotels were the legal employers of orchestral musicians. The reader will recall that the AFM was organized into over five hundred local branches by the 1980s. The bulk of work in small towns and minor cities where many of these locals were headquartered centered around playing casual jobs like weddings or funerals, or playing music in bars or restaurants. The 1982 Court of Appeals decision basically made this system of widely dispersed locals far less practical because the union no longer controlled many of these jobs.

THE AFM AND SEGREGATION

In 1964 President Lyndon Johnson spearheaded the Civil Rights Act of 1964. At that time the AFM still had thirty-six segregated locals. Black union locals had their own offices, their own officers, and collected dues. Although many of the Black locals were in the South, many large northern and western cities like Los Angeles, San Francisco, and Seattle also were segregated.

As the civil rights era unfolded, the AFM began to feel pressure both internally and externally to integrate the locals. Los Angeles did not integrate its two locals until 1953, and St. Louis and Dayton did not integrate until 1971.

There are a number of reasons that the AFM lagged so far behind the politics of the civil rights movement. Some of the Black locals had staked out their own territory and feared that integrating with the white locals would lead to a loss of power within the federation and result in a reduction in Black union leaders. They also were loath to give up their offices and treasury to a new organization that might not act in their interests. The Black Seattle local actually had some white members who were jazz musicians who preferred to play with Black musicians; instead of affiliating with the white local, they joined the Black local. This also occurred in various other cities.

Members of Black locals were also concerned that uniting the locals would lead to a loss of work opportunities for Black musicians without necessarily leading to the sharing of work that previously came to the white groups. The AFM tried to allay these fears, partly by funding Black delegates to attend the national AFM convention.

The New York Local 802 of the AFM and the Detroit local have always been integrated. However, in the 1910s New York Black composer-arranger James Europe established a Black orchestra called the Clef Club Orchestra. It was a labor exchange, booking agency, and concert hall, and Europe presented Carnegie Hall concerts with a normal wind and brass group, but added mandolins, guitars, banjos, and multiple pianos. Europe did encourage his musicians to join the integrated local, but in effect he had staked out his own territory.[11]

MUSIC AND RACISM

The AFM has generally been "behind the curve" in creating opportunities for Black musicians. For many years there were only a handful of Black symphonic musicians. To combat this situation, the union encouraged symphonies to do auditions behind a screen, so that the race and/or gender of the auditioning musician could not be discerned. The problem with this approach is that playing with other musicians is a large part of working in a symphony, and if the musician remains invisible, no sensible judgments can be made about that aspect of the musician's abilities or temperament.

The Los Angeles local practiced de facto segregation in regard to studio work. Woodwind player Buddy Collette was hired to do the Groucho Marx

TV show in 1949, and was often featured on camera by Groucho. This was four years before the Los Angeles locals were integrated, so that Collette was technically a member of the Black local.[12]

During the 1960s a number of musicians known as the Wrecking Crew played on numerous recordings. These musicians were so sought-after that they demanded double the union minimum scale for recording. There was only one Black musician, Earl Palmer, who was a regular Wrecking Crew rhythm section player, although some other musicians, notably sax player Plas Johnson, appeared on sessions where saxophone solos were utilized. On the other hand, there were dozens of Black rhythm section players in New York who worked on recording sessions. At one point a group of these New York Black rhythm players made an unsuccessful attempt to get hired as a set group, demanding double scale.

I am unable to gauge why there weren't more Black rhythm section players in Los Angeles who broke into the Wrecking Crew, nor have I found anyone who can explain it.[13]

PROBLEMS ALL DAY LONG: LOSS OF MEMBERS AND THE AFM'S INABILITY TO ADJUST TO CHANGING CONDITIONS

Rock and roll made serious inroads on the work that AFM members had been doing. The music was combo-driven, rather than orchestral. Consequently, the fifteen-or-so-member swing bands that had been popular in 1940 turned into four- or five-piece combos. Michael James Roberts, writing in his book *Tell Tchaikovsky the News: Rock 'n' Roll, the Labor Question, and the Musician's Union, 1942–1968*, focuses on the AFM's attitude toward rock and roll music, and he attributes the AFM's decline in membership to this inability to deal with rock or the young musicians who were playing the music.

Initially I found this argument convincing, because during my service on the executive boards of the Denver and Portland, Oregon locals, and at various union functions, I experienced similar attitudes. When I started to compare the exact numbers of the union's membership, a different picture emerged.

I have no argument with Roberts's general idea. Earlier in this chapter I mentioned the attitudes of the AFM toward ragtime and jazz as being a combination of musical distaste and concern by older musicians about being displaced from employment because they had difficulty in playing a (then) new style of music. Just as the imagery associated with jazz included a sort of wild lifestyle, at least for the 1920s, rock presented itself as a weird conglomeration of music by "lower-class" musicians who dressed and performed flamboyantly, in the view of older, established pop musicians. To make matters worse, many rock musicians did not read music notation, and musicians in other music genres who did read music felt that automatically made rock players inferior creatures.

The problem with Roberts's notion is that the decline in AFM membership did not occur during the time period that he covers (1942–1968). If we look back at the origins and history of rock and roll, the music entered the pop charts in the mid- and late fifties. By the end of the fifties, Elvis was in the Army, Jerry Lee Lewis was essentially in hiding due to his marrying his thirteen-year-old cousin, Buddy Holly had died in an airplane crash, and Chuck Berry was in jail for violating the Mann Act and transporting women across a state line for "immoral purposes." What happened in American pop music was the revival of American folk music, and the beginnings of Motown, which could be described as sort of R&B pop. Folk music didn't especially appeal to AFM pop musicians, and rock music as such really only returned with its repurposing by Bob Dylan and the British musical invasion highlighted by the Beatles.[14]

If we take a look at AFM membership, there were 266,000 members in 1960, and 331,000 (the highest number ever achieved) in 1976.[15] If Roberts is correct in his theory, then why did union membership actually go up during the early years of rock and roll, and not down as he suggests? (Incidentally, according to Jay Blumenthal, the then-secretary-treasurer of the union, writing in 2023, AFM membership was 57,181 in 2021 and "continued to decline" in 2022).[16]

This raises a number of issues that are difficult to explain. Why did membership continue to grow during the 1970s when, according to Roberts, musicians were turning away from the AFM because of its negative attitude toward rock and roll? And how can we account for the drastic decline in membership in the ensuing forty years?

I am puzzled by why membership would continue to increase when the union basically was eliminated from the nightclub business. It is true that symphonies continued to grow during the 1970s, in terms of the size and number of the orchestras. This cannot possibly account for the 65,000 increase in membership from 1960 to 1976. Is it simply that union members continued to remain members as a matter of habit, until at some point they became convinced that they were not receiving sufficient value for their dues?

I find it easier to account for the later forty-five-year decline in membership. Disco and hip-hop music were not musical styles that lent themselves to being unionized. Disco is essentially electronic music. If the union had a different mindset, it might have sought to organize turntable artists and DJs. Since DJs and turntable artists work with preexisting records, this would have required a different attitude on the part of union organizers. It might well have irritated instrumental players who already found themselves displaced by electronics. By this time, the reader will undoubtedly have ascertained that flexibility has never been the strong point of the AFM.

Other musical styles that appeared, such as heavy metal and punk music, represent even more extreme styles of dress and performance than early rock styles. Today, more and more recordings are being done in home studios owned by the artists or band members. In many cases these recordings are released by the artists themselves, and not by record companies. Since the artist is the owner of the recording studio and the product, no money may actually be changing hands. Although the union uses the rhetoric that registering the work with the union will protect the artist against future issue by an actual record company, this is not a compelling argument to a twenty-two-year-old rock musician who may not expect or even want to get a recording contract from an actual record label.

MISSED OPPORTUNITIES

As stated in the numbers above, the AFM has lost over 80,000 members during the course of the last thirty-five years. Basically, the union has turned back to being a guild, as it was in the early twentieth century. Worse yet, the areas where the union does have some visibility and strength do not represent growing markets. The Broadway segment of the market seems somewhat stable, but no one is scurrying to open new theatres in New York. Virtually every major city already has a symphony orchestra, so growth in that area is unlikely. The record market has become more individualized and entrepreneurial than corporate, and the symphony orchestras are mostly supported through ticket sales and increased philanthropic support. As previously discussed, the market for freelance musicians working under union contracts musicians in clubs has largely disappeared. At the very least, consideration of the union's goals and structures needs reexamination. This is not an easy task to accomplish, but the alternative is to continue on the path to oblivion or extreme specialization.

INTERVENING INTERMEDIARIES

Consolidating with other unions is one possible path. The merged unions Screen Actors Guild and the American Federation of Television and Radio Artists (SAG/AFTRA) already represents singers, actors, and voiceover talent. According to their website, they have over 160,000 members, or almost three times the current membership of the AFM. SAG/AFTRA has a somewhat different organizational model than the AFM utilizes. Instead of several hundred locals, there are twenty-five regional offices. AFM locals have territories that vary from small to gigantic. The Denver local of the AFM, for example, covers the entire state of Colorado except for Colorado Springs and Southeastern Colorado. Its territory also reaches into Utah and Wyoming. AFM locals in New Jersey cover a much smaller territory.

Other unions or guilds in the entertainment field include the American Guild of Musical Artists (AGMA), which represents singers, dancers, and staging staff in opera, choral performance, and dance. AGMA has a membership of six thousand. The American Guild of Variety Artists (AGVA) represents variety artists, self-produced shows, theme parks, and circuses. It does not disclose its number of union members on its website. AEA (Actors Equity) represents over 53,000 actors and stage managers.

If all of these groups united in a single union, there would be almost 300,000 members. This consolidation could be organized in a way that limits expenses for officers and offices, but shares governance.[17] It is quite likely that the AFM leadership would be resistant to creating such a single, unified organization, but imagine how much more power would reside in the union if its membership included actors, singers, musicians, and dancers. There would also be considerable savings possible with the combining of staff and officers into a single group.

Another music organization is NSAI (the National Songwriters Association International), a songwriters' organization which recently bought a club called the Bluebird Café in Nashville to showcase the wares of its members. NSAI, according to its website, has almost five thousand members, and although it is headquartered in Nashville, there are eighty local chapters around the United States. These chapters hold workshops and regular meetings where members meet and critique each other's work. Incidentally, the dues are two hundred dollars a year, which is comparable to the price of AFM membership in many of its locals. NARAS (the National Academy of Recording Arts and Sciences) presents the Grammy Awards and also has a relief fund for poverty- or illness-stricken musicians called Musicares. As for the AFM itself, it includes problematic intermediaries that minimize the effectiveness of the union. For example, many recording artists have personal managers, who typically take 15 to 20 percent of the artist's gross income, and in some cases as much as 50 percent. Good personal managers function as advocates for musicians, dealing with booking agents, promoters, and record companies. These are all services that the union could conceivably provide for lower fees.

Another intermediary group are the various performing rights organizations that collect money for songwriters and publishers from airplay on radio and/or television. There are almost two million members of ASCAP, BMI, and SESAC. Obviously, there are many songwriters who are not professional musicians, but even organizing 5 percent of the members of this his group would almost double the membership of the AFM. The union could also become a factor in the signing of agreements with music publishers, as it is with record companies.

At various times the union has attempted to form its own booking agency, but this would obviously compete with existing booking agents, quite a few of whom are franchised by the union. For performing these services, it would be fair and logical for the union to take a small percentage of, for example, income from bookings. Technically, the AFM has a booking agency, but I am not aware of many musicians who actually utilize its services. Those musicians who can afford it also hire entertainment attorneys to deal with such entities as record companies, music publishers, personal managers, and contractual problems.

Another intermediary that is a barrier to the union pursuing direct action is in the form of contractors. These are the people who send the emails or make the phone calls that hire musicians for recording dates. Most contractors are or were musicians themselves. Although the union technically regulates breaks at various time periods and controls overtime payments, a musician who protests that these rules are not being followed risks that the contractor will not hire her for future work. In Broadway musicals, contractors deal with some additional complexities. Every musician has a list of five approved substitute musicians that the player can call to replace her. Some Broadway shows run for years, and the musician who has the job may use subs to alleviate boredom or may take another gig in order to play something different, or to pursue less commercial but more interesting music. There are only a handful of contractors who hire musicians for Broadway shows.

They are known as music coordinators. One particular coordinator, John Miller, is apt to have five or six or six shows playing at the same time. He generally will play one of the shows, but he appears on contracts for all the shows.

Broadway shows have unique problems in terms of working conditions. Some shows use special effects, and the smoke or fog generated to produce these effects may cause musicians to have short- or long-term sicknesses. Having to play the same difficult parts day after day, and doing so in a relatively small space, can produce carpal tunnel problems. In Catherine Mulder's book *Unions and Class Transformation*, she claims that John Miller insists that musicians arrive a half hour before the actual start time. Nothing in the agreement between Broadway producers and the union has such a requirement, but arguing with a busy contactor like Miller may result in his not hiring the musician for forthcoming shows. Since Broadway shows can run from anything from a few days to several dozen years, musicians are constantly jockeying for gigs in forthcoming shows. Displeasing a music coordinator is a surefire way to avoid being hired for a future show.[18]

MISSED OPPORTUNITIES

At this writing, unions are becoming more visible and effective in the workplace. Companies like Starbucks and Amazon are currently being organized. In some instances, it will take a bit of a leap of faith to organize a particular business. The music store chain Guitar Center currently has over three hundred stores and over 10,000 employees. The employees are teachers, sales personnel, and repair people. Since the retail clerks' union has never expressed any interest in unionizing Guitar Center, and many of its employees are directly involved in musical aspects of the industry, Guitar Center seems like a logical place to organize. Organizing mom-and-pop music stores is probably more difficult than useful, but other chain stores like Music Go 'Round have a substantial number of employees and locations. There are also a number of music stores that have three or more locations, and a few superstores that have only one location but employ dozens of teachers and extensive sales personnel.

Music stores that employ teachers have widely differing agreements. Some charge no rental at all, but hold the teacher responsible for recruiting students and collecting money from them. Other stores charge the teachers a percentage of their fees, but collect all the fees and book the students. The people teaching at music stores have a varied collection of needs. For the moonlighting graduate student, income is the primary concern. Older teachers are concerned about pensions and job security. Other matters for negotiation are cancellation policies and ways of increasing summer attendance. Typically, many music students follow the example of public schools and take summers off. This represents a major problem for anyone attempting to make a full-time living by teaching lessons.

There are also private or nonprofit music schools that represent opportunities for unions to organize workers. The Old Town School of Folk Music, the largest folk-oriented music school in America, with some 350 employees, recently unionized. They were organized not by the AFM but by the American Federation of Teachers.[19]

In recent years, unions have begun to cross industrial jurisdictions. For example, the UAW represents graduate teaching assistants and part-time employees in the University of California system. They recently won a strike for the 48,000 employees in the system. The same union represents the part-time teachers at the New School for Social Research, except that the AFM represents the part-time jazz faculty.

Many part-time college teachers make far less money and have fewer benefits than full-time teachers. Part-time music teachers are an especially large segment of college teaching programs, because many of these teachers teach a particular musical instrument. It has also been my experience, as both a tenured and part-time faculty member, that tenured faculty are somewhat disinterested, to be kind, in the working conditions that part-time faculty experience. The New School model might provide an excellent opportunity for the AFM to organize college music teachers

YOU CAN TRY, TRY, TRY, BUT WILL WE EVER WIN?

A number of problems with the functioning of the AFM essentially reflect a lack of contact or understanding of the needs of today's musicians. The problem also exists in reverse: many musicians know nothing about unions, resist the notion of music as being labor, and do not understand that many rights must be negotiated, rather than granted by corporate entities. I have observed this pattern repeatedly in my service on the executive boards of two AFM locals. For example: older symphony members recall that the fight for decent wages took place over a sixty-year period, and was not an accident but a function of sometimes bitter negotiations. There are few current members that were playing in the days when symphonic work was almost always a part-time, poorly paid gig. However, many of the (now) grey musicians had mentors or teachers who were actively playing during those pre–Ford Foundation days. Other symphony members recall what their full-time pay was, in say, 1980 or 1990, and the continual struggle between the union and the symphony board members in sometimes bitter negotiations or even strikes. To a newly hired, twenty-four-year-old violinist with a starting salary of over $160,000 in the San Francisco or Los Angeles Symphonies, the struggles mentioned may not appear to represent anything relevant to their current jobs.

The AFM has always been late to recognize the validity of new or emerging musical genres. In my experience, many union officers enjoy and/or perform either classical music or swing. Bluegrass, country and western, folk, rhythm and blues, rock and roll, and urban contemporary music are a riddle that they seem unable to unlock or understand. This is obviously a generalization, and doesn't apply to every single union officer. It is simply a commentary based on my observation and active participation in the AFM.

The current generation of musicians have developed an ever-increasing level of skills in developing their skills in individual entrepreneurship. They own their own home studios, set up their own record labels and music publishing companies, and in many cases, book their own gigs. Union rules about recording minimums, pension contributions, limitations on fees paid to booking agents, and negotiations with the older big, bad, record labels are all irrelevant to these musicians.[20]

It is interesting to compare the hiring process for symphony orchestras with the university system for hiring professors. In the academic world, résumés are submitted, references are checked, and a committee boils the choice down to three or four candidates. These successful candidates are invited to campus, where they teach a sample class, and meet with deans and faculties. All of their expenses are paid—air fare, hotels, and per diem food allowances.

In the symphony world, the candidate submits a résumé, an audition tape or video is required, and a committee selects worthy candidates, as is the case with college professors. This is where the similarity ends. First of all, it is not unusual that thirty-five or forty musicians remain after the initial résumé and tape screenings. The candidates travel to the audition site at their own expense. They then play for the audition committee, and three or four candidates make the semifinals. Looking at this process from a numerical basis, that means that of the people who actually have auditioned, 2 or 3 percent of the players remain in the mix. Since the majority of candidates are coming from another city, some thirty-five people have spent a couple of thousand dollars, including airfare, hotels, food, dry cleaning, and transportation to and from the airports.

Shouldn't the AFM, and the orchestras themselves, do their preliminary screening via live Zoom? The video could be eliminated to minimize any sort of racial or gender prejudice, just as it often is in live auditions.

Now we'd be down to, say, four candidates and the musicians who have been eliminated would have spent little or nothing to make it to the audition. The Zoom auditions could be held at local music schools, most of whom have reasonable recording facilities. Even if the applicant has to rent a studio, two hours of studio time for a solo musician would cost approximately $100. Imagine that you made the final rounds in the audition process in one of the major orchestras, where salaries are now upwards of $160,000 a year. Applicants are often impoverished graduate students barely scraping by or someone currently playing in a low-paying and/or less prestigious orchestra. The chances are that a musician will not succeed at their first audition, and may have to do three or four of them before they are offered a job. Why is the candidate responsible for these expenses when a major symphony has a budget in the millions, and where orchestral players are earning well over $150,000? It doesn't seem to occur to union officials or the full-time musicians in these orchestras, that eight thousand dollars to fund four semifinalists is literally a drop in the symphonic budget, while it often represents a hardship to the auditioning musician. A musician may find himself/herself doing multiple unsuccessful auditions in a single year.

Realistically, funding for auditions should be limited to orchestras that pay a living wage, and some controls could be set up. For example, if the auditioning musician is coming from a job that pays, say, $85,000, to apply for a chair in Los Angeles, then it would seem reasonable that this musician could pay his or her own expenses.

While we are on the subject of unpaid auditions, consider the various summer classical music festivals. The ones that are unionized are generally connected to a particular orchestra, like the Boston Symphony's connection with the Tanglewood Festival or the Chicago Symphony's participation in the Ravinia Festival. Many of the nonunion summer festivals are in expensive resort areas like Aspen, Colorado, Jackson Hole, Wyoming, Bellingham, Washington, and Jacksonville, Oregon. Who plays in these orchestras? Some of the participants are people from second-line symphony orchestras operating under union contracts in cities like St. Louis or Pittsburgh. During the bulk of the year, they are earning some $80,000–$100,000 a year under union contracts, yet during the summer they pay nonunion gigs for far less money. Why doesn't the AFM organize these orchestras, and why do the musicians accept inferior wages for playing? The union has taken the attitude that they don't want to rock the boat. Many of these festivals are world-famous, and the musicians enjoy the gigs because they are often attuned to more experimental or modern music, and especially for the musicians with families, this may represent a paid vacation. It would appear to be possible to take a creative approach to housing allowances as being part of the musicians' compensation, and then to put pressure on the musicians' home local to convince players to sign a union contract. Instead, these summer festivals make a mockery of the contracts that these musicians utilize some nine or ten months a year.[21]

This is not, however, the only larcenous treatment that music festivals inflict on musicians. The International Folk Music Alliance is an organization that sponsors an annual national conference, and also oversees four smaller regional organizations that have their own annual conferences. The 2023 Folk Alliance conference costs member attendees $600, and nonmembers $675. This does not include hotel fees, food, or transportation costs. The event lasts for five days, so the hotel and food costs are considerable. The regional conferences are somewhat shorter and less expensive, but represent some of the same costs to attendees—transportation, lodging, and food.

My musician friends used to refer to such conferences as "pay to play." In other words, not only does the musician not get paid, but she has to pay in order to *get to* play. Attendees include performers, agents, managers, venue operators, and booking agents. Why would any musician spend a couple of thousand dollars to appear at such a conference? I used to refer to this phenomenon as the Jimmy Fallon syndrome. The model is that the musician is playing the world's worst bar in North Platte, Nebraska. It's all good, because no musician can possibly tell when Jimmy Fallon's sixteen-year-old nephew is going to pop in and within days the musician will be whisked to perform on Fallon's show. As the saying used to go, if you believe this fantasy, there's oceanfront property I can sell you in Arizona!

The biggest irony of the whole Folk Alliance idea is that the musicians who attend are doing something resembling American folk music, including the esteemed protest songs of Pete Seeger and Woody Guthrie. This isn't a sleazy bar in Northern Nebraska, but an upscale conference hotel in a major city.

Another oddity of Folk Alliance practices is that there actually is a local of the AFM devoted to "traveling folksingers." It is one of the rare recently organized locals, started in 1993, and it represents traveling folksingers who rarely play repeatedly in a single territory. What has Local 1000 done about pay-to-play folk music conferences? Like so many of the nonfunctioning aspects of the AFM, it does little beyond sponsoring some of their own showcases. There is no picketing, and no open complaints. The irony of musicians paying to sing songs about homeless people and coal miners seems to have escaped the musicians who perform at the Folk Alliance and those who "hire" them.

One of the many aspects of the union that has suffered as the membership has declined is the AFM/EPW Pension Fund. For a sixty-five-year-old musician, in 2003 for each $100 paid to the pension fund, the musician received $4.65. In 2007 the number dropped to $4.35, in 2009 to $3.25, in 2009 $2.00, and the current benefit, starting in 2009 is $1.00. The explanation of these reductions is relatively simple to understand. There are more and more older members who actually have taken the pension, as opposed to younger ones paying into the fund. Why the AFM's financial advisers hadn't anticipated this is anyone's guess. By March 2021 the plan had about $2 billion in assets and about $3.4 billion in liabilities. However, Congress passed legislation that in 2022 enabled the Federal Pension Guaranty Corp. to continue paying benefits. Several other unions were in this position, besides the AFM.

What remains unclear is why the union's financial advisers didn't anticipate how serious this situation was until disaster was at their doorstep. Without the relief provided by this federal legislation, benefits would have been cut for pension recipients. This is another example of the AFM's unwillingness to confront reality.

PERFORMANCE ROYALTIES FOR ARTISTS

Although many artists write or coauthor their own songs, there are many artists who do not write songs. The United States is one of the few countries in the entire world that does not pay performance royalties to artists. As such, it makes common cause with China, Iran, and North Korea! The reader will recall from our discussion of performing rights organizations that songwriters and music publishers split royalties that come from radio airplay. In the United States, only songwriters and their publishers receive this income, not the performers who made the recordings.

Radio broadcasters have argued for years that performers don't deserve such compensation, because radio play is largely responsible for successful careers in music. That may be true, to a point, but on the other hand, without music, radio stations would have little or no listeners. All radio stations can't broadcast sports radio or political commentary.

Every two years for several decades a charade occurs in the US Congress. Representatives from states where the music business is a significant factor introduce some version of what is currently the Music Fairness bill. The bill contains provisions for radio airplay split between artists and record companies, with 5 percent going to musicians and background singers on records.

The AFM and other unions and music business organizations lobby members of Congress, and the bill may or may not make it through committee hearings. Supporters include conservatives like Senator Marsha Blackburn, from Tennessee, who represents a state where the music business is a significant economic factor. Opponents include politicians who have taken contributions from broadcasters, or even themselves own or partly own radio stations.

To the credit of the AFM, it maintains a lobbyist and actively supports this legislation. Over the years the bill has become more sophisticated, with very low royalties being demanded from small-town or public radio stations. The fact that this bill is still in limbo would lead one to believe that its proponents need to take more aggressive action. It's fine to have members of Congress taking selfies with Willie Nelson, but it might be more meaningful for artist celebrities to picket Congress and the White House, perform music, distribute circulars, and publicize these efforts to music fans.

The Music Fairness Act is an unfortunate example of the AFM trying to do the right thing, but not being able to figure out how to manipulate the media and politicians in order to support its cause.

WHAT'S BEEN DID AND WHAT'S BEEN HID: CONTRACTS AND ROYALTY ISSUES

It is widely acknowledged that many blues singers never received royalties, whether or not such payments were specified in their contracts. Part of the mythology of rock and roll history is that Atlantic Records was the shining light in world of rock and roll and rhythm and blues. It makes for an inspiring, if mythical, story. The two sons of the Turkish ambassador to the United States start a company in the room of a hotel where they are living. Ruth Brown, Stick McGhee, Solomon Burke, The Drifters, The Clovers, Ray Charles, and Aretha Franklin recorded for them. Atlantic soon built its own studios, run by the brilliant engineer Tom Dowd, and the records they issued were as much R&B as pop.

To continue the fairy tale: Ahmet Ertegun and his soon-to-be partner Jerry Wexler loved the music and the artists, who in turn cared about them. And they all lived happily ever after. It is truly a wonderful American-dream story. Black artists rescued from poverty by idealistic capitalists. If only it were true.

By 1950, Ruth Brown was recording what became a series of hit rhythm and blues recordings for Atlantic Records. By the 1980s she was broke and unwell, and at one point, never having received any royalties from Atlantic Records, she wrote Ahmet a ten-page letter. He gave her a check for $1,000. Welcome to the plantation! According to the record company, she was not entitled to royalties, because they claimed that the sales of her records never recouped the costs of recording, payment to musicians, production, and promotion.

In 1983 Ruth met a corporate lawyer named Howell Begle who happened to be a longtime fan. To make a long story short, Begle agreed to represent Ruth at no cost, later signing up a number of other Atlantic Records artists. At first the company insisted that they owed no money to Ruth Brown. Because Begle was a corporate lawyer, he excelled at developing allies in and out of the music industry. He discovered written memos revealing that the company did not know how many records she had sold in Europe over a ten-year period. He enlisted the Congressional Black Caucus in the fight. AFTRA joined the party. They were fascinated to discover that Atlantic had illegally withheld payments to the AFTRA Pension Fund. This is a violation of RICO, the federal racketeering act. By 1989 Atlantic capitulated and donated $1.5 million to start the Rhythm and Blues Foundation.[22]

You may be forgiven if you wonder why I am relating this story in a paper about the AFM, not AFTRA. The AFM did not join in on this struggle. Were they really sure that the studio musicians who played on all of those recordings had received union scale? Was the AFM aware that Atlantic was doing a considerable amount of recording in Muscle Shoals and Memphis and musicians in these cities were being paid union scale for each song, regardless of whether it had been recorded in fifteen minutes or fifteen hours?[23]

Do I need to mention that this totally violated union rules about recording sessions, which were supposed to last for three hours at a time and then go into overtime? The legend of the ever-honorable Atlantic Records dies hard. In preparing this chapter I read a current book by a former Rounder Records A&R man, Scott Billington. He was at an awards dinner when the widow of Johnny Adams, one of his artists, delivered an impassioned speech railing against the thieves at record companies. She claimed that Anglo record company executives and managers consistently stole from Black artists. According to Billington, Rounder was paying her on a regular basis, and when he confronted her about this, she claimed that she was not talking about him.

A few days later he got a call from Ahmet Ertegun, who had become a board member at the Rhythm and Blues Foundation. Billington paints Ahmet as a noble citizen who contributed funds to the R&B Foundation and modified ancient contracts in favor of aging R&B stars. Ahmet confided that the accusations that Judy Adams had leveled were simply part of the territory, and Billington should not be concerned about them. It is astounding to me that this story got printed in a book published in 2022. Is it actually possible that a person who did A&R for many rhythm and blues artists was unaware of the story of Ruth Brown and Atlantic Records? It does not seem plausible, but I suppose it is possible.[24]

This brings us to the story of Arthur "Big Boy" Crudup. Crudup had recorded for the famous publisher Frank Melrose. Crudup attained far more fame as a songwriter than as an artist. One of his tunes was called "That's All Right Mama." This song was a massive hit when Elvis Presley recorded it. Not all that surprisingly, Crudup received no royalties for his songwriting work. Dick Waterman was a white blues enthusiast who took on the management and/or agency representatives of a number of rediscovered blues artists. One of his clients was Crudup. When Waterman discovered that Crudup was not receiving songwriting royalties, he arranged a meeting at Hill and Range Music in Manhattan. In the early 1970s Crudup drove from Georgia in a Model A Ford to New York. Supposedly Hill and Range was going to pay him a flat fee of $60,000 to settle the claim.

A meeting at the publisher's office ended when the company decided it would be cheaper to fight in court than to pay Crudup off. The two brothers who owned Hill and Range, by the way were refugees from the Nazis! Crudup went back to Georgia and died a few years later. Following his lawyer's advice, Waterman filed a lien against Hill and Range. When Warner Chappell Music bought Hill and Range they needed to settle Crudup's claim. Crudup had died, but his four children cashed the initial check for $250,000, and the royalties collected in the following few years exceeded $3 million.[25]

I doubt that Crudup was an AFM member. But wouldn't it have been appropriate for the union to have stepped in to support his claims? Not to mention the publishing or recording royalties of many of their other older members, who were frequently cheated out of such income.

UMAW

The purpose of this chapter is to attempt to evaluate the possible functions of the AFM, and to compare them to what the union has actually done. As I was writing the final draft, I received an email from UMAW, a new Union of Musicians and Allied Workers. UMAW was founded in 2020. They are agitating to increase payments to artists who play at the world-famous SXSW Festival. UMAW even held their own better-paying showcases at the 2024 SXSW. Where is the AFM in this struggle? UMAW is attempting to get the city of Austin to stop providing any free facilities for the festival. According to the *Austin Monitor*, the AFM has offered verbal assistance, but its primary support appears to be the belief that federal labor laws can be utilized to remedy the problem. Meanwhile UMAW has succeeded in raising the wage scale at SXSW to $350 for bands, and $150 for solo or duo acts. UMAW is pushing for a $750 flat fee.

Many of the musicians and audience for this festival are exactly the sort of prospective members the AFM claims to want to cultivate. Or not. Is there room for two unions to protect musicians? Possibly in the future UMAW can be integrated as a sort of branch of the AFM. The prospect of making additional dues payments to a second union is unlikely to excite musicians. Rather, the AFM needs to recognize the level of frustration and powerlessness that many freelance musicians confront on a daily basis.[26]

ARTIFICIAL INTELLIGENCE AND LEGISLATION

Artificial intelligence represents a threat to all creative workers—writers, musicians, and so on. The companies that promote the development of AI include major internet players like Apple, Microsoft, and Alphabet (Google). AI creates a possible loss of income for creative workers, but record companies and music publishers are in effect possible winners and losers. If the cost of producing new product and the elimination or reduction of royalties are factored in, the record companies have much to gain. On the other hand, if creative product is available without having to pay usage fees, then record companies and music publishers lose income. This creates a dilemma for record companies.

Internet companies contribute to political campaigns of candidates for both political parties. It is difficult to predict how much this financial support will influence the actions of a future Republican or Democratic administration, but clearly the contributors will expect their donations to be rewarded by legislation representing their interests. This is quite similar to the situation with radio royalties for performers. Radio station chains' contributions to Congressional campaigns certainly have some effect on the chances of performing artists receiving radio royalties. To put it another way, corporations that have serious interests in limiting royalties to creative workers have stronger financial resources for lobbying than unions that represent creative workers.[27]

To put this another way, ASCAP, BMI, the large record companies, and major music publishers all are well funded, but they are dwarfed by the major internet companies. Ultimately, governing parties will have a small appetite for opposing the interests of one of their major funding sources.

NOTES

1. There are a number of useful labor histories. Most of this information came from Melvin Dubofsky and Foster Rhea Dulles, *Labor in America: A History*.
2. Dubofsky and Dulles, *Labor in America: A History*.
3. George Seltzer, *Music Matters: The Performer and the American Federation of Musicians*, 64–67, 77–80.
4. Selzer points out that many of the musicians who played MPTF gigs were actually part-timers, and in the smaller locals elected officials of the union sometimes made sure that they got many of the gigs.
Note: Some commentators, notably Joey La Neve DeFrancesco, frame the Special Payments Fund as an effort by greedy studio musicians to grab their share of a pie that should have gone only to musicians playing live.
The Musicians Guild originally represented a group of Los Angeles studio musicians, who wanted a share of the MPTF funds, but also had various grievances against the AFM. They were especially upset that musicians played a minor role in demanding better wages and working conditions, and did not get to vote to ratify these contracts. The Guild seceded from the AFM, and formed an independent union, that lasted from 1958 until 1961, when the Guild dissolved.
5. Julie Ayer, *More Than Meets the Ear: How Symphony Musicians Made Labor History*, 59–63.
6. Seltzer, *Music Matters*, 84–85, 107, 138, 153–55; Ayer, *More Than Meets the Ear*, 155; Catherine P. Mulder, *Unions and Class Transformation: The Case of the Broadway Musicians*, 25–340.
7. Not just the recordings that a particular musician has done.
8. Michael James Roberts, *Tell Tchaikovsky the News: Rock 'n' Roll, the Labor Question, and the Musicians' Union, 1942–1968*, 206; Seltzer, *Music Matters*, 83–85, 88–92.
9. Ayer, *More Than Meets the Ear*, 101–9.
10. Seltzer, *Music Matters*, 127–35; Roberts, *Tell Tchaikovsky the News*, 38–39.
11. See Reid Baxter, *A Life in Ragtime: A Biography of James Reese Europe*.
12. See Buddy Collette with Stephen Louis Isardi, *Jazz Generations: A Life in American Music and Society*. Also mentioned in numerous obituaries online.
13. Movie, *The Wrecking Crew* (2008). A documentary film directed by Danny Tedesco, son of Tommy Tedesco, one of the most famous members of the Wrecking Crew.
14. Roberts, *Tell Tchaikovsky the News*, 12–13, 7–8, 16–17, 139–40, 152–55, 168–71, 190–91, 94–198, 202–7.
15. Seltzer, *Music Matters*, 146, 157, prints the following membership totals: 1934. 100,000; 1957. 247,000; 1960. 266,000; 1970. 300,000; 1976. 331,000; 1983. 246,000; 1984. 231,000; 1985. 223,000; 1987. 210,000. David Gaylin, in his 2015 book *A Profile of the Performing Arts Industry*, adds the following membership numbers: 2000.116,000; 2011. 85,039; and 2012. 79,700.
www.statista.com lists both the percentage of union members, and the raw numbers, from 2000–2022. The percentage of employees in 2005 was 13.7, and the number of members was 15.69 million, in 2012 these numbers were 13.1 percent and 14.37 million, in 2019 11.7 percent and 14.57 million.
16. Column by Jay Blumenthal in *The International Musician*, December 2022.
17. The numbers come from the websites of each group or union mentioned.
18. Mulder, *Unions and Class Transformation*, 31, 42, 43, 58, 74. According to various websites, including his own, as of 2022 Miller had contracted over one hundred and thirty shows.

19. To be fair, there have been and are progressive voices in the AFM that grasp the various problems outlined in this chapter. Unfortunately, their attempts to change the direction of the union have mostly failed. Examples include the seemingly abandoned attempts to organize Tejano musicians in San Antonio, and the New York local's attempt to convince venue owners to contribute funds to set up a pension fund for jazz musicians. The Portland, Oregon, local came up with the notion of Fair Trade Music, a group that would include both union and nonunion musicians. A number of interesting meetings took place, but the group lacked a core of consistent attendees. The Seattle local actually convinced twenty-five venues to sign on to a musicians' code of conduct, and they also got the city of Seattle to create parking zones for musicians. The local's website doesn't show any recent activity. Local 1000, the traveling folksinger's union, has information about Fair Trade Music on its website, but no indications of recent activity.

20. For some years a number of artists have been producing, recording, and even distributing their own records. The late Diane Sward Rapaport began writing about this in her 1974 *How to Make and Produce Your Own Record*, which went through four editions through 1999. Since then most books about the music industry in the United States discuss this option, with varying degrees of coverage. From time to time, music trade publications like *Billboard* or the *Music Connection* also publish articles about artists producing their own records. A few artists, including Ani DiFranco and Holly Near, have even started their own record companies that distribute their own work, and the music of artists that they choose to help promote.

21. Boulder has an annual summer music festival that started in 1975. In 1978 it moved to Chautauqua, a park not far from the University of Colorado. The AFM began its attempts to organize the festival in 2014, and in 2024, after 100 percent of the eligible musicians signed union cards, organized the festival. An article in the AFM's monthly publications, the *International Musician* from July 31, 2024, by Stephen Laufer describes the difficulties of organizing a workplace that only functions on a temporary basis (in the summer), and includes orchestra members from all over the United States, Canada, and even Europe. The festival did not contest this representation, which was also complicated by the fact that part of the wages for the musicians of necessity includes housing. This is because virtually none of the musicians live on a permanent basis in Colorado. Many of the other summer festivals last for only one or several weeks, and are not run as full-time orchestras with a fixed conductor, music director, or full-time fund-raising personnel.

22. There are numerous references to Brown's struggle with Atlantic in the book that she wrote with Andrew Yule, *Miss Rhythm: The Autobiography of Ruth Brown, Rhythm and Blues Legend*. Robert Greenfield's book *The Last Sultan: The Life and Times of Ahmet Ertegun* is a generally positive biography of Ertegun, but confirms Brown's story. Much of the story appears on pages 295–99.

23. Christopher M. Reali, *Music and Mystique in Muscle Shoals*, especially 53–69.

24. Scott Billington: *Making Tracks: A Record Producer's Southern Roots Journey*, 120–21.

25. Dick Waterman, *Between Midnight and Day: The Last Unpublished Blues Archive*; Tammy L. Turner, *Dick Waterman: A Life in Blues*.

26. Chad Swiatecki, "Musician Advocates Decry City's Inaction on Fair Pay for SXSW Performers," *Austin Monitor*, March 8, 2024, www.austinmonitor.com/stories-2-24/03/musician-advocates.

27. See "Interest Groups," opensecrets.org, www.opensecrets.org/industries/indus?ind=C2100 and www.opensecrets.org/industries/indus?ind=B13.

BIBLIOGRAPHY

Ayer, Julie. *More Than Meets the Ear: How Symphony Musicians Made Labor History.* Minneapolis: Syren, 2005.

Badger, Reid. *A Life in Ragtime: A Biography of James Reese Europe.* New York: Oxford University Press, 1995.

Billington, Scott. *Making Tracks: A Record Producer's Southern Root Music Journey.* Jackson: University Press of Mississippi, 2022.

Brodine, Russell V., with Virginia Warner Brodine. *Fiddle and Fight: A Memoir.* New York: International Publishers, 2001.

Brown, Ruth, with Andrew Yule. *Miss Rhythm: The Autobiography of Ruth Brown, Rhythm and Blues Legend.* New York: Donald I. Fine Books, 1996.

Collette, Buddy, and Stephen Louis Isardi. *Jazz Generations: A Life in American Music and Society.* Berkeley: University of California Press, 2000.

Cornfeld, David. *Beyond the Beat: Musicians Building Community in Nashville.* Princeton, NJ: Princeton University Press, 2015.

DeFrancesco, Joey La Neve. "When Musicians Went on Strike—and Won." Jacobin, March 6, 2022. https://jacobin.com/2022/03/1940s-musicians-strike-american-federations-of-musicians-afm-labels-streaming.

Dubofsky, Melvin, and Foster Rhea Dulles. *Labor in America: A History.* 8th Edition. Wheeling, Illinois: Harlan Davidson, 2010.

Gaylin, David H. *A Profile of the Performing Arts.* New York: Business Express, 2015. Chapter 6, "Performing Artists and Their Unions."

Gebhardt, Nicholas, and Tony Whyton, eds. *The Cultural Politics of Jazz Collectives.* New York: Routledge, 2015.

Greenfield, Robert. *The Last Sultan: The Life and Times of Ahmet Ertegun.* New York: Simon and Schuster, 2011.

Miller, Leta E. *Union Divided: Black Musicians' Fight for Labor Equity.* Champaign: University of Illinois Press, 2024.

Mulder, Catherine P. *Unions and Class Transformation: The Case of The Broadway Musicians.* New York: Routledge, 2009.

Reali, Christopher M. *Music and Mystique in Muscle Shoals.* Urbana: University of Illinois Press, 2022.

Roberts, Michael James. *Tell Tchaikovsky the News: Rock 'n' Roll, the Labor Question, and the Musicians' Union, 1942–1968.* Durham, NC: Duke University Press, 2014.

Seltzer, George. *Music Matters: The Performer and the American Federation of Musicians.* Metuchen, NJ: Scarecrow Press, 1989.

Waterman, Dick. *Between Midnight and Day: The Last Unpublished Blues Archive.* New York: Thunder's Mouth Press, 2003.

CHAPTER 7

ALL THAT JAZZ
CIA, Voice of America, and Jazz Diplomacy in the Early Cold War Years, 1955–1965

Lt. Col. (USAF, Ret.) James E. Dillard

The Cold War was a critical juncture in the twentieth century, the "American Century," and the United States refined essential elements of information warfare, including overt and covert propaganda campaigns, open-source and clandestine radio broadcasts, and soft-power diplomacy. As World War II drew to a close in 1945 with the surrender of Germany and Japan, the United States faced an uncertain future. Victory over fascism, renewed focus on the home front, and the specter of a nuclear age framed the joys and anxieties of postwar America. The lofty ideals of the war left the victors many new obligations. If, as many believed, the war had been at least in part a battle against racism, did not racial segregation and disenfranchisement belie the great sacrifices the war had wrought? The commitment to democracy had been sealed in the blood of soldiers Black and white, red and brown. Democracy, under siege throughout the 1930s and early 1940s as fascist militarists threatened the balance of power, was more than a political system. It was an ideology, a set of beliefs about the nature and moral power of the nation.

What remained to be determined, as the rest of the world watched, was the way this ideological commitment to egalitarian democracy would be put into practice as the great ideological confrontation between the United States and the Soviet Union was just beginning.[1] With the nuclear genie out of the bottle and the consequences of military conflict so dire, the two superpower antagonists would choose to keep their weapons of mass destruction on a tight leash; instead, they would try to wreak havoc on each other's systems by waging a protracted information warfare campaign leveraging both overt and covert elements. A key component of modern information warfare and the propaganda battle for hearts of minds was the coordinated State Department, Central Intelligence Agency, and Voice of America effort to use international radio broadcasts of news and music, to include overseas jazz concerts, to devise a narrative suited to US national security interests.

Meanwhile, many Americans began asking if the desire to return to normalcy would mean a renewed embrace of racial norms of segregation, disenfranchisement, and subordination—representing the legacy of two centuries of African American slavery and another century of Jim Crow "separate but equal" politics North and South. Or would international pressures paradoxically soon constrain and enhance civil rights reform as the Cold War dawned? As the new administration of President Harry S Truman cast Cold War politics in apocalyptic terms; as "McCarthyism" took hold in American politics, society, and culture; as the nation closed ranks against so-called "subversive" elements, civil rights groups walked a fine line, seeking to portray their reform efforts as closely aligned with the contours of American democracy—not as a challenge to it or a way to undermine it. Indeed, the early years of the Cold War would not accommodate strident criticism of colonialism. Western European colonial powers, after all, were America's Cold War allies.[2]

CIVIL RIGHTS AND THE COLD WAR

Only when official Washington determined it was in the United States' interest to showcase its democratic ideals as a beacon of freedom, racial equality, and opportunity did civil rights advocates begin to find common cause with powerful government and business elites. In the vanguard of a concerted effort to respond to international criticism of American race relations were the US State Department, the Voice of America (VOA), and the Central Intelligence Agency (CIA). Truman and his able Secretary of State, Dean Acheson, turned the story of race in America into a story of the superiority of democracy over communism. The government took steps to silence alternative voices, such as Paul Robeson's, when they challenged the official narrative of race and democracy in America.[3] VOA radio broadcasts by Leonard Feather and especially Willis Conover helped lay the groundwork for the emergence of jazz ambassadors such as Duke Ellington, Louis Armstrong, and Dizzy Gillespie to bring the sounds of freedom to audiences from all over the East Bloc. With the United States in the throes of a political and cultural revolution putting the Black freedom struggle at the center of domestic and international politics, the prominence of African American jazz artists proved crucial to the music's potential as a Cold War weapon of choice. High-profile concert tours allowed US officials to pursue a self-conscious campaign against worldwide criticism of US racial policies and laws. In doing so, the United States strived to build cordial relations with emerging African and Asian postcolonial states. The glaring contradiction in this strategy was that for several years after it was adopted by Truman and his successor Dwight D. Eisenhower, the United States promoted Black artists as goodwill ambassadors—symbols of the triumph of American democracy as a stark contrast to Soviet oppression—when America was still a Jim Crow nation. Race as a social construct operated culturally to project an image of American nationhood far more inclusive than the reality.[4]

The most effective response to foreign critics ultimately was to achieve dramatic social change at home. The Truman administration's civil rights efforts, including a sustained reliance on national security arguments in briefs before the Supreme Court that would overturn the constitutional basis for Jim Crow, culminated years later in the landmark *Brown v. Board of Education* case (1954), when the Supreme Court held that school segregation—a key target of foreign criticism—violated the US Constitution. *Brown* powerfully reinforced the story of race and democracy already being told in State Department propaganda and VOA radio broadcasts. Future Supreme Court Justice Thurgood Marshall's triumph in arguing the *Brown* case lent needed credibility to the notion that our democracy enabled social change and was based on principles of justice and equality.[5]

JAZZ DIPLOMACY AND VOA

In the eyes of much of the world, US credibility grew immeasurably in the wake of the landmark court case. Leveraging this renewed sense of democracy's moral superiority in the Cold War ideological arena, Conover's VOA jazz show, begun in 1955 and continuing for the next three decades, became a popular instrument of American diplomacy and African American jazz. It is tempting—and not altogether inaccurate—to claim that Conover, a mild-mannered, bespectacled white man with a deep, baritone voice made for radio, was a figure of unparalleled importance in spreading "jazz diplomacy" at the height of the Cold War.[6] As with the contributions of Radio Free Europe (RFE) and Radio Liberty (RL), US officials and media analysts invoke the experience of VOA to suggest how "soft power" can be used to "win hearts and minds" among a worldwide audience. As an instrument of CIA covert propaganda programs and State Department public diplomacy,

VOA's radio broadcasts featuring prominent African American jazz artists played a vital role in US foreign and security policy during the first three decades of the Cold War.[7]

"Propaganda," a term with an often negative connotation in the English-speaking world (especially in the wake of Joseph Goebbels's successful Nazi propaganda campaigns during Adolf Hitler's Third Reich), took on different hues during the late 1940s as the Cold War heated up. "Information with a purpose" was how many State Department and CIA officials described both overt and covert propaganda efforts—a central mission of US foreign policy as a way to counter Soviet propaganda and "misinformation" in the contest for the minds and loyalties of men and women around the world. One 1950 Senate resolution called for "international propagation of the democratic creed through a Marshall Plan in the field of ideas."[8] CIA and VOA became linchpins of the new propaganda offensive; radio, its technological instrument.

In February 1947 the VOA began its first broadcasts into the Soviet Union, shortly before the Marshall Plan—offering aid to any country willing to renounce communism—marked a major escalation in Cold War tensions in 1948. The Berlin Blockade and the communist takeover of Czechoslovakia soon prompted enhanced international broadcasting and covert propaganda efforts. In 1950 RFE emerged in Munich, Germany, broadcasting into Poland, Czechoslovakia, Romania, Bulgaria, Hungary, and Albania. While VOA stepped up overt propaganda broadcasts to the East Bloc countries, CIA channeled confidential funds and policy control to RFE. By the end of the Truman administration CIA was supporting a similar effort, Radio Liberty, broadcasting directly to the people of the Soviet Union. Both RFE and RL gained the cooperation of foreign émigrés who had fled communist-controlled countries. These émigrés delivered commentaries and led discussions, using their expertise in the arts, history, and religion. CIA considered RFE and RL a vanguard in a broad counteroffensive, using overt and covert resources, to challenge and rebut Soviet broadcast propaganda. Meanwhile, VOA gained increased power and prestige in official Washington, and its budget doubled between 1946 and 1950. The Truman administration asserted that "the propaganda effort of the USSR, now bordering on open psychological warfare, is a major threat to US foreign policy objectives" and that "a psychological offensive by the United States based on truth is essential if the United States is to succeed." The role of the VOA grew exponentially, largely because "the ability of radio to surmount the man-made barriers of censorship and suppression and to speak directly to the people" made it a crucial force multiplier globally for the State Department, CIA, and US national security interests.[9]

"THEY LOVE JAZZ BECAUSE THEY LOVE FREEDOM"

Central to the success of the VOA broadcasts to mass audiences in the Soviet Union, East Bloc, and Third World were the so-called "jazz ambassadors," who entertained and educated millions. Since many of the jazz artists also happened to be African American, they fulfilled a dual role of enhancing the American narrative of racial equality and social justice while celebrating democratic ideals of free market capitalism and freedom of expression. Among the most popular jazz musicians filling VOA's broadcast hours were Duke Ellington, Dizzy Gillespie, and Louis Armstrong.[10] US officials quickly learned that jazz was more valuable than didactic programming. Conover's show featured opening theme music from the Ellington orchestra's signature piece—"Take the A Train" by Billy Strayhorn—followed by Conover's salutation, "Time for jazz!" Broadcasting for one hour, seven days a week, fifty-two weeks a year, Conover gained enormous influence on how audiences listened to what *Time* magazine called "this valuable exportable US commodity, jazz."[11]

Several surveys indicated that by the 1960s Conover was the second most recognized American in the Soviet Union after Richard Nixon.[12] Musicians such as Ellington, Gillespie, Woody Herman, Dave Brubeck, Stan Getz, Lionel Hampton, and Oscar Peterson became foreign language students, learning words and phrases in Czech, Polish, Romanian, Bulgarian, and Hungarian. They would use these words and phrases in taped interviews with foreign disc jockeys, and the interviews were aired along with records by the featured American jazz artists. American diplomacy and soft power had no better friends than Conover and his collection of notable jazz musicians. Their music became the quintessential universal language of a free world trying to break down barriers and influence thinking and political ideas in over fifty nations under communist domination or susceptible to its influence.[13]

While Conover shunned overt propaganda, he believed deeply in the political and cultural importance of jazz. He described jazz as "structurally parallel to the American political system," an embodiment of American freedom. "Jazz musicians agree in advance on what the harmonic progression is going to be, in what key, how fast and how long, and within that agreement they are free to play anything they want." For people behind the Iron Curtain, he said, "jazz represents something that is entirely different from their traditions."[14] Conover believed that people who were denied freedom in their political culture could detect a sense of freedom in jazz. He asserted, "Jazz is a cross between total discipline and total anarchy. The musicians agree on tempo, key and chord structure, but beyond this everyone is free to express himself. This is jazz. And this is America. That's what gives this music validity. It is a musical reflection of the way things happen in America. We are not apt to recognize this over here, but people in other countries can feel this element of freedom. They love jazz because they love freedom."[15] Claimed one jazz artist, "No one did more to end the Cold War than Willis Conover."[16] How did Conover touch so many hearts in so many faraway lands? Adam Makowicz, a world-famous jazz pianist, was fourteen years old and studying classical music in Poland. One night, Makowicz recalled, "a friend brought a short-wave radio, a scarcity at the time, and a group of us congregated around it to listen to that new, enchanting, improvised music, coming from Willis's program on the Voice of America. We were hooked! From then on, every night at 11 p.m. sharp, we were tuned to shortwave to await, with anticipation, what would follow the famous 'Take the A Train' theme, and the announcement *This is Music USA— Jazz Hour*. That music, open to improvisation and coming from a free country, was our hour of freedom . . . it helped us to survive dark days of censorship and other oppression."[17]

Conover's views coincided with many Cold War–era intellectuals, such as Alfred Barr, director of the Museum of Modern Art, who claimed that "modern artists' nonconformity and love of freedom cannot be tolerated within a monolithic tyranny." For Barr, "abstract was synonymous with democracy."[18] Yet Conover and the musicians he featured on his show knew that jazz could speak to America's Achilles heel of racism in ways that a Mark Rothko or Jackson Pollock painting could not. Conover noted that jazz helps people "identify with America" and "corrects the fiction that America is racist."[19] Still, many of the Black jazz artists had views that subtly and often not so subtly differed from Conover's. For them, America's democratic ideals were something to aspire to, not something already achieved. Jazz—like democracy, freedom, and civil rights—was a work in progress, unfinished and imperfect.[20]

Even as artists and critics were promoting jazz's status as America's "classical" music—a term coined by Ellington— and its value to US Cold War diplomacy, its newfound utility was aiding its rehabilitation in mainstream popular culture. *Billboard*, which called itself the amusement industry's leading newsweekly, hailed jazz's "recently acquired vestments of legitimacy and respectability." Music critic Burt Korall wrote, "The Voice of America, Radio Free Europe, and the Armed Forces Radio Network have exposed much of Europe, Asia, and Africa to the sounds of jazz. Jazz has succeeded where American diplomats have floundered. It has created a meeting ground, been something that made for a deeper understanding of the American way of life, for to be interested in jazz is to be interested in things American."[21] Indeed, by the mid-1950s, just as Conover's VOA broadcasts were first becoming popular abroad, on US shores—from New York to California—jazz was widely celebrated in establishment and middlebrow circles alike as a pivotal cultural weapon of the Cold War, and *Newsweek*, *Variety*, and *The New York Times* all ran major feature-length stories about jazz's role in the ideological conflict between the United States and the Soviet Union.[22]

JAZZ AND THE COUNTERCULTURE OF MODERNITY

The State Department's claim that jazz embodied a unique American freedom transcending race collided with the experiences of many of VOA's Black musicians while growing up in the Jim Crow era of racial segregation and violence, including lynch-mob justice. Other Black jazz performers began to invoke what Paul Gilroy has called an African American counterculture of modernity.[23] "Modern jazz" to these Black artists connoted mobility and freedom but also meant a return to the roots of the African diaspora's intricate rhythms and sounds. Moreover, the leftist political ideologies of a few entertainers made them persona non grata with VOA tours abroad. For example, Mary Lou Williams, a talented jazz composer and pianist who had joined the Gillespie Band for a performance of the *Zodiac Suite* at the 1957 Newport Jazz Festival, was denied a visa to join a State Department tour. Many Washington officials regarded her as too "unstable," citing her "religious fanaticism." Dancer and choreographer Katherine Dunham repeatedly was rejected for State Department tours partly in response to her avant garde ballet *Southland*, which critiqued the South's history of African American lynchings.[24]

State Department and VOA cultural policy was often as improvised (though not as skillfully) as the solos of jazz artists. While arguments linking freedom and modern art helped promote the Museum of Modern Art and led to the display of Pollock's canvases in US embassies throughout Eastern Europe during the 1950s, conservatives in Congress frequently denounced new art forms as "subversive" and "un-American." Such outspoken criticism of government sponsorship of the arts led to more covert efforts by the CIA in the propaganda wars. During the Cold War, the CIA provided key support for many purportedly independent artistic and intellectual projects—in tandem with VOA radio broadcasts. Far from covert, however, the VOA jazz tours remained highly visible and celebrated in the international media. Nonetheless, state sponsorship of jazz radio programming garnered constant attacks from vocal conservatives in politics, business, and the American media. State Department officials ultimately tried to shield integrationist and modernist imagery of the jazz tours from critical audiences at home. Drawing particular criticism was Duke Ellington, whose 1940s production *Black, Brown and Beige* had challenged racial hierarchies. Ellington had also collaborated with a musical fundraiser for the Council on African Affairs, a radical anticolonial organization.[25]

Ironically, it was precisely the absence of a coherent and effective cultural policy at the State Department that created a space for VOA's unique alliance of artists, supporters of the arts, and liberals to project a jazz vision of America on the world stage. Whether fostering informal musical connections after hours or backstage, pursuing romantic liaisons, or expressing political opinions in interviews and while on stage, VOA's coterie of jazz musicians gave their own personal spin on the parallels between jazz and American freedom. The State Department jazz tours illuminated connections and collisions between domestic and foreign policy agendas . . . and between race, nation, and modernism. The immediate success of concert tours by Ellington, Gillespie, Armstrong, Hampton, and dozens of other jazz artists not only testified to the newfound importance of modern jazz, but also the vociferous opposition to the tours, especially among Southern whites and conservative congressmen, indicated deep fissures within a nation only beginning to emerge from Jim Crow political, social, and cultural paradigms. In April 1956, with a Dizzy Gillespie tour under way and four months into the Montgomery bus boycott, the White Citizens Council of Alabama, formed to resist desegregation, announced its opposition to jazz. The council called jazz a "plot to mongrelize America" engineered by the National Association for the Advancement of Colored People (NAACP). According to *Newsweek*, Asa Carter, leader of the North Alabama Citizens Council, had said that "be-bop, Rock and Roll, and all Negro music" were designed to force "Negro culture" on the South. Segregationists claimed that having the VOA send Gillespie and his kind around the world to sell overseas audiences on jazz (and to represent the nation) portended the end of the world as they knew it.[26]

They were right.

CONTROLLING THE NARRATIVE ON CIVIL RIGHTS AND AMERICA'S DEMOCRATIC VALUES

When critics of US race discrimination traveled overseas in the 1950s—before and after the Supreme Court's *Brown* ruling—they posed a powerful challenge to the US government's narrative of race in America. The Eisenhower White House determined the story of progress in race relations, measured through laws and social change, could best be protected if such challenges were contained, controlled, and managed. Paul Robeson and W. E. B. Du Bois, among others, discovered their ability to travel overseas was curtailed in the early 1950s. Robeson (through song) and Du Bois (through political organizing) generated international interest in US racial problems. Du Bois had created a stir in 1947 when he signed NAACP and Civil Rights Congress petitions claiming that African Americans "suffer from genocide as the result of the consistent, conscious, and unified policies of every branch of government."[27] Such controversial pronouncements often were exploited by Soviet propagandists and international media reporting. When Robeson and Du Bois criticized glacial progress on desegregation and education and employment policies affecting the Black community in America, the State Department confiscated their passports, effectively denying them access to an international audience.[28]

Just as the Eisenhower administration began cracking down on leftist Black critics of its civil rights policies, events in Cold War hot spots created new opportunities for jazz artists to reach international audiences in new and creative ways. The first major VOA jazz tours sent Dizzy Gillespie to the Middle East in 1956, Benny Goodman to Southeast Asia in 1957, and Dave Brubeck to Poland and the Middle East in 1958—into the very teeth of global crises where US and Soviet interests clashed. The United States used a complex array of covert and overt military and diplomatic means to enhance strategic and economic interests in Berlin, Iraq, India, the Congo, Vietnam, Poland, and Latin America.[29]

Why did US policymakers send jazz to the rescue during foreign policy crises? What was the Cold War "common sense" that made sending musicians into the preludes and aftermaths of coups d'etat seem normal to policymakers, journalists, supporters of the arts, and the artists themselves?

The story of the early VOA-sponsored jazz tours takes us into the world of postwar internationalism and the boisterous one-upmanship of the Cold War. The masculine adventurism of the 1950s elevated covert action into a cult of counterinsurgency.[30] Indeed, many of the jazz tours moved in a world of espionage where the tensions between cultural exchanges and ideological belligerence were played out. Jazz pianists and trumpeters lived in close proximity to coups and proxy wars. As European colonial empires collapsed in the decades following World War II, US policymakers opted not to supplant European colonialism but to assert that the United States had a legitimate right to lead the "free world." The nation pursued global economic integration through modernization and Third World development programs. The CIA became enmeshed in Middle East, Southeast Asian, and Latin American covert action initiatives, which pointedly overlooked the fact that not every nationalist leader or group had communist allegiances. The overthrow of popular leaders in Iran, Guatemala, Africa, and Indonesia depended on ethnocentric assumptions that limited Third World agency and independent-minded thinking by colonial peoples yearning for the same freedom and democratic values the CIA ostensibly was trying to protect and expand.

Fortunately for their State Department handlers, virtually all of the jazz musicians who toured abroad to spin the official narrative of racial equality and the free enterprise system's inherent superiority to Soviet oppression shared an abiding patriotism and pride in all things American. Gillespie himself often recounted how the unparalleled visibility of the Southern civil rights struggle—embodied in the Montgomery bus boycott and the peaceful marches of Martin Luther King Jr.—brought unprecedented national and international attention to American racism and civil rights groups. For the Black jazz artists like Gillespie, Armstrong, and Hampton, patriotism and democratic struggle went hand in hand. They looked upon the foreign tours as a way to combine a chance to work, promote a big band, serve one's country, meet fellow musicians around the world, and contribute to the civil rights cause. For national security professionals planning and implementing the new jazz diplomacy in tandem with broader policy goals, covert aspects of the VOA-sponsored tours remained opaque. As a result, neither the musicians nor State Department personnel directly involved in staging the music events were fully aware of the far-reaching objectives or political actions surrounding the tours. The full extent of the covert nature of many of the era's so-called diplomatic initiatives would not be known for decades, long after such actions had succeeded in undermining not only Soviet ambitions but also incipient democratic and nationalistic agendas in a host of Third World countries in Asia, Africa, and Latin America.[31]

The jazz artists sometimes were not necessarily welcomed with open arms by US Foreign Service personnel abroad. With government involvement in the arts anathema to many Americans, coupled with violent white resistance to the civil rights movement, musicians encountered quite a few surly segregationists among the embassy staffs. Gillespie and Brubeck often remarked that they could easily sense the political tensions and the high level of military security surrounding their every movement on foreign soil.[32]

By the same token, the Black artists also came in contact with hundreds of allies who seized upon the power of jazz to rescue the image of America and promote a liberal, internationalist vision in an egalitarian world. It was no accident that the first State Department jazz performance took place in Abadan, Iran—"to the smell of crude oil and the sound of gunfire from nearby Iraq"—at the heart of the former British Empire, in a country rich in that coveted Cold War commodity, oil. Three years earlier, in 1953, Iran had been the target of the first CIA-backed coup, which ousted Prime Minister Mohammad Mosaddegh and installed the Shah. American firms had gained entry into the Iranian oil industry and acquired big profits selling Iranian crude on the world market.[33] Over the next decade, jazz musicians would return to Iran numerous times, and the Dave Brubeck Quartet and the Duke Ellington Orchestra would even find themselves in the middle of Iraqi coups in 1958 and 1963, respectively. Beginning in Iran, Gillespie's inaugural tour traveled to Syria, Lebanon, Pakistan, Turkey, Yugoslavia, and Greece. In doing so, he and his band were navigating Eisenhower's conception of a "perimeter defense" against the Soviet Union along what later generations would call "the crescent of crisis"—from Turkey to Pakistan. In 1955 the United States had signed the Baghdad Pact, an anti-Soviet mutual defense treaty, an alliance with important new Cold War–era security partners in Turkey, Iraq, Pakistan, and Iran.[34] Gillespie's jazz diplomacy in 1956 was adding a culturally charged exclamation point to the new relationships being cultivated by embassy staffs and CIA station chiefs throughout the Middle East.

Retracing Gillespie's itinerary, one can also read US policymakers' anxieties about the coming Suez Crisis. As the twenty-two-piece Gillespie Band rehearsed in New York City in March 1956 for its State Department tour, the coordinated British, French, and Israeli attack on Egypt in the Suez War of 1956 was still more than six months away.[35] President Eisenhower and Secretary of State John Foster Dulles, however, were deeply preoccupied with Middle East tensions. They were suspicious of the nonaligned politics of Egyptian President Gamal Abdel Nasser, and they feared he was falling under Soviet influence.[36] Dulles, the architect of Eisenhower's containment policy and later an advocate of massive retaliation in the event of a Soviet first strike, had demonstrated his contempt for nonaligned politics at the time of the Bandung Conference in 1955. A year later he declared that neutrality "has increasingly become an obsolete conception" and that it was "immoral and shortsighted."[37] Still, neither Eisenhower nor Dulles wished to antagonize nationalist sentiment in the Middle East, Asia, and Africa; nor did they want to be associated with British or French colonialism in the region.[38] Such sentiments led to US defiance of its European allies when the Suez War erupted.[39] Sending Gillespie and his band on tour would be a "soft power" way to shore up the support of allies and persuade those on the fence to distinguish the United States from the declining European colonial powers. The United States also sought to rebut charges by nonaligned leaders (especially Nasser and India's Jawaharlal Nehru) that America's racism and imperial ambitions made a mockery of its claims to lead the Free World by championing democratic, free-enterprise values.[40]

With his spell-binding virtuosity, arresting trumpet solos, and egalitarian sensibility, Gillespie won over huge audiences wherever he traveled—from sophisticated fans in Beirut, to habitués of the underground jazz scene in Yugoslavia, to villagers in East Pakistan who had probably never before heard jazz. So popular was Gillespie that a Pakistani newspaper editorial argued that "the language of diplomacy ought to be translated into the score for a bop trumpet."[41] Observing Gillespie's crowds in Yugoslavia, the US ambassador wired Washington that "Gillespie's band had made our job much easier."[42] *The New York Times* reported from Beirut that the band's reception was "beyond expectations" and that US diplomats "hope the noise stays in the walls for a long time to come."[43]

THE BROTHERHOOD OF JAZZ

The State Department soon learned that with Gillespie they got a lot more democracy and a lot more action than they could have imagined. If US diplomats had already come to appreciate the failure of didactic propagandists, Gillespie's candor must have been refreshing. "I sort of liked the idea of representing America, but I wasn't going to apologize for the racist policies of America. I know what they've done to us and I'm not going to make any excuses."[44] Deeply aware of the politics behind the tours, Gillespie never hesitated to defy State Department and local convention, promoting his own vision of America. For Gillespie and his band, the tours meant long overdue recognition from a society that had failed to acknowledge the contributions of Black jazz artists. Quincy Jones, who helped with many of the band's music arrangements, said, "We were pissed off, but like the black soldiers of World War II, we kept keepin' on."[45] Overseas the band encountered patronizing ignorance on the part of embassy officials, who knew little about the history of African Americans or jazz's contributions to America's musical legacy. Jones called some of them "alcoholics who rode around in air-conditioned limousines almost too big for the dirt roads" in places like Pakistan and Greece. Jones recalled that a cultural attaché in Athens "advised his staff not to mingle with us" and "informed his female staff that in the United States, respectable girls did not mix with Black jazz musicians."[46]

Gillespie, Jones, and the rest of the band's contingent suffered the insults but enthusiastically embraced the intertwined civil rights and foreign policy agendas. However obnoxious they might become, racist US diplomats and embassy staffers could not derail Gillespie's personal civil rights agenda. Many people in Europe and Asia thought that Black musicians had no opportunities and never mingled with white artists. When those people saw that the mixed-race Gillespie band was a cohesive and extremely talented unit, they realized that what they had been hearing and thinking was off the mark.[47] The musicians were struck by the sheer novelty of what they were doing. The State Department tours took them to exotic places that simply would not have been possible without government sponsorship. Usually playing three concerts a week while on tour, the musicians found time to meet local artists. In Ankara, Turkey, tenor saxophonist Billy Mitchell and trombonist Rod Leavitt played with Turkey's top trumpeter, Muvaffak Falay, at a local hot spot. At the next night's concert, Gillespie gave Falay an engraved cigarette case "in token of the brotherhood of jazz."[48] In Ankara, Jones met Arif Mardin, who handed him a score so impressive that later, back in the States, Jones used the arrangements on Voice of America. Jones also obtained a scholarship for Mardin at Berklee College of Music in Boston.[49]

The early jazz tours' greatest value, according to many New York music critics, was the ability to portray jazz as a distinctly American idiom. Jazz was born and grew up in the United States. No other country could make such a claim on the genre. Many people in foreign lands considered jazz a new and impressive contribution to culture. Music critic Marshall Stearns wrote in his *Saturday Review* column, "Jazz is one of America's best-loved *artistic exports*."[50] For Stearns, Gillespie had not only won friends for the United States; he had succeeded in elevating the art of jazz.

On December 7, 1956, Benny Goodman and his orchestra embarked on a seven-week tour of Thailand, Singapore, Malaya, Cambodia, Burma, Hong Kong, South Korea, and Japan. Fearing that Southeast Asia would go the way of Communist China, Eisenhower and Dulles had authorized extensive covert operations in Indonesia, Burma, Cambodia, and Laos. Thailand remained a strategic bulwark against the spread of communism. Goodman's orchestra charmed the foreign audiences, and they reciprocated with decorations and honorary titles.[51]

Nothing better exemplifies the infusion of diplomatic bravado into the early jazz tours than the chaotic tour of the Dave Brubeck Quartet in 1958.

Brubeck was sent across the Iron Curtain into East Germany without a visa; then to Poland, Turkey, Afghanistan, Pakistan, India, and Ceylon; then finally straight into the Middle East crisis of 1958 and a coup in Iraq.⁵² On an artistic level, the reverence Brubeck felt for non-Western forms of music they encountered could be heard in their own evolving style.⁵³ In Iran the group played before local and expatriate elites in performances cosponsored by the Iranian Oil Refinery Company and the US Information Agency (USIA). In July, shortly after the group left Iraq, a nationalist revolt overthrew the Iraqi monarchy and established a regime friendly to the United Arab Republic, threatening the Baghdad Pact and challenging US oil interests in the Persian Gulf. Long seen as "an island in a sea of instability," Iraq had become yet another Middle East powder-keg.⁵⁴

In the early Gillespie, Goodman, and Brubeck tours from 1956 to 1958, despite logistical chaos and the backdrop of international turbulence, jazz musicians exceeded State Department expectations as ambassadors. They charmed audiences, journalists, and embassy personnel. Their irreverence, egalitarianism, and creative brilliance as musicians achieved far more in winning friends than any sanctimonious pronouncements of US superiority. For the musicians, the tours brought international cultural capital as artists and civil rights emissaries.⁵⁵

COLD WAR CRISES AND INTERNATIONAL BROADCASTING'S RESPONSE

Under the direction of President Eisenhower's administration (1953–1961), all information activities, including international broadcasting, were transferred from the State Department to the new USIA. As part of this shift, broadcasting resources grew leaner and budgets smaller. As the war in Korea reached a bitter stalemate and an armistice agreement was signed to end hostilities, which had led to more than 580,000 casualties among South Korean and US troops, bloody conflict erupted on the streets of Budapest, Hungary, in 1956. US radio commentaries via RFE and RL may have been partly to blame. When US intelligence officials gained access to the text of a historic and inflammatory speech by Nikita Khrushchev to the Communist Party Congress in which he denounced Joseph Stalin, RFE and RL rebroadcast the speech to Eastern European audiences. Within weeks mass uprisings erupted in Poland and Hungary, where thousands demanded the lifting of repressive measures linked to the Stalin regime. The Poles avoided a direct military clash with the

USSR, but in Hungary over 200,000 Soviet troops and 2,500 Red Army tanks put down open rebellion against the Soviet system, creating a wave of several hundred thousand refugees.[56]

RFE and RL were targets of harsh criticism by Hungarian émigrés in the aftermath of the failed rebellion. Socialist Party leader Bela Kovacs, for example, claimed that "U.S. radio misled Hungarians into believing they could count on effective U.S. aid in the event of trouble with the Soviets."[57] Hungarians, indeed, had been understandably encouraged and emboldened by the broadcast of Western press reviews and correspondent reports conveying (accurately) the widespread sympathy throughout the United States and Western Europe for the cause of the Hungarian rebels. European leaders fanned the flames of rebellion when RFE reported the words of Etienne de la Vallee-Poussin, chairman of the Council of Europe in Belgium, who said: "Today we are only speaking, but tomorrow we will have to act. History is marching along at increased speed. The rigidity of the Soviet system is not the same as before. Let the unity and determined attitude of the West be the answer. Only thus can we solve the essence of the question: the problem of the united, indivisible, and free Europe."[58]

This was the dilemma—as relevant today as it was in Hungary in 1956—of an external communicator who accurately conveys news and information into a region beset by a political crisis but risks its misinterpretation by the audience as signifying the promise of specific outside assistance or support for a particular cause when such is not the case. Responsible journalism can thus lead to inadvertent incitement—as happened in Hungary. The Hungarian people's belief in RFE as a symbol of American power is testimony to the influence that RFE came to assume. In the end, the historical record demonstrates that the journalistic lapses of the RFE Hungarian Service, while serious, could not by themselves have inspired, provoked, or prolonged the Hungarian Revolution or caused the Soviet Union to suppress it so brutally. Nor, by any reasonable reading, could the US government's policy guidance to RFE in 1956—and American and European expressions of sympathy—nurture the hopes of Hungarians for Western military intervention.[59]

When John F. Kennedy became president, he hired Edward R. Murrow as the new USIA director. Murrow, a legend in radio and television news broadcasting dating back to the London Blitz in World War II, elevated international broadcasting to a higher priority in US foreign policy. During the Kennedy years, VOA, RFE, and RL broadened the scope of their responsibilities and increased their budgets. The rise of Cuban dictator Fidel Castro brought East-West tensions to America's doorstep. In response, Kennedy boosted VOA's

Spanish-language broadcasts to counter increasingly strident anti-US sentiment in Latin America. The Bay of Pigs fiasco, a failed CIA-sponsored invasion of Cuba in April 1961 to overthrow the Castro regime, not only was an embarrassing foreign policy defeat for the new US president; it was also damaging to the credibility of VOA and Radio Swan, a CIA-funded clandestine station whose sole purpose was to discredit Castro. A year later the Cuban Missile Crisis pitted the United States against the Soviet Union, and Kennedy prompted the VOA to patch together a network of commercial radio stations that flooded Cuban airwaves. With the help of RFE, VOA clarified the US position on Soviet missile deployments to Cuba, and a worldwide audience listened intently as the crisis played out in the press in October 1962.[60]

Just as Americans and radio audiences around the world were taking a deep breath once the Missile Crisis was resolved, they began to hear more and more about another small country on the other side of the world, where another Cold War battleground was taking shape—Vietnam. The Cold War indeed had many faces and places, but for many African Americans—disenfranchised and impoverished after decades of slavery and segregation—the real battleground was not on the streets of Budapest or Havana or Saigon but at home in the mean streets of Detroit, Los Angeles, Little Rock, and Birmingham.

SATCHMO

The first and only official State Department tour by Louis Armstrong, known throughout the world as "Satchmo," almost never took place. Distressed by the Eisenhower administration's civil rights policies and the refusal of the Justice Department to enforce court-ordered desegregation in Little Rock, Arkansas, in 1957, Armstrong refused to become a jazz ambassador until 1960. Instead, he became involved in support of the civil rights movement's sit-ins and freedom rides. Armstrong toured Ghana as a private citizen and was quoted as saying, "The way they are treating my people in the South, the government can go to hell."[61] He also remarked after the Little Rock school desegregation crisis, "It's getting so bad a colored man hasn't got any country."[62] For obvious reasons, both Armstrong and the State Department were initially reluctant to team up for a good will tour celebrating American jazz and the superiority of America's way of life. Satchmo, however, was not the only American concerned about the Little Rock crisis. Secretary of State Dulles told Attorney General Herbert

Brownell that he was "sick at heart" and that the violence there was "ruining our foreign policy. The effect of this in Asia and Africa will be worse for us than Hungary was for the Russians."[63]

While on a commercial tour of South America, Armstrong showed how critical he could be as an unofficial goodwill ambassador. According to *The New York Times*, the "almost simultaneous" appearance of US Air Force stunt fliers and Louis Armstrong in Rio de Janeiro was "an unplanned coincidence." With US prestige suffering in the wake of the Sputnik launch, however, "jets and jazz are having a favorable impact, and the United States is again the talk of the day here."[64] Issues of civil rights had been contained in the early jazz tours of Gillespie, Goodman, and Brubeck, but Armstrong's Ghana trip and his later denunciation of Eisenhower during the 1957 Little Rock crisis illuminated the connections between domestic and foreign policy.

As State Department officials responded to charges of US racism, they also were increasingly forced to respond to criticisms of escalating US intervention in Africa. Since World War II, the United States had designs on mineral-rich Katanga Province in the Belgian Congo. So began the courtship of Satchmo to bring a positive American story to Africa. This time he accepted the challenge. When Armstrong and his band embarked on his 1960–61 tour of Africa, he, like almost all US citizens, was unaware that CIA Director Allen Dulles had ordered the CIA station chief in Leopoldville (now Kinshasa) to have the recently elected prime minister of the Belgian Congo, Patrice Lumumba, assassinated. The centrality of the Congo crisis set the tone for the Armstrong tour. Looking back on his visit to Katanga Province, Armstrong liked to comment that his jazz tour had stopped a civil war so that a daylong truce called by both sides would allow people to hear him perform. He did not know at the time of his visit that Lumumba had already been arrested and was being held and tortured by US-backed rebels. Lumumba would be assassinated in January 1961, while Armstrong and his band were still playing their jazz on the continent.[65]

For Armstrong, like the African audiences for whom he played, freedom remained an aspiration, not an achievement. The 1964 Civil Rights Act and the 1965 Voting Rights Act, while milestones on "freedom's road," were not an end but a beginning. That was because Armstrong and his generation of Black musicians, like their fellow African Americans in the auto factories, steel mills, farms, hospitals, and road construction crews across the nation, had fought too hard to quit now. The struggle would go on—in the United States and around the world.

THE SENIOR STATESMAN OF JAZZ

Less than two weeks after King's march on Washington on August 28, 1963, the Duke Ellington Orchestra left New York for Damascus, Syria, embarking on the first of many State Department tours. The tour followed on the heels of Ellington's production of *My People*, a musical revue commemorating the one-hundredth anniversary of Abraham Lincoln's Emancipation Proclamation. The Southern Christian Leadership Conference's Birmingham campaign in May and the August march on Washington provided a dramatic political backdrop for the overseas tour. Television footage of Birmingham Police Commissioner Bull Connor's vicious dogs and fire hoses turned on Black children had shocked people around the world. The turmoil in Birmingham embarrassed the Kennedy administration and pressured him to take unprecedented action on the civil rights front, which he called "a moral crisis."[66] The young president would soon find in the senior statesman of jazz the ideal ambassador for an important cultural exchange tour—now that the eyes of the world were closely watching King's stewardship of the civil rights movement's passive resistance campaigns.

Ellington, sixty-four years old when the tour began, had achieved international recognition as a composer, pianist, and bandleader. Ellington's worldliness as an international celebrity and his experience in leading a Black band in Jim Crow America meant he was uniquely suited to contend with the tensions in the Cold War cultural exchange visits to the Middle East and Southwest Asia. He was not only a patriot but also a sincere believer in his country's Cold War mission of promoting the superiority of American democracy. Along with Lionel Hampton, he was one of the very few Republican jazz musicians touring for the State Department.[67]

Ellington's tour to Damascus brought his orchestra into the most tumultuous US–Middle East relations since the overthrow of the Iraqi monarchy in 1958. The Eisenhower Doctrine had declared the need to defend the Middle East against communist aggression. Reflecting on the significance of the band's tour in Cold War hot spots, Ellington turned a *New York Herald Tribune* interview into a personal commentary on how the world viewed the progress of African Americans' civil rights struggle back home. He also noted that his State Department handlers did not require him or his band members "to restrain ourselves in the expression of our personal, political, social or religious views. As citizens of a free country, there are no restrictions on our tongues. We are to speak as free men."[68]

The assassination of President Kennedy on November 22, 1963, brought an abrupt end to Ellington's successful tour, which had also included stops in Jordan, Afghanistan, India, Ceylon, Pakistan, Iran, Iraq, Lebanon, and Turkey. Devastated by the news, Ellington stayed up late that night composing memorial music. In summing up the tour a few years later, Ellington said he hoped his audiences understood that "the music of my race is something more than the American idiom. It is the result of our transplantation to American soil, and was our reaction in the plantation days to the tyranny we endured. What we could not say openly we expressed in music. It expresses our personality." To export American culture was to export its hybrid nature, complexity, tensions, and contradictions. To export jazz was to export, in the words of Ellington, "an American idiom with African roots."[69]

COLD WAR CULTURAL LEGACIES

The goodwill ambassadors' understanding of jazz as an international music complicates the traditional characterization of jazz as "America's music," a label used by VOA's Willis Conover. Armstrong, Ellington, and Gillespie embraced the tours as opportunities to make claims on a nation that had long denied them recognition as artists, and human and civil rights as African Americans. Yet for these musicians, jazz was never solely an expression of the nation. Jazz was an international and hybrid music combining not just African and European forms but forms that had developed out of an earlier mode of cultural exchange—through the circuitous routes of the Atlantic slave trade and the overlapping diasporas created by migrations throughout the Americas.[70]

The jazz ambassadors represented America at a unique historical juncture. The Cold War, the African American civil rights movement, and the emergence of forty new African and Asian nations created the context in which the jazz ambassadors projected the optimism and vitality of Black American culture throughout the world. Through the jazz tours and through the VOA broadcasts, the music of the jazz ambassadors reached from Kabul, Leningrad, Damascus, and Tehran to Baghdad, Bombay, Karachi, and Kinshasa. The music reached even into the prisons of apartheid. For all the contradictions of Cold War internationalism, the global freedom movements of the post-1945 years helped forge an alliance of musicians, supporters of the arts, and liberals in the State Department. These policymakers and musicians gave US foreign policy an egalitarian edge. All over the world, the United

States came to be associated with jazz, civil rights, African American culture, and egalitarianism—not because the jazz ambassadors claimed to represent a free country, but because they identified so deeply with freedom struggles everywhere. In a fundamental way, the musicians were cultural translators who inspired the vision and shaped its contours, and they asserted their right to "play for the people."[71]

The story of jazz and the State Department, the CIA, and Voice of America is not the story of a nation standing apart from and unsullied by imperial power. It is the story of an America deeply implicated in the machinations and violence of global modernization: the slave trade that forced millions of Africans to voyage in chains to the Americas; the US involvement in CIA-planned coups in Iran, Iraq, Guatemala, and the Belgian Congo; and the arming of military tyrannies in Egypt and Pakistan. These events established the context for the tours. The relationship between jazz and the State Department and CIA fiefdoms reveals a Janus-faced power, at once unprecedented in its world-ordering ambitions and often too self-absorbed to understand the immediate and long-term consequences of its actions. Not only were jazz artists deployed in proximity to covert and overt military campaigns but also in the broader sense of "culture" as structures of feeling and material life. As we retrace the journeys of Armstrong and Brubeck and Ellington and Gillespie to Cold War hot spots like Iran, the Congo, and Pakistan, we also retrace the geographic patterns of those quintessential Cold War commodities, oil and uranium, along with many others critical to America's material affluence—the wealth that was so seductive to overseas audiences.[72]

The jazz ambassadors were not privy to the highly opaque and often covert political and economic agendas that accompanied their tours. Nor were they entirely innocent of them. Nonetheless, there is no doubt what side most of the musicians were on. Cheering the masses who cheered them and donning the vestments of modern African diasporic solidarity, the jazz ambassadors sided with the forces of change and innovation, liberation and true democracy. They used the global platform their country had given them to promote the dignity of Black people and their culture in the United States and abroad. For the State Department and official Washington, the jazz tours showed the power of music to legitimize and humanize, and to compel critics of our nation's policies to identify with America as an ideal. Intended as a color-blind promotion of American democracy, the tours underscored the importance of African American culture in the Cold War redefinition of America—to polish the image of American democracy and make it appear more inclusive and integrated than the reality.[73]

The jazz ambassadors projected the opposite of arrogance and belligerence that many had come to associate with US foreign policy in the wake of the Bay of Pigs, coups in Africa, and the Vietnam War. Audiences fell in love with the jazz ambassadors for all the ways they voiced their affinities with people struggling for freedom. Audiences never confused or conflated their love of jazz and American popular culture with an easy acceptance of US foreign policy. They learned to hate us less because they learned to love the message that Dizzy and Satchmo offered them: We are more alike than we are different. In spite of the fear and anxiety caused by the Cold War, as Armstrong would sing in his raspy baritone, "What a Wonderful World" it is.

💣 💣 💣

Author's Note: The views expressed in this article are those of the author and do not reflect the official policy or position of the Defense Intelligence Agency, the Department of Defense, or the US government.

NOTES

This chapter originally appeared as "All That Jazz: CIA, Voice of America, and Jazz Diplomacy in the Early Cold War Years, 1955–1965" by James E. Dillard, *American Intelligence Journal* 30, no. 2 (2012): 39–50. Copyright © 2012 National Military Intelligence Association. Reprinted with permission.

1. Mary L. Dudziak, *Cold War Civil Rights: Race and the Image of American Democracy* (Princeton, NJ: Princeton University Press, 2000), 9–11.
2. Dudziak, 11, 25–26.
3. Dudziak, 15–16.
4. Penny von Eschen, *Satchmo Blows Up the World: Jazz Ambassadors Play the Cold War* (Cambridge, MA: Harvard University Press, 2004), 5–6.
5. Dudziak, 15–16.
6. Von Eschen, 13–14.
7. A. Ross Johnson, *Radio Free Europe and Radio Liberty: The CIA Years and Beyond* (Washington, DC: Woodrow Wilson Center Press, 2010), 1–6.
8. US Department of State, *Foreign Relations of the United States* (Washington, DC: US Government Printing Office, various years), 1950, IV, 315.
9. J. Tyson, *U.S. International Broadcasting and National Security* (New York: Ramapo Press, 1983), 28.
10. Von Eschen, 18–24.
11. Von Eschen, 14.
12. Terence P. Ripmaster, *Willis Conover: Broadcasting Jazz to the World* (Lincoln, NE: iUniverse Press, 2007), 56.
13. Von Eschen, 16–26.
14. William F. Ryan, "Willis Conover: Nightspots of Washington and the World—The Seismic Jazz Underground," *Virginia Country* 14, no. 1 (1989), 68.

15. Unattributed article, "Who Is Conover? Only We Ask," *New York Times Magazine*, September 13, 1959.

16. Ripmaster, 40.

17. Alan L. Heil, *Voice of America: A History* (New York: Columbia University Press, 2003), 290.

18. Frances Stonor Saunders, *The Cultural Cold War: The CIA and the World of Arts and Letters* (New York: New Press, 1999), 256–57.

19. Saunders, 256.

20. Von Eschen, 17.

21. Burt Korall, "Jazz Speaks Many Tongues, Vaults National Barriers: Wider Jazz Market a By-Product of American Diplomatic Policy," *Billboard* (August 19, 1957), I.

22. Von Eschen, 18.

23. Von Eschen, 20.

24. "Cultural Presentations: List of Attractions—Newport Jazz Artists," October 24–November 11, 1975, Bureau Historical Collection.

25. Saunders, 256.

26. Anonymous, "White Council vs. Rock and Roll," *Newsweek* (April 23, 1956). See also Brian Ward, *Just My Soul for Responding: Rhythm and Blues, Black Consciousness, and Race Relations* (Berkeley: University of California Press, 1998).

27. Gerald Horne, *Black and Red: W. E. B. Du Bois and the Afro-American Response to the Cold War, 1944–1963* (Albany: State University of New York Press, 1986), 15, 78.

28. William C. Berman, *The Politics of Civil Rights in the Truman Administration* (Columbus: Ohio State University Press, 1970), 66.

29. Von Eschen, 27.

30. Christina Klein, *Cold War Orientalism: Asia in the Middlebrow Imagination, 1945–1961* (Berkeley: University of California Press, 2003), 19–60.

31. Von Eschen, 28–30.

32. Von Eschen, 40–42.

33. John Foran, "Discursive Subversions: Time Magazine, the CIA Overthrow of Musaddeq, and the Installation of the Shah," in Chris Appy, ed., *The Political Culture of American Imperialism, 1945–1966* (Amherst: University of Massachusetts Press, 2000).

34. Douglas Little, *American Orientalism: The United States and the Middle East since 1945* (Chapel Hill: University of North Carolina Press, 2002), 128–29.

35. Anonymous, "Dizzy to Rock India: Gillespie and Jazz Group to Tour East and Balkans," *The New York Times* (February 2, 1956), 19.

36. William Roger Louis, "Dulles, Suez, and the British," in Richard Immerman, ed., *John Foster Dulles and the Diplomacy of the Cold War* (Princeton, NJ: Princeton University Press, 1990), 134–35.

37. Thomas Borstelmann, *The Cold War and the Color Line: American Race Relations in the Global Arena* (Cambridge, MA: Harvard University Press, 1999), 113.

38. Louis, 134–35.

39. Borstelmann, 102.

40. Dudziak, 34–35 and 104–5.

41. Anonymous, "Indians Dizzy over Gillespie's Jazz," *The Pittsburgh Courier* (June 9, 1956).

42. Leonard Feather, "Norman Granz: Millionaire," *Esquire* (January 1957), 100.

43. Anonymous, "Gillespie's Band a Hit in Beirut: American Jazz, Sponsored by State Department, Packs the Middle Eastern Halls," *The New York Times* (April 29, 1956), 124.

44. Dizzy Gillespie with Al Fraser, *To Be or Not to Bop* (Garden City, NY: Doubleday, 1979), 414.

45. Quincy Jones, *Q: The Autobiography of Quincy Jones* (New York: Doubleday, 2001), 112.

46. Jones, 112.

47. Jones, 112.

48. Marshall Stearns, "Dizzy's Troupe Casts Spell over Mid-East Audiences," *Down Beat* (June 13, 1956).

49. Jones, 113.

50. Stearns, "Is Jazz Good Propaganda? The Dizzy Gillespie Tour," *Saturday Review* (July 14, 1956), 30.

51. Von Eschen, 43–44.

52. Von Eschen, 46–51.

53. Von Eschen, 46–51.

54. Von Eschen, 46–51.

55. Von Eschen, 56–57.

56. Johnson, 80–103.

57. Kovacs's allegations were reported by the American Legation in Budapest on November 19. "Telegram from the Legation in Hungary to the Department of State, November 19, 1956," Document 198, in *Foreign Relations of the United States, 1955–1957*, XXV.

58. Johnson, 115.

59. Johnson, 117.

60. P. Washburn, *Broadcasting Propaganda: International Radio Broadcasting and the Construction of Political Reality* (Westport, CT: Praeger Publishers).

61. Gary Giddins, *Satchmo* (New York: Doubleday, 1988), 160–65.

62. Giddins, 160–65.

63. Dudziak, 131.

64. Anonymous, "Hot Jazz Trails Hot Jets to Rio," *The New York Times* (November 21, 1957), 20.

65. Madeleine G. Kalb, *The Assassination of Lumumba* (London: Verso, 2001).

66. Von Eschen, 122.

67. Von Eschen, 123.

68. Von Eschen, 127–29.

69. Von Eschen, 122–25.

70. Von Eschen, 250–51.

71. Von Eschen, 252.

72. Von Eschen, 251–54.

73. Von Eschen, 251–54.

CHAPTER 8

MUSIC AS TORTURE / MUSIC AS WEAPON

Suzanne G. Cusick

EXORDIUM

This paper reports on the earliest stages of a project that began not in my musicological work but in a moment of my real life. In spring 2003, I was reading Nuha al-Radi's *Baghdad Diaries*, an account of her life before, during, and after the first Gulf War. I read "After the war ended, the Allies spent all day and all night flying over our heads, breaking the sound barrier. Just like Panama when they blasted Noriega, holed up in the Vatican Embassy with music. For fifteen days, Bush deafened the poor ambassador and Noriega with hard rock. Our torture went on for months—20 or 30 times, day or night . . ." (al-Radi 1998, 58).

"So," I thought, "perhaps it wasn't just silliness, the actions of bored or excitable soldiers who'd seen *Apocalypse Now* too many times. Perhaps it was a policy." As press reports conflating music's use on the battlefield with its use in interrogations proliferated, I began desultory research on a phenomenon of the current "global war on terror" that particularly wounds me as a musician, wounds me in that part of my sensibility that remains residually invested in the notion that music is beautiful, even transcendent—is a practice whose contemplation would always lead me to contemplation of bodies and pleasures. Not bodies in pain.

It is not my intention here to engage the moral, ethical, and political debates around torture, interesting as they are. Rather, I offer today a rough taxonomy of the complex subject denoted by my title—the US government's use of sound and music as a battlefield weapon and its use of music during the interrogation of "detainees" in the current GWOT. It is a taxonomy peppered with questions and speculations about the ways that these uses of music interact with more familiar aspects of recent musical culture in the United States.

MUSIC (OR SOUND) AS A WEAPON

"Acoustic weapons" have been in development by Department of Defense contractors since at least the 1997 creation of the Joint Non-Lethal Weapons Task Force, accounting for one-third of the Task Force's budget in 1998–99.[1] Thus, they are not peculiar to twenty-first-century wars or to the current administration. The earliest contract I know to have been let for such a weapon was on November 18, 1998, authorizing now-defunct Synetics Corporation to produce a tightly focused beam of infrasound—that is, vibration waves slower than 100 vps—meant to produce effects that range from "disabling or lethal."[2] In 1999, Maxwell Technologies patented a HyperSonic Sound System, another "highly directional device . . . designed to control hostile crowds or disable hostage takers."[3] The same year Primex Physics International patented both the "Acoustic Blaster," which produced "repetitive impulse waveforms" of 165dB, directable at a distance of fifty feet, for "antipersonnel applications," and the Sequential Arc Discharge Acoustic Generator, which produces "high intensity impulsive sound waves by purely electrical means."[4]

As far as I know, none of these have been deployed in the current wars. They have been supplanted in the nonlethal weapons arms race by a system the American Technology Corporation developed after 2000—the Long Range Acoustic Device, or LRAD.[5] Capable of projecting a "strip of sound" (fifteen to thirty inches wide) at an average of 120 dB (maxing at 151 dB) that will be intelligible for 500 to 1,000 meters (depending on which model you buy), the LRAD is designed to hail ships, issue battlefield or crowd-control commands, or direct an "attention-getting and highly irritating deterrent tone for behavior modification" (http://www.atcsd.com). As of March 2006, 350 LRAD systems had been sold—to the US Navy, the Coast Guard, various commercial shippers for marine interdiction; to the US Army and Marines for use by PsyOps units, and at checkpoints and internment facilities; to the police departments of Boston, New York, Los Angeles, Santa Ana, and Broward County, Florida. According to the US Army's 361st PsyOps company, LRADs are used "for clearing streets and rooftops during cordon and search, for disseminating information, and for drawing out enemy snipers who are subsequently destroyed by our own snipers" (Davison and Lewer 2006). It can also be set to "fire" short bursts of "intense acoustic energy" into crowds, to incapacitate people by causing spatial disorientation. Similar weapons deployed by Israel in Gaza and Lebanon produce the effect of "being hit by a wall of air that is painful on the ears, sometimes causing nosebleeds and leaving you shaking inside" (Davison and Lewer 2006).

Capable of directing "music through the use of an integrated and hardened MP3 player," and of accepting "external audio devices, like a CD or MP3 player," LRADs have been deployed with combat units since the fall of 2003. According to an ATC spokesman, they were used in Iraq in 2004 "to play both high output music and deterrent tones, evidently to great effect as a PsyOps tool, causing the insurgents to react in ways that greatly increased their vulnerability."[6] Most likely, LRADs were the means by which the 361st PsyOps company "prepared the battlefield" for the November 2004 siege of Fallujah by bombarding the city with music—supposedly, with Metallica's "Hells Bells" and "Shoot to Thrill" among other things (DeGregory 2004). PsyOps spokesman Ben Abel explained to reporter Lane DeGregory of the *St. Petersburg (Florida) Times*, "These harassment missions work especially well in urban settings like Fallujah. The sounds just keep reverberating off the walls." Abel added, "it's not the music so much as the sound. It's like throwing a smoke bomb. The aim is to disorient and confuse the enemy to gain a tactical advantage" (DeGregory 2004). Abel made clear that although the tactic of bombarding the enemy with sound was made at the command level, the choice of music was left to soldiers in the field: . . . "our guys have been getting really creative in finding sounds they think would make the enemy upset. . . . These guys have their own mini-disc players, with their own music, plus hundreds of downloaded sounds. It's kind of personal preference how they choose the songs. We've got very young guys making these decisions" (DeGregory 2004). On the battlefield, then, the use of music as a weapon is perceived to be incidental to the use of sound's ability to affect a person's spatial orientation, sense of balance, and physical coordination. It is because music is incidental that the choice of repertoire is delegated to individual PsyOps soldiers' creativity.

MUSIC AS TORTURE

Although it seems to be both more widespread and older, the calculated use of music in "detainee interrogations" is less easy to trace than the use of sound as a weapon. Evidence from the current war is spotty, based on the debriefings of released detainees by international human rights organizations and reporters, on the accounts currently detained persons have given to their lawyers, or on urban legends that circulate on the internet, some of which are corroborated by the other two kinds of accounts. Still, it is absolutely clear that music plays an important role in the interrogation of detainees in the war on terror. As early as May 2003 the BBC reported that the US Army had used Metallica's "Enter Sandman" and Barney the Purple Dinosaur's "I Love You" in the interrogation of Iraqi detainees, playing the songs repeatedly at high volume inside of shipping containers.[7] Documents obtained by the ACLU include an email from an unidentified FBI agent, dated December 5, 2003, that describes at least three incidents involving Guantanamo detainees being chained to the floor and subjected to "extreme heat, extreme cold, or extremely loud rap music."[8] The June 12, 2005, issue of *Time* included a story based on the eighty-four-page log of Mohammed al Qahtani's interrogation there from November 2002 to January 2003 (Zagorin and Duffy 2005).[9] Qahtani's interrogations began at midnight; whenever he dozed he was awakened either by water poured over his head or the sound of Christina Aguilera's music. In December 2005, Human Rights Watch posted brief first-person accounts of detainees released from a secret prison in Afghanistan, many of whom asserted that part of their experience included being held in a pitch-black space and forced to listen to music that they described, variously, as "unbearably loud," "infidel," or "Western." The same posting included the account of Guantanamo prisoner Benyan Mohammed, an Ethiopian who had lived in Britain, and who had been forced to listen to music by Eminem ("Slim Shady") and Dr. Dre for twenty days before the music was replaced by "horrible ghost laughter and Halloween sounds."[10] A long *New York Times* story on March 19, 2006, described in detail "Camp Nama," the headquarters of a multiple-agency interrogation unit at Baghdad International Airport; there, "high-value detainees"—those believed to have information directly pertinent to battlefield movements, terrorist ringleaders, or imminent terrorist attacks—were sent first to the so-called "Black Room," a garage-sized, windowless space painted black where "rap music or rock'n'roll blared at deafening decibels over a loudspeaker" (Schmitt and Marshall 2006).[11] Read together, these reports suggest that the "deafening music" is usually delivered to a detainee who has been chained into a "stress position," in a pitch-black space made uncomfortably hot or cold.

"NO-TOUCH TORTURE"

It would be possible to assume from the evidence in the popular press that the use of music in "interrogation" is (as one of the sources for the 2003 BBC story claimed) "rather new." I'm sorry to report that my reading suggests otherwise; nor is it the random, rogue behavior of particularly sadistic (or musical, or creative) interrogators and MPs. Rather, it is one component of a standard set of interrogation practices developed by the CIA (in cooperation with English and Canadian intelligence agencies) over the second half of the twentieth century—a standard set of practices that includes the hooding, stress positions, and sexual/cultural humiliation that the photos leaked from Abu Ghraib prison enabled us to see. Its advocates call this set of practices "no-touch torture."[12]

In his 2006 book *A Question of Torture*, historian Alfred W. McCoy traces the origin of "no-touch torture" to a research program funded by the OSS, the CIA, and the intelligence services of Canada and Britain in the years after World War II. Concerned by Soviet success at "brainwashing" captives and destroying their wills, these agencies supported research at Yale, Cornell, and McGill intended to learn how we might do the same.[13] In the 1950s this contract research was concentrated in three areas: 1) the Canadian government funded research at McGill that explored the devastating impact of sensory deprivation and sensory manipulation—which would eventually include hooding; continuous noise (whether loud or not) and its opposite, soundproofing; temporal disorientation, and erratic provision of food and drink; 2) the CIA funded research at Cornell and Yale on the effects of self-inflicted pain—which would eventually include stress positions, and scenarios that provoked personal, sexual, or cultural humiliation; and 3) the CIA funded research at Yale on the capacity of ordinary people to inflict lethal pain on others.

The reports of these experiments reveal a universalizing naivete and cultural bias that seems laughable now. Yet their results are the core premises of what the European Human Rights Commission described in 1976 as a "modern system of torture" (McCoy 2006, 57). This modern system aims to combine "sensory disorientation"—isolation, standing, extremes of heat and cold, light and dark, noise and silence—with self-inflicted pain, both physical and psychological, so as to cause a prisoner's very "identity to disintegrate."[14] Whether that disintegration takes the form of induced regression (to infantile behavior) or induced schizophrenia, "the effect is much like that which occurs if he is beaten, starved or deprived of sleep."[15] The prisoner becomes psychologically powerless before the authority of interrogators, both dependent and unable to resist. Moreover, the experimental data showed this "modern system of torture" to be much more efficient than beatings or starvation, producing psychological disintegration in a matter of days, rather than weeks or months. And, as one CIA researcher noted, it was hard to document, for with the exception of the standing (which can cause grotesque swelling/bruising of the feet and legs) these "techniques" leave no visible marks on the fleshy surfaces of a human body.

Institutionalized in 1963 in the CIA's Kubark Counterintelligence Interrogation Handbook, the techniques of "no-touch torture" were used—indeed, consciously tested again and again—by the CIA's counterinsurgency forces in Vietnam into the 1970s, by the English in Northern Ireland, and by police units from Uruguay, Brazil, Guatemala, the Philippines, Iran, Argentina, and Chile who were trained at the US Office of Public Safety (1962–74), the US Army Intelligence Center in Fort Huachuca, AZ, or the US Army School of the Americas (based in Panama until 1976, and now based at Fort Benning, Georgia).[16] Although the CIA's interrogation techniques are not mentioned in either the 1992 or September 2006 editions of the US Army's Field Manual for Human Intelligence Collection (HUMINT), the principal textbook for training at Fort Huachuca, they seem to be part of Army interrogators' and PsyOps units' training there. (The music most often mentioned in accounts of this training is the song "I Love You" associated with Barney the purple dinosaur.) In the field manuals, the elements of "no-touch torture" are understood to be subsumed under the heading of "additional psychological strategies" by which interrogators are encouraged to implement any of the eighteen declassified "approaches" to an informant—approaches with headings like "fear up" and "ego down."[17] If one reads the press and human rights organization accounts of "no-touch torture" carefully, these incidents can all be traced not to uniformed servicemen, but to occasions when multiple-agency teams—that is, teams that include CIA operatives, and Behavioral Science Consultants—administer the interrogations. In part because CIA operatives are specifically exempt from the provisions of the Military Commissions Act of 2006, in part because the elements of "no-touch torture" are part of what one might call the military's oral tradition, all the elements of "no-touch torture" except waterboarding and extremes of hot and cold remain permissible under the recently signed Military Commissions Act of 2006—permissible, and, to protect against international prosecution as violations of the UN Convention on Torture, retroactively pardoned.[18]

CULTURAL RESONANCES

"No-touch torture" shares with nonlethal weapons the advantage that it leaves no marks directly caused by interrogators on the visible, fleshy surfaces of the body. Thus hard to prove, and hard to jibe with images of torture familiar from visual and literary culture, "no-touch torture's" premise is nonetheless consistent with the premise behind nonlethal weapons, including those that use sound; and it is consistent with the premise by which PsyOps units use sound or music to prepare the battlefield. The common premise is that sound can damage human beings, usually without killing us, in a wide variety of ways. What differentiates the uses of sound or music on the battlefield and the uses of sound or music in the interrogation room is the claimed site of the damage. Theorists of battlefield use emphasize sound's bodily effects, while theorists of the interrogation room focus on the capacity of sound and music to destroy subjectivity. There's something here about the intersection of mind/body relationship with the distinction between private and public space, and the hierarchy of command and field operations, that I want eventually to think more about.

I also want to think much more about the eerie resonances between the aesthetics implied by theorists of "no-touch torture" and the aesthetics shared by a wide range of music cultures since the 1960s—the music cultures that formed my sensibility, and, arguably, the sensibilities of those who designed, who command, and who implement the acoustic aspects of "no-touch torture" and acoustic battle. I find two especially intriguing. First, both blur the distinction between sound and music. But whereas many composers, musicians, and scholars have tended to conceive that blurring as producing an acoustic continuum, the state's actors seem very clear that "music," with all its cultural specificity, is less important than the power of sound itself.[19] How, I wonder, might one interpret the resulting state-imposed hierarchy of sound over music? Specifically, how might inscribing such a hierarchy serve the state's interests away from battlefield and interrogation sites? Second, the state's interrogators share with many civilian musicians, composers, and scholars the notion that listening to music can dissolve subjectivity, releasing a person into a paradoxical condition that is both highly embodied and almost disembodied in the intensity with which one forgets important elements of one's identity, and loses track of time's passing. The practices and ideologies of classical music listening suggest that such music-induced ecstasy is produced by intense attention to the relationships among the sounds themselves. Such listening, Fred Maus has recently written, "seeks identification with the controlling *persona*." Maus goes on to quote Edward T. Cone: "The goal . . . must be *identification* with the complete musical persona *by making its utterance one's own*" (Maus 2004, 36).

Could this notion of listening, propagated in elite universities (including those on contract to the CIA) in the last half of the twentieth century, have influenced the architects of "no-touch torture"? Is it, in itself, another symptom of the national security state that the United States has been since the era of World War II? How might that notion of listening, which relies on its denial of both purely acoustic phenomena and nonacoustic psychosomatic experiences in the moment of listening, have interacted, in those years, with the notion that theorists of "no-touch torture" share with many vernacular proponents of psychedelic rock—the belief that music dissolves subjectivity in conjunction with other psychosomatic experiences, and always operates partly through its bodily effects? How, if at all, might the two different notions of how music ruptures subjectivity complement the distinctions drawn by the state between "sound" and "music," "command" and "field execution," "weapon" and "interrogation"? How might our own musical behaviors—as scholars and teachers especially—interact with these distinctions?

MUSIC, TORTURE, AND THE BLOGOSPHERE (OR, IS IT TORTURE, AND WHAT'S THE PLAYLIST?)

Nearly every story in the mainstream US press about music's use to "torture" detainees has prompted responses in the virtual world known as the blogosphere. I discovered these responses by accident, but quickly realized that they were at least as important to understanding the relationship of "music as torture" to civilian musical culture as thinking about classical music listening practices. In a way, I have thought, the blogosphere responses document an important aspect of the current wars' home front.

Most blog responses consist of the posted news story, followed by a handful of desultory comments. Some, however, consist of conversations that last from an hour or two (at lunchtime or in early evening) to several days. These longer conversations take one of two turns. Blogging communities who accept without question the idea that music is being used to torture detainees move quickly to political discussions of torture *tout court*, as it has been defined by recent US policy and law, and by recent international law. Generally, these conversations never return to music. But the other turn, taken by blogging communities who pose the question "But is it torture?," often stays focused on music for quite a long time, regardless of how the question has been answered.[20]

"Equating a cold room or loud music with torture is the worst kind of moral relativism," wrote MayBee this past September 29 at http://justoneminute.typepad.com, Soylent Red replied immediately "Careful, MayBee. We don't want anyone to cry or suffer from lowered self-esteem." The exchange inspired an hour's spirited competition among several bloggers about how best to torture detainees, all spinning off from Soylent Red's second posting: "But perhaps we could make some lemonade of this. Openly admit gays to the military, but only as MPs or HUMINT collectors. Turn Guantanamo into a year-round Pride Parade. Everything these people eat, sleep on, what have you will have been touched by homosexuals. Every time they take a shower they are being watched by homosexuals. Reinstitute periodic strip searches. And every interrogation begins with the words 'You know, I've been checking you out.'"

By the end of the hour, MayBee had brought the thread back to music, posting about the Red Hot Chili Peppers' song "What I got I got to get it put in you..." "Particularly if played in a camp run entirely by homosexuals with an enormous sign over the gate saying 'The Gayest Place on Earth,' I'd break before lunch." The same weekend, on the website http://volokh.com Charlie (Colorado) mocked as an "absurdity" the idea that "loud music and sexually suggestive gestures from attractive women could become 'torture,' when people not under interrogation pay substantial cover charges and tip heavily for the same experience." Strategichamlet (mail) replied "I agree.... Anyone who has talked with a professional dominatrix knows that there are a great deal of people in this country who are willing to pay to be rather brutally tortured."

Both these exchanges startle for the casualness with which they confirm an aspect of contemporary musical life that some of us worked hard to articulate in the 1990s—the easy slippage, in the minds of our contemporaries, between music and sexuality. The first exchange implies that "torture" by music could be similar to a "torture" that induced homophobia, while the second likens "torture" by music to the "torture" of desirable heterosexual fantasy play for which US men would willingly pay.

Blogs whose communities assume that music could be torture extrapolate at first from their own experience of being forced to listen to music in genres, and from cultural locations, that they find distasteful. Overwhelmingly, the conversations open with an exchange like this one, from December 19, 2005. Writing in response to Human Rights Watch's press release about the Ethiopian forced to listen to rap for twenty hours, laz wrote to The J-Walk Blog (http://j-walk-blog.com), "I used to have downstairs neighbors that would listen to rap. And let me assure you, it definitely has value as a torture device." Leonardo replied, "Twenty days? I go nuts after three minutes!" while Keith Povell commented, "Music as torture. Try listening to any commercial radio station (UK especially) and you'll get the idea." Many other bloggers understood music as torturous through memories of their own youths, or recent experiences with their adolescent children. At http://forums.military.com, a blog site for uniformed service people, peter3_1 commented on September 12, 2006, "Eminem's *Slim Shady* is enough to drive a Moslem to drink! But, then, *Iron Butterfly* did that to my parents, not to mention the *Doors*, pure torture they thought." "Oh sure! Real torture! Heavy rock turned up and the a/c cranked real low. That sounds like my daughter's room!," SGTBH wrote, adding later: "Play Village People. You can stay at the YMCA over and over again. Play Queen." Honoloulu 58 cautioned those who suggested classical music or show tunes, "Got to watch [them], they can have a calming effect and/or euphoric feeling for some."

Bloggers who accept the premise that music could be torture participate eagerly—indeed, almost gleefully—in virtual conversations aimed at producing the ideal playlist for either battlefield or interrogation-room use.[21] Two with particularly creative, sustained conversations are http://littlegreenfootballs.com, a mixed-sex, right-leaning political blog run by web designer Charles Johnson (best-known for exposing the forged documents about President Bush's military service that led to Dan Rather's retirement from CBS) and http://freerepublic.com, a sharply right-wing political blog whose musical conversations are dominated by men. "Little green footballs" staged a contest for torture suggestions in mid-May 2003, attracting nearly two hundred responses in a matter of hours. Some of the most frequently mentioned choices are "all rap music," "Horse with no name," "Alone again," "MacArthur Park," "Honey," "You light up my life," all the recordings of Cher, Yanni, Bobby Sherman, Kenny G., Harry Belafonte, YMCA and the Bee Gees, and all disco.

Whatever one might make of this playlist (it seems to me to indicate the blog's demographic rather precisely), http://littlegreenfootballs.com's competition provoked few mean-spirited comments. By contrast, Free Republic's June 10, 2005, posting of a news story about the Army's quest for a new speaker system to deliver music as a weapon or "torture" device sparked repertoire suggestions that were occasionally laced with multivalent venom. Suggestions early that evening included the music of Sousa, Welk, Donny and Marie, Barry Manilow, sound effects ranging from Tibetan chants to rabbits being slaughtered, the fantasy of Bill and Hillary singing "I got you, Babe," and "anything by Yoko Ono." Ono soon became the subject of her own racist, misogynist mini-thread. Mr Jazz wrote: "You might as well stick panties on the head of everyone in the village. At least THAT would be more human than using Yoko Ono as a weapon of torture." Straight Vermonter posted a parody of Article 13 from the Geneva Conventions to prohibit the use of her music. And Ramius wrote, "No dude . . . we gotta have some limits . . . I mean . . . just damn. I mean . . . pork fat, shredded Koran, menstrual fluids . . . I see the usefulness there. But I gotta draw the line at Yoko. I mean, we're not barbarians."

The belief that music could torture emerges, in the blogosphere, among people who feel themselves to be "tortured" by certain musics—rap music, disco, sentimental ballads, the music of Yoko Ono. Additionally, the idea that music could torture seems linked both to homophobia and to heterosexual fantasy; in fact, the most lively repertoire discussions propose as torturous popular musics easily associated with either homosexuality or the effeminacy perceived to come from being too emotionally engaged with women. These folk seem readily to imagine themselves moving from tortured to torturer, and imagine music torturing by either a racial/cultural affront or, more often, by feminizing and/or queerifying Muslim men: either way, detainees would be emasculated (and the bloggers' masculinity, presumably, strengthened). My hunch that masculinity is at issue is supported by one more blog posting, one of the last at Free Republic in June 2005, from SauronOfMordor, who, like the PsyOps spokesman, imagined sound to be more important than music. "Better yet," he wrote, "a female voice calling in Arabic, proclaiming the muj's are effeminate weaklings, and she and her sisters are waiting to kick their butts and put their soiled panties on their heads." Sauron, Ramius, and many of the bloggers at Free Republic in particular, seem among other things to use the idea of music as torture to displace onto Muslim detainees a rage rooted in their own fear that they are immersed in a culture that has become, in their words, "nancy," "pansy," and "pussy." Seen from a slightly different perspective, one might suppose the bloggers' virtual torture playlists impose on Muslim men the orientalist fantasy that Arab men are (always already) effeminate.

Interestingly, the choices of these would-be torturers from the "homefront" seem not to resemble the choices of soldiers in the field. Overwhelmingly, the field choices seem to be made from heavy metal and rap—the music in GIs' disc- and mp3-players, and wired into their helmets when they go to battle. (Recordings by Britney Spears and Christina Aguilera are said to have been used against specific detainees: the recipient of the Aguilera treatment was a fluent Anglophone, so one might assume that sexually provocative lyrics were part of the point.) Generally coded masculine in mainstream US culture, metal and rap are musics that those who don't identify with them often hear as embodying the sounds of masculine rage. Thus they may seem, to soldiers in the field, to "torture" Muslim men by creating a soundscape in which US men defeat them in a struggle of masculinities. Some of the specific songs played in battle (Metallica's "Enter Sandman," AC/DC's "Hell's Bells") seem lyrically apposite to preparing both sides for the confrontation with gruesome death that so many military memoirs liken to ecstasy. The lyrics of Eminem's "Slim Shady," played over and over for Guantanamo's "high value detainees," combine rage, misogyny, and vivid sexual imagery in ways that seem sure to offend—to confirm detainees' defeat by all that they might find loathsome about the culture of "the infidel."

But wait. The delivery of cultural offense is, from the state's perspective, only incidental to what goes on in the interrogation room. The point, the disintegration of identity, depends not on music but on sound. I want to close by trying to imagine the scene of "interrogation," and by thinking a bit further about the ways that the use of music in "no-touch torture" entangle contemporary musical culture with the aims of the national security state (that has lately become, too, a "state of exception").[22]

THE INTERROGATION SCENE

How, I have wondered, might it feel to be in one of those "interrogation rooms" for twenty hours, experiencing so-called "no-touch torture"? Could it possibly be "no-touch"? In the absence, so far, of detailed accounts from former prisoners of their experiences, I have tried to think about this practice through my own experience of high-volume rock, and, more recently, high-volume dance music. I remember from my youth the joyous feeling of the beat and guitar sounds resounding in my very bones, and from my more recent middle age the feeling of Junior Vasquez's disco beats all but pushing me onto and across the floor, forcing me to move. For me, both kinds of experience produced the feeling of being touched, without being touched by anyone; all of us who sang or danced were physically touched by the same force, which sometimes moved, sometimes enveloped, sometimes caressed us. From that shared experience of being touched-without-being-touched by the vibrating air in which we all moved, I drew a deeply sensual, erotic (though not explicitly sexual) feeling of communion with the friends and strangers around me, even as the music blessedly silenced, temporarily, my individual thoughts. My experience, of course, was not only psychological or sensual; it was enhanced by the adrenalin rush, the raised blood pressure and heart rate, the "ringing" that would last for hours in my bones that were the best-known, immediate physical effects of loud music.

A detainee, too, must experience himself as touched without being touched, as he squats, hands shackled between his shackled ankles to an I-bolt in the floor, in a pitch-black room, unable to find any position for his body that does not cause self-inflicted pain. Surely, among many other things, the experience creates a nexus of pain, immobility, unwanted touching (without-touch);

and of being forced into self-hurting by a disembodied, invisible Power. A dark ecstasy, the experience must be neither isolation nor communion, but a relationship that mimics the effects of the chains—the relationship of being utterly at the mercy of a merciless, ubiquitous Power. I imagine it, sometime, as being plunged into it something like the postmodern, post-Foucauldian dystopia where one is unable quite to name, much less resist, the overwhelmingly diffuse Power that *is* outside one, but also *is* inside, and that operates by forcing one to comply against one's will, against one's interests, because there is no way—not even a retreat to interiority—to escape the pain. What better medium than music to bring into being (as a felicitous performative) the experience of the West's (the infidel's) ubiquitous, irresistible Power?[23]

In the last few days, thinking about this panel's overall focus on the relationship of musical culture to the state that is the USA, I've been pondering the gradual institutionalization of this scene in the global imagination—through, for instance, its visual representation in the film *The Road to Guantanamo*. I've been thinking that the scene, both as drastically real for interrogators and detainees, and as virtual for filmgoers, press readers, bloggers, and me, bears thinking about as an artifact of the global war on terror, itself an artifact of the United States' newly unabashed effort to project itself as global sovereign. I'm struck, for instance, by the fact that "no-touch torture" using music to dissolve others' subjectivities has been imposed on persons picked up in Afghanistan, Bosnia, Egypt, Ethiopia, Gambia, Indonesia, Iraq, Mauritania, Pakistan, Thailand, and the United Arab Emirates, including British and Canadian citizens. Thus, the performative scene in which music is the medium of ubiquitous, irresistible power that touches without touching has been imposed on representatives of the entire Muslim world. Music, then, is not only a component of "no-touch torture" but also a component of the United States' symbolic claim to global sovereignty—but in a way that is almost the polar opposite of the Louis Armstrong "good will ambassador" tours of the 1950s.[24] At the same time, however, the United States has given the detainees thus treated over to its own soldiers as scapegoats, toward whom their choice of music linked to working-class masculinities can channel their rage at the economic and political forces that make them—like their captives—human beings that the state allows to be killed with impunity. Moreover, because media representations on the one hand and the technologies of "new media" on the other allow the scene to be widely imagined and responded to at home, the United States has, perhaps inadvertently, given the same detainees over to a certain swath of the homefront, where they can be scapegoats for a different kind of rage. Believing they cannot be killed with impunity, the homefront bloggers at littlegreen footballs and freerepublic do more than express their rage at the feminized position they occupy as nonwarriors in an increasingly warrior-worshipping public culture. They create (and occupy) as homophobic, racist, and misogynist the subject position of virtuous, justified torture—a subject position identified with, and occupied by, the global national security state that has, in its most recently passed law on the treatment of detainees, declared itself exempt from international law. All the while, the scene—at least as one can currently know it—allows certain kinds of repertoire to stand for the violence of "Western," "infidel" conquest, leaving repertoire that is more likely to be valued by elites both innocent and intact.

But I freely confess here that I have barely begun this work. I do not yet know who makes the choices in detainment facilities, and on what basis. Nor do I know whether guards and interrogation teams hear, or listen to, the music played. What do US personnel think about this practice, and what do they feel? What do detainees think and feel? What does either group think and feel about the specific repertoire chosen? How, if at all, has the experience changed the musical behaviors of either group?

What equipment delivers the sound? At what decibel level? Is it engineered so as to afflict without causing permanent hearing loss?

Has music proven to be useful in "breaking" detainees for interrogation?

Thinking culturally, I wonder what the musical ideas and practices of those who designed "no-touch torture" might have been? If the torture scene is "performative," what relations of power are brought into being? How might this use of music to serve the national and imperial agenda of the United States as a "state of exception" affect twenty-first-century musicalities?

For now, I offer this paper only as a way of beginning.

NOTES

This chapter originally appeared as "Music as torture / Music as weapon" by Suzanne G. Cusick, *TRANS-Transcultural Music Review* no. 10 (2006), www.sibetrans.com/trans. This article is published under a Creative Commons license (Attribution-NonCommercial-NoDerivs 2.5), https://creativecommons.org/licenses/by-nc-nd/2.5/.

1. For an introduction to acoustic weapons in the context of nonlethal weapons research, see Davison and Lewer (2006), Wright (1999), and Aftergood (1994).

2. The contract can be found at https://www.armysbir/com/awards/sbir_fy99_phaseii_company.htm.

3. http://dictionaryofwar.org/en-dict/node/418. The company claimed at the time that its system could cause eardrum rupture at 185dB, lung injury at 200dB, and death at 220dB.

4. http://defense-update.com/features/du-1-05/NLW-DEW.htm See also http://www/global.security.org/military/systems/munitions/accoustic.htm [sic].

5. On American Technology Corporation, the LRAD, and its several applications, see the company's website, http://www.atscd.com. For a profile of Elwood "Woody" Norris, the inventor of LRAD technology and founder of ATC, see Sella (2003).

6. Personal email to the author from James Croft III, Chief Technology Officer, ATC, 26 October 2006.

7. "Sesame Street breaks Iraqi POWs," 20 May 2003, http://news.bbc.co.uk/2/hi/middle_east/3042907.stm.

8. For a complete overview of the material gathered by the American Civil Liberties Union, see http://www.aclu.org/safefree?torture/torturefoia.index.html.

9. Excerpts from the interrogation log on which the story was based are online at http://www/time/com/time/magazine/article/0,9171,1071202,00.html.

10. Http://hrw.org/english/docs/2005/12/19/afghan12319_txt.htm.

11. Details of similar procedures (including the uses of the other colored rooms) can be found in Sifton (2006).

12. The most complete account of this congeries of techniques is McCoy (2006).

13. For a description of these experiments see McCoy (2006) chapter 2, "Mind Control."

14. McGill University researcher Donald Hebb, cited in McCoy (2006, 35).

15. Lawrence E Hinkle Jr., "Consideration of the Circumstances under Which Men May Be Interrogated, and the Effects That These May Have upon the Function of the Brain," File: Hinkle, Box 7, CIA Behavior Control Experiments Collection, National Security Archive. Washington. Cited in McCoy (2006, 42 and note 60).

16. Declassified parts of the Kubark manual can be found online at http://www.kimsoft.com/2000/kubark/htm. See McCoy (2006, chapter 2) for details of the way various US agencies have trained other nations' security forces. For a comprehensive gathering of documents pertaining to US torture of detainees that were available up to 2005, see Greenberg and Dratel (2005).

17. The most recent US Army Field Manual for Human Intelligence Collection, issued in September 2006, can be found online at http://www.army.mil/references/FM2-22.3.pdf.

18. The full text of the Military Commissions Act of 2006 is online at http://www.loc.gov/rr/frd/Military_Law/MC_Act2006.html. See also the Detainee Treatment Act of 2005, part of the Defense appropriations bill, online at http://jurist.law.pitt.edu/gazette/2005/12/detainee-treatment-act-of-2005-white.php.

19. On the musical side, I mean to evoke both to a very wide spectrum of musical composition, ranging from *musique concrete* to the improvisatory works of John Cage and Pauline Oliveros and the rich scholarly and creative literature that has emerged in response to R. Murray Schaefer's 1977 book *The Soundscape: Our Sonic Environment and the Tuning of the World* (see Schaefer 1997).

20. Readers who doubt that these practices constitute torture may wish to consult Borchelt et al. (2005).

21. Florida reporter Lane DeGregory wrote a sidebar, entitled "Anything but 'MacArthur Park'!," to his November 2004 report of music's use during the siege of Fallujah. The sidebar exemplifies this kind of media response that invites ordinary Americans to imagine themselves as torturers. He or his colleagues at the *St. Petersburg Times* "asked (Tampa) bay residents which songs they would play to drive the insurgents out of Falluja, break down Iraqi prisoners, or just drive their neighbors nuts." The results, published November 21, 2004, are reported at http://sptimes.com/2004/11/21/Floridian/Anything_but_MacArth.shtml

22. I mean to allude to Agamben's book *State of Exception* (see Agamben 2005), as well as to the ideas in that book's prequel, *Homo Sacer: Sovereign Power and Bare Life* (see Agamben 1998).

23. The phrase "felicitous performative" refers to J. L. Austin, *How to Do Things with Words* (see Austin 1962), especially to Lecture II, which seeks to define performative speech that actually works—that is "felicitous."

24. On these tours, see Eschen (2004).

REFERENCES

Aftergood, Steven. 1994. "The soft-kill fallacy." *Bulletin of the Atomic Scientists* 50(5): 40–45, http://www.thebulletin.org/article.php?art_ofn=so94aftergood.

Agamben, Giorgio. 1998. *Homo Sacer: Sovereign Power and Bare Life*. Palo Alto, CA: Stanford University Press.

Agamben, Giorgio. 2005. *State of Exception*. Chicago: University of Chicago Press.

al-Radi, Nuha. 1998. *Baghdad Diaries: A Woman's Chronicle of War and Exile*. New York: Vintage.

Austin, John L. 1962. *How to Do Things with Words*. Cambridge, MA: Harvard University Press.

Borchelt, Gretchen, et al. 2005. *Break Them Down: Systematic Use of Psychological Torture by US Forces*. Cambridge, MA: Physicians for Human Rights. http://www.pegc.us/archive/Authorities/PHR_psych_torture_20050501.pdf.

Davison, Neil, and Nick Lewer. 2006. *Bradford Non-Lethal Weapons Research Project, Research Report No. 8*. http://www.brad.ac.uk/acad/nlw/research_reports/docs/.

DeGregory, Lane. 2004. "Iraq'n'roll." *St Petersburg Times* online. *Floridian*, November 21, 2004. http://s[times/com/2004/11/21/Floridian/Iraq_n_roll.shtml.

Eschen, Penny M. Von. 2004. *Satchmo Blows Up the World: Jazz Ambassadors Play the Cold War*. Cambridge, MA: Harvard University Press.

Greenberg, Karen J., and Joshua L. Dratel, eds. 2005. *The Torture Papers: The Road to Abu Ghraib*. Cambridge and New York: Cambridge University Press.

Maus, Fred Everett. 2004. "The Disciplined Subject of Music Theory." In *Beyond Structural Listening? Postmodern Modes of Hearing*, ed. Andrew Dell'Antonio, 13–43. Berkeley: University of California Press.

McCoy, Alfred W. 2006. *A Question of Torture: CIA Interrogation, from the Cold War to the War on Terror*. New York: Metropolitan Books.

Schaefer, Murray. 1997. *The Soundscape: Our Sonic Environment and the Tuning of the World*. Rochester, VT: Destiny Books.

Schmitt, Eric, and Carolyn Marshall. 2006. "Task Force 6-26: Inside Camp Nama; In Secret Unit's 'Black Room,' A Grim Portrait of US Abuse." *New York Times*, March 19, 2006.

Sella, Marshall. 2003. "The Sound of Things to Come." *New York Times*, March 23, 2003.

Sifton, John. 2006. "'No Blood, No Foul': Soldiers' Accounts of Detainee Abuse in Iraq." *Human Rights Watch* 18 (3-G). http://hrw.org/reports/2006/us0706/.

Wright, Steve. 1999. "Hypocrisy of 'nonlethal' arms." *Le Monde diplomatique*, December 1999. http://www.mondediplo.com/1999/12/09wright.

Zagorin, Adam, and Michael Duffy. 2005. "Inside the Interrogation of Detainee 063." *Time*, June 12, 2005. http://www.time.com/time/magazine/article/0,9171,1071284,00.html.

CHAPTER 9

MAINTAINING A RACKET
How the Contemporary Music Business Keeps On Keepin' On

Jim Rogers

THE MUSIC BUSINESS 2024: "IT'S TAYLOR SWIFT'S ECONOMY, AND WE'RE ALL LIVING IN IT"

"[Taylor] Swift manages to be both authentic singer-songwriter and unabashed hyper-capitalist," writes Dorian Lynskey in *The Guardian* (June 1, 2024). The astounding success of Swift's 2024 album *The Tortured Poets Department* cemented her classification as a global phenomenon whose net worth now exceeds $1 billion. The album shattered streaming records on Spotify (achieving 300 million streams in a single day), held the top fourteen spots on the *Billboard* Hot 100 chart, and sold 2.6 million copies in its first week of release in the United States alone, outselling all of the other Top 10 albums of the year-to-date combined (Lynskey 2024; McIntyre 2024; Millman 2024). Swift's Eras Tour across 2023–24 (ongoing at the time of writing) sees her perform more than 150 shows across five continents and has become the highest-grossing concert tour in history, the first ever to generate revenues in excess of $1 billion. *Billboard* estimated that the early months of the tour saw Taylor Swift merchandise gross approximately $2 million per show (Peoples 2023). Universal Music claimed its overall merchandise revenues grew by 12 percent during the first three months of the tour as a direct result of Swift's "strong performance" (Parodi 2023). Moreover, Swift's TAS Rights Management company owns approximately two hundred federal trademark registrations allowing the artist to exercise control over, and exploit the rights to, her name, song titles, catch phrases, and more (Kondoudis n.d.). *Billboard* stresses that putting a precise figure on the overall wealth generated through the Swift "brand" is tricky due to the difficulty in accessing data, such as synchronization royalties from the use of her songs in films, TV, and advertising, as well as income from sponsorships and merchandise sales through her website and licensing agreements (Peoples 2023). The *Financial Times* highlights similar problems (Ashworth 2023). But all agree, the wealth being generated is vast, and the methods through which it is being accumulated are many, across a diverse spectrum of music rights domains. The terms "Swiftonomics" and "Taylornomics" have become common parlance in discussions not only about the economic impact of popular music, but in broader economic discourse (see, for example, Mitra 2024). The *Wall Street Journal* indubitably announces: "It's Taylor Swift's Economy, and We're All Living in It" (Pisani 2023).

So how does this picture of super-profit relate to the music economy as a whole? Leaving aside that the nature of her contractual arrangements with various facets of the music industry are often celebrated in the media as being singular or exceptional (for example, Bruner 2021; Wang 2018), does the Taylor Swift story reflect broader trends across core music sectors? Let's take a quick snapshot. In 2023, the overall global value of revenues emanating from music copyrights was estimated at $41.5 billion by prominent British economist Will Page, reflecting an increase of 16 percent year-on-year, and an effective doubling in value over the previous eight years (Smith 2023; Thomas 2023). Within this picture, global record industry revenues alone reached $28.6 billion, a 10 percent rise on the previous year (IFPI 2024). The latest financial results (at the time of writing, Q2 2024) appear to show no obvious clouds overshadowing the horizon. Overall, the Universal Music Group, the Warner Music Group, and Sony Music Entertainment (the three major corporations that dominate the global phonographic and music publishing industries) all continue to perform strongly. Universal reports a revenue of $3.2 billion for this period, reflecting a near 9 percent increase compared to the same period in the previous year, fueled by growth across all core segments (Aswad 2024a; Peoples 2024b). Sony posted a remarkable 22.5 percent year-on-year increase for Q2 2024, with revenues for that quarter fractionally shy of $3 billion (Smith 2024). In the equivalent period, we see Warner Music's revenues effectively hold steady year-on-year, but nonetheless, the company's stock rising by 6 percent on the back of sustained growth in publishing and digital (Aswad 2024b). This is in the wake of Warner posting record revenues of more than $6 billion across its music in 2023 (Paine 2023). When it comes to live music, some sources place the value of global concert ticket sales at almost $25 billion, with an additional $6 billion generated through live music sponsorship (Statista 2024).

All things considered, this is surely a good time to own and administer music rights in all their forms? The mid-2020s sees the global music industries in peak economic condition . . . yes? Well, no, according to many key industry sources and commentators. Rather, we are being warned of a very dark cloud that looms large on the horizon, one that threatens to take the bloom off the rose of the music business as a site of creative enterprise and commercial innovation. Drawing on the nineteenth-century French economist Frederic Bastiat, a recent *Financial Times* opinion column offering commentary on the "Swiftonomics" phenomenon carries some cautionary advice: "[We have a] tendency to value what we see, over what is hidden. Just because we witness or measure certain economic activities does not mean they are net value-creating or productive" (Parikh 2024). So, what is it that lurks in the background threatening to take the edge off productivity in the music business and devalue music?

IT'S THE END OF THE WORLD AS WE KNOW IT . . . AGAIN . . .

Celebrating eight years of steady growth, Frances Moore, the then-CEO of the International Federation of Phonographic Industries (IFPI), introduces her organization's 2023 *Global Music Report* with a tone of satisfaction: "Music continues to grow globally," she proclaims, and "artists are increasingly interconnected with fans as a result of the worldwide infrastructure and investment from record companies" (IFPI 2023, 5). Moore proudly underlines how her industry has produced "new and diverse opportunities for artists" helping them to "achieve their greatest creative and commercial potential . . . whilst enabling fans to seize the[se] expanding opportunities" (IFPI 2023, 5). However, her tone quickly becomes cautious, even gloomy, as she warns that: ". . . record companies must work to ensure that the value of the music artists are creating is recognised and returned. This challenge is becoming increasingly complex as a greater number of actors seek to benefit from music whilst playing no part in investing in and developing it" (IFPI 2023, 5). The specific (seemingly greedy and opportunistic?) "actors" Moore refers to are not immediately identified, but their recent arrival in the music business is also noted by Will Tanous, Universal Music's executive vice president in a subsequent section of the same report: "Everybody I work with got into this business because working with artists and music is not merely a job, it's a calling. There are a lot of new and different players in the ecosystem now that the industry has returned to growth ... who are solely in this to seize financial opportunities in a growing market. Where were those people when the industry was in decline and needed help? We were here, and we were investing all through the difficult years" (IFPI 2023, 17). So, an industry that is widely regarded as having endured years of economic hardship as a result of digital "piracy" now sees its party potentially crashed and spoiled by opportunistic looters eager to help themselves to the hard-earned returns on the investments of labor and finance committed by Universal and their allies that have returned the music industry to growth in recent years?

The identities of the dark forces at play are soon revealed, however. Michael Nash, Universal Music's chief digital officer, pinpoints the culprits a couple of pages later: "The bottom line is, a lot of AI developers are just ignoring the ethics of ingesting the creative work of others, or they're simply justifying it with what we view as a dangerous distortion of the idea of fair use ..." (IFPI 2023, 19).

The centrality of AI to current industry discourse is reflected in the frequency with which it is referenced in the subsequent (and what is, at the time of writing, the most recent) IFPI *Global Music Report* (2024). The term artificial intelligence/AI appears precisely fifty-five times in a fifty-five-page document, pervading across conversations (on artistic development, musical innovation, technological advancement, global financial growth, and fan engagement) where ultimately, the industry professes its primary role to center on protecting artists and fostering an environment that allows them to fulfill their creative potential. As Rob Stringer, CEO of Sony Music Entertainment, advances: "We're at a major inflection point in the music industry once again, with the advent of generative AI.... Our music drives the development of new technology and innovation, shaping cultural moments across tech, gaming, TV, film, and more.... The fight to have partners recognize music's true value is relentless. With any new advancements, we will continue to ensure they are creator-friendly, that artists are always put first and that art is protected" (IFPI 2024, 2). Additionally, the IFPI point out that: "International treaties, free trade agreements, and national laws worldwide ensure that copyright works and recordings cannot be used without authorization from rights-holders. They also require that any exceptions to these rights must be limited and must not unreasonably prejudice rights-holders.... Using copyright-protected materials to train an AI system is not 'fair use' and there is no justification for governments to create new exceptions to copyright for the purpose of AI training" (IFPI 2024, 51).

So, let no one be in any doubt—AI is the latest digital kid to appear on the block who requires firm discipline and tight regulation if cultural and economic catastrophe is to be avoided. The global phonographic industries deliver this message loud and clear.

The recording industry also links the evolving AI domain to a more pernicious and sinister problem that they claim will plague the music industry and stifle commercial and creative innovation unless government and lawmakers act fast. In a written submission to the UK government in October 2023, the British Phonographic Industry (BPI) assert that: "AI will increase cyber fraud in the form of hacking and content theft—particularly theft of valuable prerelease content that can be sold to the highest bidder—and aggravate issues such as unlicensed music distribution or streaming manipulation, both resulting in losses to the legitimate rights holders" (BPI 2023, 5). What's more, BPI argue that internet and social media "providers" enable such "fraud" as they deliver the platforms through which these "malicious activities" are executed. "This is not," they insist, "a sustainable model for the music industry or any IP-rich industry" (BPI 2023, 5).

Further stark warnings have started to emanate from the financial sector. In autumn 2021, the Universal Music Group (UMG), the world's biggest music label, floated on the Amsterdam Stock Exchange. The label, whose artists and catalogues include The Rolling Stones, Bob Dylan, and Paul McCartney, was spun off by its owners, Vivendi, in a move that saw shareholders acquire a 60 percent stake in the company. The first day of trading saw shares in UMG jump by 39 percent (Fielder 2021). On April 1, 2023, UMG market capitalization value was in excess of $46 billion, solidifying its position as one of the top 400 most valuable companies in the world (CompaniesMarketCap.com). However, in the wake of this valuation came a clear caution from a key financial intermediary on Wall Street. Equity broker BNP Paribas Exane double-downgraded Universal, citing the ramifications of AI in the music industry as a significant cause for concern, not only for UMG but for all major actors in the music business per se. Such developments create a quandary for the intellectual property rights regime (Huppe, 2022), with AI now standing as "the most disruptive technology for the music business since the Napster era of piracy" (Hu, cited in Epstein 2023).

Music industry news and analysis website *Music Business Worldwide* poses the following question: "What happens to major record company streaming market share when the dam breaks, and we start to see millions of songs, all made by AI, distributed to Spotify et al each day?" (Ingham 2023b). "Will artificial intelligence wreck the music industry?" asks songwriting blog *Two Storey Melody* (Anderson 2023). "How can we prevent AI-generated music from displacing human artists and musicians?" asks *Rolling Stone* in an article dedicated to "the impacts and disruption of AI on music industry stakeholders" (*Rolling Stone* Culture Council n.d.). Elsewhere, the *Daily Telegraph* tells us that "AI music is a danger to artists," and highlights the concerns of UMG Chair Lucien Grange, regarding the urgent need for the UK government to "crack down" on AI-generated music (Warrington 2023). The same article warns that without immediate political intervention, Britain is in danger of becoming "less committed to basic property rights than the Chinese Communist Party" (Warrington 2023).

Even Taylor Swift is not immune. International media outlets carried reports of "Protect Taylor Swift" trending on social media after fans reacted to fake images of the star circulating widely in early 2024 (see, for example, Cooper 2024; Patrick 2024). Even the White House responded to these developments with the Biden administration's Press Secretary Karine Jean-Pierre telling media outlets of her government's "alarm" over the issue and emphasized the necessity for Congressional legislative action to combat AI threats (Sarnoff 2024; Srivastava 2024). Yes, the story relates to images and not music, but image and likeness rights have come to form an increasingly important revenue stream for the music business and form part of the commercial strategy of labels and artists (Drott 2018; Morrow 2018). This comes at a moment where a plethora of high-profile music artists are pointing toward impending disaster for the music economy and music culture per se at the hands of AI. An open letter published by a coalition of some two hundred musicians and songwriters in April 2024 paints an apocalyptic picture of music's future:

> AI poses enormous threats to our ability to protect our privacy, our identities, our music and our livelihoods. . . . AI models . . . are directly aimed at replacing the work of human artists, with massive quantities of AI-created "sounds" and "images" that substantially dilute the royalty pools that are paid out to artists. For many working musicians, artists and songwriters who are just trying to make ends meet, this would be catastrophic. . . . AI will set in motion a race to the bottom that will denigrate the value of our work . . . and destroy the music ecosystem. (Artists Rights Alliance, 2024)

The letter's signatories include Aerosmith, Billie Eilish, Bon Jovi, Ja Rule, REM, and the Estate of Frank Sinatra.

Notwithstanding the potential nightmare scenario of which the letter forewarns, it is surely curious and peculiar to note such names appear in the context of "artists and songwriters who are just trying to make ends meet"? Nevertheless, such concerns resonate strongly on Capitol Hill. In 2018,

Congress enacted the Orrin G. Hatch-Bob Goodlatte Music Modernization Act (MMA) with the professed intention of delivering a fairer and more efficient system for statutory music licensing and royalty distribution, promising increased benefits to artists and digital music platforms alike. Now, prominent policy makers tell us that such lofty ideals risk being swept away by the latest digital current. "The stakes could hardly be higher," says Republican Congressman Darryl Issa, as "AI . . . could very well render . . . the Music Modernization Act obsolete" (cited in Roseborough 2023).

As all of this continues to unfold, summer 2024 sees Universal, Warner, and Sony (under the umbrella of the Recording Industry Association of America) pursuing two generative AI music services, Suno and Udio, through the courts. The lawsuits aim to secure rulings on mass copyright infringement, orders to halt any further infringement, and compensation for previous infringements (Resnikoff 2024; Tencer 2024). The main accusations focus on the unauthorized reproduction of sound recordings on a mass scale for the training, development, and operation of Suno and Udio's services.

So, in contrast to the vibrant and burgeoning economic landscape painted by recent financial reporting on the industry's core sectors of activity, we now stand on the edge of a potential economic and cultural abyss? Or more pointedly, we now stand on the edge of a potential economic and cultural abyss, once again? Because we have been here before with earlier digital innovations. Perhaps it possible that the industry itself, and some of those who opine and comment on it suffer from digital amnesia? In the sections that follow below, let me illustrate why the discourse surrounding AI is nothing new, and why whatever changes AI may unleash on the creation and production of music, and how it gets marketed, discovered, or recommended, it is, in the long term, unlikely to fundamentally alter the power structures underpinning the global music business.

TALKIN' 'BOUT A REVOLUTION: MEDIA FRAMING OF THE DIGITAL MUSIC ECONOMY

The evolving discourse around AI in music is starting to reflect the features and characteristics of commentary and discussion on earlier digital innovations. A headline-level overview of the past twenty-five years of mainstream media coverage of the music business shows a recurring narrative, one which inextricably links successive developments in the digital realm to seemingly insurmountable challenges for the music industry. What follows here is not news; in fact, it's been in the news (to a greater or lesser degree) since the tail end of the 1990s. Nevertheless, let us briefly reconstruct that narrative, as it is potentially instructive in the context of more recent coverage of developments around AI.

Conventional wisdom tells us that various "waves" of digital innovations since the late 1990s (both illicit and legal) have combined to threaten and challenge traditional music business power structures, and greatly impair the scope of artists and labels to make money from their creative and commercial endeavors. Concomitantly, twenty-first-century audiences are perceived as having cheaper or free access to greater quantities of music than ever previously possible. In short, the value of music (at least in economic terms) would appear to have been severely compromised by successive "advancements" in the digital domain. As Rasmus Fleischer asks, "if the song has no price, is it still a commodity?" (2017, 146).

Mainstream journalistic discourse around the implications of digital for the music business is characterized by the incessant representation of technology as antagonist, bringing widespread disruption and disorder to a previously thriving cultural industry sector. It perseveres across changing technological contexts—initially emerging with the evolution and subsequent proliferation of peer-to-peer file-sharing sites from the late 1990s onward, but persisting into the streaming era, and now raising its head once more in the AI milieu.

Consistently, media accounts privilege the capacity of technology companies (and the new and evolving music platforms they design and administer) to deliver a "new music order"—one in which, almost exclusively, the control and influence of major record labels is deemed to have been undermined. Within mainstream media coverage, a small number of themes emerge and consistently recur over time. What follows here is just a small handful of illustrative examples dotted across the past quarter-century (see Preston and Rogers 2010; Rogers 2013, 2020, for a more detailed overview of such media accounts).

First, free peer-to-peer file-sharing platforms emerged as the archvillain of the industry from the turn of the century, threatening to collapse the industry and deprive artists and performers of the means of making a living. This narrative held sway in mainstream media for almost two decades. Of note in such coverage, is the persistent representation of "industry" as an "organic life form," and the overwhelming tendency for technology to be seen as impairing core music industry actors or depriving them of life. We've witnessed the media anthropomorphize music labels as "would-be victims" of an aggressive assailant seeking to destroy them. For example, in naming 2003 as "the year that music dies," *Wired* magazine tells us that "[R]ecord labels are under attack from all sides—file sharers . . . and good old-fashioned customers—and it's killing them. A moment of silence, please" (Mann 2003). Elsewhere we are told that "Piracy continues to cripple the music industry" (*The Guardian*, January 21, 2010), and shown "[H]ow one generation was single-handedly able to kill the music industry" (*Elite Daily*, June 6, 2014). These are but a few examples, but they epitomize the delineation of the music business in news, trade, and popular media across the 2000s.

Across this period we also witnessed the recurring theme of "crisis" around the issue of peer-to-peer activities. Take, for instance, the following examples from 2008: "The music industry . . . knee deep in a downloading crisis" (*The Sunday Business Post*, April 6, 2008); "Want a snapshot of an industry in crisis? Take a look at the music business right now" (*Globe and Mail*, January 31, 2008); "Industry crisis as album sales drop" (*The Irish Independent*, January 14, 2008).

"Destruction" is another enduring characteristic of what the media have served up on the digitization of music across the years: "Digital streaming threatened to destroy the industry while downloads could be pirated" (*BBC News*, June 8, 2024); "The MP3 destroyed the old record industry model . . . a tectonic shift . . . that's helped to destroy the personal relationship between a listener and their music collection" (*Attack* magazine, July 4, 2020).

Also, the long-term ramifications of changing consumer behavior for the welfare of recording artists in the context of digital flux are emphasized across many accounts. For example: "Twenty years ago, the idea of free music was so compelling that up to 80m users downloaded Napster and broke the law. The aftershocks are still being felt today" (*The Guardian*, May 31, 2019). And, the picture of the "starving artist" has become a well-established motif: "[I]n the music industry, albums can cost thousands of dollars to produce and . . . they should not come for free. . . . Pirates scour the web . . . to take artists' music and profit illegally" (*Forbes*, February 1, 2016). In this context, recording artists are conceptualized as an endangered species, in need of rescuing and conservation. Take, for example, this desperate plea issued by music producer and DJ, Sahpreem A. King in *Digital Music News*: "Everyone thought that Napster was the second coming of Christ—and the beginning of the music revolution; however, in the midst of this transformation, the fans became increasingly desensitized to the fact, that . . . artists . . . have to make a living from their music. . . . Artisans should be able to make a living from their work no different from a nurse or auto mechanic. . . . For God's sake, something has to give. . . . Let's save the music by starting the conversation" (King, cited in Resnikoff 2013).

About a decade ago, music streaming entered the fray as the apparent panacea for the industry's ills. Initially, we see streaming characterized as a "good Samaritan," bringing the music industry back to life in the aftermath of the peer-to-peer explosion. For example: "How Streaming Saved the Music Industry" (*Financial Times*, January 16, 2017); "The Lazarus Effect . . ." (*New Statesman*, January 9, 2019). But, such generous portrayals of the "outcomes" of streaming platforms were short-lived, and these online delivery services soon assumed the role of antagonist previously occupied by file-sharing sites. Spotify enjoys "an exploitative relationship with musicians," writes Laura Snapes in *The Guardian*; "[A]ny platform that intimidates the creators that underwrite its business is truly dystopian" (Beaumont-Thomas and Snapes 2018). And in this context, the "killing/death" analogy reappears: "Streaming Sites Are Killing The Music Industry" is the headline of Isaac Herron's *Youth Time* magazine article, which proceeds to describe what he perceives as "the streaming plague" where artists like himself "starve for revenue" (Herron 2020). Elsewhere we read that "Music legends warn streaming is killing the industry, with artists driving Ubers to survive," *Birmingham Mail*, March 24, 2021); and "Why is the music industry dying in 2023? . . . [because] streaming companies [are] making handsome gains at the expense of the artist" (*Gemtracks* 2023). It's worth noting that what is often absent from this narrative is an examination and analysis of the role of the major record labels and publishers that, as the primary "rights-holders" who act as intermediaries between artists and streaming platforms (see Hesmondhalgh et al. 2021 for an analysis of the dynamics and distribution of music streaming revenues).

As outlined above, the latest perceived digital menace to surface comes in the form of artificial intelligence (AI). But this also comes accompanied by the resurgence of another older enemy, as a 2023 story in *Billboard* magazine reminds us that "Digital Piracy Still Plagues Music Industry" (Barrionuevo 2023). The accompanying text that highlights a recent USTR report that claims illicit sites for music and film were visited more than 140bn times across the first eight months of 2022, highlighting, according to RIAA CEO Mitch Glazier, "the devastating impact of copyright theft on American creators" (Barrionuevo 2023).

Overall, there is clarity and consensus in journalistic accounts on the continuously disruptive nature of digital distribution technologies in the music domain, and the recurring threats to the welfare of artists and labels posed by the successful diffusion of such technologies across society. Such accounts often carry pleas from artists and industry that policy makers act to tame these dangerous digital innovations and protect a vulnerable cultural sector that is at risk. But this also raises a fundamental question: are there other competing narratives that don't make the news?

COMPLICATING THE NARRATIVE OF DIGITAL DESPONDENCY: WHAT'S NOT MAKING THE NEWS

Academic literature on the implications of unfolding digital developments for the music industry forms a more bemusing and baffling narrative.

The gloomy depiction of internet-induced music industry decline is reinforced in numerous academic publications stretching across a decade or more (for example, Blackburn 2004, 2007; Rob and Waldfogel 2004; Liebowitz 2006a, 2006b, 2008; Zentner 2006; Elberse 2010; Bustinza et al. 2013) among others. These studies span various disciplines, but are primarily situated in the realms of law, economics, and management. They broadly agree that, from the late 1990s onwards, the widening availability of peer-to-peer file-sharing technologies on the internet was a key factor in driving recording industry revenues on a steep downward trajectory.

However, a body of research quickly surfaced to problematize and complicate the piracy narrative. We initially saw the emergence of a few dissenting voices to challenge the dominant perception of "illegal" file-sharing and waning industry revenues. Notably, Burkart and McCourt (2003, 2004) drew our attention to the timing of such actions as the Napster case, which they saw as conveniently arising to deflect attention away from ongoing antitrust investigations by US federal and state agencies into price fixing in the compact disc (CD) market. Furthermore, such a strategy served as a "successful stalling tactic" that allowed major music labels "to reorganize their business relationships and sort out on-line delivery systems in a way that will preserve their de facto oligopoly of production and distribution" (2003, 345).

More significantly, the precise economic implications and outcomes of file-sharing pursuits became much less clear as the phenomenon itself came under more widespread and critical scrutiny. For example, a three-year study of the Canadian recorded music market concludes that there is "no direct evidence to suggest the net effect of P2P file-sharing is either positive or negative" (Andersen and Frenz 2008, 24). In a follow-up study that adopts an evolutionary economics approach, the same authors offer evidence that "P2P file-sharing behaviour may not be bad news for the industry, because such activities create a range of new business opportunities" (Andersen and Frenz 2010, 736).

Elsewhere, a Swedish-based study that conducted a comparative analysis of the effects of evolving digital distribution platforms on the music, software, and book publishing industries claimed that there was "no consensus on the exact extent of ill effects of file-sharing" (Andersson et al. 2009). Furthermore, it asserts that music conglomerates are using alliances, mergers, and acquisitions "in order to consolidate their positions in an attempt to slow down change" (Andersson et al. 2009).

In his critique of an extensive range of existing research on music piracy, Volker Grassmuck (2010) concludes that "the nearly eighty empirical studies under review cannot support allegations by IFPI that illegal file-sharing has been a major factor in the decline in music sales" (Grassmuck 2010, 1). Equally, in investigating the economic and cultural outcomes of file-sharing in the music, film, and games industries, Poort et al. find that "the increased accessibility of culture renders the overall welfare effects of file-sharing robustly positive" (Poort et al. 2010, 35).

Elsewhere, Waldogel (2012) argues that despite the perceived implications of file-sharing on music revenues, evidence "suggests that the quantity of new consequential recorded music has not declined since Napster" (91), implying that "copyright protection is not vital to ensure continued supply in music" (97). And while Hammond's (2014) analysis of the effects of prerelease file-sharing on the album sales of individual artists finds that illegal downloading produces an overall negative impact on record industry revenues, he equally determines that it differentially affects established and new artists. His key finding is that "file sharing benefits more established and popular artists who are signed to major labels" (Hammond 2014, 387).

Ultimately, on the question of "piracy," we are left with a distinct lack of agreement in the halls of academia. Different research illustrates that illicit file-sharing is simultaneously detrimental, beneficial, or irrelevant to the economic health of the music business. However, in many respects, this is now a redundant question. Piracy is out of fashion, surpassed by streaming and later AI as the predominant topics for discussion in considering the health and welfare of labels and artists alike.

Regarding streaming, in a study designed to assess its effects on music industry revenues, Wlömert and Papies (2016) observe the behavioral patterns of 2,500 music consumers across a period of a year. Their ultimate findings signal that "the negative effect of free streaming on industry revenue is offset by the positive effect of paid streaming" (Wlömert and Papies 2016, 314).

In a comparative study of five major music streaming services, Rahimi and Park (2020) illustrate the significant impact of streaming on recording industry growth in recent years, and predict the "exponential growth of this contribution in the years to come" (5–6).

In his economic analysis of the effects of streaming platforms on the music business, Zehr (2021) concludes that not only is streaming enabling the industry to return to pre-P2P levels of profit, it is also successful in "drawing consumers to other areas of the music market" (51).

So again, as with file-sharing, a confusing image is starting to emerge regarding streaming. On one hand, a dominant media narrative emphasizes its dangers to music artists and industry, and on the other, a growing body of studies that contradict that.

However, the usefulness of a continuing story of digital turmoil to major music labels is perhaps most starkly advanced by David Arditi, who sees the aforementioned narrative of industry decline at the hands of digital piracy as "a rhetorical construct that helps to obscure the material reality of the recording industry" (2014, 14). Such a narrative enabled the record industry to significantly expand the spectrum of spaces and places where it could usefully exploit the intellectual property rights it managed and controlled. As Arditi subsequently advances: "[B]y arguing that digital music harmed musicians, record labels successfully convinced musicians, music listeners, journalists, legislators, and the general public that the recording industry needed to develop new sources of revenue in order for musicians to be able to eat" (Arditi 2019, 3). So, let us briefly consider how just such a strategy played out for the major labels, and what its implications have entailed for those companies themselves and for the artists on their rosters.

THE REVITALIZED MAJOR MUSIC LABEL: BUILT BIGGER AND STRONGER THAN ITS PREDECESSORS

If we take stock of how the world's major music rights holders (principally, the major labels) responded to earlier digital developments, it might provide some insight into their resilience, and what we might expect in years to come, once the dust settles on the AI landscape.

The scenario we briefly laid out at the start of this chapter regarding the various sources of Taylor Swift's fortune is instructive here. However distinctive the nature of her contracts with Universal and other key industry actors may be (see, for example, Théberge 2021), the business model is very much reflective of general music sector developments. The past decade has seen a body of scholarly literature emerge that describes the form and nature of how the transnational music business has expanded, and the implications and outcomes for the labels themselves, artists, and music audiences (see, for example, Arditi 2014, 2019; Marshall 2013; Rogers 2013, 2020; Wikström 2020, among others). Here, we become aware of the (economic) value of music as both a primary and a secondary medium. On one hand, music represents a stand-alone media form—one that sees rights owners sell and license recordings to their final consumers via a range of physical and digital distribution and retail platforms (CDs, vinyl, licensed downloads, streaming services, and so on). Equally, music is a core element of all forms of audiovisual media (traditional and new), and music rights owners generate value from licensing their catalogues to the abundance of such outlets that now exist. Moreover, we start to understand the increasing number of ways in music that brands and trademarks are commodified and monetized. What's crucial to grasp here is how the transnational music label has changed its form as the "digital revolution" has been unfolding. In essence, the structure and organization of large music firms have altered significantly as they adjust and adapt to new modes of music production, distribution, and consumption in the changing digital ecosystem.

At the heart of this restructuring process lies a fundamental reenvisioning of the "recording contract," the legally binding agreement between label and artist, that sees the label now routinely acquire ownership and control over an unprecedented (and expanding) range of rights emanating from the performers and songwriters on their roster. What this means for the contemporary major music label is access to a far broader set of potential revenue streams than their historic predecessors would have enjoyed. Labels now derive income from the sale and licensing of recorded music in a range of contexts (digital and physical sales, streaming, broadcast, synchronization); the exploitation of music publishing rights across a broadening spectrum of outlets; a share of their artists' live revenues; proceeds from merchandising (which had a global retail value of $3.5 billion in 2018 [Cochrane 2021]) and the range of spaces and places where music "trademarks" can realize a return; and beyond that, any other conceivable source of revenue generated by the artists on their roster.

Such arrangements are facilitated by "multi-rights" recording contracts (often referred to as 360-degree deals) which evolved in the late 2000s and have subsequently been normalized as industry standard. While, historically, artists signed multiple contracts with different actors in different music industry subsectors (recording, publishing, live, merchandise, other), now a single contract with their record label can cover all (or many) facets of an artist's career. In essence, the majors ceased being just "record" labels and, rather, extended their scope to generate revenue from exploiting rights across the breadth and depth of all areas of their artists' careers, with their investment strategies shifting to increasingly privilege licensing, synchronization, and merchandise (see, for example, Marshall 2013; Rogers 2017; Tschmuck 2016; Guichardaz et al. 2019, for a critical unpacking of multi-rights deals, and the expanding range of revenue-generating opportunities they provide to labels). As such, their interests now extend far beyond those associated with the traditional concept of a record label as we might have known and understood it to be across the twentieth century. As *Rolling Stone* puts it: "the major record companies ... are pinning their futures on the broadness of their menu" (Ingham 2019). Warner was initially "the label most aggressive in pursuing 360s," and operates a policy only to sign new artists to such multi-rights contractual agreements (Marshall 2013, 83). All three labels have been "reorienting themselves towards this new approach, utilising various combinations of acquisition and internal reorganization to support the model" (Marshall 2013, 83).

Beyond this, ventures such as Universal's UMusic Hotels reflect broader industry trends of monetizing music and music brands in nontraditional ways. Universal opened its first resort in Madrid in 2022, promising its guests an "immersive music experience" that includes concerts, themed events, and various leisure environments (Dalugdug 2023). In essence, it represents a further extension of Universal's music and brands into the domains of lifestyle and hospitality and provides another example of how major labels keep developing new sources of income. Additional UMusic resorts are being planned in Biloxi, Mississippi; Atlanta, Georgia; and Orlando, Florida, in the United States, as well as in various locations across Europe and Latin America (Jones 2023).

While all of this has been unfolding, it is also interesting to observe the frequency with which the major labels turn to the judicial system to tame the technological platforms that carry disruptive potential and turn them into sources of licensing revenue. One way of telling the story of the music business in the twenty-first century would be to chronicle the many instances where they sought recourse to the courts. As Aram Sinnreich (2015) notes: "[E]nforcement of copyright became the linchpin of music cartelization, and industry practices and economics morphed to reflect its ascendancy over distribution.... [P]ower no longer resided in monopolizing access to finite retail shelf space or limited radio airtime or scarce consumer dollars and attention; instead, it found purchase in the threat of crippling and sustained litigation against any unsanctioned commerce ..." (617).

The twenty-first century has seen music labels pursue several high-profile legal actions against the producers, suppliers, and users of various technology platforms on the basis of copyright infringement with huge success. Initially, these cases focused on different forms of peer-to-peer sharing technologies (for example, Universal Music v. MP3.com [2000];

A&M Records v. Napster [2001]; MGM v. Grokster [2005]; Capitol Records v. Limewire [2010]). Other cases focused on the users of these services (for example, Capitol Records v. Brianna LaHara [2003]; Capitol Records v. Jammie Thomas-Rasset [2006]; RIAA v. Whitney Harper [2008]; Sony Music Entertainment v. Joel Tennenbaum [2009]). Subsequently, the major music companies brought legal proceedings against internet service providers in an effort to have them held legally responsible for policing online music copyright infringement (for example, BMG Rights Management v. Cox Communications [2015]; Sony Music Entertainment v. Grande Communications [2017]; Warner Bros. Records v. RCN Telecom Services [2019]; Universal v. Bright House Networks [2019]). Streaming services have also ended up in court, (for example, Universal v Grooveshark [2010]; Wixen Music Publishing v. Spotify [2018]; National Music Publishers' Association v. Peloton [2019]), as have stream-ripping services (Warner-Chappell Music v. YouTube-MP3.org [2016]; BPI v. Yout.com, Flvto, 2Conv and Others [2021]). Furthermore, sites like Flvto find themselves on the US government's "Notorious Markets List" and on the European Commission's "Counterfeit and Piracy Watch List" (*Music-News.com* 2021). And as we noted earlier, 2024 saw Universal, Warner, and Sony engage in litigation against AI music services Suno and Udio. The above list offers a small but indicative sample of cases taken by the music industry as digital innovations continue to reshape how music gets distributed and consumed. The IFPI website has, over the years, published a litany of such accounts. With each major digital innovation comes a fresh wave of copyright lawsuits. As Sinnreich notes: "[T]he [music] industry came to view its litigious crusade as analogous to the civil rights movement" (Rosen 2003) and frequently compared its P2P-using customers to shoplifters (Meza 2007), drug dealers, and terrorists (Van Buskirk 2008; no mere idle rhetoric, considering that the film industry and the FBI invoked the Patriot Act to pursue a fan of the TV show SG-1 for allegedly infringing copyrights on his website [Doctorow, 2004])" (Sinnreich 2015).

Moreover, in Sinnreich's earlier book *The Piracy Crusade* (2013), he summarizes the response of the major music companies to the advent of digital distribution as a process that moves through a series of stages with the objective of nullifying the threat from illicit sites before (legally) bringing them under their control. Initially, the industry's biggest labels responded with litigation, then moved toward settlements, followed by licensing deals, and eventually acquisition of many of the "rogue" digital platforms as part of their strategy to manage and control digital distribution.

OUTCOMES OF THESE DEVELOPMENTS: FEATURES AND CHARACTERISTICS OF THE 2020s MUSIC BUSINESS

Let us briefly consider the outcomes of this new major label approach in terms of revenue generation, and the implications regarding their overall position in recording and music publishing markets. As we noted above, the total global value of music copyrights (encompassing phonographic recording, and all facets of music publishing) rests at more than $41 billion, prompting Will Page, the former chief economist at Spotify and PRS for Music to proclaim: "music copyright has never had it so good" (cited in Dredge 2022). Page estimates that that figure breaks down approximately 66/34 percent in favor of recording.

At the time of writing, the trade value of the global recording industry alone is reported to be $28.6 billion (IFPI 2024), a record high. In 2023, the three major labels, Universal, Warner, and Sony were collectively generating more than $2.9 million per hour (Ingham 2023b). As such, these three companies combine to account for approximately 70 percent of the global market (Dredge 2023; Royalty Exchange 2024). However, within the United States, those same three majors accounted for as astonishing 83.5 percent of the recorded music market (Rys 2023). And we must also realize that these major labels also have interests in the 30 percent of the global market not directly under their control. For example, the Alternative Distribution Alliance, owned and operated by the Warner Music Group, represents one of the largest worldwide distributors of independent music, as well as providing marketing, merchandising, and music licensing services to more than 150 "indie" labels. Equally, Sony owns The Orchard, an international digital distribution company that provides services to independent music labels.

A consistent feature of the music business over many decades has been a trend toward ever-greater concentration of ownership. This has continued unabated in the twenty-first century with takeovers, mergers, and joint ventures still characterizing the sector. In many cases, this involves intense and ongoing political lobbying at state and superstate level to secure the go-ahead for buyouts and alliances. A recurring argument advanced by the major record labels has related to the necessity for consolidation in light of digital threats. Key examples include the Sony–BMG merger of 2004, the Live Nation–Ticketmaster merger of 2011, and the breakup of EMI and its takeover by Universal and Warner in 2012. Moreover, the three majors continue to acquire or partner with smaller companies in the recording and music publishing sectors, and they have extended their interests in such domains as music merchandising, production music, and other facets of audiovisual production with ongoing acquisitions across these domains, as well as consumer digital. For example, Sony spent $1.4 billion on takeovers during the first half of 2021 alone (Stassen 2021). As such, they are growing bigger in traditional areas of activity (recording and publishing) and extending and expanding into newer areas of pursuit.

Here, it's worth briefly considering the scale and extent of political lobbying engaged in by music industry organizations. Music companies and representative bodies invested almost $15 million on political lobbying in the United States in 2022, with the Recording Industry Association of America (RIAA) accounting for nearly $7 million of this (Open Secrets 2023). The Universal Music Group and Sony Music Entertainment were the second and third biggest spenders, with a combined outlay of approximately $3.1 million. Across the preceding decade the overall industry spend on lobbying in the United States exceeded $130 million (Open Secrets 2023). Key recipients include members of the Subcommittee on Communications, Technology, and the Internet, and Subcommittee on Privacy, Technology, and the Law, with the aim of influencing intellectual property legislation and gaining support for mergers and alliances.

In the EU context, the IFPI identifies copyright reform, geo-blocking, performers rights, digital services, and AI as some of the areas in which it strives to shape discourse and influence policy (Lobbyfacts EU 2023). The EU Transparency Register shows that between 2014 and 2022, IFPI attended more than seventy meetings with EU commissioners, their cabinet members, or directors-general at the European Commission (cited in LobbyFacts EU 2023). Here too, we consider the extension of real-space intellectual property mechanisms into cyberspace across the past two decades, and the bolstering of music copyright law. This is most recently illustrated by the Music Modernization Act (MMA) of 2018, a landmark piece of US legislation that makes a series of provisions to further protect and enhance music rights holders. Key developments relate to the establishment of a new type of blanket licensing for digital music services (that simplifies the procedure for acquiring licenses for streaming music); and the extension of federal protection to sound recordings made prior to 1972 ("Classics Act").

What we have witnessed across the digital era is ongoing consolidation across core music business sectors, with money and power increasingly centralized. Back in the 1990s, six major companies dominated the global marketplace (Polygram, Sony, Warner, BMG, EMI, and Universal). Within twenty years, the field diminished to just three (Universal, Sony and Warner). And the past ten years has witnessed the ongoing expansion of all three labels. With its operational headquarters in California, Universal has facilities operating in more than sixty countries, and boasts in excess of two hundred separate music labels under its umbrella. Sony Music operates in forty-three territories with approximately 140 labels under its direct or indirect control; and Warner has a direct presence in more than fifty countries, with a series of five "umbrella" labels that combine to own or control some eighty-nine additional music companies.

The distribution of wealth among recording artists is also highly polarized. *The Medium* (2018) cites an earlier report that shows how the top 1 percent of artists account for 77 percent of global recording income. *The Guardian* report such concentration of revenue as the "superstar artist economy" (Ellis-Petersen 2015). Equally, a Scandinavian study of music streaming (Maasø 2018) resonates strongly with these findings, demonstrating how a small minority of superstar acts account for most plays on Spotify. The "star system" remains very much intact, with the promotional and marketing strategy of labels and media outlets focusing on a few highly visible and marketable artists.

The reported global value of music publishing was $6.8 billion in 2022, with predicted growth to $10 billion by 2028 (Precision Reports 2023). However, Page (cited in Dredge 2022) notes that these estimations fail to take into account synchronization revenues and direct deals engaged in between publishers and streaming services. So as such, the actual income from publishing is significantly higher. Like the recorded music sector, music publishing illustrates a similar picture of high concentration, with the same three major companies—Universal, Warner, and Sony—combining to account for approximately 60 percent of the global market (Dredge 2023). However, this becomes 73 percent if we include the two largest "independent" music publishers, Kobalt and BMG (Statista 2023).

Here too it is important to acknowledge the size and scale of the live concert industry, as multi-rights recording deals have resulted in major labels often taking a share of their artists' live performance revenues, which can be as much as 20 percent. Across the twenty-first century, the global concert industry has significantly risen in value. In one of the first studies to collate data from a range of international sources to present a "global" overview of the domain, Dave Laing (2012) estimated the value of the live music industry to be approximately $25 billion in 2010. Notwithstanding the interruptions visited on live music by the COVID-19 pandemic, in 2023 the overall value of the global concert industry in 2024 was estimated to be in excess of $31 billion (Statista 2024). Goldman Sachs predict that this figure could exceed $51 billion by 2030 (Paine 2024a). As live music revenues increase, so too does the share claimed by major labels. And as with the recording domain, wealth here is becoming ever more polarized. The late economist and former US Assistant Secretary of the Treasury Alan Krueger (2019) estimated that since 1982, the share of concert revenues taken by the top 1 percent of performers has increased from 26 percent to 60 percent. And the top 5 percent of performers lay claim to 85 percent of global revenues (Krueger 2019). As with the recording sector, fewer superstar acts now lay claim to a bigger share of a bigger pie.

As all of the above has been unfolding, the music industry has been experiencing an increasing financialization, where established and successful music catalogues are treated as financial assets. Music labels, but also private equity firms, have invested heavily in acquiring the rights to existing music recording and music publishing repertoires, effectively betting on their future revenue-generating potentials. This reflects a shift from viewing music as a cultural product to a financial asset. Some of the most notable acquisitions in recent years include Universal's 2020 purchase of Bob Dylan's full collection of songs (more than six hundred) for a reported $300 million (Sissario 2020; Valinsky 2020); Sony's procurement of Bruce Springsteen's entire master recordings and publishing rights in 2021 (Savage 2021; Thomas 2021); and Queen's 2024 sale of recording, music publishing, and name, image, and likeness assets to Sony for an estimated $1.2 billion (Edward 2024). Moreover, investment companies such as Hipgnosis Song Fund have invested hundreds of millions of dollars acquiring rights to bodies of work by such artists as Neil Young (Greene 2021), Barry Manilow (Brandle 2020), Shakira (Millman 2021), the Red Hot Chili Peppers (Aswad 2021) among many others. 2024 saw Hipgnosis itself acquired by US-based independent music company Concord for $1.4 billion (Shabong 2024).

MONOPOLY POWER

The continuing global expansion of the major labels is epitomized by Warner's recent acquisition of Mumbai-based artist management and live events company E-Positive, who represent some of the biggest stars of the Indian music market and is predicted to reach a value of $4 billion by the end of 2025 (Basoruy 2023). The steady year-on-year growth of Indian music markets (recorded, publishing, and live) over recent years is making it increasingly attractive to the global majors. Moreover, India is set to surpass the United States as the biggest streaming market in the world (Stassen 2024). Prior to buying E-Positive, Warner had already launched Warner

Music India in 2020 and subsequently forged alliances with Tips Music (one of the largest distributors of Bollywood music and film in India) and Sky Digital India (Stassen 2023), as well as purchasing a controlling stake in Indian digital media and music company Divo (WMG 2023). Sony and Universal have much longer histories in the Indian market, having opened operations there in the late 1990s. UMG represents some of the biggest Indian music stars on the global stage, including A. R. Rahman, Arijit Singh, and Leslee Lewis, while the UMG India website highlights the ever-growing presence of Western pop acts in Indian streaming and sales charts, with Lady Gaga, Justin Bieber, Rihanna, and Taylor Swift featuring prominently. Sony has grown to become the largest global major operating in India, with a market share of 25 percent (Agarwal 2022).

Also, reflecting their shared diversification and acquisition strategies, the size of the workforce at all three majors has steadily increased across the past decade. Cumulatively, employee headcount at these labels grew by more than 43 percent since 2013 (Ingham 2023c).

For all three majors, what we have seen is "relatively" consistent growth (albeit with some fluctuations) across the past twenty years. The Universal Music Group's combined revenue intake across all core industry sectors exceeded $12 billion in 2023 (Peoples 2024a), bolstering its position as the biggest music label in the world (and "propelled" by the success of Taylor Swift [Peoples 2024b]). Sony Music Entertainment ranked second with 2023–24 revenues of $10.2 billion, marking a 17 percent increase on the previous year (Paine 2024b). Warner's 2023 intake surpassed $6 billion for the first time (Paine 2023). As such, we can conclude that somewhere close to 70 percent of these labels' income came from the phonographic recording sector, with the remainder spread across other areas of activity.

The net effect of such major label restructuring has been to strengthen and reinforce the market dominance of the global majors, in a context where overall phonographic recording, music publishing, and live concerts revenues have grown exponentially across the past two decades (despite the dire prophesies inherent in media and policy discourse regarding successive waves of digital innovation). Size matters, and the three major music corporations are bigger than earlier incarnations of themselves (and their predecessors) in a number of key ways: they operate more offices in more territories around the world than ever before; their respective rosters of labels are larger than was previously the case; they have aggressively expanded their combined workforce across recent years; they are active in more industrial contexts than "traditional" record labels and engage in a broader range of revenue-generating activities; they control more areas of their artists' careers than their predecessors; and they are making more money.

Here too, it's worth paying attention to relatively recent developments in the live music industry. Its value to the overall music economy has proliferated across the past three decades. By 2019, the value of the live concert industry in North America was estimated at $9.4 billion with the average price of concert tickets for the one hundred top-grossing tours in the United States rising to $94.83, representing a 120 percent increase over a fourteen-year period (Apruzzese et al. 2021, 159). And as we have noted above, the global value of the concert industry for 2023 is estimated at $30 billion. As revenues have increased, so too has monopoly power in this arena. Here, two actors have evolved to dominate the world stage—Live Nation Entertainment (LNE) and the Anschutz Entertainment Group (AEG). Combined they accounted for roughly 70 percent of global concert ticket sales in 2019 (Wayte 2023), with LNE claiming approximately 50 percent. As with the recording industry, takeovers, mergers, and alliances have grown to characterize the global live music industry. LNE's evolution as the global superpower has seen it extend and expand its interests both horizontally across and vertically down the live industry value chain on a worldwide scale. The Beverly Hills–based company is the world's biggest touring agent and concert promoter, and its interests also span venue operation, festival operation, ticketing (primary and secondary), and artist management. 2022 saw LNE host 44,000 shows for 7,800 acts across forty-eight countries, to an overall audience of 121m people (LNE Annual Report 2023). LNE currently produces 147 festivals globally, owns and/or operates 338 concert venues, provides management services to some 410 artists, and provides ticketing services (via Ticketmaster) to some 9,300 clients around the world. Its revenue intake from concerts for 2022 was $13.5 billion, with just under $1 billion more generated from related advertising and sponsorship. In terms of sheer scale (in the scope of its operations and the extent of the wealth it generates), such global dominance is unprecedented.

REFLECTIONS

Yes, AI is different from earlier digital innovations that affected the music industry due to its advanced capabilities in automation and creativity. But peer-to-peer file-sharing was also radically different when it first emerged as a technology of mass distribution. Digitized files made for the loss of "scarcity" (once digitized, music can be copied and shared limitless times). Yet successive waves of innovation in peer-to-peer networks, from Napster through decentralized networks like Kazaa and Gnutella, and the subsequent BitTorrent protocol did not collapse the music industry. Each of these technologies, in turn, increased the resilience of file-sharing networks against legal takedowns. Later, we saw the evolution of "pirate" streaming sites and streaming ripping tools. Yet, despite such a coalition of seemingly pernicious technological forces, the mid-2020s see the music business in rude economic health across all its core sectors. Moreover, the fundamental power structures that underpin and influence the domain of music remain largely unaltered from predigital times. In this context, the term *digital revolution* is a misnomer. Yes, the ways in which music gets made, distributed, and consumed have all evolved tremendously over the twenty-first century, but despite the prospects and possibilities emanating from technological developments, all core music sectors continue to reflect strong oligopolistic trends, with a handful of very large companies and a relatively small number of superstar artists yielding most of the revenue. As we have seen, the strategies and tactics by which the biggest labels now produce these revenues have expanded as they continue to evolve a broader and more diverse range of profit sources from the various music "rights" under their control. Furthermore, such concentrated power in phonographic recording, music publishing, and live music, respectively, continues to give "the few" substantial control over what music gets produced, promoted, distributed, and performed around the world. If this is the situation after twenty-five years of digital disruption, why then should we assume that AI will explode this universe?

Those labels that currently dominate the global marketplace are also markedly different in form and nature from their appearance at the turn of the millennium. Too little attention has been paid to their changing modus operandi as our focus remains on the fast-moving technological environment. A key aspect of transnational major label strategy has involved shaping and controlling mainstream media accounts of the digital shift that have functioned to accommodate, and make palatable, institutional and organizational-level reconstruction of the music business per se. Controlling the media narrative has meant that mergers, joint ventures, and acquisitions aimed at preserving the dominant position of major labels have proceeded with little scrutiny or pushback from within policy circles, and the reach of copyright law has extended.

We have witnessed the creation of "realities" through language use and media discourse, realities that ultimately serve the corporate interests and agendas of the biggest players in the global music business. Over recent decades, we have seen mainstream media largely skew to the ideological agenda of global music industry power bases. However, what specific criteria of "truth" apply to test these claims? It is not clear that journalism has worked this out. Media commentary offers little if any acknowledgment of scholarly research that challenges the dominant narrative. The predominantly one-track approach to how the mainstream media cover the evolving music/digital convergence implies that many in the field of journalism operate with an overly simplistic agenda. And here, we must be particularly attentive to the warnings received from Stuart Hall et al. (1978) regarding the central role of powerful sources in shaping media discourse. Elite media, Hall tells us, construct consensus. However, ". . . it is a consensus structured in dominance. This happens . . . through journalists seeking 'accredited sources'—the institutional spokesperson—to provide truth claims, so that power is reproduced through the media" (Hall 1978, 58; cited in Daniele 2010). The outcome of the media's partiality toward the perspectives of those in power is that the major music labels themselves, and their representative trade bodies, become the key authorities (or "primary definers," to use Hall's term) in shaping discourse.

But, perhaps the outcome-to-date of the music industry in the context of digital distribution could have been more accurately predicted had we paid greater attention to the history of the business. American academic, author, and critic Isaac Goldberg, in his 1930 work *Tin Pan Alley: A Chronicle of the American Popular Music Racket*, provides a clue: "Seeking to capture, for profit, the ear and heart of the American public, the music industry . . . is an industry tainted by commercialism and insincerity" (Goldberg 1930, 332). "[T]he moving pictures did not destroy it; the radio poured new life into its veins; the talkies adopted it . . . the coming of television can have no adverse effect upon this singing fool" (Goldberg 1930, 330). Dealing with new media technologies is nothing new to the music business, nor has it ever held any genuine fear for its most powerful actors. When needed, the state has always been at hand to legislate and administer the required "justice."

So, what next? We are offered a further clue from what is perhaps an unlikely source—celebrity fashion and lifestyle magazine *Vogue*: "If anyone can stop the coming AI hellscape, it's Taylor Swift" (Specter 2024).

REFERENCES

Andersen, B., and M. Frenz. (2008). *The impact of music downloads and P2P file-sharing on the purchase of music in Canada*. Working paper. Dynamics of Institutions of Markets in Europe. http://www.dime-eu.org/files/active/0/WP82-IPR.pdf.

Andersen, B., and M. Frenz. (2010). "Don't blame the P2P file-sharers: the impact of free music downloads on the purchase of music CDs in Canada." in *Journal of Evolutionary Economics* 20: 715–40.

Anderson, J. (2023). 'Will artificial intelligence wreck the music industry?" in *Two Storey Melody*, January 23. https://twostorymelody.com/artificial-intelligence-in-the-music-industry/.

Andersson, B., L. Lahtinen, and P. Pierce. (2009). "File-sharing—A threat to intellectual property rights, or is the music industry just taking us for a spin?" *ECIS 2008 Proceedings*. http://aisel.aisnet.org/ecis2008/3.

Apruzzese, J., P. G. Barretta, and T. Tompkins. (2021). "Impact and Hope for the Live Music Industry." *Ethnomusicology Review* 24. https://ethnomusicologyreview.ucla.edu/sites/default/files/er_v24_16barretta_etal.pdf>.

Arditi, D. (2014). "Downloading is Killing Music: The Recording Industry's Piracy Panic Narrative." *Civilizations (The State of the Music Industry)* 13: 13–32.

Arditi, D. (2019). "Music is everywhere: setting a digital music trap." *Critical Sociology* 45, no. 4–5: 617–30.

Artists Rights Alliance (2024). *Stop Devaluing Music*. https://artistrightsnow.medium.com/200-artists-urge-tech-platforms-stop-devaluing-music-559fb109bbac.

Ashworth, L. (2023). "Why is it so hard to work out how much money Taylor Swift is making?" *Financial Times*, November 2. https://www.ft.com/content/630a62f2-7117-43e5-89a3-3e16e73c99b6.

Aswad, J. (2020). "Red Hot Chili Peppers to Sell Song Catalog to Hipgnosis for Upwards of $140 Million." *Variety*, May 3. https://variety.com/2020/music/news/barry-manilow-songs-hipgnosis-merck-mercuriadis-1234723318/.

Aswad, J. (2024a). "Universal Music Posts $3.2 Billion Revenue in Second Quarter, Publishing up 10 percent as Streaming Revenue Dips." *Variety*, July 24. https://variety.com/2024/music/news/universal-music-second-quarter-2024-streaming-revenue-down-1236083074/.

Aswad, J. (2024b). "Warner Music Stock Jumps After Big Streaming Boost in Third Quarter." *Variety*, August 7. https://variety.com/2024/music/news/warner-music-stock-jumps-streaming-boost-2024-third-quarter-1236098558/.

Basoruy, T. (2023). "Value of the music industry in India 2007–2025" Statista, May 15. https://www.statista.com/statistics/235845/value-of-the-music-industry-in-india/.

Barrionuevo, A. (2023). "Digital Piracy Still Plagues Music Industry as Criminals Employ New Tactics, Says New Report." *Billboard*, February 1. https://www.billboard.com/pro/online-piracy-plagues-music-industry-new-methods/.

Beaumont-Thomas, and L. Snapes. (2018). "Has 10 years of Spotify ruined music?" *The Guardian*, October 5. https://www.theguardian.com/music/2018/oct/05/10-years-of-spotify-should-we-celebrate-or-despair.

Blackburn, D. (2004) *Does File Sharing Affect Record Sales?* Cambridge MA: Harvard University, Department of Economics Working Paper.

Blackburn, D. (2007). *The Heterogeneous Effects of Copying: The Case of Recorded Music*. Cambridge, MA: Harvard University, Department of Economics Working Paper.

BPI (2023). *Written Evidence Submitted by the British Phonographic Industry (BPI)*.

Brandle, L. (2020) "Hipgnosis Songs Buys Barry Manilow Catalog." *Billboard*, August 3. https://www.billboard.com/pro/hipgnosis-songs-buys-barry-manilow-catalogue/.

Bruner, R. (2024). "Here's Why Taylor Swift Is Re-Releasing Her Old Albums." *Time*, August 2. https://time.com/5949979/why-taylor-swift-is-rerecording-old-albums/.

Burkart, P., and T. McCourt. (2003). "Infrastructure for the Celestial Jukebox." *Popular Music* 23, no. 3: 349–62.

Bustinza, O., F. Vendrell-Herrero, G. Parry, and V. Myrthianos. (2013). "Music business models and piracy." *Industrial Management and Data Systems* 113, no. 1: 4–22.

Cochrane, L. (2022). "I'm with the brand! How merch saved the music industry." *The Guardian*, October 21. https://www.theguardian.com/music/2022/oct/21/im-with-the-brand-how-merch-saved-the-music-industry.

Companies Market Cap. (2023). "Market capitalization of Universal Music Group." *CompaniesMarketCap.com*, April 11. https://companiesmarketcap.com/universal-music-group/marketcap/#:~:text=Market%20cap%3A%20%2444.83%20Billion,cap%20according%20to%20our%20data.

Cooper, A. (2024). "'Protect Taylor Swift' trends as X removes inappropriate AI images." CBC News, January 26. https://www.cbc.ca/kidsnews/post/protect-taylor-swift-trends-as-x-removes-inappropriate-ai-images.

Dalugdug, M. (2023). "Universal launches its first music-based experiential hotel in Madrid." *Music Business Worldwide*, January 10. https://www.musicbusinessworldwide.com/universal-music-group-opens-its-first-music-based-experiential-hotel-in-madrid/.

Daniele, L. (2010). "What is the nature of the relationship between journalists and their sources? Who controls it?" Linda Daniele, Adventures in Writing. https://lindadaniele.wordpress.com/2010/0/25/what-is-the-nature-of-the-relationship-between-journalists-and-their-sources-who-controls-it/.

Dredge, S. (2022). "Will Page says 'music copyright has never had it so good' as global revenues reach almost $40 billion." *Music Business Worldwide*, November 4. https://archive.completemusicupdate.com/article/will-page-says-music-copyright-has-never-had-it-so-good-as-global-revenues-reach-almost-40-billion/#:~:text=By%20Chris%20Cooke%20%7C%20Published%20on,now%20almost%20%2440%20billion%20worldwide.

Dredge, S. (2023a). "DIY and non major/Merlin music now accounts for a quarter of Spotify streams." *Music Ally*, February 3. https://musically.com/2023/02/03/diy-artists-now-account-for-a-quarter-of-spotifys-music-streams/.

Dredge, S. (2023b). "Music and Copyright publishes its market share analysis for 2022." *Music Ally*, April 26. https://musically.com/2023/04/26/music-copyright-publishes-its-market-share-analysis-for-2022/.

Drott, E. (2018). "Music as a Technology of the Self: A Social History of Listening in the Twentieth Century." *Critical Inquiry* 45, no. 1: 23–48.

Edward, T. (2024). "Queen reportedly closing on $1.2 billion sale of their music catalogue." *Smooth Radio*, February 19. https://www.smoothradio.com/artists/queen/music-catalogue-sale-billion/.

Ellis-Petersen, H. (2015) "Adele's 25 set to make UK chart history as sales of new album soar." *The Guardian*, November 22. https://www.theguardian.com/music/2015/nov/22/adele-25-uk-charts-album-sales-record.

Epstein, M. (2023). "How will AI impact the future of music?" *Complex Volume*, March 22. https://www.complex.com/pigeons-and-planes/how-will-ai-change-the-music-industry.

Fielder, J. (2021). "Universal Music Group flotation: Five things you need to know." *Euronews*, September 21. https://www.euronews.com/culture/2021/09/21/universal-music-group-flotation-five-things-you-need-to-know.

Fleischer, R. (2017). "If the Song Has No Price, Is It Still a Commodity? Rethinking the Commodification of Digital Music." *Culture Unbound* 9, no. 2: 146–62.

Fraser, D. (2024). "How 'Swiftonomics' is impacting the music industry." BBC News, June 8. https://www.bbc.com/news/articles/cleex2epjn8o.

Grassmuck, V. (2010). *Academic Studies on the Effect of File-Sharing on the Recorded Music Industry: A Literature Review.* Projeto de Pesquisa de Grupo de Pesquisa em Política Pública para o Acesso à Informação Escola de Artes, Ciências e Humanidades Universidade de São Paulo.

Greene, A. (2021) "Neil Young Sells Catalog Rights to Merck Mercuriadis' Hipgnosis." *Rolling Stone*, January 6. https://www.rollingstone.com/pro/news/neil-young-music-catalog-hipgnosis-investment-1110037/.

Guichardaz, R., L. Bach, and J. Penin. (2019). "Music industry intermediation in the digital era and the resilience of the Majors' oligopoly: the role of transactional capability." *Industry and Innovation* 26, no. 7: 843–69.

Hammond, R. G. (2014). "Profit Leak? Pre-Release File Sharing and the Music Industry." *Southern Economic Journal* 81, no. 2: 387–408.

Hesmondhalgh, D. (2018). *The Cultural Industries*. 4th ed. London: Sage Publications.

Hesmondhalgh, D., R. Osborne, H. Sun, and K. Barr. (2021). *Music Creators' Earnings on the Digital Era*. Newport: Intellectual Property Office.

Hickey, S. (2008). Industry crisis as album sales drop." *The Irish Independent*, January 14. https://www.independent.ie/irish-news/industry-crisis-as-album-sales-drop-by-10pc/26344592.html.

Honeyman, T. (2014). "How One Generation Was Single-Handedly Able to Kill the Music Industry." *Elite Daily*, June 6. https://www.elitedaily.com/music/how-one-generation-was-able-to-kill-the-music-industry/593411.

Huppe, M. (2022). "Artificial Intelligence has big implications for ownership in the music industry." *Forbes*, December 12. https://www.forbes.com/sites/forbesbusinesscouncil/2022/12/12/artificial-intelligence-has-big-implications-for-ownership-in-the-music-industry/.

IFPI, (2023). Global Music Report 2023 [online]. https://www.ifpi.org/wp-content/uploads/2020/03/Global_Music_Report_2023_State_of_the_Industry.pdf.

IFPI. (2024). *Global Music Report 2024*. https://globalmusicreport.ifpi.org/.

Ingham, T. (2019). "Every Music Company Is Morphing into the Same Thing." *Rolling Stone*, March 22. https://www.rollingstone.com/music/music-features/every-music-company-is-morphing-into-the-same-thing-811329/.

Ingham, T. (2023a). "Analysts are starting to believe that AI may be an existential threat for the major labels. Is that overly pessimistic?" *Music Business Worldwide*, April 11. https://www.musicbusinessworldwide.com/ai-may-be-an-existential-threat-for-the-major-labels-overly-pessimistic/.

Ingham, T. (2023b). "The 3 major music companies are now jointly generating approximately $2.9m per hour." *Music Business Worldwide*, May 15. https://www.musicbusinessworldwide.com/the-3-major-music-companies-are-now-jointly-generating-approximately-2-9m-per-hour/.

Ingham, T. (2023c). "The three major labels employed more than 27,000 people between them last year—up by 6,660 on 2017." *Music Business Worldwide*, June 28. https://www.musicbusinessworldwide.com/the-3-major-music-companies-employed-over-27000-people-between-them-last-year-up-by-over-7000-on-2017/.

Ingram, M. (2008). "Want a snapshot of an industry in crisis? Take a look at the music business right now." *Globe and Mail*, January 31.

Jones, B. (2023). "How UMusic Hotels plans to disrupt the industry with live events and community engagement." *Hospitality Investor*, January 24. https://www.hospitalityinvestor.com/strategy/how-umusic-hotels-plans-disrupt-industry-live-events-and-community-engagement.

Kondoudis, M. (n.d.). *Taylor Swift Trademarks: A Complete Guide*. https://www.mekiplaw.com/taylor-swift-trademarks-explained/.

Krueger, A. (2019). *Rockonomics: A Backstage Tour of What the Music Industry Can Teach Us about Economics (and our Future)*. London: John Murray.

Liebowitz, S. (2006a). "Economists Examine File-Sharing and Music Sales." In G. Illing and P. Waelbroeck (eds.), *The Industrial Organization of Digital Goods and Electronic Markets*, 145–74. Cambridge, MA: MIT Press.

Liebowitz, S. (2006b). "File sharing: Creative destruction or just plain destruction?" *Journal of Law and Economics* 49(1): 1–28.

Liebowitz, S. (2008). "Testing file-sharing's impact on music album sales in cities." *Management Science* 54(4): 852–59.

Live Nation Entertainment. (2023). *Live Nation Entertainment 2022 Annual Report*. https://investors.livenationentertainment.com/sec-filings/annual-reports/content/0001335258-23-000048/0001335258-23-000048.pdf.

Lobbyfacts EU. (2023). *IFPI Representing recording industry worldwide*. https://www.lobbyfacts.eu/datacard/ifpi-representing-recording-industry-worldwide?rid=60394321918-91&sid=177564#data-card-data-info.

Lynskey, D. (2024). "It's the age of Swiftonomics—but will Taylor Swift's phenomenal success trickle down?" *The Guardian*, June 1. https://www.theguardian.com/music/article/2024/jun/01/its-the-age-of-swiftonomics-but-will-taylor-swifts-phenomenal-success-trickle-down.

Maasø, A. (2018). "Music streaming, festivals and the eventisation of music." *Popular Music and Society* 41, no. 2: 154–75.

Machin, D., and T. van Leeuvan. (2007). *Global Media Discourse: A Critical Introduction*. Abingdon: Routledge.

Mann, C. (2003). "2003: The Year That Music Dies." *Wired*, February 1. https://www.wired.com/2003/02/dirge/.

Marshall, E. (2023a). "Sony Music Posts $10B in Annual Revenue as Profits Jump 25%." *Billboard*, April 26. https://www.billboard.com/pro/sony-music-fiscal-2022-earnings-revenue-profit/.

Marshall, E. (2023b). "Universal Music Revenues Jump 21% on Recorded Music Subscriptions, Streaming in 2022." *Billboard*, March 2. https://www.billboard.com/pro/universal-music-q4-2022-earnings-streaming-publishing-umg-financials/.

Marshall, L. (2013). "The 360 deal and the 'new' music industry" *European Journal of Cultural Studies* 16(1): 77–99.

McCourt, T., and P. Burkart. (2003). "When Creators, Corporations and Consumers Collide: Napster and the Development of On-line Music Distribution." *Media, Culture and Society* 25, no. 3: 333–50.

Medium. (2018). "The Top 1% of Artists Earn 77% of Recorded Music Revenue." *Medium.com*, May 8. https://medium.com/@volareo/the-top-1-of-artists-earn-77-of-recorded-music-revenue-abb267b25ccd.

McIntyre, H. (2024). "Taylor Swift's New Album Is Up More Than 1,200% In Sales." *Forbes*, July 20. https://www.forbes.com/sites/hughmcintyre/2024/07/20/taylor-swifts-new-album-is-up-more-than-1200-in-sales/.

Millman, E. (2021). "Shakira Sells Her Music Catalog to Hipgnosis Songs Fund." *Rolling Stone*, January 13. https://www.rollingstone.com/pro/news/shakira-sells-catalog-to-merck-mercuriadis-hipgnosis-songs-fund-1113586/.

Millman, E. (2024). "Taylor Swift's 'Tortured Poets Department' Outsells Rest of 2024's Top 10 Albums Combined." *Rolling Stone*, July 16. https://www.rollingstone.com/music/music-news/taylor-swift-the-tortured-poets-department-best-selling-album-2024-so-far-1235061422/.

Mitra, M. (2024). "Swiftonomics: The Economic Influence of Taylor Swift." *Investopedia*, March 8. https://www.investopedia.com/swiftonomics-definition-8601178.

Morrow, G. (2018). *Artist Management: Agility in the Creative and Cultural Industries*. London: Routledge.

Mulligan, M. (2023). "Recorded music market 2022 | Reality bites." *Midia Research*, March 16. https://midiaresearch.com/blog/recorded-music-market-2022-reality-bites.

Music and Copyright. (2022). "SME and WMG the biggest market share winners in 2021." *Music and Copyright*. https://musicandcopyright.wordpress.com/2022/04/05/sme-and-wmg-the-biggest-market-share-winners-in-2021/.

Music-News.com. (2021). "Record industry wins double landmark UK court victory in new cyberlocker and stream-ripping piracy cases." *Music-News.com*, April 21. https://www.music-news.com/news/Underground/138494/Record-industry-wins-double-landmark-UK-court-victory-in-new-cyberlocker-and-stream-ripping-piracy-cases.

Open Secrets. (2023). *Recorded Music and Music Production: Lobbying, 2022*. OpenSecrets.org. https://www.opensecrets.org/industries/lobbying.php?cycle=2022&ind=C2600.

Paine, A. (2023). "Warner Music Group tops $6 billion in revenue for the first time in its history." *Music Week*, November 16. https://www.musicweek.com/labels/read/warner-music-group-tops-6-billion-in-revenue-for-the-first-time-in-its-history/088863.

Paine, A. (2024a). "Music in the Air 2024: Live, publishing and superfans boost Goldman Sachs' global growth forecast." *Music Week*, May 3. https://www.musicweek.com/labels/read/music-in-the-air-2024-live-publishing-and-superfans-boost-goldman-sachs-global-growth-forecast/089723#:~:text=Live%20music%20is%20forecast%20to,of%2047.3%25%20over%20that%20period.

Paine, A. (2024b). "Sony Music reports 17% revenue increase in 2023–24 financial year." *Music Week*, May 14. https://www.musicweek.com/labels/read/sony-music-reports-17-revenue-increase-in-2023-24-financial-year/089774.

Parikh, T. (2024). "Taylor Swift and the fallacy plaguing modern economics." *Financial Times*, July 26. https://www.ft.com/content/93a3eed4-a42d-4822-948c-de75aeb5b0d2.

Parodi, A. (2023). "Taylor Swift merchandising sales boost Universal Music's results." *Reuters*, July 26. https://www.reuters.com/business/universal-music-reports-higher-than-expected-core-profit-helped-by-strong-sales-2023-07-26/.

Patrick, H. (2024). "'Protect Taylor Swift' trends on X/Twitter after 'disgusting' AI photos posted on platform." *The Independent*, January 26. https://www.independent.co.uk/tv/culture/taylor-swift-ai-photos-twitter-b2485437.html#:~:text=Taylor%20Swift%20fans%20started%20a%20powerful%20online%20movement,Taylor%20Swift%22%20to%20drown%20out%20the%20nonconsensual%20images.

Peoples, G. (2023). "Taylor Swift Grossed Almost $2B This Year from Her Music, Movie, Touring and Concert Merchandise." *Billboard*, December 13. https://www.billboard.com/business/business-news/taylor-swift-earned-2-billion-music-movie-touring-1235555994/.

Peoples, G. (2024a). "Universal Music Annual Revenue Crosses $12B After Strong Q4 for Recorded Music." *Billboard*, February 28. https://www.billboard.com/business/business-news/universal-music-q4-2023-annual-earnings-umg-financials-1235617508/.

Peoples, G. (2024b). "Universal Music Group Revenue Up Nearly 9% on Taylor Swift Sales, Publishing and Merchandise Gains." *Billboard*, July 24. https://www.billboard.com/pro/universal-music-earnings-q2-2024-revenue-up-taylor-swift-merch/.

Pisani, J. (2023). "It's Taylor Swift's Economy, and We're All Living in It." *Wall Street Journal*, July 23. https://www.wsj.com/arts-culture/taylor-swift-taylornomics-concert-eras-tour-local-economy-9fa1d492.

Poort, J., P. Rutten, and N. van Eijk. (2010). "Legal, Economic and Cultural Aspects of File Sharing." in *Communications and Strategies* 77: 35–54.

Precision Reports. (2023). *Emerging Music Publishing Market Analysis by Region and Music Publishing Market Size 2023–2030*. Barchart.com. https://www.barchart.com/story/news/19258937/emerging-music-publishing-market-analysis-by-region-and-music-publishing-market-size-2023-2030.

Preston, P., and J. Rogers. (2010). "The Three Cs of Key Music Sector Trends Today: Commodification, Concentration and Convergence." In Dal Yong Jin, ed., *Global Media Convergence and Cultural Transformation: Emerging Social Patterns and Characteristics*, 373–96. Hershey, PA: IGI Global.

Rahimi, R., and K. Park (2020). *A Comparative Study of Internet Architecture and Applications of Online Music Streaming Services: The Impact on The Global Music Industry Growth.* Paper presented at International Conference of Information and Communication Technology (ICoICT), Yogyakarta, Indonesia, June 24–26.

Resnikoff, P. (2013). "Technology Didn't Kill the Music Industry. The Fans Did." *Digital Music News*, November 14. https://www.digitalmusicnews.com/2013/11/14/technologydidntfans/.

Resnikoff, P. (2024). "DMN Pro Weekly Report: Could the Major Labels Lose Against Suno and Udio? A Pressing Look at Where These Critical Cases Stand." *Digital Music News*, August 8. https://www.digitalmusicnews.com/pro/udio-suno-legal-update-weekly/?utm_source=Daily+Snapshot&utm_campaign=994bd97db1-Daily_Snapshot_August_8th_2024&utm_medium=email&utm_term=0_-77cac1fdfd-%5BLIST_EMAIL_ID%5D&mc_cid=994bd97db1&mc_eid=a931092497.

Rogers, J. (2013). *The Death and Life of the Music Industry in the Digital Age.* New York: Bloomsbury.

Rogers, J. (2020). "Re-conceptualising the record industry: Audio-visual nexus in an evolving digital environment." In E. Encabo, ed., *My Kind of Sound: Popular Music and Audiovisual Culture*, 60–78. Cambridge Scholar.

Rolling Stone Culture Council. (n.d.), "Unveiling the Impacts and Disruption of AI on Music Industry Stakeholders." *Rolling Stone.* https://council.rollingstone.com/blog/the-impacts-and-disruption-of-ai-on-music-industry-stakeholders.

Roseborough, V. (2023). "Music industry sounds alarm over AI threat, calls on Congress to act." in *The Hill.* https://thehill.com/homenews/house/4070544-music-industry-sounds-alarm-over-ai-threat-calls-on-congress-to-act/.

Rys, D. (2023). "Record Label Market Share Q4 2022: Republic's 'Midnights' Run Outpaces a Surging Sony." *Billboard*, January 11. https://www.billboard.com/pro/record-label-market-share-q4-2022-republic-surges-sony-big-year/.

Sarnoff, L. (2024). "Taylor Swift and No AI Fraud Act: How Congress plans to fight back against AI deepfakes." *ABC News*, January 30. https://abcnews.go.com/US/taylor-swift-ai-fraud-act-congress-plans-fight/story?id=106765709.

Savage, M. (2021). "Bruce Springsteen sells his entire music catalogue for $500m." *BBC News*, December 16. https://www.bbc.com/news/entertainment-arts-59680797.

Shabong, Y. (2024). "Hipgnosis agrees sale to Concord in $1.4 bln music rights deal." *Reuters*, April 18. https://www.reuters.com/business/media-telecom/concord-chorus-buy-music-investor-hipgnosis-songs-fund-14-bln-2024-04-18/#:~:text=April%2018%20%28Reuters%29%20-%20Nashville-based%20independent%20music%20company,catalogues%20of%20artists%20including%20Shakira%20and%20Neil%20Young.

Sinnreich, A. (2013). *The Piracy Crusade: How the Music Industry's War on Sharing Destroys Markets and Erodes Civil Liberties.* Amherst and Boston: University of Massachusetts Press.

Sinnreich, A. (2015). "Music Cartels and the Dematerialization of Power." In A. Bennett and S. Waksman, eds., *The Sage Handbook of Popular Music*, 613–28. London: Sage.

Sissario, B. (2020). "Bob Dylan Sells His Songwriting Catalog in Blockbuster Deal." *New York Times*, December 7. https://www.nytimes.com/2020/12/07/arts/music/bob-dylan-universal-music.html.

Smith, D. (2023). "The Music Industry's Valuation—Excluding Live Shows—Hit $41.5 Billion During 2022, According to a New Analysis." Digital Music News, November 6. https://www.digitalmusicnews.com/2023/11/06/music-industry-value-2023/.

Smith, D. (2024). "Sony Music Entertainment Reports Double-Digit Calendar Q2 Revenue Jump Amid Publishing Growth and Favorable Exchange Rates." *Digital Music News*, August 7. https://www.digitalmusicnews.com/2024/08/07/sony-music-earnings-q2-2024/.

Specter, E. (2024). "If Anyone Can Stop the Coming AI Hellscape, It's Taylor Swift." *Vogue*, January 26. https://www.vogue.com/article/taylor-swift-deepfake-x-possible-legal-action#:~:text=Now%2C%20Swift%20is%20reportedly%20considering,singer%20told%20the%20Daily%20Mail.

Srivastava, A. (2024). "White House sounds alarm over explicit AI-generated Taylor Swift photos, 'Congress should take . . .'" *Hindustan Times*, January 27. https://www.hindustantimes.com/entertainment/music/white-house-sounds-alarm-over-explicit-ai-generated-taylor-swift-photos-congress-should-take-101706315044440.html.

Stassen, M. (2021). "Sony spent $1.4bn on acquisitions in the last six months, and Rob Stringer's not stopping there." *Music Business Worldwide*, May 27. https://musicbusinessworldwide.com/sony-musics-spent-1-4bn-on-acquisitions-in-the-last-six-months-and-rob-stringers-not-stopping-there/.

Stassen, M. (2023). "Warner buys India-based management and live events company E-Positive, home to superstar Darshan Raval." *Music Business Worldwide*, October 10. https://www.musicbusinessworldwide.com/darshan-raval-warner-acquires-e-positive-in-india/.

Statista. (2022). *Total Recorded Music Share Worldwide, by Label, 2021*. Statista. https://www.statista.com/statistics/947107/recorded-music-market-worldwide-label/#:~:text=Share%20of%20global%20recorded%20music%20market%20in%202021%2C%20by%20label&text=According%20to%20the%20source%2C%20music,share%20between%202018%20and%202020.

Statista. (2023a). *Revenue market share of the largest music publishers worldwide from 2007 to 2022*. Statista. https://www.statista.com/statistics/272520/market-share-of-the-largest-music-publishers-worldwide/.

Statista. (2023b). *Music events—worldwide*. Statista. https://www.statista.com/outlook/dmo/eservices/event-tickets/music-events/worldwide.

Statista. (2024). *Live music industry revenue worldwide from 2014 to 2024, by source*. Statista. https://www.statista.com/statistics/1096409/live-music-industry-revenue-worldwide-by source/#:~:text=According%20to%20a%202020%20study,billion%20U.S.%20dollars%20in%202024.

Théberge, P. (2021). "Love and Business: Taylor Swift as Celebrity, Businesswoman, and Advocate." *Contemporary Music Review* 40, no.1: 41–59.

Thomas, D. (2023). "Annual revenue from music copyright climbs to $41.5bn." *Financial Times*, November 5. https://www.ft.com/content/ff370cd2-1f4c-4935-92b1-da33eadb7485.

Thomas, L. (2021). "Bruce Springsteen sells his music catalog to Sony in massive deal." *CNBC*, December 16. https://www.cnbc.com/2021/12/16/bruce-springsteen-is-selling-his-music-catalog-in-massive-deal-report.html.

Tschmuck, P. (2016). "From Record Selling to Cultural Entrepreneurship: The Music Economy in the Digital Paradigm Shift." In P. Wikström and R. DeFillippi, eds., *Business Innovation and Disruption in the Music Industry*. Dordrecht and Cheltenham: Edward Elgar.

Valinsky, J. (2020). "Bob Dylan sells his entire catalog of songs to Universal." CNN Business, December 7. https://edition.cnn.com/2020/12/07/media/bob-dylan-song-catalog/index.html.

Waldfogel, R. (2012). "Music Piracy and Its Effects on Demand, Supply, and Welfare." *Innovation, Policy and the Economy* 12, no. 1: 91–109.

Wang, A. X. (2018). "Taylor Swift's New Record Deal Affects Thousands of Other Musicians." *Rolling Stone*, November 19. https://www.rollingstone.com/pro/news/taylor-swift-universal-republic-deal-spotify-758102/.

Warner Music Group. (2021). *Annual Report 2021*. https://investors.wmg.com/static-files/17781830-b658-41f5-94fc-eac9cffe9edd.

Warner Music Group. (2023). *Warner Music India Signs Deal to Acquire a Majority Stake in Divo, the Largest Digital Media and Music Company in South India*. February 8. https://www.wmg.com/news/warner-music-india-signs-deal-to-acquire-a-majority-stake-in-divo-the-largest-digital-media-and-music-company-in-south-india#:~:text=Warner%20Music%20India%20has%20signed%20a%20deal%20to,in%20the%20entertainment%20sector%20across%20the%20whole%20country.

Warner Chappell Production Music. (2022). About Us. https://uk.warnerchappellpm.com/about.

Warrington, J. (2023). "AI music is danger to artists, Universal chief tells Hunt." *The Telegraph*, May 21. https://www.telegraph.co.uk/business/2023/05/21/ai-music-danger-artists-universal-jeremy-hunt/.

Wayte, L. (2023). *Pay For Play: How the Music Industry Works, Where the Money Goes, and Why*. University of Oregon Libraries. https://opentext.uoregon.edu/payforplay/.

Wikström, P. (2020). *The Music Industry: Music in the Cloud*. 3rd ed. Cambridge: Polity Press.

Wlömert, N., and P. Papies. (2016). "On-demand streaming services and music industry revenues—Insights from Spotify's market entry." *International Journal of Research in Marketing* 33, no. 2: 314–27.

Zehr, Hugh. (2021). 'An Economic Analysis of the Effects of Streaming on the Music Industry in Response to Criticism from Taylor Swift." *Major Themes in Economics* 23: 51–63.

Zentner, A. (2006). "Measuring the effect of file-sharing on music purchases." *Journal of Law and Economics* 49, no. 1: 63–90.

CHAPTER 10

"THE WAY WE PUT AN END TO WAR"
Song and War

Franz Andres Morrissey and Britta Sweers

A protest song is a song that's so specific that you cannot mistake it for bullshit.
—Phil Ochs[1]

INTRODUCTION

War and song are clearly linked. Music in the time of World War I—mainly the music hall songs as well as contemporary sheet music of popular ditties—is a case in point of how, as a manifestation of hegemonic discourse in music, young men were encouraged, if not coerced, into signing up to "play their part" or "do their bit" as the euphemistic usage was in the day (Andres Morrissey 2020), neatly glossing over that the duty to "King and Country" actually meant fighting merciless battles, often sustaining life-changing injuries or dying for mostly meaningless territorial gains or losses along the front lines.

Music as an accompaniment to troops marching is another instance of its use in preparation for or in times of war. It could be said that there are few ways as effective at creating a feeling of belonging and power as falling in with the strong, slightly up-tempo beat of a march or a marching song. Like the music hall and popular songs of that period, marching tunes represent a hegemonic use of music, furthering the objectives of the powers-that-be, of the "lofty goals" of the state. This would be reflected in lyrics of "Your King and Country Want You," sung by female artists with these words:

We don't want to lose you
But we think you ought to go
Your King and Country
Both need you so. (Rubens 1914)

In contrast to such material, instances of hegemonic discourse, there was a very different type of lyric, far from duty to King and Country, the gung-ho patriotism of songs aimed at recruitment. As Priestley put it, "[t]he First World War ... produced two distinct crops of songs: one for patriotic civilians, like the drivel [of 'We Don't Want to Lose You'] ... ; the other, not composed and copyrighted by anybody, genuine folk song, for the sardonic frontline troops" (Priestley 1962; quoted in Palmer 1990, 15). Brophy and Partridge describe these songs as "com[ing] from the ranks, especially from the private soldiers without ambition to bear office or social responsibility" (1930 [1965], 15), thus representing the antihegemonic discourse of the day as it was expressed in music and song. Interestingly, many of these music hall songs and sheet music ditties (or at least their usually quite lengthy choruses) were used for parodies, the lyrics either completely replaced or often skillfully adapted from the original lines. They would be in circulation among the troops, spreading rapidly through the trenches (Andres Morrissey 2020) thanks to the familiarity of the tunes, thus disseminating their bitterly sarcastic criticism of authorities, staff officers, and politicians, as well as depicting the conditions of the squaddies in tones varying between sardonic descriptions of conditions (being shelled, catastrophic circumstances in the trenches, differences in precariousness between officers and enlisted men, and so on) and longing to return to a life of peace and safety.

These examples show that while there is a tradition of music and song being used by the authorities to mobilize troops and encourage sacrifice, there is also a tradition of protest against such mobilization, and resentment against the expectation of the authorities that willingness for sacrifice is readily offered.

This chapter documents this aspect of music and war, with the inclusion of popular music that falls in with the political mainstream of the day, in our case during the Korean War (1950–1953) and its aftermath as well as the Vietnam War and aspects of the Cold War. In the context of the Korean War, we can observe a clearly formulated, musical support for war and the Bomb in line with hegemonic messages (cf. subsection "Patriotic Songs"), mixed in with some material deploring the loss of (American) life. This stands in some contrast to the Vietnam War, where the popular music of the day was more clearly and starkly opposed to American politics in Indochina (cf. subsection "Song as Antihegemonic Discourse Against the War").

However, to begin with, we shall have a look at a number of early examples of popular music being in opposition to the hegemonic discourse of the day. Here, as in our other discussions of materials, we have needed to be highly selective for reasons of space and succinctness, focusing on songs that most forcefully bring out the points we want to make.

HISTORICAL ANTIWAR SONGS OF THE OLD WORLD

The first song to consider, the Scottish "Floo'ers o' the Forest," referring to the Battle of Flodden of 1513, but sung also during and after the Jacobite Rebellion, is an antiwar song in the sense that it thematizes *loss of loved ones*, presenting the plight of widows and young women in this poignant lament:

> I've heard them lilting, at our yowe-milking,
> Lasses a-lilting afore the dawn o' day;
> Noo they are moaning on ilka green loaning;
> "The Floo'ers o' the Forest are a' wede away." (Anonymous, ca. 1513)

The "flowers of the forest," the husbands and young unmarried men have all gone, leaving the women to mourn.

Another type of song, which could carry an antiwar message, presents what life for soldiers in various armies would have been like. An example is "O Frankerych," a song associated with Swiss mercenary armies, soldiers for the king of France in this case but similar or almost identical descriptions of the miseries of ordinary troops exist with reference to other countries and rulers, Prussia for instance.

> *Oh Frankerych, oh Frankerych, elendes Jammertal*
> Oh France, oh France, miserable vale of tears,
> *In dir isch nüt zu finden als luuter Angst und Qual.*
> Nothing can be found in you but utter fear and pain.
> . . . .
> *Elendig ischt das Leben, das me hier füeren muss.*
> Miserable is the life that one is forced lead here. (Anonymous, 1917)

The song lyrics contain elements of Swiss German dialect, hence the association with Swiss soldiers. In other variants different localized forms of German would be in evidence, indicating the origins of the soldiers in question. The song drastically illustrates the ill-treatment the common soldier had to endure.

A song that fits a similar mold is the Scottish ballad "Bonnie Woodhaa," which also presents a take on war from the *point of view of a soldier* with the additional perspective of being separated from loved ones.

> Doon by yon green bushes by Calder's clear stream
> where me and my Annie oftimes we hae been.
> the hours swiftly passed an' happy were we.
> It was little she thocht that a sodger A'd be.

After the soldier is wounded and taken behind the lines, he muses on his life as a miner and thinks longingly of his love:

> If my Annie was here, she would bind up my wounds
> One kiss from her sweet mouth would staunch aa the stounds
> But if heaven protects me an I do return
> A will sport wi you Annie by Calder's clear burn (Anonymous 1977)

Separation and reunion, uncertain in the previous song, are also a theme in the next example, "The Plains of Waterloo." It starts with a narrator observing a young woman out walking in the field lamenting that despite the war being over, her lover, William, has not returned from the eponymous plains. The narrator asks her about her lover's name and then tells her that he saw the young man, his brother-in-arms, die in battle, calling out for her. She is distraught, and the young man, actually William himself, realizes that the separation has not diminished her love for him and pulls out half a ring:

> "Oh see here is the ring that between us was broken,
>   In the depth of all dangers, love, to remind me of you."
> And when she saw the token, she fell into his arms, saying,
>   "You're welcome, lovely William, from the plains of Waterloo."

What we find here is that the two lovers have a symbol, usually a broken ring, more rarely two halves of a coin, to aid in mutual recognition, which is why these types of songs are called "broken-token" ballads.[2]

Another motif we have in this genre are songs about *forced recruitment*. Press gangs or recruiting sergeants would force young men on board warships or into serving with regiments, sometimes by plying them with drink or bribing them with money (the "King's Shilling," receipt of which was taken as a solid commitment to serve). One example is "The Recruited Collier":

> Oh what's the matter with you me lass and where's your darling Jimmy?
> The soldier boys have taken him and sent him far far from me.
> Last payday he went into town and them red-coated fellows.
> Enticed him in and made him drunk and is better gone to the gallows.

The lamenting woman's father tries to free the young man from the recruitment agents:

> . . . my father would have paid the smart and he ran for the golden guinea
> but the sergeant swore he'd kissed the book and now they've got young Jimmy.
> (Anonymous [1952] 1978)

It is noteworthy that this song presents the woman's perspective in the first person. The same applies to the next example, "Here's the Tender Coming," a woman exhorting her husband in a dire warning to hide from the press gang on the "tender," a holding vessel, lying off in Shields' Bar near Newcastle.

> Hide thee, canny Geordie, hide theeself away.
> Hide thee till the tender makes for Druid's Bay.
> If they catch thee, Geordie, who's to win our bread?
> Me and little Jacky'd better off be dead. (Anonymous 1882, 126)

All these examples date back to the nineteenth century or earlier. The last example of Old World antiwar songs dates back to World War II and is called "The D-Day Dodgers," referring to the Allied, in this case British, soldiers, who were fighting their way up the Italian peninsula, the misconceived "soft underbelly" of the continent under Axis control. It is not clear who came up with the moniker "D-Day Dodgers"; sometimes Lady (Nancy) Astor is blamed for it although there is no evidence that she ever used the phrase.

The song mordantly comments on the perception among the squaddies that their sacrifices were belittled by those safely back at home, including the politicians. The sarcasm is very powerful. The references to particularly bloody battles make it appear as if the campaign in Italy was a pleasure cruise:

> Naples and Casino were taken in our stride.
> We didn't go to fight there, we just went for the ride.
> Anzio and Sangro were just names we only went to look for dames.
> The artful D-Day Dodgers way out in Italy.

Unsurprisingly, Winston Churchill's foil, Lady Nancy Astor, one of the first women Members of Parliament, comes in for a scathing attack:

> Dear Lady Astor we like you all a lot.
> Standing on that platform talking Tommy Rot.
> Your England sweetheart and her pride, we think your mouths too bloody wide .
> We are the D-Day Dodgers in sunny Italy.

The song ends quite somberly with a reference to the many soldiers who died during the campaign:

> Look around the mountains in the mud and rain.
> You'll find scattered crosses some that have no name.
> Heart-break, toil and suffering gone the boys beneath them slumber on.
> They are the D-Day Dodgers who stayed in Italy. (Pynn & Anonymous 1944, 227)

These three verses show the spectrum of the *soldiers' anguish and disdain in the bitter sarcasm* expressed, which is of a very similar nature to the self-penned songs of World War I. But the sarcasm will also be present in some of the later antiwar songs, as we shall see (cf. subsection "Song as Antihegemonic Discourse Against the War").

What all these songs have in common, apart from their antiwar stance in its different facets, is that they are all anonymous,[3] a point we will return to later (section "Rounding Off").

ANTIWAR SONGS IN RECENT HISTORY

The Korean War: Historical Background

Before turning to the Vietnam War, with its rich vein of antiwar songs, historically during a very fertile counterculture period, we will turn our attention to a period roughly five years after the end of World War II, and a war fought for similar reasons in a relatively similar part of the world: the Korean War.⁴ The whole history of that region of Asia, be it Korea or be it Vietnam, is thoroughly entangled, which makes it rather difficult to figure out where to start from because these East Asian conflicts all have their origin in colonial history of one kind or another, starting in the late nineteenth century with French colonial aspirations, and in the early twentieth century with the Japanese rule of the Korean peninsula. A significantly complicating factor, however, was that they both, at least at the outset, were proxy wars resulting from the Cold War, which was framed in the West as Western powers being the champions of values such as democracy, political liberty, and free market capitalism, and having to keep in check, ideally even defeat, the malevolent forces of Communism, in other words, a clear "us vs. them" narrative pitting (Western) good against (Communist) evil. The attempts at preventing a Cold War from flaring up into a direct confrontation cast a long shadow over both political spheres of influence, underpinned, on the one hand, by the threat that such a direct confrontation would result in a devastating nuclear war, a fear present in literature and film as well as in the political discourse (see subsection "Songs and the Cold War"), but also in everyday life of the generations between 1945 and 1989. On the other hand, it initially meant material support for, but soon afterwards military involvement at the side of, the proxies who had initially fought the conflicts between Communism and the West, for which the Korean War and the Vietnam War, with its spread into neighboring Laos and Cambodia, were stark examples.

The Korean War lasted three years, from 1950 to 1953, with Japan playing a central role. The Japanese, part of the Axis in World War II, had found themselves confronted with the communists, not dissimilar to Nazi Germany fighting the Soviet Union. In other words, communists, the latter enemies, were initially on the side of the forces against the Axis, although these useful alliances very quickly soured after the cessation of hostilities when the former Allies carved up the spoils into occupation zones. These occupation zones were the starting point of Cold War conflicts that later resulted in fixed borders, in the case of Korea with the Republic of Korea (South Korea) and communist North Korea under Kim Il-Sung. The dividing line between the two countries is the 38th Parallel, which was proposed at the Potsdam Conference in 1945.

In 1948, in short succession the Republic of Korea and the Democratic People's Republic of Korea were established with the same border between the two entities. However, in 1950 the North launched an invasion, having first secured the support of Stalin and Mao, which marked the beginning of the three-year war. Under the leadership of the US and Western allies, with support of the UN, there was fierce fighting, with Seoul being taken at various times by both sides; eventually the armies of the North, supported by troops of the Chinese People's Volunteer Force, were pushed back to the 38th Parallel, and a demilitarized zone, the DMZ, was established under the armistice agreement.

To sum up, it is significant that this war was perceived in the West as the US and Western powers, with the support of the UN, representing the democratic stance against the communist world under the leadership of the Soviet Union. And yet, at the time there was a similar line of argumentation in the United States that underlay the reluctance to get involved in World War I and World War II, an isolationist attitude that could be summed up as "why should we fight wars far away for others?" The Korean War clearly represented this view for many.

Songs of the Korean War

Investigating the mindset of the Korean War and how it influenced political discourse, we came across a veritable treasure trove of a web resource (History on the Net n.d.). It boasts a great collection of soldier's graphic novels addressing the Korean War, which were very popular among the troops. One such graphic novel was called *War Heroes*, its cover depicting two GIs, one wounded, the other shooting some North Korean soldiers he refers to as "Gooks" in a speech bubble. Interestingly enough, it already takes up some depictions of the Vietnam War with very similar depictions.

The same web resource also features material referring to psychological warfare, with strategies of how to counteract enemies with some rather more subtle means. Music plays a central role here, not so much in the Korean War yet but definitely in the Vietnam War, where the United States used music to fight against the North Vietnamese troops, a point we shall come back to below (subsection "A Brief Historical Overview of Indochina").

So what kind of music do we find here? The web resource, which is one of the few that actually focuses on music in the Korean War, makes a division of four different types:

- patriotic songs
- the lot of soldiers in battle
- a main focus on religious faith
- emotional distress caused by fortunes of war

Patriotic Songs

We shall start with *patriotic songs* because, similar to the WWI (music hall) songs representing hegemonic discourse, we find the same combination of religion and patriotism, whereas the antiwar stance would be more along the lines mentioned above, addressing the question of "what are we fighting this war in foreign lands for?"

One of the major voices of the Korean War was Jimmy Osbourne (1923–1958), who wrote a large number of songs at a time when, pre-rock 'n' roll, a dominant genre was country music. This genre quite often reflects a more nationalist, perhaps even a Republican stance, and provides a pertinent insight into an American mentality of mainly poorer white populations. Jimmy Osborne was often called a Kentucky folk singer; Kentucky, alongside Nashville, Tennessee, was the heartland of the genre. He was also quite a successful radio DJ, which was an important element in a musical career at that time.

What is interesting and relevant for us is that most of his songs, mainly comments on the Korean war, were his own. We prefer not to use the term *singer-songwriter* because that has somewhat different political connotations, and he represents a tone considerably more in step with hegemonic representations of America. One of his early songs, written before the start of the war, was a song called "God, Please Protect America" (released July 26, 1950). It combines patriotic duty with the "God on our side" rhetoric.

> We read in the newspaper, hear on the radio
> They're fighting in Korea, the boys are called to go
> To meet the enemy as he comes across the line
> God please protect America in this troubled time

Connected with said rhetoric, there is also a call to prayer for a victory:

> Oh people let's start prayin' as we never prayed before,
> We need the hand of God to lead us through this war,
> Give us victory in Korea and save our boys so fine,
> God please protect America in this troubled time

Nevertheless there is also an indication of war-weariness, reflected in the line, "How can we stand another war to take our loved ones dear?"

Osborne is also a commentator on later events of the Korean War. Whenever there is a report of a victory of some sort he hears about, he turns this into song. So, after a brief pushback of North Korean troops, he writes "Thank God for the Victory in Korea" (released October 2, 1950). Once again the religious stance is important here.

> Thank you dear God for victory in Korea.
> We're grateful that the battle is won.
> We give you the praise for victory in Korea.
> We thank you dear God for what you've done.

However, there is also a reflection of the sacrifices the Americans and Americans soldiers made:

> All the boys gave their lives, left their children and wives,
> They were willing to die for you and me.
> At night and day they did fight for the cause that is right
> for America and its liberty.

Here too, we find the hegemonic stance discussed above, that all these sacrifices are part of the victory of good over evil, of America and its liberty triumphing over an enemy, with the help of God.

This kind of political stance becomes more problematic when, in the defense of Western values during the course of the Korean war, there is a serious debate about, once more, waging nuclear war. General McArthur, a prominent figure during World War II, supported the idea of dropping fifty atomic bombs on Korea, which was thought would stop the war. This was a significant issue as the shock about Hiroshima and Nagasaki was still very present in many minds. This debate and support for McArthur was commented on by musicians. Jackie Doll and his Pickled Peppers came out with the song "When They Drop the Atomic Bomb" (1951).[5]

> There will soon be an end to this cold and wicked war.
> When those hard-headed communists get what they are looking for
> only one thing that will stop them and their atrocious bunch,
> if General McArthur drops an atomic bomb.

While in the first line we have a critical voice against the "cold and wicked war," the Bomb is viewed very positively indeed. The song goes on:

> There will be fire dust and metal flying all around
> And the radioactivity will burn them to the ground.

If there's any communists left they'll be all on the run
If General McArthur drops an atomic bomb.

This represents a completely different stance from what we will see in the anti–Vietnam War movement and the Campaign for Nuclear Disarmament, but it is useful to recall how these weapons were viewed in line with the hegemonic discourse before anti–nuclear war protests set in.

Because McArthur kept up the pressure to use nuclear force, President Truman sacked him in 1951 as there was a justified fear of Soviet nuclear retaliation, which would most probably have resulted in the above-mentioned Mutual Assured Destruction. However, interestingly enough, the popular reaction was to celebrate MacArthur, the WWII war hero. There are quite a few songs about his final speech "No/Old Soldiers Never Die," which is a reference to a soldier's ditty with the lines "Old soldiers / Never die, never die / Old soldiers never die / They simply fade away."[6] Quite a few country musicians use this phrase as a tribute to McArthur. Gene Autry, one of the most famous country musicians of the period, used the phrase in the chorus of a 1951 song, in which he goes on to sing:

> On the seventh of December in the year of '41
> The free world met disaster at the hands of the Rising Sun
> From the bastions of Corregidor, Pearl Harbor, and Bataan
> Came the sound of war and fury and the death march of free man

It is interesting that the view of World War II, and the threat it represented to the world order, is limited to the American perspective here. It also needs to be said that this song represents a form of resistance, aimed at the Truman government, which sacked this popular and highly decorated commander.

We also have references harking back to the Jimmy Osborne song "The Voice of Free America," from 1951, which is reminiscent of the WWII patriotic song "There's a Star-Spangled Banner Waving Somewhere."

> Like The Voice of Free America I am pleading now with you
> Let's all shout the word of freedom throughout Europe and Asia too.
> There is no place like our nation, it is led to God's own hand,
> Let's defeat the aggressor and bring peace to every land.

The theme of bringing freedom to the whole world as well as the American Way of Life and that all this is a gift from God, manifests itself in the following lines:

> Oh, The Voice of Free America it beams throughout the world
> Tells the honest way of life to man and woman, boy and girl.
> Let's thank God for all our freedom he's been good to you and me
> Let's unite the willing nations and keep the whole world free.

To summarize, emphasis on the United States as being led and of being ordained by God to bring freedom and Western values to the world, if necessary by military means, doubtlessly reflects a hegemonic American worldview.

To round off discussion about the patriotic stance, there were also similar views outside the genre of country music. Sister Rosetta Tharpe, the gospel/jazz/blues singer, recorded "There Is Peace in Korea," which came out in 1953 after the signing of the Armistice. It has that electric bluesy sound that has resulted in her being considered a precursor of rock 'n' roll, but the same notions are present here too, admittedly a little less gung-ho than in the previous examples, America bringing the real values to the world and God being on their side.

> I'm so glad at last, there's peace in Korea
> ....
>
> We're hoping there will be no more misery, and no more sadness
> No no no no no no dying, there'll be, in the land
> Hope we'll have happiness, and joy, and peace of mind

The lyrics culminate in the knowledge the singer expresses that "God has made this world / And made it for the good and kind," but the understanding the song also conveys is that peace is linked to American military victory.

Songs of Soldiers in Battle

However, what the songs discussed so far have in common is that they largely exclude the actual suffering of the young men sent to bring that military victory about. This aspect is present in the more sobering *songs of soldiers in battle*, reflecting the fact that these projections of military might also meant that American soldiers lost their lives or had to endure serious hardships.

One example is Stewart Powell's "The Rotation Blues" from 1951, about soldiers wanting to end their time on the front line. This song also belongs to the country music genre, and its content is reminiscent of the squaddies' songs from World War I by focusing on the hardships of the simple soldiers on the front line.

I got the rotation blues.
I'm the lonely soldier sitting in Korea.
But rotation's coming so I shouldn't have no fear.

Just a few more weeks rotation's gonna set me free.

The same can be said about "A Brother in Korea" (1952) by Sonny Osborne, which sounds a considerably more critical note and represents a more serious reaction to having to go and fight in Korea. It starts with a wry observation that ". . . it's sad but it's true . . . / The people aren't happy unless they're fighting in a battle somewhere." Apart from presenting a much less heroic and altogether rather harsher picture of young men having to go and do their duty as soldiers, what is also alluded to here is the perspective discussed above: American boys fighting wars in far-flung parts of the world.

It was on the 27th of November Uncle Sam sent for him to go
He said "bring your clothes for three days, until you're signed up for more"
. . . .

He's in Korea today, he's fighting for the loved ones back home
He's far across the sea, he may never come home

Nevertheless, here too we find at least an allusion to hegemonic discourse, i.e., that the war in Korea is fought "for the loved ones back home."

The same theme is also present, albeit more subtly, in "Heartbreak Ridge" from 1951, performed by the Delmore Brothers, and although it clearly depicts the enemy, "the Reds," as representing "hatred and sin," it also is quite explicit about the enormous loss of life at this crucial battle in the chorus:

On Heartbreak Ridge I stand tonight
Nothing but wounded and dying in sight

A similar stance is presented in Elton Britt's 1951 song "Korean Mud," of the less than glorious death of the unknown soldier.

An American soldier lay dying
Out in the Korean mud
And all that was needed to save him
Was a pint of someone's blood

The song continues with the sad observation that "there was no blood to save him / And this poor boy had to die."

Clearly, songs like these are explicit about the horrors of the war, even if the tone strikes us as somewhat sentimental, and their criticism is rather different in what they project from the kinds of antiwar songs we will find about ten years later. Nevertheless, like the latter, these songs also represent a degree of antihegemonic perspective, albeit relatively muted.

Songs About Religious Faith

We can deal with this topic somewhat more briefly because many of the songs already discussed contain strong elements of religious fervor, including the belief that God is on America's side. The ones from that period we are considering here reflect faith above all, with the actual Korean War playing much less of an explicit role. One is Jimmy Osborne's 1950 song "The Old Family Bible." What is remarkable in this context is that it only obliquely refers to the current political situation as ". . . these gray restless days, with the clouds overhead / And the rumble of the thunder far away." The chorus also hints at problems in the world but the focus is very clearly on faith:

> I'll cling to the old family bible
> The book that is my guiding light
> When the world is full of troubles and every burden doubles
> The old family bible makes things right

The Louvin Brothers' "Weapon of Prayer" of 1951 is quite a compelling example of the notion of Americans being warriors of God.

> In that land across the sea there's a job for you and me
> Though our presence there may not be found.
> We must stay each night and day on the battle line and pray.
> We must never lay our weapons down.

What makes this song extraordinary is the suggestion that you may not personally need to be fighting in Korea, but that you will help the efforts of the United States by praying for success.

> We don't have to be a soldier in a uniform
> To be of service over there

> While the boys so bravely stand with the weapons made by hand
> Let us trust and use the weapon of prayer

In this second excerpt, the song actually suggests that actual joining the troops is not needed and that prayer will work toward victory just as well. In other words, faith is as good as military force.

To conclude this short overview, it can be said that these types of songs in their Christian focus as a mainstay of the United States also represent a hegemonic stance, albeit somewhat more obliquely so.

Emotional Distress

If we look at songs that may not or only partially reflect hegemonic discourse, in other words, songs that present a position slightly more critical of war, these mainly deal with personal issues. Kay Kellum's "When I Get Back" (1950) refers to patriotic duty and fighting for the "Red, White and Blue," but the main concern appears in these lines:

> Will your love still be for me when I get back from oversea
> Will you love me forever, my darlin'?
> Will you care to hold me tight under a starry night?
> Will you love me like you used to do?

Ernest Tubb's 1951 song "A Heartsick Soldier on Heartbreak Ridge,"[7] while taking on the theme of the carnage of that battle "across from the river of sighs / where the shells burst around me," interestingly has a mostly emotional focus:

> Does she know how I long for the sound of her voice
> And the love letters that never came?

J. B. Lenoir's "I'm in Korea," recorded in 1954, although it reflects similar feelings, is a departure from the acoustic folky material of most the songs discussed above, being an almost textbook example of a blues, played on an electric guitar with piano and sax accompaniment. The worry about the relationship with the woman back home is that of a married man thinking about "my kids and you / If I die, what you goin' do" and it ends with the exhortation "Don't let nobody lay their head down in my bed."

Another departure from the acoustic feel is Joni James's string-drenched "I'll Be Waiting for You," a reassuring response to worries and fears of being forgotten, in which the lover fighting across the sea receives the promise that the young woman's love is not in any question whatsoever.

However, apart from these songs in which longing for a loved partner is the central concern, there are a few songs that at least hint at a more critical view of the soldiers' plight. Jim Eanes's 1951 song "Missing in Action," once again a typical country song, tells the story of a soldier returning home, having been wounded, taken prisoner, and managing to escape from a POW camp. He realizes on coming home that his lover has married someone else, a frequent theme in similar songs, but she had been informed that he was "missing in action" and therefore assumed he was dead. The song ends with the young man looking toward a life of loneliness and longing.

Another Jim Eanes song, "A Prisoner of War" from 1952, portrays the heartache of longing for one's lover, but it also paints a very bleak picture, once again in the form of a country waltz, of the harsh conditions in a POW camp, where the only consolation is the thought of one's love. Perhaps the most touching lyrics are these:

> Sometimes I wonder if they'll set me free
> And if the good Lord has forsaken me
> Time and again I have called your sweet name
> Only to wake up and find things the same

The verse is fairly unique in that it questions the protection of God in the face of the emotional and physical hardship.

Lastly, we move forward to 1956, three years after the Korean armistice: the song "Forgotten Men" in acoustic old time style performed by Don Reno and Red Smiley. This song, somewhat reminiscent of "Floo'ers o' the Forest," is a lament for the dead. The last verse is very downbeat:

> Their picture hangs upon the wall
> But their names are not mentioned back home
> As the year go by our memories dim,
> We forget our loved ones are gone

There is patriotism in the chorus, but it is clearly muted:

> Forgotten men who lie asleep across the ocean waves
> Who fought and died for the flag that waves across their lonely graves

However, the main focus is certainly on the sacrifices of those "who fought and died" and how they are now being forgotten.

To sum up, the songs in the present subsection are clearly different, more critical of what the war does to young men, and they lack the gung-ho patriotism and self-assuredness of God being on the side of America, but their criticism is focused on individual suffering, heartache, and fading memory rather than on the more powerful fundamental antiwar stance of later years. This may partly be explained by the fact that in the period between 1950 to 1956 the antileft hegemonic discourse was embodied by McCarthy and the House Committee on Un-American Activities (HUAC), which mercilessly persecuted real and perceived leftists. A more direct criticism of the war in Korea or its aftermath would have led to being investigated and most likely blackballed for communist sympathies, as happened to a considerable number of actors and musicians, quite a few of whom with a communist background or sympathies fled the United States at that time, including Alan Lomax in 1950 and Peggy Seeger, Pete Seeger's half-sister, in 1956. Workers' movement activists were also under suspicion and subjected to harassment, as were proponents of Black emancipation. Antihegemonic discourse could be a reason for anything from loss of employment or performance opportunities to thuggish harassment to imprisonment. Under these circumstances it is no real surprise that voices critical of the war effort in Korea were muted at best.

Protest Against War as an Antihegemonic Stance

In the following we shall focus on voices in music speaking out against armed conflict, which typically represents the antihegemonic perspective. To begin with there were a number of antiwar songs in the States about World War II, sung by performers like the Almanac Singers on the seminal album *Songs for John Doe*. Pete Seeger later wrote on a copy "John, a collector's—songs made in 1940 and early 1941—one could argue for days about it!" (Sweers and Andres Morrissey 2019). This indicates what Seeger and his contemporary protest singers had experienced at that time.

The Almanac Singers were initially very vociferous on American nonintervention in World War II, as evidenced by the album. What would later prove to be a problem was that they were linked, rightly or wrongly, to the Communist Party of the USA. After appearing at the American Youth Congress in February 1941, they became quite a success. But then Pearl Harbor happened. In this context the likes of Woody Guthrie and Pete Seeger, both members of the Almanac Singers, changed their tack because a) American neutrality was no longer an option, and b) this was no longer noninvolvement in a war not fought near or on American soil. Their activism, originally pacifist in nature, underwent a 180-degree turn: they now supported the war effort, but they did so because it was viewed as an antifascist struggle. In fact, Woody Guthrie had written on his guitar, "This machine kills fascists."

Clearly, in terms of antihegemonic attitudes expressed in music, a lot more would need to be said about Woody Guthrie, but in terms of a long-term protest song icon, we would like to focus on Pete Seeger. His career spanned a lifetime and he was a powerful voice, so much so that he led the public at Obama's inauguration in Woody Guthrie's song "This Land Is Your Land," together with—among others—Bruce Springsteen. Seeger's conviction had always been to unite people in song (Winkler 2009; Seeger and Reiser 1986), and he lives up to this conviction in this performance too, leading the approximately 400,000 people attending the ceremony at the Lincoln Memorial.

This conviction was also mirrored in his songwriting. One of the songs, at least attributed to him even though it is actually an adaptation of a hymn or gospel song, sung at many rallies and during civil rights marches, is "We Shall Overcome" (Seeger and Reiser 1986, 194ff). In fact, Seeger changed the modal verb *will* in the original version from earlier singing to *shall*. It was published in the *People Songs Bulletin*, a publication of activist songs to be sung communally, a publication that had Pete Seeger as a director (for an in-depth discussion, cf. Lynskey 2010, 65ff).

A similar example is "Where Have All the Flowers Gone" (1955) (Hutchinson 2013). Like "We Shall Overcome," it is structurally and melodically a very simple song with consistently repeated lines ("long time passing"), which makes it easy to learn, easy to sing along with, and easy to remember. It was taken up by a long list of singers including the Kingston Trio, Joan Baez, Peter, Paul and Mary, Harry Belafonte, Dolly Parton, and so on, but also by Marlene Dietrich, who famously sang it in German as well as in English and French.

The origin of this anthem is the Cossack song "Koloda-Duda" (Hutchinson 2013). Pete Seeger found the lines in the novel *And Quiet Flows the Don* (Тихий Дон) by Mikhail Sholokhov. Although he says "I never got around to looking up the song," Seeger wrote these three original lines down in his notebook:

Where are the flowers? The girls have picked them.
Where are the girls? They have all taken husbands.
Where are the husbands? They are all in the army.

Pete Seeger's final version takes up the idea of the Cossack original, also a theme in the novel, which contains references to the Cossacks being drafted into the Tsarist Army, and develops it into a compelling pacifist song narrative, compelling in its simplicity and its circularity, starting with flowers, which the girls pick, their husbands who go off to be soldiers, then end up being buried in graveyards, and the graveyards are covered in flowers. The repeated lines, "long time passing" and the chorus-like "when will we ever learn" came to him later. He sang the song at Oberlin College in 1955, and one Joe Hickerson added the two verses, i.e., "where have all the soldiers gone / gone to graveyards . . ." and "where have all the graveyards gone," emphasizing the circular nature of the song with "covered with flowers every one."[8]

In contrast to some of the songs discussed presenting the hegemonic perspective, such pacifist/antiwar sentiment clearly represents an antihegemonic discourse. It was in part this political stance, associated with left-wing views, that led to Pete Seeger's being ostracized by mainstream media and venues in the wake of his bout with the HUAC, and his later being found to have been in contempt of Congress.[9]

Such antihegemonic views were clearly critical of the state and the readiness to project military power for ideological reasons. They also stood in contrast with the fundamentalist Christian attitude that such international interventions were guided by God. Both critical perspectives are in evidence in a number of songs, which came out of a surge of singer/songwriters or protest singers with rather pointed antihegemonic, if not explicitly left-wing stances.[10] In Britain this would have included the likes of Ewan MacColl and Ian Campbell; in the States, to name but a few, Phil Ochs, Tom Patton, Steve Earle, and, of course, Bob Dylan—although he would even then probably not accept the label "left-wing" and later distanced himself from the image of being a protest singer.[11]

Two of his songs are worth mentioning in this context. "With God on Our Side" (1964, on *The Times They Are A-Changin'*) most obviously questions that the above-mentioned fundamentalist conviction of American projection of military power, including the nuclear option prevalent in many of the hegemonic songs of the Korean War, is doing God's will:

But now we've got weapons of chemical dust
If fire them we're forced to, then fire them we must
One push of the button and they shot the world wide
And you never ask questions when God's on your side

However, in his earlier song "Masters of War"[12] (1963, on *The Freewheelin' Bob Dylan*), he focuses on another aspect, the armament industry (cf. Lynskey

2010, 65 ff). The criticism of making money from selling death and destruction is formulated most poignantly in the "one question" in the penultimate verse, which is also an indictment of the profit motive of capitalism. Dylan asks,

> Is your money that good
> Will it buy you forgiveness?

To this he answers,

> All the money you made
> Will never buy back your soul

The Vietnam War and the Music Associated with It

In comparison to the complex Korean War, the Vietnam War could be said to be in a league of its own, both in terms of political complexity and in the forms of protest against it, which developed with the rising dissent, most probably because, despite the geographical distance, coverage on television made the horrors very immediate. We will consider how that protest manifested itself in a few exemplary songs, but in order to clarify the political background we briefly need to consider the historical background to the Vietnam War.

A Brief Historical Overview of Indochina

Precolonial history of Vietnam[13] is tangled, characterized by domination from China, who developed some of the regional infrastructure, followed by a period of various dynasties of what could be called Vietnamese rulers, although this period, from the tenth century onward, was anything but characterized by political stability. Western colonialization, initially a Christianization effort, began in 1516 with the Portuguese, who failed, however, to establish more permanent control over the region. The French followed, also with the intention of establishing Christianization; one of the French missionaries, Alexandre de Rhodes, developed a Roman script for Vietnamese in the sixteenth century, which is in use to this day. But in 1857, under Napoleon III, the French set out to conquer Vietnam militarily and to make it a French colony. It took thirty years for France to establish its colonial hold over Indochina (including Laos and Cambodia), a process with numerous setbacks. A contributing factor was that the French had no interest in developing the region, being solely focused on exploiting its resources, with Vietnamese locals employed only in menial positions and fired at whim. In other words, from the outset, French colonialization was characterized by all power being in the hands of the French and Chinese, and, unsurprisingly, it was persistently subject to rebellion and resistance.

In 1925 Ho Chi Minh initiated the Revolutionary Youth League of Vietnam, which would develop into the Indochinese Communist Party. Through cunning maneuvering and exploiting the changing political situations, which included a French colonial administration under Japanese rule, as well as cooperating with the Allies toward the end of World War II, Ho Chi Minh's comrades secured a firm foothold in the area. With the Japanese surrender in August 1945 and no other local force to oppose the "Viet Minh," they seized control over Hanoi, forcing the puppet ruler, Emperor Bai Dai, to abdicate.

Despite a negotiated settlement with the French, who were fundamentally opposed to Vietnamese independence, an increasingly successful communist guerrilla campaign eventually led to the First Indochina War (1946–1954), with the US supporting the French with aid because of fears about the spread of Asian Communism. With the fall of their garrison in Dien Bien Phu, in 1954 the French agreed to a temporary partition along the seventeenth parallel separating the Democratic Republic of Vietnam (North Vietnam) and South Vietnam, with an anticommunist regime in Saigon.

This regime was infamous for its persecution of opposition, by no means all communist, but it proved incompetent in addressing social woes as well as in curbing the activities of the Viet Cong. The United States supported South Vietnam from 1955 onward (the beginning of the Second Indochina War), first with advisers, but increasingly more militarily, with President Johnson ordering bombing raids on North Vietnam in 1965, Operation Rolling Thunder, to stop incursions of and the supply of weapons to the Viet Cong. Johnson's decision marked the official US entry into this complicated war, once again, framed as a conflict between the democratic West and the communists, North Vietnam and by proxy China and the USSR.

By 1968 there were half a million US soldiers in South Vietnam. It was also the year of several important battles: Khe Sanh in January with the heaviest US air raids so far, Hue from January to March, the first battle of Saigon in March, Kham Duc in May, and the traumatic North Vietnamese Tet Offensive. This was followed by Operation Dewey Canyon, the last major US offensive of US Marine Corps, from January till March 1969. By 1971 with the Easter Offensive and the unstoppable progress of North Vietnamese troops, the situation had become increasingly untenable for the United States. Political pressure at home was on the increase, no doubt as a result of a "televised" war; North Vietnam and the Viet Cong were showing no signs of being defeated; the death toll amongst US soldiers was mounting; and at the same time there was a growing awareness of notorious massacres against Vietnamese civilians (for instance, My Lai). Further compounding the situation was the increasingly manifest ecological impact of Agent Orange on the jungles, the local population, as well as on the US troops that administered it. Eventually, continuing the war was no longer an option. Nixon signed the Paris Peace Treaty on January 27, 1973, with the North, South Vietnam, and the Viet Cong. On April 29, 1975, the last remaining US personnel were airlifted from a rooftop in Saigon, a traumatic moment for the American psyche, witnessed all over the US—and the world—on the evening news. In May 1975 the communist troops marched into Saigon; September 2, 1976, marks the foundation of a reunified Socialist Republic of Vietnam.

The Cultural Impact

The impact of this war and many of the battles mentioned found its way into popular culture—music as well as film. Its coverage on worldwide television led to protests worldwide. But the impact on the human beings involved and the loss of lives was staggering: about 58,200 US soldiers died, 45,000 under forty-five and one-third around twenty.[14] In addition, there were around 60,000 suicides resulting from trauma and in the region of 40,000 veterans who became heroin addicts in Vietnam; the social impact was dramatic. But the impact on Vietnam dwarfs these figures, with millions of civilians killed and a country that to this day struggles with the disastrous environmental fallout from Agent Orange, not to mention Laos and its continued casualties due to unexploded bombs from the American attempts to cut off supplies along the so-called Ho Chi Minh Trail.

In this war too, we have different ways of music being involved. Clearly, once again, there were patriotic songs, which were seen as being central to upholding morale of and solidarity among the soldiers.[15] But besides songs reflecting the hegemonic discourse, there were others that came out of Vietnam similar to songs of the Korean War, reflecting the daily experiences of the common soldier, one example being Bill Ellis's "Grunt." But of course with the counterculture back in the United States, there was a considerable presence of antihegemonic music (see the following subsection). This counterculture also had an impact on the GIs, most of whom were very young and of the same generation as those of the so-called Summer of Love and later

Woodstock, a young generation that grew up with rock 'n' roll. By contrast, the music on military radio stations was still often old-fashioned crooner songs and in no way reflected the musical taste of the soldiers.[16] Many of the young soldiers brought tape recorders to cater for their own musical preferences. Incidentally, the music of the era is also reflected in military slang of the day, for instance "rock and roll" for the machine guns or semiautomatic weapons. The term for planes with weapons was "Puff the Magic Dragon," from the folky sixties hit record.

But music was also an element of psychological warfare: American troops would play loud music from their helicopters, hoping to confuse the enemy as well as to draw fire in order to locate enemy troops and to eliminate them from the air.

US troops would also play Vietnamese and Buddhist funeral music in the naïve assumption that this would confuse and demoralize the local population, with little to no impact. Similarly ineffective was the attempt to destabilize Vietnamese morale by dropping pamphlets encouraging the population to surrender, or sheet music with anticommunist songs.

Song as Antihegemonic Discourse Against the War

As it became increasingly unlikely that the American military involvement in Vietnam could be kept under wraps, a whole raft of songs was composed that addressed this fact. One of the first examples is the iconic "Universal Soldier" by Canadian singer/songwriter Buffy Sainte-Marie (1962). During a layover in San Francisco on her way to Toronto, she got talking to medics on a transport plane arriving with wounded soldiers from Vietnam; the song was her reaction to what she witnessed. At the time there was a total official denial that military operations were taking place in Indochina, but Sainte-Marie recalls that "[t]he medics assured me there was indeed a huge war going on. I started writing the song in the airport and on the plane, and I finished it . . . in Toronto."[17] What is significant about this song is that it focuses on who soldiers are and how they are eternal participants in war, irrespective of period, creed, or nationality, but also that without them "all this killing can't go on." This makes it a somewhat oblique anti–Vietnam War song at a time when *officially* there was no US involvement in Vietnam.

The protest became explicit in "the first protest song directly to refer to Vietnam by name" (Auslander 1981, 108), Phil Ochs's "Talking Vietnam Blues" (for a detailed summary, see Songtell 2023). Not only was it a scathing comment on the ineptitude of the powers supporting South Vietnam, but it did so lampooning the (hegemonic) discourse used by officials aiming to downplay the scale of US involvement, referring to "trainees" rather than soldiers and even using the verb *train* euphemistically instead of *fight* in the line "Friends, the very next day we trained some more." What was actually involved is presented in a way that does not mince words:

> We burned some villages down to the floor
> Yes, we burned out the jungles far and wide
> Made sure those red apes had no place left to hide

The indictment of the American engagement in Indochina, and its impact on the local population, is stated, on the one hand, in the stark line "Threw all the people in relocation camps / Under lock and key," and on the other hand, by returning to mocking the hegemonic stance: "made damn sure they're free," in other words, that this was for their own good.

What makes this song even more poignant is the fact that it came out in April 1964, a full four months before the Gulf of Tonkin incident and the first major escalation of the American presence in Vietnam (Auslander 1981). A small detail, but a possible indication of a reference to an attitude discussed earlier, "why should American boys fight wars in far off lands," is the short guitar figure, three notes, repeated four times, only at the beginning of the song, reminiscent of a bugle but also part of the tune of the American WWI song "Over There," exhorting Americans to take up arms at the side of the allies. What is also in evidence, harking back to the Korean War, is the dehumanization of the communist enemy.

Another example of explicit protest against the Vietnam War has been immortalized by the *Woodstock* movie. Country Joe McDonald arguably had his great moment in the limelight in the acoustic solo performance of "I-Feel-Like-I'm-Fixing-to-Die Rag" (cf. Linskey 2010, 109ff.). Like Ochs's "Talking Vietnam Blues," this song is a bitterly sarcastic comment, mockingly encouraging young men to give up their education in order to fight in Vietnam; urging the military (generals) to go out and "get those reds / 'cause the only good Commie is the one that's dead"; pointing out to Wall Street "that there is plenty good money to be made / by supplying the army with the tools of the trade" (with a reference to dropping the Bomb only "on the Viet Cong"); and lastly to tell parents that having shipped off their sons to Vietnam they would earn respect by being "the first ones in your block / To have your boy come home in a box." The chorus has the same sarcastic upbeat, gung-ho mock optimism:

And it's one, two, three, what are we fighting for?
Don't ask me, I don't give a damn, next stop is Vietnam
And it's five, six, seven, open up the pearly gates
Well there ain't no time to wonder why, whoopee! we're all gonna die

In the footage, it seems many of the 400,000 in the audience at Woodstock lustily sang along.[18]

The song created some strong reactions. Arguably the last one was an acrimonious lawsuit in 2003 brought by Babette Ory, Kid Ory's daughter, because in his chorus MacDonald had used the chord sequence and elements of the tune of Ory's trad jazz "Muskrat Ramble." The lawsuit had at its inception Kid Ory's private judgment, allegedly made in 1968, that the lyrics were "rude, *unpatriotic*, and obscene" (emphasis mine), as reported by his daughter in the 2003 filing of a complaint about infringement of copyright. According to Cronin's (n.d.) comment on the case, Judge Nora Manella was of the opinion that Babette Ory was primarily concerned with "erasing the defendant's song from the planet" and that the suit for copyright infringement was mainly a means to that end. It is striking to consider that, even thirty-five years after Kid Ory allegedly made the remark about the song being unpatriotic, the anti–Vietnam War protest was still anathema to patriotic Americans, even if the same state is notorious for the racist treatment of African Americans well into the sixties and until today, and Kid Ory would have experienced this racism all his life.

It is a fact that many lower-class people could not avoid the draft and subsequently were sent to Vietnam, whereas the socially better placed, including the likes of Donald Trump, managed successfully to avoid that tour of duty, because they had ways and means of dodging the draft.[19] In this context Arlo Guthrie's "Alice's Restaurant" is remarkable in that it approaches draft dodging with a satirical and humorous twist by suggesting that draftees should approach their recruiting officers, representatives of the state, singing the rather quirky and apolitical chorus of this song as a creative way of indicating counterculture dissent and opposition to serving in Vietnam. Guthrie's "Alice's Restaurant," thus, like Ochs's and McDonald's songs, used satire and sarcasm rather than finger-pointing for antiwar protest.

Another example, which perhaps is a little counterintuitive to think of as an anti-Vietnam song, is Scottish Australian singer/songwriter Eric Bogle's "The Band Played Waltzing Matilda." Its theme is the WWI Gallipoli campaign, when the ANZAC troops (alongside other Allied units) were trying to secure the Dardanelles for the Royal Navy.[20] The losses were staggering;

in the entire campaign there were "over 220,000 casualties out of a force of nearly 500,000. From [the Allies'] point of view, the campaign was a disaster" (National Army Museum n.d.).

Bogle's 1971 song tells the story of a young itinerant farm worker who loses his legs fighting in Suvla Bay in the Dardanelles and, taken back to Australia, every April watches his "old comrades" Remembrance Day Parade marching with pride and nostalgia ("reliving the dreams of past glories"). The scene created toward the end of the song is reminiscent of "Forgotten Men" discussed above. The man marching "bent, stiff and sore" are

> The forgotten heroes of a forgotten war
> And the young people ask
> What are they marching for?
> And I ask myself the same question

The repetition of *forgotten* is a stark reminder up the futility of both the sacrifices of the young men and that the celebrations refer to a campaign that is gradually becoming less than relevant.

In an interview with *The Scotsman* in 2009, Bogle described the song as being ". . . an oblique comment on the Vietnam War, which was in full swing . . . but while boys from Australia were dying there, people had hardly any idea where Vietnam was. Gallipoli was a lot closer to the Australian ethos—every schoolkid knew the story, so I set the song there" (Scotsman 2009).

Perhaps unsurprisingly, there was a fair amount of pushback against the song. "At first the Returned Service League and all these people didn't accept it at all; they thought it was anti-soldier, but they've come full circle now and they see it's certainly anti-war but not anti-soldier" (Scotsman 2009). This last distinction is quite crucial for a lot of antiwar songs discussed so far, but they are all too often seen as a threat to hegemonic perspectives and therefore criticized as denigrating the powers that be, which they often do, as well as the men and women who are sent to fight for their country, which they actually do not.

"Counterculture" as a Background of Antiwar Protest

The sixties and seventies were decades where youth culture became increasingly politicized and antihegemonic. This includes such phenomena as the so-called "Summer of Love,"[21] the increasing impact of the civil rights movement, the widespread student unrest in Europe, the upheavals during the Democratic National Convention in Chicago, but also the assassinations of Martin Luther King Jr. and Robert Kennedy in 1968. It also is the period of sexual liberation, of an increasingly powerful women's liberation movement, and of gay rights. These movements, often associated with hippie culture, overlapped with and supported one another. In other words, in terms of strong antihegemonic initiatives, this was a very fertile age, which is reflected in its music. It has to be said, however, that the counterculture, its fashion, and its music, like the anarchy of punk in the seventies, was quite swiftly commercialized and in this exploitation integrated into the mainstream and, one could argue, tamed.

The state did not remain impassive: there was forceful suppression of protest and instances where resistance was quelled brutally. One notorious example was in Ohio, where there were several deaths and bullet injuries. Symptomatically, once again the narrative was one that pitted American values against communist aggression, in this case the communists being American students. The brutal actions of the state and the National Guard and the support they enjoyed from President Nixon, received vociferous "liberal" and counterculture condemnation and became the subject of the song "Ohio" by Crosby, Stills, Nash and Young (Linskey 2010, 203ff).

But it was the early 1980s that really brought out reflections on Vietnam and what it meant for the American psyche. This is apparent in songs of the period. On the one hand, there is Stan Ridgeway's "Camouflage" of 1986, a ballad (in the sense of the song telling a story) that in its focus on GI heroics, admittedly with a twist, can easily be (mis-)read as perpetuating the myth of noble American sacrifice in necessary foreign wars. Earlier songs, however, are less ambivalent: Paul Hardcastle's 1985 "19" focused on the youth of the soldiers that had fought and died in Vietnam. The title is a reference to the average age of American military personnel in Vietnam. But probably the best-known example for the reflection on what Vietnam meant for young, lower-class Americans is Bruce Springsteen's 1981 hit "Born in the USA" with these memorable lines:

> I had a brother at Khe Sanh
> Fightin' off them Viet Cong
> They're still there, he's all gone

This laconically underlines how the war failed to achieve what the hegemonic political discourse had advocated and what this failure had done to young soldiers. That "Born in the USA" has been used by politicians of the right in campaigns to instill patriotism shows how a song can be profoundly misunderstood, mainly because of the hook line, thereby missing the biting irony of that hook line as well as the searing indictment of both the so-called American Dream and the projection of American values in far-flung foreign lands (cf. also Inskeep et al. 2019).

Songs and the Cold War

Vietnam and Korea were classic proxy wars, which reflected the Cold War mind-set, the ongoing struggle against communism, the most persistent threat to the Free World, the West, and real political, economic, social, and cultural values, implicitly or explicitly "with God on [their] side." In order to defend these values and assure the supremacy of the Free World any means was acceptable, including the threat of nuclear warfare. As both sides had huge nuclear arsenals—and increasingly more powers acquired them as well—there was the doctrine of Mutual Assured Destruction (MAD), which was a cause for serious concern worldwide. It also had a range of cultural manifestations in literature and film, the best known perhaps being Nevil Shute's 1957 novel *On the Beach* and the 1959 film.

The fear and the madness of Mutual Assured Destruction is also starkly expressed in Stanley Kubrick's 1964 film *Dr. Strangelove or: How I Learned to Stop Worrying and Love the Bomb*, a biting satire that inexorably launches a course for the destruction of all human life at the very end. That the eponymous Dr. Strangelove, one of several roles played by Peter Sellers, has hardly controlled, Tourette-like outbursts of Nazi saluting and language adds another mordant satirical layer to this film with its clearly antihegemonic content attacking the nuclear doctrine current during the Cold War.

The threat of nuclear annihilation fostered a great deal of existential angst not unlike present-day concerns about the climate crisis. Unsurprisingly, then, a central antihegemonic movement in the Cold War years came from the Campaign for Nuclear Disarmament (CND), and its symbol, a circle around a stylized missile, became fairly ubiquitous among mainly younger people in the sixties and seventies.

The British folk scene in the sixties was, in fact, closely linked to the CND and to leftist small parties (cf. Bean 2014). Robin Dransfield, a British folk singer and musician, recalls the mood of the day and this close link in the case of North Yorkshire's Harrowgate folk club: "Harrowgate folk club . . . was started by people who were members of the Young Communist League and the CND. (. . .) My education, in particular my political education, began there because it was the heyday of the CND, the world was going to come to an end tomorrow. Then finding out about Woody Guthrie and people like that. It was an amazing time" (Bean 2014, 133ff).

One of the early members of the Campaign for Nuclear Disarmament in Birmingham was Ian Campbell, who wrote "The Sun Is Burning" in 1962 and recorded it in 1963. It was covered by Simon and Garfunkel on their 1964 album *Wednesday Morning 3 am*. This very powerful song starts almost idyllically:

> The sun is burning in the sky
> Strands of clouds go slowly drifting by
> In the park, the lazy bees are droning
> In the flowers among the trees

In the last line, there is a constant return to "the sun," beginning with a mildly disconcerting verb *burns*, "And the sun burns in the sky." This last line becomes more threatening as the song progresses until the climax in the last two verses, which ends with stark images, reflecting that Cold War fear of nuclear annihilation.

> Now the sun has come to Earth
> Shrouded in a mushroom cloud of death
> Death comes in a blinding flash
> Of hellish heat and leaves a smear of ash

Once again, the last line mentions the sun, "And the sun has come to Earth," but it also alludes to how the H-bomb reproduces the way the sun creates energy. The results are stark:

> Now the sun has disappeared
> All is darkness, anger, pain and fear
> Twisted, sightless wrecks of men
> Go groping on their knees and cry in pain

It is in the last verse that "the sun has disappeared," an allusion to the nuclear winter that would follow a nuclear war.

Twenty years later, Scottish singer Dick Gaughan wrote "Think Again," slightly more obliquely about the potential catastrophe of a confrontation with the Soviet Union. It was inspired by Yevgeny Yevtushenko's "Do the Russians Want War?," an antiwar song from 1956 (Macalester College n.d.). Gaughan writes that he came up with the song in 1981 on the platform at

Friedrichstrasse, at the time "no-mans land between East and West Berlin . . . during the period when Ronald Reagan and Margaret Thatcher were heightening the Cold War rhetoric in cynical attempts to increase their domestic popularity by John Wayne–esque posturing. I found it quite incredible that most people seemed to think there was absolutely nothing wrong with these lunatics being prepared to risk leading humanity over the edge of the nuclear abyss in order to get themselves re-elected" (2008). The song raises a lot of questions, but also exhorts listeners to consider the horrors of a potential World War III. The chorus expressed the polarization, but also the impossibility of anything but a disastrous outcome:

> In the name of humanity, bitterly torn
> In the name of our children as yet to be born
> Before we do that which can never be undone I beg of you
> Think, think again, and again and again and again and again

This sentiment, as well as the certainty of global destruction for essentially ideological reasons alluded to in the quote above, is powerfully addressed in the last verse, which begins with the title of Yevtushenko's song "Do you think that the Russians want war?"—the first of several questions, all concerned with the notion of how insane it would be to risk "the destruction of all humankind . . . because you don't like their political system." The ending could not be more explicit:

> There will be no survivors you know
> No one left to scream in the night and condemn our stupidity

ROUNDING OFF

We conclude this chapter with a few considerations on our topic. To begin with, any attempt to consider the impact of music as a means of projecting political power and the protest against such attempts in a format of the present kind cannot be but sketchy and highly selective. Thus, it is inevitable that some readers may miss a name or a song that they deem essential. The intention, however, was not to provide the definitive account of songs about and, more importantly, *against* war, but to tease out some features that make them and what they protest against as relevant as they are, not least when they stand in contrast to the hegemonic discourse then and now.

However, we would also like to address two issues that have been left out of our considerations so far: firstly, *songs as narratives* and, related to this, *narrator perspectives* (including whether their authorship is or is not known),[22] and, secondly, the question as to the *artistic quality of protest songs*.

Let us begin with songs as narratives. Winkler (2009) describes Seeger's view that "singing songs in unison could foster a common commitment to work for social and political change" (40). Why songs are such a powerful element in the struggle between hegemonic attitudes and antihegemonic discourse is indicated by Frith's (1996) convincing observation that "[a]ll songs are implied narratives. They have a central character, the singer; a character with an attitude, in a situation, talking to someone (if only to herself)" (169ff).

We have discussed such "implied narratives" and considered their appeal, both in anonymous songs and those with identified authorship. In the former category we have seen several overarching themes, mainly the complaint against recruitment, the plight of those involved in the fighting, and the lament of those about to be or having been left behind. On the other hand, in our examples, predominantly songs written by well-known songwriters, we have seen actual narratives with often explicit criticism of authority/ies, as well as songs aimed at mobilizing audiences or at least giving them food for thought.

What is interesting in this context is narrator perspective. That the voices of singers fall into three categories, the two dominant ones being first person and third person focalization respectively. *I-narratives* are characterized by a directly affected person telling the listeners about her or his conditions and emotions. These were in evidence for example in "O Frankerych," "The D-Day Dodgers," as well as in many of the WWI soldiers' songs representing the plight of the men in the trenches. Issues like the fear of women being left behind and the fear of partners' recruitment were voiced in "Here's the Tender Coming" and "The Recruited Collier."

On the other hand, we have songs with a third-person perspective, such as "Floo'ers o' the Forest," also with the lament of women left behind or the "broken-token ballads," even though the story is often told in the dialogue between the characters in the story, with an I-narrator who frames the narrative (such as "Plains of Waterloo").

In contrast to these anonymous songs, there are those with attributable authorship. Here, we also have first-person perspectives as in "Masters of War" and "Born in the USA" as well as third-person perspective as in "Where Have All the Flowers Gone," "The Sun Is Burning," "Universal Soldier," "The Band Played Waltzing Mathilda," and so on. But among such songs with attributable authorship we also find narratives with a second-person focus.[23] The *you* addressed in those can be an implied addressee, in "Masters of War" the Industrial Military complex, in "I-Feel-Like-I'm-Fixing-to-Die Rag" prospective recruits, Wall Street, the general staff, and parents.

However, the addressee can also be an audience, a wider public. In "Think Again" Gaughan seems to want to shake the general public and through them the powers that be into a realization that we should not let our mistrust of the Soviet Union lead all of us into a confrontation that will only bring untold misery. It is probably not a coincidence that a large number of songs addressing labor conflicts, but also other issues that may best be faced by mobilization, use this form of second-person perspective. From a point of view of discourse and register, this tentative exploration may well be a topic for further exploration.

Lastly, we should also consider the notion *artistic quality*. In the Prologue to his *33 Revolutions per Minute: A history of Protest Songs*, Linskey makes the following observation:

> Protest songs are rendered a disservice as much by undiscerning fans as by their harshest critics. While detractors dismiss examples as didactic, crass or plain boring, enthusiasts are prone to acting as if virtuous intent suspends the usual standards of musical quality (...) The best protest songs are not dead artefacts, pinned to a particular place and time, but living conundrums. The essential, inevitable difficulty of contorting a serious message to meet the demands of entertainment is the grit that makes the pearl. (...) the political content is not an object to greatness but the source of it. They open a door and the world outside rushes in. (2010, xiiff)

To what degree the songs discussed here meet Linskey's criteria is clearly a matter of debate—and taste. What is striking is that some of the songs are still in the consciousness of music aficionados, admittedly in some cases rather a small group, and that these songs are more likely to reflect the anti-hegemonic perspective. By contrast, hardly any of the songs mentioned in the context of the Korean War, certainly not the jingoistic ones, have made it into a canon of any kind. The question one might have to address in future research is whether interest in the protest songs we have looked at has morphed to a purely historical perception with the growing distance to the events they referred to.

NOTES

1. Quoted in Lynskey 2010, 76.
2. For more information cf. https://mainlynorfolk.info/shirley.collins/songs/plainsofwaterloo.html.
3. There is a caveat for "D-Day Dodgers," however. It is sometimes claimed that it was originally written by Lance Corporal Harry Pynn in 1944 (Palmer 1990, 227), but that several verses were added anonymously because, clearly, the squaddies' feelings about their sacrifices being eclipsed by the D-Day Landings were very strong.
4. The factual information in the following account is based on Millet (2024) and Editors, History.com ([2009] 2022). The interpretation of the underlying ideologies is ours.
5. For an insightful discussion of the song's historical and political context, see Voices and Visions (n.d.).
6. This lyric is based on an old gospel song called "Kind Thoughts (/Words) Never Die."
7. Wesley Tuttle, Ken Marvin, and Gene Autry also covered this song.
8. According to the same source (Hutchinson 2013), Joe Hickerson received 20 percent of the total royalties.
9. Seeger's comrade Woody Guthrie was already exhibiting serious symptoms of Huntingdon's disease in the mid- to late fifties, which may have been the reason for him not being treated with the same harshness as Seeger, even though the FBI had him on file.
10. This is not to say that the epithet could not be applied to earlier antihegemonic singers, songwriters and performers like Joe Hill, Sarah Ogan Gunning, Sis Cunningham, Seeger, Guthrie, Lee Hayes, and others. But the term is more readily applied to the younger performers, where the music in some cases played a more central role than direct activism.
11. This happened around the same time as he "went electric," allegedly to the disappointment of Pete Seeger.
12. Whereas "With God on Our Side" has the same tune as Irish poet and songwriter Dominic Behan's "The Patriot Game" and there is a debate about who used whose melody, the origin of the tune to "Masters of War," "Nottamun Town," is undisputed and attributable to Dylan's fascination with the old English folk idiom.
13. The following is a summary of factual information is based on Turley, Osborne, Duiker, and Buttinger (2023).
14. See also the reference to "19" by Paul Hardcastle below (subsection "'Counter Culture' as a Background of Antiwar Protest").
15. The film *Full Metal Jacket* very graphically depicts the use of music.
16. *Good Morning Vietnam* illustrates this clash in musical tastes.
17. Quoted by More (2021) from a conversation between Buffy Sainte-Marie and Juliette Jagger on *Amplify*, in early 2020.
18. In the film version, the lyrics are included in footage with a moving dot to indicate how an audience might want to sing along.
19. This was famously lampooned in Ochs's "Draft Dodger Rag."
20. There is a very patriotic song called "Boys of the Dardanelles," composed by Marsh Little (1880–1958) in 1915, aimed at recruiting young Australian men for that campaign (National Film and Sound Archive of Australia NFSA n.d.).
21. The term that was imposed, which is interestingly commented on and deconstructed by Callahan (2017).
22. For a more detailed discussion of these issues, cf. Watts and Andres Morrissey (2019).
23. In fact, a lot of traditionals and songs written in the folk idiom quite often begin with a line inviting an audience, "Come all ye . . . ," and to exhort them to "listen to my song." However,

this way of addressing a potential audience is often limited to the opening of the song with the rest focusing on either first- or third-person perspective.

WORKS CITED

Andres Morrissey, F. (2020). "Plucky Tommies, Angelic Nurses and the Others: Identity constructions in hegemonic and antihegemonic discourse of First World War songs." In J. Andres, B. Rozema, and A. Schröder (Eds.), *(Dis-)Harmony: Amplifying Voices in Polyphone Cultural Productions*, 9–33. Bielefeld: Aisthesis.

Anonymous (1843). "Floo'ers o' the Forest." In *The Book of Scottish Song*, A. Whitelaw, Ed. Glasgow: W. G. Blackie and Co.

Anonymous (1882). "Here's the Tender Comin'." *Northumbrian Minstrelsy: A collection of the Ballads, Melodies and Small-Pipe Tunes of Northumbria*, J. Collingwood Bruce and J. Stokoe, Eds., 126. Newcastle: Society of Antiquaries of Newcastle-upon-Tyne.

Anonymous (1917). "O Frankerych, o Frankerych." *Das Schwyzerfähnli: Ernste und heitere Kriegs-, Sodaten und Volkslieder der Schweizer III*, H. in der Gand, Ed., 23–26. Biel, Bern, Zürich: Ernst Kuhn.

Anonymous ([1952] 1978). "The Recruited Collier." *Come All Ye Bold Miners: Ballads and Songs of the Coalfields*, A. L. Lloyd, Ed., 114–15. London: Lawrence and Wisehart.

Anonymous (1977). "Bonnie Woodhaa." *The Rambling Soldier*, R. Palmer, Ed., 229–30. Harmondsworth: Penguin.

Auslander, B. H. (1981). "'If Ya Wanna End War And Stuff, You Gotta Sing Loud': A survey of Vietnam-related protest music." *Journal of American Culture* 4 (Summer).

Bean, J. (2014). *Singing from the Floor: A history of British folk clubs*. London: Faber and Faber.

Brophy, J., and E. Partridge. (1930 [1965]). *The Long Trail: Soldiers' songs and slang, 1914–1918*. 4th ed. London: André Deutsch.

Callahan, M. (2017). *The Explosion of Deferred Dreams: Musical Renaissance and Social Revolution in San Francisco 1965–1975*. Oakland: PM Press.

Cronin, C. (n.d.). *Ory v. Country Joe McDonald*. Retrieved from George Washington University Law Blogs: Music Copyright Infringement Resource: https://blogs.law.gwu.edu/mcir/case/ory-v-country-joe-mcdonald/.

Editors. ([2009] 2022, [9] 11 [November] May). *Korean War*. History.com. https://www.history.com/topics/asian-history/korean-war.

Frith, S. (1996). *Performing Rites: On the value of popular music*. Cambridge, MA: Harvard University Press.

Frith, S. (2008, November 10). "'The magic that can set you free': the ideology of folk and the myth of the rock community." Retrieved January 29, 2022, from https://doi.org/10.1017/S0261143000000970.

Gaughan, D. (2008). "Think Again." Retrieved from Dick Gaughan's Song Archive: https://web.archive.org/web/20180918204039/http://www.dickgaughan.co.uk/songs/texts/thinkaga.html.

History on the Net. (n.d.). *Music About the Korean War: 1950–1954*. The Authentic History Center. https://www.historyonthenet.com/authentichistory/1946-1960/2-korea/3-music/index.html.

Hutchinson, L. (2013, May 3). "Happy Birthday, Pete Seeger!" Performing Songwriter. http://performingsongwriter.com/pete-seeger-flowers-gone/.

Inskeep, S., V. Pearson, and B. Gordemer. (2019, March 2). "What Does 'Born in the USA' Really Mean?" American Anthem: Music that challenges, unites and celebrates. NPR. https://www.npr.org/2019/03/26/706566556/bruce-springsteen-born-in-the-usa-american-anthem.

Lynskey, D. (2010). *33 Revolutions per Minute: A History of Protest Songs*. London: Faber and Faber.

Macalester College. (n.d.). "Do the Russians Want War?" (1956). Seventeen Moments in Soviet History: An online archive of Soviet history: https://soviethistory.msu.edu/1954-2/hydrogen-bomb/hydrogen-bomb-music/do-the-russians-want-war-1956/.

Millet, A. (2024, August 3). "Korean War." *Encyclopedia Britannica*. https://www.britannica.com/event/Korean-War.

More, R. (2021, August 2). "Behind the Song: Buffy Sainte-Marie, 'Universal Soldier.'" American Songwriter: The Craft of Music. https://americansongwriter.com/buffy-sainte-marie-universal-soldier/.

National Army Museum. (n.d.). "Gallipoli Campaign." National Army Museum UK. https://www.nam.ac.uk/explore/gallipoli.

National Film and Sound Archive of Australia (NFSA). (n.d.). "Boys of the Dardanelles." National Film and Sound Archive of Australia. https://www.nfsa.gov.au/collection/curated/asset/82247-boys-dardanelles.

Palmer, R. (1990). *"What a Lovely War!" British Soldiers' Songs from the Boer War to the Present Day*. London: Michael Joseph.

Priestley, J. B. (1962). *Margin Released: A Writer's Reminiscences and Reflections*. New York: Harper and Row.

Pynn, H., and Anonymous. (1944). "D-Day Dodgers." In Palmer (1990).

Rubens, P. A. (1914). "Your King and Country Want You." London: Chappell and Co.

The Scotsman. (2009, May 19). "Eric Bogle interview: And the man sang Waltzing Matilda." *The Scotsman*. https://www.scotsman.com/news/eric-bogle-interview-and-the-man-sang-waltzing-matilda-2466934.

Seeger, P., and B. Reiser. (1986). *Carry It On! A history in song and picture of the working men and women of America*. Poole: Blandford Press.

Songtell. (2023, June 28). "Meaning of Talking Vietnam Blues (Live) By Phil Ochs." Songtell.com. https://www.songtell.com/phil-ochs/talking-vietnam-blues-live.

Sweers, B., and F. Andres Morrissey. (2019). "Community Building Through Anti-hegemonic Performances." Lecture course Singing Social Friction. Bern: University of Bern. https://www.morrissey.unibe.ch/arcpod/Lecture_SSF_SS19/11_SFF_Antiwar_Songs/11_SFF_Antiwar_Songs.html.

Turley, W., M. Osborne, W. Duiker, and J. Buttinger. (2023, October 30). "History of Vietnam." Britannica.com. https://www.britannica.com/topic/history-of-Vietnam.

Voices and Visions. (n.d.). "'When They Drop the Atomic Bomb' | 1951." Retrieved March 23, 2023. https://vandvreader.org/jackie-doll-and-when-they-drop-the-atomic-bomb-1951/.

Watts, R. J., and F. Andres Morrissey. (2019). *Language, the Singer and the Song: The Sociolinguistics of Folk Performance*. Cambridge: Cambridge University Press.

Winkler, A. M. (2009). *To Everything There Is a Season: Pete Seeger and the Power of Song*. Oxford: Oxford University Press.

CHAPTER 11

"IT DON'T MAKE SENSE"
Willie Dixon, the Blues, War, and Peace

Steven Garabedian

In 1983, in the midst of Ronald Reagan's first term, and at a height of the president's hardline Cold War rhetoric, blues statesman Willie Dixon released his tenth album, *Mighty Earthquake and Hurricane*. It included "It Don't Make Sense (You Can't Make Peace)." Dixon called it his "favorite song out of all the hundreds of songs that I've written."[1] In that same year, Ronald Reagan had intensified the Cold War with his "evil empire" speech about the Soviet Union, and American viewers had tuned in to the World War III television nightmare *The Day After*. Dixon sang:

> You have made great planes to scan the skies;
> You gave sight to the blind with other men's eyes
> You even made submarines stay submerged for weeks
> But it don't make sense you can't make peace[2]

In live performance, the artist took the composition further. Over a meditative musical backing, Dixon preceded the verses with a blues sermon that built to a crescendo of admonition on the senselessness of war in a world of miracles. He chided: "When you think about the various nations of the earth. . . . We have been able to make anything that we want to make, and do anything that we want to do. Have created miracles. . . . Suppose you had spent half as much money on trying to make peace as you have in making war. We wouldn't have to worry about nothing. But, it don't make sense! It don't make sense! It don't make sense, when you can't make peace."[3]

There is no indication that Ronald Reagan was listening, and in fact, right or left, center or politically disinterested, many in the dominant culture have seemed deaf to the wisdom of the blues. In the "blues revival of the 1960s," the genre crossed over from Black to white as a mass popular phenomenon.[4] Unfortunately, much of its ongoing political vernacular was lost in translation. Still today, the music is celebrated for its artistry, but rarely taken as seriously for its political wisdom and social commentary.

This article begins and ends with Willie Dixon, but it is addressed to broader concerns than strictly blues biography or discography. Branching from Dixon to other African American blues artists, many of them equally legendary in their musical reputations, it highlights an overlooked tradition of Black expressive protest on US war and peace from the 1940s to the 1970s.

In the decades after World War II, the Cold War blanketed modern American life in a cloud of absurdity. The arms race, the Iron Curtain, Mutual Assured Destruction (M.A.D.), the Cuban Missile Crisis, and the hot fronts in Korea and Vietnam raised the stakes for human survival. Originating in African American vernacular communities of the South "just as the false dawns of emancipation and Reconstruction gave way to the long debilitating darkness of Jim Crow and disenfranchisement," as historian Brian Ward puts it,[5] the blues had already evolved to a full and varied maturity by the middle of the twentieth century. Besides just plain sounding good, being danceable and emotionally moving, blues was adult music for adult realities. Indeed, owing to its historical development in the tortuous crucible of racism, the genre was suited by nature to handle the contradictions, ambiguities, and hypocrisies of life generally, whether in the heat of the US South or the nuclear winter of the global Cold War.

Scholar-theologian James Cone has written that the "important contribution of the blues is their affirmation of black humanity in the face of immediate absurdity." With its sophisticated fusion of bitter and sweet, blues was a music of resistance in the face of those who would "destroy physical bodies with guns, whips, and napalm," Cone stated in *The Spirituals and the Blues* in 1972.[6] Well before the age of the American superpower, people of color had long endured a litany of indignities and absurdities. Blues was a music made for surviving, even transcending, the extremes of everyday human experience in a land where slavery was a foundation for freedom, white was right, and violence was touted as a logical path to peace. If Vietnam came to break the hearts of many young middle-class white Americans in the 1960s, Black Americans had been suffering broken hearts in America for generations.

The blues has been underappreciated as part of a global movement culture for peace. Willie Dixon was just one of multiple African American blues artists articulating a collective wisdom and critical consciousness that few outsiders in the dominant culture seemed to hear. Even as the 1960s were becoming "The Sixties," even as Willie Dixon was becoming a household name among musicians, fans, and critics in that key era of blues crossover, blues songs on peace appear to have been off the record of awareness. Ultimately, this article begs the question of why this wisdom of the blues remains largely unacknowledged. Besides a twelve-bar musical sequence, searing guitar technique, sexual swagger, and romantic release, the world still has much it could learn from the music. "The blues are the true facts of life expressed in words and songs and inspirations with feeling and understanding," held Willie Dixon. "Everything that's been done wrong on the face of the earth *happens* because of evil, ignorance and stupidity," he insisted. "The wisdom of the blues can be used all through life and that's why most blues songs are written as a statement of wisdom. I'd say that from 95 percent up to 99 percent of the world believes that it don't make sense you can't make peace."[7]

HEAVY-HITTER: WILLIE DIXON AND THE BLUES

Willie Dixon was a blues heavyweight. He is credited as the author of more than five hundred titles, many of them indelible classics. These include "Little Red Rooster," "I'm Your Hoochie Coochie Man," "You Shook Me," "Back Door Man," "I Just Want to Make Love to You," "Spoonful," and "Wang Dang Doodle," as performed by such artists as The Rolling Stones, Muddy Waters, Led Zeppelin, The Doors, Howlin' Wolf, and Etta James.[8] A Mississippi native who moved to Chicago and became the essential in-house songwriter, arranger, musician, and producer at the famed Chess Records of the 1950s and 1960s, Dixon called both his 1969 solo album and his 1989 autobiography *I Am the Blues*, after the title of one of his signature compositions. There were legions of fans who believed it.

But, in addition to blues hit-making, Willie Dixon "felt he was on a higher mission," as his recent biographer stresses.[9] "It Don't Make Sense" is not an aberration or novelty in the artist's career. During World War II, Dixon was imprisoned for refusing the draft on the grounds that he was a "conscientious objector" and "wasn't gonna fight for nobody." In the mid-1960s, he marched in Chicago with Martin Luther King Jr.[10] In 1971, the musician titled an entire album *Peace?* and released it on his own Yambo Records label. The LP featured an evocative hand-drawn cover illustration of a tearful dove perched on a globe of snakes at war, and it included the topical songs "Peace" and "It's in the News."[11] In 1988, Dixon cowrote "Study War No More" with his grandson,

Alex. His final feature recording as a performer was an AIDS awareness campaign single, "AIDS to the Grave." Willie Dixon died in 1992 at age seventy-six. He was eulogized by Louis Farrakhan. Family members said the artist "did not know Farrakhan personally but admired him."[12] As is clear from a lifetime of words, music, and action, Dixon did not shrink from politics. He took his art and his convictions seriously, and he melded the two in an organic blues philosophy that he stressed determinedly for years.

FIGHTING SPIRIT: THE BLUES AND AFRICAN AMERICAN PROTEST

Willie Dixon is no fringe figure, and protest was never marginal to African American blues tradition. Whether addressed to issues of race, gender, sexuality, labor, war, or peace, and whether coded, subtle, or more direct, lyrics of social and political comment, derision, or defiance were common in the genre, even at a time when Black voices were severely constrained in most other spheres of public visibility. In their classic *Long Memory*, Mary Frances Berry and John W. Blassingame state, "Since most forms of black music received little consideration from whites when they first emerged, the musicians could articulate an unadulterated call for freedom before segregated black audiences. More than any other creative artist, the black musician sang his song of protest to the black masses."[13] Protest was not the exclusive function of the blues, of course. No mass popular form could thrive on such narrow terms. Still, the blues, in its original racialized context of creation and appreciation, was always more than entertainment alone. In this, James Baldwin's stinging proposition rings true: "It is only in his music, which Americans are able to admire because a protective sentimentality limits their understanding of it, that the Negro in America has been able to tell his story."[14]

Blues entered the commercial recording arena in 1920. For the first half of the decade, the blues queens Gertrude "Ma" Rainey and Bessie Smith dominated the field. In her important *Blues Legacies and Black Feminism*, Angela Davis interprets the music of popular artists Rainey, Smith, and successor Billie Holiday. In their day, when the avenues for formal political action were nominal and highly dangerous, Davis argues that these blues women's recorded output was radical in its open articulation of "class exploitation, racism, and male dominance."[15] In 1928, the reigning "Empress of the Blues," Bessie Smith, recorded her original composition "Poor Man's Blues." In part, the lyrics read:

> Mister rich man, rich man, open up your heart and mind
> Mister rich man, rich man, open up your heart and mind
> Give the poor man a chance, help stop these hard, hard times[16]

In the 1930s, tunes on the themes of Red Cross relief, the WPA, and welfare troubles were common coin in the blues industry.[17] Successful artists Josh White and Bill Broonzy, at work as commercial professionals from the 1920s forward, contributed their own versions and came to record even more noteworthy original blues of overt protest and social commentary. In 1940, White put out an eight-song album called *Chain Gang*. His backing group, the Carolinians, included Bayard Rustin, already an active socialist, pacifist, and civil rights worker. The following year, White released *Southern Exposure: An Album of Jim Crow Blues*. "Jim Crow Train" was just one of its six political songs:

> Now, hear that train whistle blow
> Can't you hear that train whistle blow? (2x)
> . . .
> Oh, Lord, this train is Jim Crow!
> Damn that Jim Crow![18]

William Lee Conley Broonzy, or "Big Bill" as he came to be popularly known to audiences on both sides of the Atlantic, wrote "Black, Brown and White" after World War II. It is perhaps the most famous African American blues song of protest:

> They says, "If you was white, you'd be all right.
> If you was brown, stick around,
> But if you's black, oh brother, get back, get back, get back."[19]

The above song examples are artful renderings of blues protest, many by artists who were at the center of the commercial industry. As Steven Tracy relates in *Write Me a Few of Your Lines: A Blues Reader*, however, the question of protest has long been a point of contention in blues scholarship.[20] In this, interpreters in the mode of Berry and Blassingame, Baldwin, and Davis, for instance, have been generally cast as "alternative" in the revivalist consensus that has dominated since the 1960s. I have written elsewhere on what I would assert as the fact of African American blues protest,[21] and my intent here is not to argue the historiographic issue. Suffice it to say, for some listeners, the blues is fundamentally about love and sex. Songs with social protest, they conclude, are exceptions to the general rule of blues authenticity, and any connection drawn between blues poetics and direct politics is a stretch. Certainly, for Willie Dixon, though, to return to our opening figure, the blues and protest made perfect sense. "[P]olitics carry the whole world today," he stated. "Everything today is political, one way or the other.... If you make blues and don't make 'em about world affairs or something pertaining to political things, yours are too far gone."[22]

Currently, the leading documenter of direct blues of social protest and political commentary is Dutch researcher Guido van Rijn. Since 1997, van Rijn has published six books on the subject, all periodized around the administrations of the US presidents—from Roosevelt to Obama—and all accompanied by CD anthologies.[23] As the author readily grants, "Blues songs with political comment are very rare; they may have been infrequently recorded because of the singers' fears of possible consequences." Accordingly, he suggests, a strict accounting of numbers can be deceiving. Of the stream of protest within blues recording generally, the "corpus is small," he acknowledges. Yet this expressive subset represents a "quantitatively modest, but qualitatively impressive musical response to the struggle for African American freedom." It is "one which is probably the visible and audible sign of a larger body of unrecorded protest songs," he concludes.[24]

Blues protest did not surface directly in Willie Dixon's career until the 1960s and 1970s. Even then, his output of songs with direct commentary is small in number relative to his entire body of work. Still, Dixon was a rebel throughout his life. His daughter, Shirli Dixon, said, "All of his work, he thought, was message music," and his biographer, musicologist Mitsutoshi Inaba, takes as his main subject the connection between Dixon's deep social convictions and seemingly apolitical blues hit-making in *Willie Dixon: Preacher of the Blues*. The "missing link," Inaba determines, is the collective heritage shared by the African American interpretive community Dixon intended as his primary audience. When Dixon wrote "Hoochie Coochie Man" or "Spoonful," for instance, he meant the songs as more than idle commercial efforts or sexual boasting. Dixon envisioned blues performers as secular preachers, Black community spokespersons who could impart wisdom, affirmation, and healing through a mass popular medium.[25] Blues historian, folklorist, and activist Worth Long has called Dixon a "poet-philosopher." In an interview, Dixon told him: "When I write a song, I hope that people like it well enough to dance to it. Because most of the time if people dance to something—ten to one—they learn something about the words of it that gives them a certain education they wouldn't learn otherwise. Blues is the greatest, because blues is the only one that, along with the rhythm and the music, brings wisdom."²⁶ Although he was not always singing songs of direct lyrical protest, Willie Dixon's blues always carried a spirit of solidarity and agitation. This has too often been missed by many of his most ardent celebrants in the dominant culture. As we will see, so has the connection been missed between the blues, war, and peace.

THE RIGHT TO FIGHT, OR NOT: AFRICAN AMERICANS AND US WAR

Willie Dixon's life and work opens a broader window on the blues interpretive community, African American social history, US war, and American countercurrents for peace in the twentieth century, from World War II to Vietnam. At the end of 1941, after Pearl Harbor, Dixon was arrested on stage during a live engagement in Chicago. "The army had been sending me a personnel notice off and on for a long time," Dixon explains in his autobiography, "but I made up my mind I wasn't going no damn where." He recounts:

> They started my trial and I told them I didn't feel I had to go because of the conditions that existed among my people.... A lot of people in Chicago felt like this, you know. Under the conditions that existed at that particular time, what the hell did you have to fight for? They were mistreating every damn body all over the world, especially our people.... They claimed I must have been educated somewhere else and all like this but the only education I had was from the actual experience up and down the highway.

Dixon ultimately did prevail in his stance avoiding service, resuming his life in Chicago under the terms that he stay quiet and not seek defense work. "The guy said, 'Man, you don't even trust the government,'" Dixon remembers. "I said, 'No, the government don't trust me.'"²⁷

Willie Dixon was not alone. If he was not yet preaching the kind of full-blown pacifism of "It Don't Make Sense" from some forty years later, he was expressing a shared critical ambivalence. Dixon said that he was not afraid to fight and not opposed to violent confrontations with bigotry or aggression. "If the country had treated me right," he insisted, "I would have been glad to go."²⁸ Dixon's antiwar sentiments were situational and political, not absolute and philosophical. He simply doubted the sincerity of his own nation and government in its fight for freedom. For African Americans, the blinders had been off as far as US rhetoric from the beginning. Such forced skepticism could lead in radical political directions, from antiracism to antiwar to pacifism and global justice.[29] Willie Dixon was not to that point yet in his consciousness in World War II, but like many other marginalized Americans, he was primed to see things differently and to respond in kind.

As in any community of millions, there is no single African American story of which to speak definitively. But, as historians have shown, Kimberley Phillips most recently, the condition of minority status in a nation structured by racial oppression did generate broad contours of collective experience for Black Americans. In the experience of war in the twentieth century, the double bind of citizenship and exclusion led to a conflicted Black collective outlook. On the one hand, from World War II to Vietnam, African Americans served, through voluntary enlistment and the draft, in the US military in higher proportions than other American population groups; at the same time, they developed stronger objections to war, and sooner too, than their peers in US society. By the 1960s, African American servicemen and their families constituted a vanguard of the rank-and-file of the "long civil rights movement" as well as the antiwar, antidraft movement opposing Vietnam. It was this community on the ground that pushed Martin Luther King Jr. to come out against the war in Vietnam in 1967.[30]

This restive Black social force at a focal point of power in the age of the American superpower was never uncomplicated or without paradox, however.[31] The line from service to resistance was not straight. Following years of racial denigration as "unfit" for combat, many Black Americans took pride in a record of courage under fire when they were finally integrated at the front in Korea and Vietnam, even if they were sooner to cynicism and scrutiny in both wars than others in American life. In World War II, while they insisted on a "Double V" campaign of victory against racism abroad and at home, many in the African American community and civil rights leadership continued to argue, as they had in World War I, for the "right to fight" as a path to full citizenship. By World War II, W. E. B. Du Bois, once an advocate, had already renounced such a call to arms; by the end of the war, he would be joined by other disheartened converts. Langston Hughes went from encouraging Black military participation in World War II to denouncing it as a modern form of impressment for poor people of color. James Baldwin expressed a similar dismay. As the soaring rhetoric of freedom gave way to the return of racism following World War II, a "certain hope died," Baldwin wrote, "a certain respect for white Americans faded."[32]

In the 1950s and 1960s, despite the strictures of Cold War containment and conformity, some Black Americans voiced their worry over the possibility of a nuclear World War III and doubted the wisdom and worth of hot fronts in Korea and Vietnam. Although President Truman had desegregated the armed forces on paper in 1948, it appeared the imperatives of war rather than conscience were what truly impelled integration in Asia. From World War II through the Cold War 1960s, mainstream civil rights organizations—the NAACP, most prominently—maintained the "right to fight" policy that encouraged Black military service, but all along outspoken ordinary African Americans and alternative leaders pressed the dual causes of racial freedom and global peace. In 1951, in the throes of the Korean War and McCarthyism, for instance, William L. Patterson of the dissident Civil Rights Congress drew a fearless parallel. "The lyncher and the atom bomb are related," Patterson asserted. "White supremacy at home makes for colored massacres abroad. Both reveal contempt for human life in a colored skin." By Vietnam, a young boxer was putting it his own way. "Man, I ain't got no quarrel with them Vietcong," quipped Muhammad Ali.[33]

The disquiet and dissent of a collective Black critical vernacular on war is reflected in the world of the blues. Willie Dixon was exceptionally accomplished at musical expression, but he was hardly unique in his attitudes. As referenced earlier, Bessie Smith recorded her composition "Poor Man's Blues" in 1928. The song is about race and class inequality, but it also includes two concluding verses on war:

> Poor man fought all the battles, poor man would fight again today
> Poor man fought all the battles, poor man would fight again today
> He would do anything you ask him in the name of the U.S.A.
> Now the war is over, poor man must live the same as you
> Now the war is over, poor man must live the same as you
> If it wasn't for the poor man, mister rich man, what would you do?[34]

Willie Dixon never wrote a song about the experience of race in World War II, but Bill Broonzy did, in his famous "Black, Brown and White" from 1946. Again, this song, introduced above, has verses about war fused alongside its verses protesting race and class inequality:

> I helped to win sweet victories
> With my little plow and hoe
> Now, I want you to tell me, brother
> What you gonna do about the old Jim Crow?[35]

"POST-WAR FUTURE BLUES"

The years of the early Cold War saw the first spike in African American blues protest of US war and peace. In surveying the material from the end of World War II to the end of the Korean conflict, one discerns an arc that moves from high hopes to trepidation to disappointment in this period. In 1945, a New Orleans artist under the name "Cousin Joe" recorded "Post-War Future Blues." The song was an optimistic ode to the return to normalcy. The chorus and concluding verse are indicative:

Chorus:
That's my post-war future, when I get back home,
Now that it's all over, no more battlefields will I roam.
...
We gonna raise two little boys, and we gonna raise a little girl,
So we can live our happy lives, in this free and peaceful world.[36]

But already, in the years 1949–1951, hope had turned into fear in a string of blues addressed to the theme of World War III and nuclear apocalypse. John Lee Hooker recorded "Build Myself a Cave" in 1949; David "Honeyboy" Edwards released "Build a Cave" in 1950; and Frankie Ervin, Sam "Lightnin'" Hopkins, Jimmy Rogers, Robert Lockwood and Albert "Sunnyland Slim" Luandrew, and Arthur "Big Boy" Crudup put out "I'd Rather Live Like a Hermit," "War New Blues," "The World's in a Tangle," "I'm Gonna Dig Myself a Hole," and another version of "I'm Gonna Dig Myself a Hole," respectively, in 1951. Guido van Rijn summarizes that in each of these songs, these artists had "sung about burrowing underground either to escape (nuclear) bomb attacks, or to escape the draft."[37] English contemporary Bob Groom highlights the case of Crudup as particularly noteworthy. The bluesman is the Mississippi artist whose "That's All Right" from 1946 inspired the famous 1954 rock 'n' roll cover by Elvis Presley. During World War II, as Groom points out, Crudup recorded the "intensely patriotic" blues "Give Me a 32-20"; Crudup wanted to fight with a "red, white and blue flag in my hand." By the time of "I'm Gonna Dig Myself a Hole" in April 1951, Crudup was singing a far different tune:

I'm gonna dig myself a hole, move my baby down in the ground;
You know, when I come out, there won't be no wars around.[38]

Earlier in the year, Frankie Ervin, a California blues singer, had extended the metaphor of escape and survival in his popular "Dig Myself a Hole" song cycle. In "I'd Rather Live Like a Hermit," Ervin sang:

> I'd rather live like a hermit in the forest,
> With Mother Nature on my side.
> . . .
> Because when those bombs start falling,
> It might be too late.[39]

Nuclear brinkmanship, Ervin suggested, was a strange measure of progress and civilization.

From the late 1940s through the 1970s, Texas blues singer, guitarist, and composer Sam "Lightnin'" Hopkins enjoyed a renowned career in postwar commercial blues. He was also one of its more frequent exponents of topical material.[40] In "Sad News from Korea" in 1951, as the war dragged into a bloody stalemate and public support for Harry Truman dropped to the lowest of his presidency,[41] Hopkins sang:

> Whoa, I got sad news this morning; people havin' trouble over in Korea.
> . . .
> Ain't it sad, ain't it sad, when the rain come fallin' down,
> Well, when you got a lot of playmates in this world somewhere;
> they can't be found.[42]

In 1950 and again in 1954, Chicago artist J. B. Lenoir recorded two fatalistic blues on the Korean War.[43] In 1952, L. B. Lawson, with famous accompanist James Cotton on blues harmonica, recorded two similar songs of death and despair. In "Missing in Action," Lawson sang:

> Yes, now you know the day they captured me, and I fell down on my knees,
> I said: "I want everybody just to hear me, Lord, I wanna pray one time, if you please."
> I said: "Lord, have mercy, will you please make a way?"
> Yes, you know I was missing in action, Lord, I was helping the ROK.[44]

In "Got My Call Card," Lawson's lyrics culminated in direct address:

> Well, I got my questionnaire, yes, I got my call card too,

. . .
> Yes, my brother's gone to the army, Lord, and they tryin' to get me too.
> Ooh, oh, oh! Lord, now what I'm gonna do?
> Yes, I swear he's missing in action, Lord, and they're coming after you.[45]

Both songs were produced at the Sun label in Memphis, owned by Sam Phillips.[46] In that same year, a third blues on the subject was recorded at Sun. In "Lost in Korea," Sherman Johnson concluded dolefully of the war: "World War Two was bad, but this is the worst I've ever seen, Every time I think it's over, I wake up and find it's just a dream." Producer Phillips added audio effects approximating the "whistlings, shudderings, and far-off rumblings" of battle "he heard in his imagination."[47]

Specialist van Rijn finds "a remarkable rise in political songs from 1950 to 1953 occasioned by the Korean War, in a period when the total record sales did not show a similar peak."[48] On a parallel track, Groom states: "Failure to progress significantly, either socially or economically, over the next ten years, plus involvement in another bloody war far away in Asia, turned that optimism to pessimism. . . . A decade of disillusion had produced a long series of relevant recordings, some indulging in caustic comment, some humorous, others more simply reportage. Those about the Korean War, however, were increasingly ambivalent and several unequivocally antiwar, anticipating the stand of boxer Muhammad Ali on the Vietnam War issue."[49] In American popular lore, "the fifties" were a "golden age" of abundance and tranquility. But, some in the decade clearly had reason to sing the blues.[50]

"THE DANGER ZONE"

In the sixties, counterinsurgency efforts in Indochina were undertaken during the presidency of John F. Kennedy. But, much closer to home, Cuba proved the major front of Cold War crisis that grabbed world attention. From the Bay of Pigs to the Cuban Missile Crisis, artists who were more and less known issued blues of immediate topical resonance. Lightnin' Hopkins recorded "War Is Starting Again"; Ray Charles recorded "The Danger Zone"; Luke "Long Gone" Miles recorded "War Time Blues"; "Sleepy John" Adam Estes recorded "It Was a Dream"; and Eddie Carson recorded three different versions of his blues monologue "The Devastating Bombs." Of these, Ray Charles's performance of "The Danger Zone" from 1961 and Carson's "The Devastating Bombs" from 1962 are perhaps the most striking.

Now a legendary figure, Ray Charles was only just beginning as an international crossover star in 1961. "The Danger Zone" was written by Percy Mayfield, and it followed the same melody and musical structure as Mayfield's famous hit from 1950, "Please Send Me Someone to Love." Charles sang:

> Sad and lonely all the time,
> That's because I've got a worried mind.
> Chorus: You know the world is in an uproar,
> The danger zone is everywhere, everywhere.[51]

Far less famous, but equally noteworthy for its Cold War timeliness, is "The Devastating Bombs." Eddie Carson released the song in 1962, likely in direct response to the Cuban Missile Crisis in October:

> Now you know those bloody, those bloody, bloody bombs, that hangs high, high over our heads,
> They may someday, someday destroy the world, and make our own, our own death beds.
> Now you can hide, you can hide in your bomb shelters, and if you do, and if you do survive,
> You can see the world, the whole world of today, destroyed before your very eyes.[52]

Again, as these songs attest, the nuclear peace of the Cold War arms race and global containment was a dangerous proposition.

"DAMN NAM (AIN'T GOIN' TO VIETNAM)"

After 1965, fear and confusion turned to outright distrust and opposition for some in America. Escalation to full-scale US combat operations in Vietnam precipitated a corresponding escalation in African American blues protest, in terms of both frequency of songs and frankness of lyrics.[53] As the nation politicized over the Vietnam War and domestic social issues, so did US popular culture. African American blues was at the cutting edge of this overall politicization, and the immediacy with which some artists commented, in *real time*, on Vietnam developments is startling. In the earliest stages of escalation, a number of blues songs were released bemoaning the war and chastening its architects. Of these, two blues songs by J. B. Lenoir stand out. On March 5, 1965—only three days after Lyndon Johnson launched the "Rolling

Thunder" bombing campaign and three days before the first two Marine battalions landed to commence ground combat operations in Vietnam—Lenoir recorded an updated version of his "Korea Blues" from 1950. In the song "Vietnam," Lenoir ponders not heroism and medals but instead compulsory service, death, and whether his son will be forced into the same cycle of war and loss.[54] On a tour with the American Folk Blues Festival in October 1965, the artist issued an even more trenchant critique of US policy abroad and at home in his second blues song on the war. In the live recording, "Everybody Is Crying About Vietnam," Lenoir sang:

> Vietnam, Vietnam, everybody's crying about Vietnam,
> Long as they killing me down in Mississippi,
> Nobody seemed to give a dime.[55]

With his high voice and loud tiger-print tuxedo, singer-songwriter and guitarist Lenoir was a notable live performing and recording artist in Chicago through the 1950s and 1960s until his untimely death at age thirty-eight in 1967. Lenoir is known for his 1954 boogie hit "Mamma Talk to Your Daughter," but his legacy of original blues songs of protest bears perhaps even more remembering.

In that same initial year of escalation, and similarly responding in the moment to ongoing developments, a female vocalist shared the experience of war for those left behind. "Viet Nam Blues," from 1965, is credited to singer Sylvia Maddox and composer "Sylvia Crite," likely the same woman, although little else is known about her. Like Lenoir's "Vietnam," the song casts the war as a story of personal loss, not one of righteous sacrifice or heroic duty in the name of freedom. For Maddox, Vietnam means that ordinary peoples' lives will be broken with little understanding of "what it's all about" and "if you're right or wrong":

> Uncle Sam has took my baby, yes, shipped him to Vietnam,
> Ain't it blue, blue, girls, ain't it lonely here, when he takes so many mothers' sons?
> Well, I know you don't know what it's all about, oh, if you're right or wrong,
> So many things have passed and gone, but you never left me, left me all alone.[56]

One year into escalation, in spring 1966, John Lee Hooker recorded an eloquent song of peace titled "This Land Is Nobody's Land." Hooker is surely among the most well known of modern blues superstars, with his resonant guitar style and voice that is instantly recognizable. His 1949 record debut,

"Boogie Chillen," is a blues classic, but like Willie Dixon and so many of these other artists under consideration, it is hardly the sole measure of his interests or ability. With "This Land Is Nobody's Land," Hooker delivered a blues sermon with a pacifism on the order of Dixon's "It Don't Make Sense":

> This land is no one's land,
> This land is your burying ground,
> I wonder why they're fighting over this land,
> God made this world, everything that's in[57]

As these blues suggest, African Americans questioned the means and ends of the war in Vietnam sooner and in greater numbers than other American communities. In a war noted particularly for its pain and divisiveness, the Black experience of Vietnam was particularly bitter, especially in the war's early years. While many young Americans in the white mainstream were only just awakening to a crisis of conscience in Southeast Asia, socially and economically disadvantaged Americans on the margins were already forced into the maelstrom. Vietnam, more than World War II or Korea, was a "working-class war," drawing disproportionately on poor whites and people of color for its combat ranks. In World War II, nearly all eligible men were called up for US military service; in Korea, the number was still high at 70 percent of all able American males. But, from the mid-1950s into the 1960s, details Christian Appy, what had been a relatively universalized burden of war became the experience of a marked "military minority." African Americans were overrepresented in terms of national income inequality, and Black men came to be overrepresented in army frontline combat units in Vietnam. At the beginning of the war, these disparities were acute and deadly. Between 1965 and 1967, African Americans accounted for 11 percent of the total US population, but Black fatalities were 20 percent of the US combat total. These figures were an embarrassment for American officials, and the army gradually brought down Black casualty rates to where they were proportional. Nevertheless, the lesson of Vietnam was clear. Some Americans were expected to do the "dirty work" of the nation, abroad and at home, in greater numbers and at greater cost than others. Although African American induction and enlistment rates were historically higher than that of white Americans, a distinct Black response was registered as escalation peaked in Vietnam. In 1968, the bloodiest year of the war, Black reenlistment dropped by more than half (to 31.7 percent) of what it was the previous year (66.5 percent).[58]

The Black critical backlash to war was not reflected only in Vietnam reenlistment and participation. The provocative Nina Simone conveyed a stark radicalization of sentiment in "Backlash Blues" in 1967. With lyrics written by Langston Hughes, the song is antiracist, antiwar, and anti-imperialist:

Mr. Backlash, Mr. Backlash, just who do you think I am?
You raise my taxes, and freeze my wages, and send my son to Vietnam.
You give me second class houses, and second class schools,
Do you think that all colored folks are just second class fools?[59]

On the ground and in the leadership community, many African Americans had tired of US war. Despite its indirect philosophical tone, John Lee Hooker's "This Land Is Nobody's Land" was nonetheless left off of Hooker's 1966 album for Chess Records, perhaps owing to its political resonance. Two years later, in the more overtly polarized political environment of 1968, Hooker got straight to the point with "I Don't Wanna Go to Vietnam":

Sitting here thinking, I don't wanna go to Vietnam,
United States have so much trouble of their own,
Why they wanna fight in Vietnam?[60]

Hooker recorded "I Don't Wanna" with the 1960s blues hippies Canned Heat. Into the 1970s, blues artists continued to sing out, in even stronger terms, on Vietnam, injustice, and peace. There was T-Bone Walker's "Vietnam" in 1969; Memphis Slim's "Chicago Seven" and "Youth Wants to Know" in 1970; Leon Thomas's "Damn Nam (Ain't Goin' to Vietnam)" in 1969 and again in 1970; Robert Pete Williams's "Vietnam Blues" in 1970; and Champion Jack Dupree's "Vietnam Blues" in 1971. Still, blues protest did not seem to capture the hearts and minds of the rock counterculture the way acoustic blues about hard traveling, hard drinking, or hard love did. Canned Heat played Woodstock in 1969, but John Lee Hooker was not with them. In fact, no major African American blues heroes appeared at the fabled three-day festival of "peace and music." In the collective hearing of "the sixties generation," the blues was a roots music. It was rural and folky, or electric and sexually charged, but it was not political. Rock could evolve to a higher stage of artistic and intellectual sophistication and revolutionary engagement, but the blues did so, indicated its most committed revivalist adherents, only at peril to its true meaning and authenticity.[61]

THE BLUES AND WAR: PROTEST AND DENIAL

In the 1960s, Willie Dixon and the blues crossed over to mainstream visibility, but African American blues protest did not. Samuel Charters is commonly cited as the founding figure in the white mainstream discovery of the blues in the 1960s. Many date the formal beginnings of "the blues revival" to 1959, with the publication of Charters's seminal *The Country Blues*. In 1963, in his second book on the subject, Charters issued a summary statement that has proved widely influential. "There is little social protest in the blues," he maintained. "[S]ometimes the poverty and the rootlessness in which the singer has lived his life is evident in a word or phrase, but there is little open protest at the social conditions under which a Negro in the United States is forced to live. There is complaint, but protest has been stifled."[62] What Charters and other revivalist leaders and fans heard in the music was the romance of the outsider and the promise of cultural redemption in the Atomic Age.[63] Going back to before World War II and the rise of US hegemony and the Cold War, political consciousness and activism had been central to the nascent dominant cultural "discovery" of Black and white southern folk music. By the time the blues hit the mainstream in the 1960s, however, the ground had shifted. "Of the early centrality of the left in the revival there can be no doubt," explains Robert Cantwell in looking back. "But for those of us whose revival began around 1958, these associations were absent and would have been, in our naive and compliant youth, a barrier to any enthusiasm for folksong. What is most interesting about the revival is not its political affiliations, but the absence of them."[64]

Meanwhile, African American blues protest was hiding in plain sight all along. It was in these key crossover years, *Living Blues* magazine cofounder Jim O'Neal recalls, that Dixon began to feel the urgency to get the word out about the deep wisdom of the blues. The artist's passion to preach in part "arose from his feeling that many books about the blues—written by scholars of the time—failed to discuss what he felt the blues truly meant for African Americans," O'Neal elaborates. Although Dixon spoke out directly in interviews, communicated through song, and published an autobiography and a collection of his own lyrics, his was a message too often lost on the disciples. "Rather foolishly," admitted Mick Jagger, for instance, "I didn't take notice of more of his work."[65]

Willie Dixon was not just a blues visionary; he was an apostle for peace. The unstated assumption among observers is that blues songs of protest means blues songs protesting racial injustice. There are indeed many songs in that vein, but the concerns of people of color ran the full range of American issues, and this breadth is reflected in their blues. A systematic look into the striking tradition of African American blues protest reveals an impressive number of songs on US war and peace by mainstream artists at the center of the tradition. If Willie Dixon was singing "It Don't Make Sense" in the Cold War of the 1980s, Arthur Crudup was singing "I'm Gonna Dig Myself a Hole" to avoid Korean War service and the threat of the nuclear annihilation in 1951, Ray Charles was singing about being a "worried man" in the acute Cold War crises of the Kennedy years in "The Danger Zone" in 1961, and John Lee Hooker was singing, flat out and unmistakably, "I Don't Wanna Go to Vietnam" in 1968. Certainly, blues songs of protest on racial inequality have been overlooked and undervalued, but blues on the politics of war and peace have been subject to an even more severe and enduring denial.

The denial of blues protest is part of the same mental operation that takes a nation to war and denies the possibility of peace as a just and rational goal for humanity. Unfortunately, this is the collective thinking that too often conditions US dominant culture. For some, "common sense" holds that blues is *just* music—just about men, women, love, and sex. It is not political. It is not philosophy. It is no big deal. For some, as well, war is inevitable—human nature is destructive, and peace is futile. To some dissenters all along, none of this makes sense. "The blues being the true facts of life," stated Willie Dixon, "we know it has been a fact of life that the people in the world have always made whatever they wanted. In making the many things of the world, we have made everything but peace. If you accept the wisdom of the blues, we can definitely have peace."[66]

NOTES

This chapter originally appeared as "It Don't Make Sense: Willie Dixon, the Blues, War, and Peace" by Steven Garabedian, *Peace and Change* 40, no. 3 (2015): 287–312. Copyright © 2015 Peace History Society and Wiley Periodicals, Inc. Reprinted with permission.

1. Willie Dixon and Don Snowden, *I Am the Blues: The Willie Dixon Story* (London: Quartet Books, 1989), 228; Willie Dixon, *Mighty Earthquake and Hurricane*, 1994, Mighty Tiger B00000DRL6, compact disc.

2. Dixon and Snowden, 228.

3. Willie Dixon, *I Am the Blues*, directed by Robert Schwartz (Heart Productions, 1984). http://www.youtube.com/watch?v=Yil7_XsLN1M.

4. Bob Groom, *The Blues Revival* (London: Studio Vista, 1971); Jim O'Neal, "I Once Was Lost, But Now I'm Found: The Blues Revival of the 1960s," in *Nothing But the Blues: The Music and the Musicians*, ed. Lawrence Cohn (New York: Abbeville Press, 1993), 347–88; and Ulrich Adelt, *Blues Music in the Sixties: A Story in Black and White* (New Brunswick, NJ: Rutgers University Press, 2010).

5. Brian Ward, *Just My Soul Responding: Rhythm and Blues, Black Consciousness, and Race Relations* (Berkeley: University of California Press, 1998), 72.

6. James Cone, *The Spirituals and the Blues: An Interpretation* (1972; Maryknoll, NY: Orbis Books, 1991), 114, 118.

7. Worth Long, "The Wisdom of the Blues—Defining Blues as the True Facts of Life: An Interview with Willie Dixon," *African American Review* 29, No. 2 (Summer 1995): 210; Dixon and Snowden, 229.

8. Dixon and Snowden, "Appendix 2," 247–49.

9. Mitsutoshi Inaba, *Willie Dixon: Preacher of the Blues* (Lanham, MD: Scarecrow Press, 2011), ix.

10. Dixon and Snowden, 54, 178.

11. Willie Dixon, *Peace?* 1971, Yambo Records 777–15, 33 rpm.

12. Inaba, 57, 295, xi.

13. Mary Frances Berry and John W. Blassingame, *Long Memory: The Black Experience in America* (New York: Oxford University Press, 1982), 369.

14. James Baldwin, "Many Thousands Gone," *Partisan Review* 18, No. 6 (November–December 1951): 665.

15. Angela Y. Davis, *Blues Legacies and Black Feminism: Gertrude "Ma" Rainey, Bessie Smith, and Billie Holiday* (New York: Vintage Books, 1998), 119.

16. Davis, 327–28; Bessie Smith, "Poor Man's Blues," 1928, YouTube, http://www.youtube.com/watch?v=Ykl6o4GAEq8.

17. Ronald D. Cohen and Dave Samuelson, *Songs for Political Action: Folk Music, Topical Songs, and the American Left, 1926–1953*, 1996, Bear Family Records, BCD 15720 JL, compact disc box set; and Neil Slaven, *Ain't Times Hard: Political and Social Comment in the Blues*, 2008, JSP Records, JSP 77109, compact disc box set.

18. Josh White, "Jim Crow Train," 1941, YouTube, http://www.youtube.com/watch?v=O_lb4Ig5esw. On White, see Elijah Wald, *Josh White: Society Blues* (Amherst: University of Massachusetts Press, 2000); also, Cohen and Samuelson, *Songs for Political Action*.

19. The first appearance of the song on record was by Walter "Brownie" McGhee in 1947. Although he performed it often from 1946 on, Broonzy did not record the song himself on a commercial label until 1951. William Lee Conley "Big Bill" Broonzy, "Black, Brown and White," 1951, YouTube, http://www.youtube.com/watch?v=koc1coZsTLA. For the McGhee version and more on the history of the song, see Cohen and Samuelson, *Songs for Political Action*; also, see Bob Riesman, *I Feel So Good: The Life and Times of Big Bill Broonzy* (Chicago: University of Chicago Press, 2011).

20. Steven C. Tracy, ed., *Write Me a Few of Your Lines: A Blues Reader* (Amherst: University of Massachusetts Press, 1999), 339–41.

21. Steven Garabedian, *A Sound History: Lawrence Gellert, Black Musical Protest, and White Denial* (Amherst: University of Massachusetts Press, 2020). On Gellert and white collecting, see Benjamin Filene, *Romancing the Folk: Public Memory and American Roots Music* (Chapel Hill: University of North Carolina Press, 2000); and Marybeth Hamilton, *In Search of the Blues: Black Voices, White Visions* (London: Jonathan Cape, 2007). For a view that differs from my own, see Bruce M. Conforth, *African American Folksong and American Cultural Politics: The Lawrence Gellert Story* (Lanham, MD: Scarecrow Press, 2013).

22. Dixon and Snowden, 227.

23. Guido van Rijn, *Roosevelt's Blues: African-American Blues and Gospel Songs on FDR* (Jackson: University Press of Mississippi, 1997); van Rijn, *The Truman and Eisenhower Blues: African-American Blues and Gospel Songs, 1945–1960* (New York: Continuum, 2004); van Rijn, *Kennedy's Blues: African-American Blues and Gospel Songs on JFK* (Jackson: University Press of Mississippi, 2007); van Rijn, *President Johnson's Blues: African-American Blues and Gospel Songs on LBJ, Martin Luther King, Robert Kennedy and Vietnam, 1963–1968* (The Netherlands: Agram Blues Books,

2009); van Rijn, *The Nixon and Ford Blues: African-American Blues and Gospel Songs on Vietnam, Watergate, Civil Rights and Inflation, 1969–1976* (The Netherlands: Agram Blues Books, 2011); van Rijn, *The Carter, Reagan, Bush Sr., Clinton, Bush Jr. and Obama Blues: African-American Blues and Gospel Songs, 1976–2012* (The Netherlands: Agram Blues Books, 2012).

24. Van Rijn, *Roosevelt's Blues*, xv–xvi; and *The Truman and Eisenhower Blues*, 153, 70.

25. See Inaba; Shirli Dixon qtd. in Inaba, 297.

26. Long, 211.

27. Dixon and Snowden, 44, 53–55; Inaba, 31, 52. Autobiographical statements like that of Dixon's are, of course, to be taken with some scrutiny. In this case, readers should note that the artist's autobiography is coauthored with music writer Don Snowden, who opens each chapter with independently researched passages meant to provide clarifying or corroborating information. Also, I have relied on additional secondary source material for cross-checking—namely, the biography by Mitsutoshi Inaba and interview article by Worth Long.

28. Dixon and Snowden, 55.

29. Although beyond our present purposes, the distinctions and overlap between pacifist and antiwar movements and histories are significant. See for instance, Charles Chatfield, *The American Peace Movement: Ideals and Activism* (New York: Twayne Publishers, 1992); Staughton and Alice Lynd, eds., *Nonviolence in America: A Documentary History* (Maryknoll, NY: Orbis Books, 1995); Peter Brock and Nigel Young, *Pacifism in the Twentieth Century* (Syracuse, NY: Syracuse University Press, 1999); James Tracy, *Direct Action: Radical Pacifism from the Union Eight to the Chicago Seven* (Chicago: University of Chicago Press, 1996); John D'Emilio, *Lost Prophet: The Life and Times of Bayard Rustin* (New York: Free Press, 2003); and Marian Mollin, *Radical Pacifism in Modern America: Egalitarianism and Protest* (Philadelphia: University of Pennsylvania Press, 2006).

30. Kimberley L. Phillips, *War! What Is It Good For? Black Freedom Struggles and the U.S. Military from World War II to Iraq* (Chapel Hill: University of North Carolina Press, 2012), 245–48. See also James E. Westheider, *Fighting on Two Fronts: African Americans and the Vietnam War* (New York: New York University Press, 1997); C. L. R. James et al., *Fighting Racism in World War II* (New York: Pathfinder Press, 1980); Nelson Peery, *Black Fire: The Making of an American Revolutionary* (New York: New Press, 1994); and Terry Whitmore, *Memphis Nam Sweden: The Story of a Black Deserter* (1971; Jackson: University Press of Mississippi, 1997).

31. Contrary to Phillips and others, Michael Cullen Green argues that Black soldiers were willing and enthusiastic participants in US imperialism after World War II. See Green, *Black Yanks in the Pacific: Race in the Making of American Military Empire after World War II* (Ithaca, NY: Cornell University Press, 2010). For opposing viewpoints, tracing the lines of affinity and coalition between Black Americans and other nonwhite oppressed peoples abroad, see Penny M. Von Eschen, *Race Against Empire: Black Americans and Anticolonialism, 1937–1957* (Ithaca, NY: Cornell University Press, 1997); Winston James, *Holding Aloft the Banner of Ethiopia: Caribbean Radicalism in Early Twentieth-Century America* (New York: Verso, 1998); Cedric J. Robinson, *Black Marxism: The Making of the Black Radical Tradition* (1983; Chapel Hill: University of North Carolina Press, 2000); Carole Boyce Davies, *Left of Karl Marx: The Political Life of Black Communist Claudia Jones* (Durham, NC: Duke University Press, 2007); Robin D. G. Kelley, *Freedom Dreams: The Black Radical Imagination* (Boston: Beacon Press, 2002); and Timothy B. Tyson, *Radio Free Dixie: Robert F. Williams and the Roots of Black Power* (Chapel Hill: University of North Carolina Press, 1999).

32. Phillips, 9–10.

33. Phillips, 10, 209; Dave Zirin, *A People's History of Sports in the United States: 250 Years of Politics, Protest, People, and Play* (New York: New Press, 2008), 141.

34. Davis, 328.

35. Broonzy, "Black, Brown and White," 1951, YouTube, http://www.youtube.com/watch?v=koc1coZsTLA.

36. Van Rijn, *The Truman and Eisenhower Blues*, 7; Bob Groom, "Beyond the Mushroom Cloud: A Decade of Disillusion in Black Blues and Gospel Songs," in *Ramblin' on My Mind: New Perspectives on the Blues*, ed. David Evans (Urbana: University of Illinois Press, 2008), 332.

37. Van Rijn, 94.

38. Groom, 338; Arthur Crudup, "I'm Gonna Dig Myself a Hole," 1951, YouTube, http://www.youtube.com/watch?v=Jpice5hFE0c.

39. Van Rijn, 37–38.

40. Groom, 335; van Rijn, *The Nixon and Ford Blues*, 108.

41. See David Halberstam, *The Coldest Winter: America and the Korean War* (New York: Hyperion, 2007); and Bruce Cumings, *The Korean War: A History* (New York: Modern Library, 2010).

42. Groom, 339–40; Sam "Lightnin'" Hopkins, "Sad News from Korea," 1951, YouTube, http://www.youtube.com/watch?v=-Lj8zQowebI.

43. Van Rijn, *The Truman and Eisenhower Blues*, 78–80.

44. Van Rijn, 80.

45. Van Rijn, 81.

46. In 1954, Phillips would break Elvis Presley to world fame with Presley's cover of Crudup's "That's All Right."

47. Van Rijn, 83; Groom 341; Sherman "Blues" Johnson, "Lost in Korea," 1952, YouTube, http://www.youtube.com/watch?v=UsFvl2wfurE.

48. Van Rijn, 151.

49. Groom, 347–48.

50. On the postwar dreams and anxieties, the Cold War and "the fifties" generally, see Tom Engelhardt, *The End of Victory Culture: Cold War America and the Disillusioning of a Generation* (Amherst: University of Massachusetts Press, 2007); George Lipsitz, *Rainbow at Midnight: Labor and Culture in the 1940s* (Urbana: University of Chicago Press, 1994); Lary May, ed., *Recasting America: Culture and Politics in the Age of the Cold War* (Chicago: University of Chicago Press, 1989); Elaine Tyler May, *Homeward Bound: American Families in the Cold War Era* (New York: Basic Books, 1999); Pete Daniel, *Lost Revolutions: The South in the 1950s* (Chapel Hill: University of North Carolina Press, 2000); and John Lewis Gaddis, *The Cold War: A New History* (New York: Penguin Books, 2005).

51. Van Rijn, *Kennedy's Blues*, 39; Ray Charles, "The Danger Zone," 1961, YouTube, http://www.youtube.com/watch?v=9v1TqDm8uoc.

52. Van Rijn, 43.

53. For two of the most comprehensive and penetrating accounts of Western conflict in Vietnam, see Marilyn B. Young, *The Vietnam Wars, 1945–1990* (New York: Harper Perennial, 1991), and Mark Philip Bradley, *Vietnam at War* (Oxford: Oxford University Press, 2009).

54. Van Rijn, *President Johnson's Blues*, 75–76; J. B. Lenoir, "Vietnam," 1965, YouTube, http://www.youtube.com/watch?v=LkRzFcoxfVA&list=PLC3CC3-B67E0C986B5&index=13. Readers will note this link connects them to the wonderful "Vietnam War Song Project" YouTube channel.

55. Van Rijn, 93–94; J. B. Lenoir, "Everybody Is Crying about Vietnam," 1965, YouTube, http://www.youtube.com/watch?v=97uEgyHbq-c.

56. Van Rijn, 74–75; Sylvia Maddox, "Viet Nam Blues," 1965, YouTube, http://www.youtube.com/watch?v=rnWeLd4gWp0.

57. Van Rijn, 104–5; John Lee Hooker, "This Land Is Nobody's Land," 1966, YouTube, http://www.youtube.com/watch?v=SL5vC-B_zq4.

58. Christian G. Appy, *Working-Class War: American Combat Soldiers and Vietnam* (Chapel Hill: University of North Carolina Press, 1993), 18, 20, 7; Phillips, 218.

59. Nina Simone, "Backlash Blues," 1967, YouTube, http://www.youtube.com/watch?v=2Pj9AucSc9Y&list=PLC3CC3B67E0C986B5. For a transcription of the live performance of the song, see van Rijn, 140. Also, see Phillips, 230; and Nadine Cohodas, *Princess Noire: The Tumultuous Reign of Nina Simone* (New York: Pantheon Books, 2010), 202.

60. Van Rijn, 89; John Lee Hooker, "I Don't Wanna Go to Vietnam," 1968, YouTube, http://www.youtube.com/watch?v=NsEtybJk2fk&feature=c4-overview-vl&list=PLC3CC3B67E0C986B5.

61. Sixties blues revivalists loved their blues heroes as symbols, not contemporaries. Musicologist Jeff Todd Titon, who was one of them, has reflected incisively on the dynamic. See Titon, "Reconstructing the Blues: Reflections on the 1960s Blues Revival," in *Transforming Tradition: Folk Music Revivals Examined*, ed. Neil V. Rosenberg (Urbana: University of Illinois Press, 1993), 220–40; and Charles Keil, *Urban Blues* (Chicago: University of Chicago Press, 1966). More recently, see Marybeth Hamilton, *In Search of the Blues: Black Voices, White Visions* (London: Jonathan Cape, 2007); and Barry Lee Pearson, *Jook Right On: Blues Stories and Blues Storytellers* (Knoxville: University of Tennessee Press, 2005). By contrast, on the evolution of "rock 'n' roll" into rock and revolution, see Peter Doggett, *There's a Riot Going On: Revolutionaries, Rock Stars and the Rise and Fall of '60s Counter-Culture* (Edinburgh: Canongate Books, 2007).

62. Samuel Charters, *The Poetry of the Blues* (1963; New York: Avon Books, 1970), 152. Of late, Charters has reexamined this position. See "The Blues' Angry Voice," in *Walking a Blues Road: A Selection of Blues Writing, 1956–2004* (New York: Marion Boyars, 2004): 131–42.

63. Grace Elizabeth Hale explicates these dynamics in their multiple iterations, musical and otherwise, in *A Nation of Outsiders: How the White Middle Class Fell in Love with Rebellion in Postwar America* (New York: Oxford University Press, 2011).

64. Robert Cantwell, *When We Were Good: The Folk Revival* (Cambridge, MA: Harvard University Press, 1996), 21–22.

65. Jim O'Neal qtd. in Inaba, xxvi; Mick Jagger qtd. in Inaba, 301; Dixon's book of lyrics is *Willie Dixon: The Master Blues Composer*, published in 1992.

66. Dixon and Snowden, 229.

CHAPTER 12

COMPARED TO WHAT?
Representing and Misrepresenting American Music

Mat Callahan

In 1966 Gene McDaniels copyrighted "Compared to What?" The song went on to become a worldwide hit for Les McCann in 1969. Making veiled reference to the war in Vietnam, the lyric calls out "the President," who has "got his war," and speaks in the name of the "folks" who don't know "just what it's for," concluding with the prophetic and oft-quoted lines:

> Nobody gives us rhyme or reason
> Have one doubt and they call it treason
> We're chicken-feathers, all without one nut
> Tryin' to to make it real, compared to what?[1]

Trying to make it real is a challenge. The real must contend with the fake, the genuine with the phony, the actual with the illusion, the true with the false. The discrepancy McDaniels's song calls attention to is what concerns the present chapter. In this case, the discrepancy between common perceptions of American music, and what those perceptions obscure or erase. How were these common perceptions formed, and by whom? What were the interests of particular historical actors, and what were the results of their efforts? How was a "canon" formed, and what criteria were applied to include or exclude music and musicians? How did geographical and historical factors interact with musicological ones to produce both the music as it actually existed and that which was promoted and disseminated by various agents, be they official (state), commercial (private publishers), or scholarly (song collectors, folklorists, and so on). In short, what was identified with America as a geographical, demographic, and political unit?

The problem can be posed in another way: the national aspect of "American Music" is self-evident. American music can be compared with Brazilian or Cuban, Iranian or Ghanaian, or indeed, the music of any other country. It can also be compared with music that preceded the emergence of the United States as well as music that has resulted from American influence subsequent to the rise of the United States to international dominance in the last century. Thus we can compare the music English settlers brought to Massachusetts in 1640 with music made in Massachusetts by people born there in 1740 and music made after 1776. Likewise, it is possible to compare music made by enslaved Africans at different stages of the historical development of the British colonies that became the United States with music in various African countries from which slaves were transported. It is also possible to compare the music of the native peoples met and conquered by European empires with that produced since the United States was founded. But this is only one dimension of the problem.

Another, equally important dimension is historical and political, whereby music was used in the process of building the United States and promoting its interests worldwide. Here the complex interactions between music and politics have to be examined in a different light. The overarching frame, in this case, is the claims made by the United States as an historical novelty and ideal. There can thus be no comparison between American music and that of other countries because no other countries have made the claims the United States has made to being a "light among the Nations," a "city on a hill," a bastion of freedom, and so forth. The rhetoric is so well known it need not be recalled at the moment. The point here is that claims of liberty, democracy, free enterprise, and the separation of church and state were extolled by music and increasingly so over time. This was, in part, because between 1776 and 1959, the United States kept expanding, incorporating more territory and more people who, not surprisingly, made their own music. These new people did not, however, fit neatly into the European-African frame that defined, and to a large extent still defines, American music. (Indeed, music in the Southwest and Hawaii, while undoubtedly influenced by European and African sources, is by no means dependent or merely an extension of those sources. They can thus only be incorporated into what is called "American Music" by using political, not musical, criteria, that is, citizenship in the country.)

Perhaps more significant, however, is that the very process of nation-building that began in earnest following independence from Great Britain not only made extensive use of music but began the selection that concerns us here. This is most obvious and egregious in the case of slavery and the conflict surrounding slavery's maintenance and eventual abolition. From a musical point of view, however, distinctions were never simply a question of Black and white, European vs. African (or African American). If anything, the distinctions ran along the lines of secular vs. religious music or between the music of cultivated, urban elites and the music of the populace at large, urban and rural alike. Such distinctions, moreover, included diverse musical practices, how music was performed and composed. The view that music should uplift morally and spiritually was widely held and invoked deliberately in combatting the vulgar and profane. Music education was energetically promoted, and well before there was a music industry to speak of, there were teachers, composers, instrument builders, and compilers of songbooks actively engaging practitioners of the craft.

Yet the lofty phrases of the Declaration of Independence and the Constitution did not correspond to the reality faced by the great majority of people. The conflicts arising from the disparity were many and frequent, so too the necessity of ever more forcefully promoting the ideal vs. the reality. While the rights to life, liberty, and the pursuit of happiness were upheld as the endowment of all, and while a Republic, free from the tyranny of monarchs and pontiffs, aristocrats and priests, was established, native peoples, slaves, women, and men of no property were systematically excluded.

Nevertheless, the promise had a powerful appeal. Arguments made by and on behalf of all the excluded frequently invoked the promises made by the Constitution. Reading today the statements made by Native leaders, abolitionists, advocates for women, small farmers, and workers, we see they continually refer to the promises that remained unfulfilled. In the case of abolitionism and women's suffrage, these arguments were the intellectual bulwark of massive popular movements. In the case of the labor movement, they went further still, insisting on addressing the underlying conflict between labor and capital.

It should not surprise us that these conflicting viewpoints were expressed in song. But it is precisely those songs that expressed popular resistance to the depredations of the state and the capitalist economy that have been marginalized to the extent of erasure. It is those songs, of which many remain, and indeed are still being produced, that our attention must turn if we are to form a more comprehensive, more accurate account of American music.

Yet even if this premise is accepted and the evidence presented elsewhere in this volume helps accomplish the task of reclaiming and restoring, there is still the broad category "American music" that needs to be accounted for.

In other words, there is the actual development of music as it was composed, performed, and heard, and there is the way music was written about by historians, critics, and publicists. As we shall see, these endeavors don't always coincide.

DESCRIBING AND DEFINING

Attempts to describe the music made in North America began with the first encounters between European and Native peoples. These descriptions were soon extended to the music of enslaved Africans whose numbers grew increasingly as colonization proceeded. Descriptions of the music European settlers brought with them proliferated as well. These focused especially on the music of dissenting Protestants but also included the ballads, sea-chanties, work songs, and dance tunes that disseminated spontaneously among the populace at large. Not long after colonization had begun in earnest with the settlement of towns like Boston, New York, and Charleston, descriptions of music began to take note of the difference between the urban and the rural, as well as between the religious and the profane. Early on, moreover, a distinction between "highbrow" and "lowbrow," or the music of cultivated elites and plebeian masses, was frequently made.

Attempts to *define* American music, however, only began in the period following the American Revolution and the founding of the United States. These were by and large attempts to differentiate the music made in the United States from that of Europe, England in particular. They were as much attempts to define a national character as a musical one and were not, in any case, rigorously scientific. Frequent reference to American's youthful vigor or lack of inhibition, was as much an ideal as a reality, and music was used as proof. After all, the instruments, the melodies, harmonies, and common usages were European- or African-derived (the Native element was often mentioned as a precursor and separate body of music, sometimes imitated but largely unassimilated into what the new inhabitants brought with them). Nonetheless, these attempts continued and were renewed at various intervals, which mark defining moments in American history. Specifically musicological definition rose to prominence with ragtime, followed by the massive popularity of jazz, not only in the United States but in Europe following World War I. The concurrent rise of the United States as a world power and the export of jazz is no accident; in fact, the parallels between America's rise and representations of America's music are interdependent. Indeed no account that fails to correlate musical development with the expansion from thirteen original colonies to continental and imperial power can be complete.

LIMITS—ARBITRARY, GEOGRAPHICAL, POLITICAL

Description and definition of American music is usually limited at the outset both by arbitrary distinctions having no musicological significance and by geographical and political facts that can only be set aside by decision. These limits are, in fact, obvious and not controversial in and of themselves. But before presenting a survey of the literature concerned with American music, it is worth recalling them and how they limit or influence the core of what the world views as American music, that is, European and African influences combining to produce the various genres most often associated with the United States.

1. Native peoples of North America made music. Indeed, in virtually every account recorded by a European observer, music and dance are mentioned as important social practices. These practices of music and dance ranged from ceremonial to religious to festive, but were found everywhere throughout the continent. Though frequent references were made and some composers took inspiration from Indian sources, this music remains a marginal reference in descriptions or definitions of American music. [2]

Hawaiian and Polynesian music is another question altogether. Sometimes it is mentioned but most often as itself, a music of a people that are only uneasily included in the "melting pot." This is due to the embarrassing fact that Hawaii was a sovereign nation-state that was conquered by the United States. The last queen, Lili'uokalanhi, was herself an accomplished musician and composer; the ukelele and slack-key guitar are instruments closely associated with Hawaii, and Hawaiian music gained worldwide renown in the late nineteenth and early twentieth centuries. Indeed, the pedal-steel guitar made a great impact, eventually being incorporated as an essential component of country music. Nevertheless, Hawaiian music is only infrequently mentioned as an integral part of American music, stemming from the fact that Hawaii, like Mexico, was an independent country, with its own musical traditions, that was conquered and absorbed into the United States (in the case of Mexico, it was half of that country).

2. While French, Dutch, and Spanish colonies were all established in what is now the United States and Canada, passing reference is all that is usually made of these European influences on American music. It is well known, of course, that music of French derivation flourished in Louisiana (Cajun,

opera, and so on), and that remnants still flourish in Quebec and the Atlantic Provinces of Canada.³ Nevertheless, with the exception of Cajun, which is considered a regional component, French-derived music is usually referred to as distinct, side by side, with American music.

So is the Spanish and Mexican influence, especially as it affects the music of the Southwest. In spite of the fact that this influence is almost ubiquitous in the region, it is only briefly mentioned in most descriptions of American music. To some extent this is due to the Spanish language being predominant (American music is virtually 100 percent English language–based). But the fact that the music, as melody, harmony, instrumentation, group formation, and composition, has long been enormously popular (to the present day) is revealing of the difficulties presented by any attempt to define or describe American music.

Since Puerto Rico was acquired by the defeat of Spain in the Spanish-American War (1898), its music has played an important role, perhaps most famously in Leonard Bernstein's *West Side Story*. By the time the present volume is published, Puerto Rico may have voted to become a state. A referendum of the question was authorized by the US House of Representatives December 16, 2022. In any case, the music of Puerto Rico, which shares influences with that of Cuba and other Caribbean countries, is undoubtedly a component of the broader category of Latin that is acknowledged, at least to some extent, by most musicologists and historians of American music. The problems this presents are partly linguistic (Spanish vs. English), partly ethnic-Latin vs. Anglo- or Afro-American, and partly the result of irreducible hybridity. In short, once Puerto Rican music is included, American music necessarily includes music that does not originate in the continental United States. (See below for Leonard Bernstein's comments on this point.)

The Dutch influence is minimal but is evident in one song: "Yankee Doodle."

Once these limits are taken into account, one can proceed to what are considered in the literature to be foundational influences, namely Protestant music and African/African American.

PROTESTANT MUSIC

The Protestant influence is symbolized by the earliest English-language book printed in America, the *Bay Psalm Book*, 1640, in Cambridge, Massachusetts, but it goes much further. Indeed, it is evident that, from the earliest English settlements to the present day, the influence of the music of Puritanism and the English Revolution (1640–1660) was perhaps the greatest overall in shaping what has come to be known as American music. This is largely derived from religious hymns sung by various dissenting groups: Quakers, Presbyterians, Methodists, Shakers, and Baptists. It includes, however, hundreds of songs by notable composers such as Isaac Watts, Isaacher Bates, William Billings, and Phillip Hayes. It was transmitted to the broad masses in three distinct ways and three distinct waves.

First, the organized churches which presided over birth, marriage and death, as well as weekly services. These also provided education, psalm books, and organized singing.

Second, circuit riders, or preachers who traveled a circuit to bring to rural populations not only the word of god but the songs of praise and the assemblies, be they in people's homes or tents or out in the open, which constituted the church.

Third, camp-meetings. These began in earnest at the turn of the eighteenth century. Thousands would come, some great distances, pitch their tents, and stay three or more days to join in spiritual festivities. These revivals were full of excitement, singing, and dancing. The preaching was noted for its emotionalism and theatricality. Appeals were made to the body, not the intellect, and conversion was the goal. By all accounts, this goal was regularly achieved. The wild and uninhibited atmosphere was created partly by the outdoor setting, partly by the multiple sermons going on simultaneously, and partly by the abandonment of formal rules for singing. Indeed, a new mode of singing was born at these revivals. Simpler lyrically and in melodic range, more rhythmic and repetitive in performance, this mode of singing produced involvement, immersion, and spiritual deliverance.

The divergence from the staid, church-based psalm singing was considerable, leading to this new style being denounced by some among the elders of denominations as varied as the Methodists, Baptists, and Presbyterians. Of course, the elders could not object to so many people being filled with grace and brought into the fold. Indeed, most supported and encouraged the camp-meetings in general. But controversies arose over the singing: What was the correct method? To what extent was it allowed to deviate from the printed words and notes? What were acceptable limits to bodily movements? Hand-clapping, foot-tapping, swaying, spinning, and wilder gesticulations were the common responses evoked among the congregants singing this way. This is still evident in the music sung in certain churches to this day. Its influence is more broadly evident in gospel, soul, and derivatives such as rock and roll.

There is considerable evidence proving that Black people, slave and free, were in attendance in significant numbers. There is some dispute about this because debate about the origins of the Negro Spiritual were at stake. Outraged by injustices that endured and even intensified in the early decades of the twentieth century, many Black scholars rejected the idea that the Negro Spiritual was influenced by the spirituals sung by whites. This was justified in one sense by the fact that great contributions to music were undoubtedly made by enslaved people, individually and collectively. Furthermore, the arguments were not confined to music but to the characterization of African and African American people as inferior used to justify their enslavement.[4]

Nevertheless, the evidence that there was not only interaction but that many lyrics and song titles did originate in Protestant hymnody is clear and unmistakable. This does not, however, in any way reduce the influence and contribution made by African Americans. On the contrary, there is considerable testimony written by participants and observers to convince us not only of the presence of large numbers of Black people at these camp-meetings but to the particularity of their style of singing and how it was transmitted to other participants. This interaction need not, any longer, be downplayed in the interests of justice.[5]

It should further be noted that policies of slaveowners varied over time and location. In some cases, slaveowners encouraged their slaves to go to camp-meetings; in others, they were forbidden. Prohibition became more general following the Nat Turner rebellion of 1831, in part because Turner was well known to have convened prayer meetings of his own, using them to recruit and inspire his fellows in bondage.[6]

The three waves referred to above were, the First, Second, and Third Great Awakenings, which swept across the United States in episodes that can be clearly traced. There is general agreement among historians that the First Great Awakening occurred 1730–1750, the Second 1790–1840, and the Third 1855–1930. The religious, social, and political outcomes of these movements were considerable but are beyond the scope of this book to relate. However, from a musicological perspective they were of incalculable importance. Not only did these movements spread a large body of song to the populace, urban and rural, slave and free, but to a much larger extent than is often acknowledged, they established forms of song and practices of singing that were shared by everyone and that endure to this day.

This raises other questions regarding song-collecting, the music business, and journalism. Whatever the motives, the outcome was paradoxical. On the one hand, Protestant music was known by all and practiced by many. On the other hand, authorities of all sorts—academic or commercial—acted as though this were irrelevant, promoting instead the idea that the people had no music, that traditional songs were disappearing, and that an interest in music had to be revived, cultivated, and esteemed by other means. At the very least, this suggests motives other than simply musical ones. What was at stake was not music per se but the organization of society. The authorities, cognizant of the importance of music to social life, sought to direct music toward their own ends. While this may not be unique to the United States, it is unavoidable when considering how the United States developed and, moreover, how the United States has been represented. Within the first half century after the founding of the country, the clamor had begun. The proliferation of books, journals, essays, and articles expanded rapidly. What follows is a chronology of books and essays devoted to the history of American music. Most are explicitly directed toward that aim, others are included because they are vital to the controversies that arose in the process, and still others because they comment on the process as it unfolded.

♦ ♦ ♦

Histories of American Music chart this progression as seen in the following examples:

1838—*The Musical Review*, a journal published in New York, calls for the writing of a History of Music in America. Nothing comes of it.

1846—G. Hood publishes A Musical History of New England.

1847—Mr. Brough's Musical Lecture on the United States, "A transcript of impressions left upon the memory during a Musical Tour with Mr. and Mrs. Wood, in 1835 and part of 1836, and again in 1840; with subsequent random recollections up to 1846, in the United States of America." Mr. Brough delivered these musical lectures in Dublin, Ireland, in 1847.

While these lectures presented a broad range of observation not confined to music, the songs included were not merely decorative. Instead, they were representative of the people and conditions encountered during Mr. Brough's tour. Laments of Irish and German immigrants recount the experience and feelings of recent arrivals to the United States, while songs purporting to be Indian and Negro depict conditions faced by these constituent parts of the general population Mr. Brough personally witnessed.

The fact that such musical-lectures were popular and frequently repeated in Ireland, even at the height of the Great Hunger (1847 was known as Black '47, when more than a million people died and a million more left the country, the largest number to the United States), indicates the growing interest in America as a land of opportunity, refuge, and novelty.

1853—Nathaniel D. Gould publishes A History of Church Music in America.

1854—John W. Moore publishes *An Encyclopaedia of Music*.

1867—*Slave Songs of the United States* is published. The work of three abolitionists, William Francis Allen, Lucy McKim Garrison, and Charles Pickard Ware, *Slave Songs* was the first published collection of African American music of any kind. It marks a watershed moment in the study of music in general and African American music in particular. It remains an important resource today.

1875—Dr. Frederic Louis Ritter sets out to write a History of Music in America. He eventually does—in 1883.

1878—James Monroe Trotter publishes *Music and Some Highly Musical People*. A landmark work, first for its biographies of a large number and wide range of African American musicians, and second, for providing a sweeping overview of music's history and one that preceded those that would later become "classics." Noted musicologist Eileen Southern wrote that Trotter's book was: "the first time that anyone, black or white, had attempted to assess a body of American music that cut across genres and styles."

1880—J. B. T. Marsh publishes *The Story of the Jubilee Singers*. This book recounted the 1871 tour of the world-renowned group that would, in one sense, define the Negro Spiritual. This story, important in its own right, was the wellspring of enduring controversies and misapprehensions that persist. (In brief: Thomas W. Higginson's seminal report on the Spirituals, thus named by the Negro troops Higginson commanded in the Civil War, introduced the Spirituals to a wide readership. The Spiritual thus became intertwined with folk song due the growing interest in folk songs in general and the folk songs of the Negro in particular. The Jubilee Singers, however, presented a highly refined and polished version that captivated cultivated, urban audiences. Its musical quality is not disputed, but its classification is.) In any case, Marsh's was and remains an important source of historical as well as musical information.

1883—The aforementioned Ritter publishes *Music In America*, which would be republished several times, including posthumously in 1900. Ritter acknowledges Trotter's contribution, quoting him extensively, in the context of an exploration of popular music. Ritter begins the chapter "The Cultivation of Popular Music" by saying: "The people's-song—'an outgrowth from the life of the people, the product of innate artistic instinct of the people, seeking a more lofty expression than that of every-day speech for those feelings which are awakened in the soul by the varied events of life'—is not to be found among the American people" (the quotation marks indicate an excerpt from Ritter's own essay, "Some Famous Songs"). Ritter goes to great lengths to support his claim. His views were widely shared, becoming the fulcrum of the debate that would eventually lead to their total refutation (see Sonneck, 1905).

1904—Louis Elson publishes *The History of American Music*, which becomes a classic in two senses: first, because it was widely read, becoming a reference book; second, because it established a classificatory system that made a lasting impression. Not only did it describe but it attempted to define American music. This distinction will be explored further on.

1905—Oscar Sonneck, from 1902–1917 head of the music department at the Library of Congress, publishes *A Bibliography of Early Secular American Music*, (H. L. McQueen, 1905). In his preface Sonneck states his purpose: "Historians, popular and unpopular, have steadily (and with surprisingly uncritical methods) guided the public into the belief that a secular musical life did not exist in our country during the eighteenth century. To be sure, these pages throw little more than side-lights on the formative period in our musical history, but possibly they will help to undermine an absurd theory and strengthen the opposite position correctly held by a few writers, as, for instance, Henry Edward Krehbiel."

The reason to highlight this here is that the evidence supports Sonneck's claims and that the prevailing norms that did, eventually, change. But it took much longer than might be expected. Indeed, some changes had to wait until the tumultuous sixties, six decades later, to be effective. Sonneck, however, never wrote a general history. His five books covered different aspects of the subject, early secular American music, providing much valuable data previously overlooked or unacknowledged by historians of music.

1908—W. L. Hubbard, ed., publishes *History of American Music* (Toledo: Irving Squire, 1908).

1914—Henry Edward Krehbiel publishes *Afro-American Folksongs: A Study in Racial and National Music*. An immensely influential work by an eminent musicologist and critic, it was noteworthy for taking seriously the folks songs of African Americans and for situating these within the larger body of American music.

1915—*Music in America* (New York: National Society of Music,1915), Arthur Farwell and W. Dermot Darby, eds. Noteworthy for the attention paid to modern American composers. This was the conscious effort of Arthur Farwell, himself a composer, to promote the independence and originality of America as a nation and to champion its musical pioneers. This agenda became a norm in subsequent histories.

1915—John Wesley Work publishes Folk Song of the American Negro. It followed the earlier publication of New Jubilee Songs as Sung by the Fisk Jubilee

Singers (1901) and *New Jubilee Songs and Folk Songs of the American Negro* (1907), which established Work as the first African American song collector (at least to be published; in fact, others had assisted earlier collecting done by the founders of the Fisk Jubilee Singers). Work's collection is important for his methods of classification and for containing songs previously unavailable.

1922—Thomas Talley publishes *Negro Folk Rhymes Wise and Otherwise*. It circulated widely enough to be noted in various other surveys of American music and it was influential to some extent. For example, it was mentioned along with numerous other "standard" collections: Howard Odum, George Pullen Jackson, Guy Johnson, Dorothy Scarborough, and John Lomax, and by Harry Smith in Smith's idiosyncratic collection *The Anthology of American Music* (1952). Yet Talley's name was not mentioned when I visited the Library of Congress and sought out every single book that contained slave songs. He was not mentioned in queries I made to other musicologists and folklorists at other institutions, either. In short, Talley's work is largely forgotten while others of his contemporaries remain widely known.

1930—Isaac Goldberg publishes *Tin Pan Alley: A Chronicle of the American Popular Music Racket* (John Day, 1930) The book was a landmark study in two ways. First, it took the music industry and its products seriously, as previous histories of American music did not. Second, it was thorough and comprehensive enough to stand the test of time, serving as one of the foundational texts of David Suisman's *Selling Sounds* published in 2006, one of the inspirations for the present project. While Goldberg accepts capitalism as a natural, inevitable, and generally positive development, he is nonetheless aware of some of the negative consequences. An example is the term *racket* used in the title. This play on words was used at a time when "racket" commonly described organized criminal activity (the numbers racket, the drug racket, and so on). Simultaneously, it humorously referred to the racket (noisy sound) made by the popular ditties sold by Tin Pan Alley.

1931—*Our American Music: Three Hundred Years of It* is published (New York: Thomas Y. Crowell Co.). Its author, John Tasker Howard, continued the well-established pattern, albeit with a framing twist based on Euterpe, one of the nine Muses. The book is thereby divided into three parts, "Euterpe in the Wilderness" (1620–1800), "Euterpe Clears the Forest" (1800–1860), and "Euterpe Builds Her American Home" (1860–1931). This periodization remains useful insofar as it takes note of key political and technological changes that surrounded music-making in the United States. There are, however, problems that this periodization does not address. Some of them are evident in the "Wilderness," "Forest Clearing," and "American Home" metaphors. Needless to say, these tropes have in recent years been critiqued not only because they are clearly biased but because they fail to include much that should be, even according to its own logic. Such oversights follow a common pattern.

1940—"Folk Music As a Source of Social History" by Charles Seeger was published in Caroline F. Ware, ed., *The Cultural Approach to History* (New York: Columbia University Press, 1940). This essay was a product of Seeger's work at the Federal Music Project and as chief of the Pan-American Union's music division. Seeger's theoretical contributions had enormous impact, which is felt to this day. He argued that musicology must include the study of "the field of music as a whole," that full account must be taken "of music as a social and cultural function," and that "the relationships between written and unwritten" music be fully explored. This text was by no means the first Seeger had written; indeed, Seeger was a founding member of the American Musicological Society in 1934 and had already written extensively on related subjects. The significance of this particular essay is that it was the inspiration for subsequent treatments of American music, in particular the work of Gilbert Chase.

1955—Gilbert Chase publishes the first edition of *America's Music: From the Pilgrims to the Present*. This book, to a great extent inspired by the work of Charles Seeger (Chase's own predecessor at the Library of Congress) and Oscar Sonneck, is today a textbook used in many courses of musicology, American Studies, and related fields. It has been republished three times, the latest being in 1998.

1958—"What Is American Music?" written by Leonard Bernstein for a television program. Original CBS Television Network broadcast date: February 1, 1958. Following on the unparalleled success of *West Side Story*, Bernstein delivered this lecture, which concluded:

> In fact, there are so many different qualities in our music that it would take much too long to list them; there are as many sides to American music as there are to the American people—our great, varied, many-sided democracy. Maybe that's the main quality of all —our many-sidedness. Think of all the races and personalities from all over the globe that make up our country; and when we think of that we can understand why our own folk music is so complicated. We've taken it all in, French, Dutch, German, Scotch, Scandinavian, Italian, and all the rest, and learned it from one another, borrowed it, stolen it, cooked it all up in a melting pot. So what our composers are finally nourished on, is a folk music that is probably the richest in the world, and all of it is American, in spirit, whether it's jazz, or square-dance tunes, or cowboy songs, or hillbilly

music, or rock and roll, or Cuban mambas, or Mexican huapangos, or Missouri hymn-singing. It's like all those different accents we have in our speaking; there's a little Mexican accent in the Texas accents, and a little Swedish to be heard in our Minnesota accent, and there's a little Slavic in the Brooklyn, and a there's a little Irish in the Boston accent. But they're all American accents. They've been absorbed.

From a purely musical perspective, Bernstein is correct. The melting pot does describe the cross-pollinating that characterizes much music in America. In spite of the criticism of folk revivalists/traditionalists, modernist composers, and defenders of classical music, the melting pot metaphor prevailed until a few short years later when the sixties erupted and the whole construct was called into question. This was largely a result of political struggle—the anti-war movement, the civil rights movement, and the New Left.

1963—LeRoi Jones (aka Amiri Baraka) published *Blues People*. This book of essays contributed mightily to breakdown of the shibboleth "American" by demanding that an accounting be made of history, specifically, the oppression and exploitation of slaves and their descendants. Written in the context of a burgeoning civil rights movement, Jones draws distinctions between poor and middle-class Negroes as well as the Negro intelligentsia, regarding defense of the "American system," its premises and policies. This distinction had particular significance in musical terms since it was evident in divergent styles, settings (urban and rural, concert halls and night clubs, respectable/bourgeois, and disreputable/bohemian) and between audiences and ambitions. Jones observed:

> The young Negro intellectuals and artists in most cases are fleeing the same "classic" bourgeois situations as their white counterparts—whether the clutches of an actual Black bourgeoisie or their drab philosophical reflectors who are not even to be considered a middle class economically. The important development, and I consider it a socio-historical precedent, is that many young Negroes no longer equate intelligence or worth with the tepid values of the middle class, though their parents daily strive to uphold these values. The "New Negroes" produced a middle-class, middle-brow art because despite their desired stance as intellectuals and artists, they were simply defending their right, the right of Negroes, to *be* intellectuals, in a society which patently denied them such capacities. And if the generation of the forties began to understand that no such "defense" or explanation was necessary, the young Negro intellectuals of the fifties and sixties realize—many of them perhaps only emotionally—that a society

whose only strength lies in its ability to destroy itself and the rest of the world has small claim toward defining or appreciating intelligence or beauty.⁷

1968—Sterling Stuckey publishes "Through the Prism of Folklore: The Black Ethos in Slavery" in the *Massachusetts Review*. This seminal essay challenged prevailing views of slavery and the character of slave songs. Stuckey used the "prism of folklore" to critique not only the methods and assumptions of folklorists but those of historians as well. He presented both songs and perspectives that would be confirmed and expanded upon by *Songs of Slavery and Emancipation* (2022).

1972—James Lovell Jr. publishes *Black Song: The Forge and the Flame*. While this book never received the attention of the others in this list, it is included here for two reasons. First, it is significant in its claims regarding the revolutionary character of many Negro Spirituals. Lovell claims that there are at least six thousand Negro Spirituals that explicitly call for freedom and justice and that prophesy the abolition of slavery. This poses a challenge for all scholars concerned with American music, be it African American or not.

Secondly, *Black Song* is the culmination of a life's work extending at least as far back as the publication of an essay "The Social Implications of the Negro Spiritual" in the *Journal of Negro Education* (October 1939, 634–43). As a result of decades of effort, Lovell's book is a treasure trove of song but also of controversy. If scholars or the general public want to know what animated key debates in musicology, history, and politics in twentieth-century America, this is an important source.

1983—Charles Hamm publishes *Music in the New World*, perhaps as widely read and influential as Gilbert Chase's *America's Music*, Hamm is credited with winning scholarly acceptance of the study of popular music. In one sense this is the culmination of a controversy that ran through the two centuries after America was founded. Hamm's work did not end all disputes and certainly did not end the publication of histories of American music, but it did in one sense close debate on whether or not music that was commercially sold could be considered music of the populace. Furthermore, it flatly disproved the notion that everything that was commercial was of inferior quality when compared with either "classical" or traditional music. It could not only be genuine, it could be good. (As obvious as this may be to musicians and music-lovers, among scholars and purists the old arguments refuse to go away.)

1998—Gilbert Chase's 1955 classic is posthumously republished with many additions Chase made before his death. Overall, these not only embrace Hamm's position regarding popular music, but further expand on Charles

Seeger's original claim that music be considered as a whole and be viewed in terms of its social and cultural function. It should be noted that Seeger's thesis was radical when it was proposed in the early 1930s. Today this is widely accepted, albeit in a context in which the terms of debate have changed.

Serious criticisms came to prominence in the tumultuous sixties: Adorno's *Culture Industry*, Debord's *Society of the Spectacle*, and a host of other theoretical critiques of capitalist domination of all circuits of communication. (Adorno's were published in 1944 but only began to circulate in the English-speaking world after 1972.) From Jaques Attali's *Noise: The Political Economy of Music* (1977), to Simon Frith's *Sociology of Rock* (1978), to Dave Harker's *One for the Money: Politics and Popular Song* (1980), music, and especially popular music, was critically reappraised. As musicologist Susan McClary wrote in the afterword to *Noise*, criticism exposed the complicity of musicology itself in concealing "that from which we sought to hide—political control and money."[8]

The list, already very long, is lengthening at a prodigious clip to this day. Such criticism has no doubt rendered obsolete any account claiming to be objective or neutral. Whether driven by political, academic, or commercial interests, hidden agendas or ulterior motives are always lurking, waiting to be exposed. It's no longer possible to speak of the old categories—folk, popular, classical, jazz, highbrow, lowbrow, middlebrow, and so on—without qualifying them. Indeed, one cannot speak of American music with the patriotic fervor that was at one time taken for granted, as evidenced in the earliest of books listed above right down to Chase's work. After all, "The Star-Spangled Banner," alone, raises controversies no longer possible to ignore.[9]

Such qualifying, moreover, has largely left music itself behind as it focuses entirely on the political, and not, as was the case in the histories mentioned above, on the religious, philosophical, aesthetic, or educational dimensions of music and music-making practices. Such concerns, once the norm, are often rejected *tout court* on the basis that they have no bearing anymore on what "really matters." The triumph of capitalism is complete. It therefore reduces all the old controversies to one question: how many? That is, how many units are sold, be they records, CDs, downloads, concert tickets or paraphernalia?

From this perspective, the history of American music itself may appear quaint and dated. Yet questions persist due to the intrinsic quality of music made in the United States. The practices and criteria used to make and measure that music exist in a quarrelsome relation to the state and the apparatuses of the academy, the music industry, and music journalism. Not exactly autonomous, but not entirely subservient either, music-makers and the public keep doin' what they're doin', hearkening back to the way dissenting Protestants and enslaved Africans used music to keep their spirits alive for a better day to come.

INTERROGATING REPRESENTATION

> It's not what you look like when you're doin' what you're doin'
> It's what you're doin' when you're doin' what you look like you're doin'
> —"Express Yourself," Charles Wright

One issue, however, deserves closer attention: representing music as a practice in its own right. Kofi Agawu's work, *Representing African Music*, is instructive in that he interrogates the frameworks and suppositions of ethnomusicology, folklore studies, postcolonial studies, and anthropology as they have developed over the last century in relation to Africa and that continent's music. Not only does he ask penetrating questions; Agawu identifies problems, theoretical and practical, that arise from these questions not being posed. Indeed, Agawu's effort brings us back to the questions with which this chapter began when he writes: "My aim, quite simply, is to stimulate debate about modes of knowledge production by offering a critique of discourse about African music. Who writes about it, how, and why?"[10] Agawu's effort plays a doubly important role in that it clarifies a great deal about African music while providing tools that can be applied to music in general. In other words, many of the observations Agawu makes about the misapprehension of African music apply to misapprehensions that are common in the study of American music. For example, in defending the usefulness of comparison as an approach to knowledge and the consequences of the failure to apply it, Agawu states:

> Allied to the retreat from comparison is a retreat from critical evaluation of African musical practice. The pious dignifying of all performances as if they were equally good, of all instruments as if they were tuned in an "interesting" way rather than simply being out of tune, of all informants as if a number of them did not practice systematic deception, and of the missed entries and resulting heterophony in dirge singing as if they did not result from inattentiveness or drunkenness: these are acts of mystification designed to ensure that the discourse about African music continues to lack the one thing that would give it scientific and hence universal status, namely, a critical element. (61)

This applies in every detail to the ways vernacular music in the United States has been written about for at least a century. The publicist and the patriot have fulfilled their agendas by creating mystique where it need not arise. They have been aided in this by the work of scholars who, though no doubt sincere, were nevertheless prey to certain views that can now be evaluated according to their practical effects and not merely in abstract argument. Thus, ideas of genetic predisposition reinforce concepts of inbred talent or genius to bring about a view of music-making that is fundamentally racist in the strict sense of that term. That is, we are not all human beings according to simple criteria such as: we procreate, we share blood, we die of the same injuries and diseases, and we have the same mental capacities. Instead, we are forever and eternally at war with one another in an unequal battle between the mighty and the meek.

Such argument ignores the fact that conquest always entails an apprehension of the conquered by the conqueror that is not only ranking and dehumanizing but also specifically equates musical ability with inferior status. For example, this statement by Gerald of Wales who, as a chronicler for his Norman masters, wrote about the Irish:

> The only thing to which I find that this people apply a commendable industry is playing upon musical instruments . . . they are incomparably more skillful than any other nation I have ever seen. For their modulation on these instruments, unlike that of the Britons to which I am accustomed, is not slow and harsh, but lively and rapid, while the harmony is both sweet and gay. . . . It must be remarked . . . that both Scotland and Wales strive to rival Ireland in the art of music. (Giraldus Cambrensis, *The Topography of Ireland*, 1187, Chapter XI, 71)

Compare that to this quote from Richard Jobson, in his 1623 book about the slave trade: "There is, without doubt, no people on the earth more naturally affected to the sound of musicke then these people . . ." (Richard Jobson, *Golden Trade*, 105–8 [London, 1623]).

(Jobson's sentiment has been repeated so often that I could have chosen from dozens of sources making identical claims. Kofi Agawu supplies numerous examples including those made not only by Europeans but by Africans themselves. Indeed, these are beliefs held by some to this day. It is therefore worth mentioning that the symbol of the United Irishmen, who rose in revolution against their British conquerors in 1798, was the harp. The instrument was beribboned with the words: "Equality, It is new strung and shall be heard.")

Differentiation, while necessary and productive in and of itself, is nonetheless harnessed by those with ulterior motives. Differentiation does not necessarily imply ranking or hierarchizing but differentiation *has* been applied to support other claims such as those mentioned above regarding the superiority or inferiority of populations. Music-making itself has in many instances militated against this ranking, especially when common people are thrown together by occupation or migration. A great deal of the world's music can be traced not to a single, ancient source but to the combination and intermingling of influences shared by disparate groups, be they sailors, soldiers, traders, slaves, or populations displaced by war, famine, or political oppression. This is certainly the case in the United States.

CONTESTING DIFFERENCE / EMBRACING SAMENESS

Agawu takes differentiation to task, contesting its claims and providing an alternative. The argument is made under three headings: *Is Difference Real?*, *Resisting Difference*, and *Embracing Sameness?* Following this reasoning, Agawu goes so far as to suggest: "These are tough questions . . . they advocate the eventual disappearance of the ethnomusicologist" (166).

The point is not to deny difference but to question how difference is constructed and the purposes that construction serves. This inevitably poses questions of ethics, politics, and ideology. Eliding these questions or hiding behind a veil of ineffability, primordiality, and unknowability is itself a political position with consequences. Often this reasoning simply dissolves into a question of ownership and property, the fundamental division between capitalism, the capitalist state, and all they wiped out in the process of their ascendancy. This is as true in the United States as it is in Africa.

Furthermore, where music originates is not more important than where it is going. The obsession with preserving the past can occlude music's sonic existence as a productive activity. But not only the object "music" or "tradition" is at stake. Always present is the question of the future and where the people making music are seeking to go, be that overcoming the legacies of imperial conquest, slavery, or other forms of oppression, or be that simply seeking to enter into conversation with the rest of humanity. This is why Agawu says: "It is time to restore a notional sameness to our acts of representation" (171).

Agawu lays the basis for arguing that American music, as it actually exists, could be one among many, equal and edifying, just as Ghanaian, Brazilian, Indonesian, or Russian musics are. Instead of the presumptions and pretensions of American "exceptionalism" we might share and enjoy the richness and variety of music made in the United States in conversation with the world. It would then be possible to apply Agawu's ethical and political criteria as they appear in, for example, the UN Charter of Human Rights. Despite the manifest failure to apply these standards by governments and special interests, musicians and music lovers can nonetheless appeal to the aspirations expressed and apply them at the very least to the appreciation and respect of diverse musical traditions and practices.

There is one further point to be made about representation in this regard: musical instruction uses representation even as it prepares for music's presentation. When a teacher speaks of rhythm, melody, of techniques specific to any instrument, to accepted norms for the performance of a composition, or even to composition itself, they are necessarily referring to universality even as they provide particular direction. This universality resides in the particular in a living dynamic precisely because, at root, music is an activity and not a product. Yes, music-making does produce and some of its products are timeless, exemplary compositions. But the universality of rhythm, melody, timbre, voice, and instrument are present throughout if only in particular form.

The importance of this distinction is that it highlights the clash between presentation and representation and perhaps suggests a solution that would benefit both. If the purpose of music is ultimately to serve human sociality, to uplift and inspire human endeavor toward a more just and peaceful world, then its representation should more closely reflect and consciously serve the presentation of music made in that spirit. Instead of lording it over musicians and music teachers, it would better serve the critic or the musicologist to study and improve the appreciation of music from the perspective of the maker and not only the publisher or propagandist.

NOTES

1. "Compared to What," words and music Gene McDaniels, Longport Music Corp., November 3, 1966. Catalog of Copyright Entries: Third Series, Library of Congress.

2. Sound recordings of the music of the Omaha and other tribes were made by Alice C. Fletcher and Francis La Flesche. Between 1880 and 1910 hundreds of wax cylinders were compiled, which now reside in the Library of Congress. Beginning in 1933, William N. Fenton made recordings of the Iroquois that became *Songs from the Iroquois Longhouse*, an album which is part of the Anglo-American Ballads collection, also at the Library of Congress.

3. See La Bottine Souriante, https://en.wikipedia.org/wiki/La_Bottine_Souriante.

4. See James Lovell, *Black Song: The Forge and the Flame*, Macmillan (1972). For the position Lovell was arguing against, see Guy Johnson, "The Negro Spiritual: A Problem in Anthropology," *American Anthropologist* 33 (2) (April 6, 1931).

5. Anne Wheeler, "The Music of the Early Nineteenth-Century Camp Meeting: Song in Service to Evangelistic Revival," *Methodist History* 48: 1 (October 2009); see also: Dena J. Epstein, *Sinful Tunes and Spirituals*, 199 (quoted in "A Sonic Palimpsest," chapter in this volume, note 7).

6. See Stephen B. Oates, *The Fires of Jubilee* (Harper Perennial, 2016). See also: Catherine Locks, Sarah Mergel, Pamela Roseman, Tamara Spike, and Marie Lasseter, "Religious Reforms in the Antebellum United States," LibreTexts, https://human.libretexts.org/Bookshelves/History/National_History/United_States_History_to_1877_(Locks_et_al.)/13%3A_Antebellum_Revival_and_Reform/13.01%3A_Religious_Reforms_in_the_Antebellum_United_States.

7. Amiri Baraka, *Blues People*, 230–32.

8. Jaques Attali, *Noise: The Political Economy of Music* (Minneapolis: University of Minnesota Press, 1985; original publication date 1977, in French), 154.

9. Lyrical controversies concern Key's phrase "hirelings and slaves" in the rarely sung third verse. Ironically, the music was composed by an English man named James Stafford Smith. It is an English drinking song. The question arises: is the national anthem of the United States American music? See https://www.ask.com/culture/understanding-controversies-surrounding-lyrics-star-spangled-banner and: https://en.wikipedia.org/wiki/John_Stafford_Smith.

10. Kofi Agawu, *Representing African Music* (New York: Routledge, 2003), xii. All other page references are to this book and are made in the text.

REFERENCES

Agawu, Kofi. *Representing African Music*. New York: Routledge, 2003.
Attali, Jacques. *Noise: The Political Economy of Music*. Minneapolis: University of Minnesota Press, 1985 (original publication date 1977, in French).
Cambrensis, Giraldus. *The Topography of Ireland* (1187).
Epstein, Dena J. *Sinful Tunes and Spirituals: Black Folk Music to the Civil War*. Urbana: University of Illinois Press, 1981 (originally published 1977).
Frith, Simon. *The Sociology of Rock*. London: Constable, 1978.
Harker, Dave. *One for the Money: Politics and Popular Song*. Hutchinson, 1980.
Hugill, Stan. *Shanties from the Seven Seas*. Guilford, CT: Mystic Seaport Museum, 1961.
Jobson, Richard. *Golden Trade*. London, 1623.
Miller, Karl Hagstrom. *Segregating Sound*. Durham, NC: Duke University Press, 2010.
A Wesleyan Methodist, *Methodist Error or, Friendly Christian Advice To those Methodists Who indulge in extravagant emotions and bodily exercises*. D. and E. Fenton, 1819.
Wheeler, Anne. "The Music of the Early Nineteenth-Century Camp Meeting: Song in Service to Evangelistic Revival." *Methodist History* 48: 1 (October 2009).

HISTORIES IN CHRONOLOGICAL ORDER

Flood, George. *History of Music in New England*. Boston: Wilkins, Carter, 1846.
Brough, Mr. *Mr. Brough's Musical Lecture on The United States of America*. Dublin: R. Carrick, 30, Bachelor's Walk, 1847.
Gould, Nathaniel D. *History of Church Music in America*. Boston: Gould and Lincoln, 1853.
Moore, John W. *Complete Encyclopaedia of Music*. Boston: Oliver Ditson, 1854.
Allen, William Francis, Charles Pickard Ware, and Lucy McKim Garrison. *Slave Songs in the United States*. New York: Dover Publications, 1995 (originally published 1867).
Trotter, James Monroe. *Music and Some Highly Musical People*. Charles T. Dillingham, 1878.

Marsh, J. B. T. *The Story of the Jubilee Singers with Their Songs*. New York: Houghton, Mifflin, 1880.
Ritter, Dr. Frederic Louis. *Music in America*. New York: Charles Scribner's Sons, 1883.
Elson, Louis C. *The History of Music in America*. New York: Macmillan, 1904.
Sonneck, Oscar. *A Bibliography of Early Secular American Music*. H. L. McQueen, 1905.
Hubbard, W. L., ed. *History of American Music*. Toledo, OH: Irving Squire, 1908.
Krehbiel, Henry Edward. *Afro-American Folksongs: A Study in Racial and National Music*. New York and London: G. Schirmer, 1914.
Farwell, Arthur, and W. Dermot Darby, eds. *Music in America*. New York: National Society of Music, 1915.
Work, John Wesley. *Folk Song of the American Negro*. Nashville, TN: Press of Fisk University, 1915.
Talley, Thomas W. *Negro Folk Rhymes, Wise and Otherwise: With A Study*. New York: Macmillan, 1922.
Goldberg, Isaac. *Tin Pan Alley: A Chronicle of the American Popular Music Racket*. New York: John Day, 1930.
Howard, John Tasker. *Our American Music: Three Hundred Years of It*. New York: Thomas Y. Crowell, 1931.
Seeger, Charles. "Folk Music as a Source of Social History." In Caroline F. Ware, ed., *The Cultural Approach to History*. New York: Columbia University Press, 1940.
Chase, Gilbert. *America's Music: From the Pilgrims to the Present*. Champaign: University of Illinois Press, 1955.
Bernstein, Leonard "What Is American Music?" Original CBS Television Network broadcast date: February 1, 1958.
Jones, LeRoi. *Blues People*. New York: William Morrow, 1963.
Stuckey, Stirling. "Through the Prism of Folklore: The Black Ethos in Slavery." *Massachusetts Review* 9, no. 3 (Summer 1968): 417–37.
Lovell, John, Jr. *Black Song: The Forge and the Flame*. New York: Macmillan, 1972.
Hamm, Charles. *Music in the New World*. New York: W. W. Norton, 1983.

SUMMARY REFLECTIONS
On Responsibility, Academia, and Asking Questions

Britta Sweers

It was in late May 2023, when my colleague, American Literature Professor Thomas Claviez, I, and ten students from our institutes followed the traces of the blues through the Deep South from Nashville, via Memphis, Clarksdale, Cleveland, Jackson, down to New Orleans. Guided by late music producer and blues musician Leon Burnette (aka "Mr. B."), who had founded one of the few independent African American tour companies[1] specialized on civil rights themes, we delved deep into the culture of the blues. Yet we were also profoundly educated in the surrounding politics, and repeatedly witnessed the still obvious dividing lines that kept pushing African American cultural legacies to the margins. At the same time, we came across alternative narratives by visiting newly founded educational spaces, such as the Nashville Museum of African American Music, opened in 2021, or the Mississippi Civil Rights Museum in Jackson, which was opened in 2017. Stories told in these institutions clearly differed from those conveyed globally in textbooks and by music journalism, which had shaped the perception of "American music" for decades. Reading music histories through African American eyes, and listening to the music as well as to the stories surrounding these musics, we started to recognize different music historical lines. African American music became a major story of its own, not a subordinated side story to the history of (white-dominated) popular music. And the exact replica of John A. and Alan Lomax's 1939 Ford Deluxe car in Jackson's Delta Blues Museum was a further reminder of the fluidity and politics of what had been termed "folk music." The Lomaxes' recording activities and collections had repeatedly contributed to a counternarrative to dominant white American folk music concepts that were strongly based on idealized Appalachian-based British folk music traditions, against which the Lomaxes had promoted cowboy songs and, later, African American music of the Deep South.

> Having undertaken my main research on electric folk or folk rock in England (Sweers 2005a), my research inevitably dealt with the impact of American music, the music industry, collectors and collections, and dominant discourses that were strongly shaped by debates on authenticity. Not only did folk rock bands like Fairport Convention and Steeleye Span collide with dominant ideals of authentic (acoustic) folk music (in opposition to electric instruments being perceived as representing the commercialized ideals of the music industry), but the debates also concerned "acceptable" repertoires. For instance, American folk music of the 1950s/60s had become an opposite against which the hard-core folk clubs had set the rule that only songs from one's own (British) region should be performed. And yet, I had come across some of the best revival recordings of various Child ballads by US-American folk musicians, such as Joan Baez, Bob Dylan, or Jean Ritchie. But there was also a further strain that completely dissolved the seemingly clear distinctions: British ballads had found their way into African American repertoires and were thus popularized globally, while some of the strongest folk songs that had been adapted by white American or English folk musicians actually came from African American performers or had been adapted into global protest repertoires such as the African American gospel "We Shall Overcome." How did this fit together? Who had set up these categories, boundaries, and opposites?
>
> Born close to Hamburg in Northern Germany, I had repeatedly been asked by British musicians why I would research on English, not on German folk music. Due to the political instrumentalization of German folk song during the Nazi era, I, as well as many of my generation, had been extremely suspicious of anything relating to German folk music (Sweers 2005b, 2023). While we sang traditional local children's songs, we nevertheless completely rejected German folk music as an idea of a national folk music. It appeared contaminated, and it might come of little surprise that the German folk revivalists of the 1960s first drew strongly on German revolutionary repertoires, satires, and other critical political repertoires. This was fused with US-American, British, Irish, and Scottish folk repertoires, instruments, and arrangement styles. And, on a popular music level, American music was central to my generation's identity anyway, but we did not understand the internal processes that had shaped the global presence of these repertoires at that time.

As this autobiographical account indicates, the perception of music is shaped for numerous reasons by educational-academic ideas, commercial interests, and political intentions alike. Mat Callahan's Introduction thus started out by quoting Jeremy Collier that "music is almost as dangerous as gunpowder" (3). And, as the chapters in this book have demonstrated, it indeed is—in multiple and opposite ways. It can become a powerful force of resistance and protest, as the chapters by Mat Callahan, Steve Garabedian, or Franz Andres Morrissey, and myself have illustrated. But it can likewise be used as a political means of control toward becoming a destructive force, as particularly Suzanne Cusick's gripping examination of "Music as Torture" (ch. 8) has demonstrated. As her study illustrates, the same piece of music can be enjoyed as a form of entertainment, but it could also become a means of resistance and might even be used for torture.

As chapter 10 on folk songs related to war contexts has illustrated, music is used as a means of control, but in the same situations as a means of protest. The utilization of music for a specific purpose thus appears Janus-faced: Armies might be controlled and coordinated by heavy rhythms of related marching songs, but the same rhythms and even melodies have likewise been used by hiking and protesting groups. This indicates that there is no such thing as an utterly negative, manipulative, and destructive music that can immediately be recognized as such without contextualization. This was also a realization of the Columbine High School massacre from April 20, 1999. The shooters might have listened to a specific musical repertoire, as of Marilyn Manson, but it was not his music or a specific song with a specific texture that caused the shooters to commit their crime.[2] Yet this is the actual power of music: It is a floating, ever-changing object that can adapt to any situation and can become anything in any context. This has probably always been the case.

MULTIPLE LAYERS OF MANIPULATION

However, as the various chapters have outlined, particularly since the emergence of capitalism after the Industrial Revolution in the nineteenth century, music has been manipulated and controlled to an unprecedented extent by politics, as well as by the music industry, journalism, and the academy, which Callahan termed "the unholy trinity" (see Introduction in this volume) and which most often intertwine in their different power strands. While the music industry likewise evolved in Europe, these developments have particularly become apparent with US-American music. But because American music has been received, consumed, and adapted in many countries of the world, the processes depicted in this book are not confined to the US mainland or even to North America. It actually tells a global story.

As this book's chapters highlighted, music has been manipulated on multiple levels: This concerns *politically shaped* processes such as *replacement*, as Callahan (ch. 1) illustrated in the case of African American music that was, as part of the Jim Crow legacy, consciously pushed out of public notice. Similar processes are apparent in many other situations, as, for instance, with the Jewish presence in European music life during the Nazi era from which it never really recovered. These processes also relate to issues of *representation*, in which academia has been playing a central role, as became evident with Steve Garabedian (ch. 2), who wondered who actually collected the repertoires we take for granted nowadays. This also relates to issues of *power* that have been at the core of postcolonial and cultural-theoretical debates (such as Geeta and Nair 2013). We thus constantly need to ask who is in power to decide what is selected—and taught. We mostly have white Americans, often from privileged positions, who created the collections, also of African American music. As Franz Andres Morrissey (ch. 3) highlighted, however comprehensive they might appear, collections are never neutral, due to the choices that were shaped by audiences, national politics, moral issues, nostalgia, or commercialism. And even criticism of related collections, as undertaken by Dave Harker (1985), for instance, is likewise shaped by a political agenda.

Yet, as was also highlighted in various chapters, music has likewise been strongly subjected to interests of *commercialism*. As Jim Rogers (chs. 5 and 9) highlighted, understanding the history of the (American) music industry appears essential for a profound perception of the power mechanisms into which music has been embedded since the nineteenth century. We easily connect the issue of commercialism to recorded and digitalized music, but these processes already started out with much more conservative media formats, such as Sheet Music and Tin Pan Alley, and go way beyond specific popular music genres, as Elissa Stroman (ch. 4) exemplified.

This relates back to the issues of *communication* and, again, the factors of *inclusion/exclusion*. As particularly Stroman (ch. 4) illustrated so succinctly, *media coverage* has been playing a major role in communicating musical knowledge. Yet, as the example of *The Etude* magazine highlighted, journalism has likewise been central in shaping canons, tastes, and identities through music. Music writing has been exerting an impact on the public representation and exclusion of genre, gender, race, or class for a long time. This chapter also points to the impact of domineering nominal concepts like the ideal of "High Art." But who decides about such categorizations? Here, universities and schools have been playing a major role by setting up curricula that have, in turn, been implementing related standards and ideals in broader society. Again, the question emerges of who actually decides about these inclusive and exclusive choices. And who decides what is played in the radio, on TV, or in social media? This likewise applies to the protest musics covered in this volume.

As all authors illustrated, related choices and societal positions of musics are not natural processes, and rarely involve the musicians or musical communities themselves. The same applies to genre categories, such as folk music or popular music. A good example are, for instance, the English or British folk music collections of Cecil Sharp and particularly of Francis James Child, as Andres Morrissey illustrated in chapter 3. Also, related genre categories are rarely set up by the performers themselves, but are likewise created by theorists, journalists, or the music industry and are shaped by individually selected criteria, ideals, counter-identities, or sales figures.

WHO DECIDES WHAT TO INCLUDE AS "AMERICAN MUSIC"

We hereby return to the question of how power structures have been shaping the perception of American music, and, specifically, folk music. As Callahan pointed out in his Introduction, there would have been myriads of possibilities, such as the vast range of migrant cultures in the emerging urban spaces. These were quickly targeted by the music industry in the nineteenth century, which initially recorded a vast variety of migrant music because these repertoires sold best among these growing communities (Stokes 2020). There were the African American musics that had already developed into a rich range of styles at that point. There would have also been the music of the American Indians—which was pushed into a separate category, into an *Other*. While African American music was likewise othered, particularly during the Jim Crow era, it nevertheless maintained an in-between state because of its major impact on and crossover into the broader (white) popular music market that could not be fully ignored. In short, there would have been a greater musical richness, complexity, and hybridity than is usually acknowledged. Yet, what remained of this vast range of options was basically Appalachian-based music. Even in the politically shaped revival movements this repertoire in particular became more prominent. Despite the integration of African American spiritual songs like "We Shall Overcome" into an overarching protest hymn repertoire, knowledge of the broader musical and historical context was in danger of vanishing. At the same time, other formats, such as blues protest forms, as depicted by Garabedian (ch. 11), vanished from public knowledge.

As the specific situation of African American musics illustrates, interrelated political agendas, educational and journalistic representations, as well as marketing decisions have been playing a major role here. This concerned silencing musicians, genres, performative practices and contexts, as well as allowing and denying access to spaces of visibility. However, this also happened with artists connected to the Workers' Movements or CPUSA activities, such as Pete Seeger, in the McCarthy era. At the same time, the above-mentioned factors have been key to shaping the outer picture of American music that completely differed from the situation in the States. As James E. Dillard (ch. 7) demonstrated so succinctly, to the outside, jazz was promoted as *the* American music—not any vernacular music, while the music industry's commercial agenda and its opposition conveyed further ideas, also of "authentic" American music.

UNDERSTANDING THE UTILIZATION OF CONCEPTS OF POWER: AUTHENTICITY

The utilization of concepts is a way of exerting power in this context, which I would like to exemplify in the case of "authenticity" that appears at the core of many discourses surrounding music. This key word also emerged in relation to many issues debated in this collection, be it working-class music, national music-related concepts, folk song collections, or in journalism. By classifying music as "authentic," it becomes elevated to special value and importance; by accusing it of the opposite, it becomes false, treacherous, as the debate surrounding Bob Dylan's electrified appearance on the Newport Folk Festival in 1965 illustrates. It thus is also a means of dominance. But, what, actually, is "authentic" music?

The expression denotes, among others, the idea of "conforming to an original" or "true to one's own personality, spirit, or character."[3] As art historian Denis Dutton (2003) pointed out, "authenticity" should not be taken as an absolute or essentialist concept, but as a relational term that is always defined by an opposite. In other words, "authenticity" should only be approached by asking under what conditions, by whom, and for whom the concept of authenticity is debated and who profits from it (Claviez et al. 2020a). It hereby becomes evident that the idea of "authenticity" played a central role for the validation of a genre, a song, or performance, or an artist.

As Dutton further clarified, authenticity discourses mainly center on two different yet often intertwined perspectives (Dutton 2003, 259–61, 266–68). One approach, described by Dutton as an *authenticity of provenience* (or *nominal authenticity*), relates an object, in this case music, to a historic point of origin. This perception emphasizes a historic transmission line that is connected to a local identity formation. The opposite position is shaped by the idea of *expressive authenticity*, which perceives works of art as genuine expressions of an individual or a society's values and beliefs. Due to its fluid, performative nature, nominal authenticity is much more difficult to be determined in music than in art, which can relate this concept to an existent physical object. In contrast, musical authenticity of provenience is established by references to musical versions preserved in notated or printed collections or ethnic identities that are taken as reference points. Both concepts cannot be fully separated. Nominal concepts of authenticity (for example, rebellion or historical workers' songs) are often also intertwined with the idea of an expressive authenticity that could, for instance, relate to the values of modern workers' unions, protest movements, of folk revival scenes. Similarly, since the nineteenth century, art music scenes have been identifying via certain repertoires, hereby excluding others, even if this is historically vague or wrong. However, as Thomas Claviez (2020b), with whom I had followed the traces of the blues in the introductory account, argued, the idea of authenticity always requires an external authentifier, a referential authority that is given the power to decide what is accepted as "authentic." Within the processes described in this book, this authority, and thus power, was given to journalism or music publishing, (music) education, or the music industry that has likewise been using this concept as a label for validation.

CONSTRUCTED MUSICAL IDEALS

Thus, rather than approaching "authenticity" by searching for the most authentic American music genre, artist, or other category, the utilization of "authenticity" should be read as signifier of identity constructions. Quite often, the most heated debates emerge where related world views collide. Mat Callahan pointed to the political sphere and academia, but this also concerns music journalism, which, by selecting the coverage of related artists and genres, has the power to decide on visibility—to the extent that it can create its own myths. A good example is Bob Dylan's above-mentioned electric guitar performance at the Newport Folk Festival in 1965 (cf. ch. 1). The myth that Dylan was booed for his electric appearance prevails, although the reconstructed tapes also point to the bad amplification system and too short appearance of Dylan (Sweers 2005, 21–23). While Dutton's approach contributes to a deeper understanding of the central lines of arguments and misunderstandings, Claviez's observation raises an awareness of the manipulative forces at work, an issue taken up by Andres Morrissey's chapter on "Curating Music," as well.

This also applies to the idea of (authentic) folk music that has been a recurring issue in this book. As outlined in Cole (2021) and Sweers (2025), folk music exists and is a myth at the same time. This seems to be a contradiction at first sight, but understanding related mechanisms might help to decipher what we actually listen to (or think we are listening to). There is no denying that traditions exist, such as seasonal or life-circle events or specific performance practices and contexts. Some of these traditions have indeed been practiced for a long time. But how far have these been national traditions? American or English folk songs were not necessarily considered by their tradition bearers as "American" or "English folk songs," but as songs sung in the kitchen, in the evening, alongside popular songs. This might have been in a style differing from church choir singing, but not as a conscious part of a large body of repertoire labelled as *the* Child Ballads, for instance. This only came later, after the songs had been collected and bundled into collections.

How did collectors decide about what to include and what to exclude? Choices were often influenced by individual preferences and hidden agendas. For example, quite often collecting and disseminating activities were strongly shaped by the intention to create a national identity. And this resulted in the creation of specific historical narrations in the sense of a nominal authenticity in which academia could exert a strong impact, as the debate surrounding the origins of the spirituals also illustrates.[4] This likewise applies to definitions. As a scholar, I have learned how to read definitions, such as outlined by the International Folk Music Council (IFMC) in 1955, where folk music was defined as oral, shaped by generation-long transmission processes, selection, many variants, and so on. And while I still perceive this definition as useful (Sweers 2023), I know that it is not neutral, but has been shaped by pre-assumptions. Based on the work of the English folk song collector Cecil Sharp, the definition excludes popular and art music, for instance, although this music might follow the same patterns as outlined here. Furthermore, the perception that folk music is shaped by selection is a Darwinist perspective. Yet, most importantly, this concept only includes the traditions of rural working classes that were idealized as carriers of the unspoiled essence of "the people," as Johann Gottfried Herder (1778/79; cf. Sweers 2023) saw it—or, since the nineteenth century, a nation. Again, this practice—which also applies to the idea of "American folk music"—excluded numerous practices, such as those of urban working classes, be it work-context related (such as factory songs), thematic repertoires, or natural fusions with popular music.

Finally, this definition indirectly contained the assumption of a local white or European culture, which excluded migrant and indigenous cultures.

Again, this does not deny the existence of folk music traditions but argues for perceiving the concept of folk music as a body of music shaped by ideas, visions, intentions. It is manipulated and consciously altered. Consequently, it does not make sense to search for the most authentic (old or original) version, but to embed a body or piece of music into a different set of questions, as outlined by Dutton and Claviez: What is chosen for which purpose? Who (scholars, politics, journalism) decides and has the power to decide what (also in relation to gender and ethnicity) is chosen? What kind of authenticity is postulated for which purpose? Against which opposition is authenticity placed (such as other nations, globalization, the music industry)? And who is, by academic training, political or economic power, able to look beyond these concepts, narrations, or myths? While I exemplified this in the case of folk music, this applies to many other phenomena discussed in this book. The better we understand these contexts, the better we can recognize processes of manipulation—and this is where academia comes in in a positive way, as this is the place to obtain related tools to dissect these strategies. Yet, this also calls for a broader communication of this knowledge into the public.

THE ISSUE OF NOSTALGIA

As Jim Rogers's chapter on the current situation of the music industry revealed, we also need to question narratives, particularly those coming from dominant positions that utilize notions of nostalgia. For, as folk music scholar Ross Cole argued, ideas of nostalgia are always tied to utopian visions that have likewise strongly shaped our perception of various musics and categories. While nostalgia seems to be an almost natural sentiment, it can, likewise be instrumentalized by the politics, the academia, and the music industry alike, as I will illustrate with regard to the idea of "American folk music." And, again, notions of authenticity play a powerful role here.

Nostalgia is often described as an "excessively sentimental yearning for return to or of some past period or irrecoverable condition."[5] We can detect this form of nostalgia in revivals of working songs that were initially tied to specific contexts and fell out of use, for example, due to functional changes of production or working practices (Korcynski et al. 2013). This might include preindustrial songs that were silenced through the industrial mechanization of work, as well as mining or industrial weaving songs—and here we are back to Andres Morrissey's chapter. However, historian Svetlana Boym (2001) further differentiated between *restorative* and *reflective nostalgia*. *Restorative nostalgia* can be described as the attempt at a complete reconstruction of, in this case, monuments of the past, accentuating the idea of nominal authenticity. Characterized by a serious stance, restorative nostalgia dwells on ideas of a lost national past (see also Hobsbawm 1992). Here we might be reminded of songs like The Band's "The Night They Drove Old Dixie Down" (1969). In contrast, what Boym characterizes as *reflective nostalgia* is much more ironic and humorous, as was also evident with various electric folk bands. By playing with the "patina of time" from a more self-reflective stance, this alternative form of nostalgia "dwells on the ambivalences of human longing and belonging and does not shy away from the contradictions of modernity," aiming more intensely at individual and cultural memory (Boym 2001: xviii). Furthermore, "nostalgia is not always about the past; it can be retrospective but also prospective" (Boym 2001, xvi) by creating an ideal utopian vision. Therefore, by analyzing the nature of utilized nostalgic concepts, we can obtain further insights into the mechanisms of inclusion and exclusion. This applies to collections as well as to historical references.

If we accept, as Cole (2021) further argued, that folk musics, as they appeared in the nineteenth century, were nostalgic visions that were created through, for example, collecting and archiving, interrelated notions of authenticity need to be taken as indicators of central personal, communal, or commercial values tied to the idea of "folk music." Thus, rather than understanding these activities as exclusively natural communal or neutral scientific activities, there are again other forces at work that manipulate and use related emotions and concepts of nostalgia—even in musicians' union debates—to their own end, such as the music industry or politics. This is the reason why it is important to ask who actually is in power to decide what to include/exclude in utopian visions created by notions of authenticity and nostalgia—perhaps *especially* in the context of union debates, as Richard Weissman (ch. 6) so convincingly revealed.

Focusing on the (in-)visibility of gender and ethnicity in folk and popular music here, was it really the community that decided to exclude female or African American artists, or was a community manipulated by the extremely strong and prevailing conservative ideas of nostalgia on gender and ethnicity (such as in blues music)? How far are African American traditions included at all? What about Asian migrants—and the presence of Native Americans in these visions? Some strikingly slow alterations might be explained by the domineering impact of the extremely strong nostalgic notions and utopian counter-ideas against global modernity, which allowed little space for even other than local European white identities and romanticized rural and working-class cultures. This might explain why issues of race (or postcolonial perspectives) have often been ignored in theoretical and journalist writings on folk music.

For example, until the popularity of world music in the late 1980s, little attention was paid to the impact of migration and/or performers with migrant (or slave) backgrounds who adopted relating repertoires: One early English example were the Child ballad performances of singer Sheila Chandra, while the Imagined Village project, together with Jamaican writer and musician Benjamin Zephaniah, reinterpreted "Tam Lyn" as "Tam Lyn Retold" in an electronic rap style in 2007 and transferred the fairy-tale content of the original ballad into a migrant context.[6] Yet, significant mind-changing approaches—such as the African American old-time string band Carolina Chocolate Drops that, together with singer Rhiannon Giddens, drew attention to overlooked Black folk music repertoires, influences, and adaptations—are still rare. As I would like to argue, these kinds of approaches that have strongly contributed to a broader awareness of the discrimination and invisibility of non-European migrant performers, repertoires, and female artists only occurred at a point when prevailing restorative nostalgic concepts were clearly loosening up or shifting toward a more reflective stance in the new millennium. And, to return to this book, Richard Weissman's chapter reminds us to question nostalgic explanations, such as for diminishing membership in unions.

DEVELOPING A DIFFERENT MIND-SET

As the chapters in this book highlighted from multiple perspectives, our perception of American music is affected on multiple levels, not only due to the power of politics and record labels, but also due to academic, and, thus, school classroom teaching. Who decides which music is covered in the classroom? What is deemed as suitable (for example, white art music)? What is excluded and thus forgotten? Developing a mind-set that enables one to question those manipulations so clearly dissected by Mat Callahan and Steve Garabedian is challenging. Due to my specific ethnomusicological training, I am able to look beyond surface images, yet I likewise have to rely on and have been shaped by canons conveyed in textbooks or by the music industry—and consciously need to question these myself. Callahan's chapters clearly reveal how much was manipulated by the music industry and even by academia due to choices that were made. Furthermore, as Callahan pointed out, the enormous musical skills of the slaves were covered up by fakery and blackface imagery, which was, musically speaking, as Andres Morrissey and Garabedian indicated, actually shaped by British-Scottish-Irish traditions. To discover different canons one needs to, first of all, find access to and listen to alternative narrations. Seeing through this imagery with any confidence is not easy, even for me as an academic.

After my return from the US trip, I decided to teach a class on African American popular music in Switzerland. I aimed at creating a narrative different from what had been taught in central European popular music history books at school and university, but also by journalism. I was able to do so because Leon Burnette had guided us to related museums, had used the road trips to educate us with stories and further documentaries, was always open for questions and had facilitated many fascinating personal encounters. Without Burnette we would have listened to country music only, or directly rushed to Graceland, or would have experienced Sun Records as a purely white label without being able to tell the background story. During the tour, our vision changed.

It already started with H. Wiley Hitchcock's book on music in the United States, which, first published in 1969, still maintains a central position as one of the first comprehensive historical introductions to American music. Yet, the utilization of William Sidney Mount's painting The Power of Music *(1847) on the front cover of the fourth edition becomes contradictory from an altered mind-set. The painting depicts an African American laborer listening to a white fiddle player through an open barn. While Mount was known for his respectful stance toward the African American population, clearly contrasting the many caricatures of that time, a contextless utilization of this painting in the twenty-first century also signals power imbalances—that of a passive, subordinated African American culture outside the active white musical sphere.*

Listening to a classic blues song like "When the Levee Breaks" (Kansas Joe McCoy and Memphis Minnie, 1929), students started to read the song as a document not only of natural disaster,[7] but likewise of racial injustice, as lyrics like "I works on the levee" could also indirectly be read as pointing to the situation of many African Americans who had been forced to repair the breaking levees and paid with their lives. Students increasingly started to look beyond labels and related processes of separating and downgrading through categorization, such as race, but even R&B music, as well as the position of African American composers. This not only concerned their public (in)visibility, but concerning further downgrading strategies due to genre categorization. (Where do you classify Scott Joplin? Entertainment or art music? Or both? Or even something else?)

> *Learning about the specific forms of crossovers between Black and white music cultures also led to a questioning of the actual story of rock 'n' roll music. In European popular music history narrations, it is a history of white active figures. It is still Bill Haley ("father of rock 'n' roll") and Elvis Presley ("king of rock 'n' roll") who are depicted as the innovators. It rarely tells us the story of Louis Jordan's jump blues hit "Caldonia" (1945) or "Saturday Night Fish Fry" (1949), Roy Brown's "Good Rocking Tonight" (1947), rerecorded by Elvis Presley in 1954, or Jimmy Preston's "Rock the Joint" (1949), covered by Bill Haley in 1952. Or Ike Turner's "Rocket 88" (1951) that counts as one of the earliest rock 'n' roll songs and was recorded by Sam Phillips. Or, most prominently, Big Mama Thornton's "Hound Dog": Written by Jerry Leiber and Mike Stoller for Thornton in 1952, it became a #1 hit in the R&B charts in 1953, but appeared a modest success compared to the rerecorded version by Elvis Presley in 1956.*

These stories point to the invisibility of the "original" performers and the one-sided narration of popular music. Yet barriers were also broken, even by small individual activities of white audiences, such as listening to R&B music in car radios or visiting (forbidden) Black record shops. Again, this highlights the power of music, but also of the individual that can, even by small actions, break the force of the "unholy trinity." However, with regard to my academic context, it also points to the necessity of separating education from mere economic monetizing and political interests as much as possible—and the need for alternative knowledge spaces, such as the African American museums mentioned in the introductory autobiographical account. I was able to create such a course, because I did not have the obligation to only teach a certain canon, but had the liberty to experiment and to create new perspectives at a liberal and open-minded, publicly financed university in Bern, Switzerland. Had I been under the neoliberal obligation to teach (financially more lucrative) multiple-choice knowledge suitable for large student bodies or to fulfill a certain political agenda, this would have been difficult.

OUTLOOK: ASKING QUESTIONS

Revealing the various interacting forces and processes of (mis-)representation (ch. 12) appears essential for an understanding of the mechanisms that have been shaping value systems and visibilities. Developing an awareness of and listening to alternative voices is clearly likewise central here, as this could, in the end, lead to an alternative perception of musics that actually matter for its protagonists, communities, and audiences alike. This also is the reason why this concluding summary has been asking so many questions. And this is a starting point—to raise the awareness by questioning what is presented in curricula, covered by the music industry and in media coverage, or described as authentic, national, and the like. The following just summarizes a selection of potential questions as a starting point:

- . . . such as the *classic journalistic questions*: Who did what under which circumstances for which purpose? For what purpose is what collected and displayed? What are the aims of a collection? Concepts of authenticity and nationality can be taken as a marker of central points of conflict, identity construction, or other interests.
- As this situation relates to *power issues*? Who is making judgmental values? Who is in power or is given the power to decide and to what or whose benefit?
- What is actually *included* and what is *excluded*? Gender, class, race are central analytical criteria here but should not, therefore, lead to the neglect of other designations such as religion or children, which are defining characteristics of entire bodies of music.
- How is the music *represented*? Following the analytical practice of discourse analysis: How do people talk about music? Which language, which images are being used, also to promote certain ideas, such as those related to national, economic, and similar values?
- What are the *mechanisms behind visibility and audibility* of genres, artists, and the like? For example, are decisions in the music industry shaped by specific commercial interests? What are the background stories?
- What purpose do *concepts* and *categories* (such as popular music) serve?
- How are *canons* created and what purpose do they serve?
- Which (national, cultural, and so on) *myths* are created and perpetuated through music? If *nostalgic visions* are utilized—what kind of aspects are valorized and idealized?

Yet, there is more to ask:

- How does music represent and reflect on war and politics? How does the state use music?
- What narratives are being used to what purpose (for example, with regard the financial situation of the music industry)?

- What are the dynamics or formats that have emerged specifically in the context of capitalism and commodification (for example, copyright)?
- Where are conflict points? Authenticity debates can be taken as a marker here, as in the opposition of acoustic folk versus electric popular music. Are they really opposites or do they serve a purpose?

As Mat Callahan indicated in his concluding chapter, we, and specifically academia, have a responsibility to look beyond these mechanisms. Academic knowledge is power that is much too often withheld from those needing it, due, in many cases, to financial reasons. I thus understand the task of us music scholars to uncover these mechanisms, to challenge established narratives as researchers—by asking more questions. This also applies to teaching. It is not enough to just teach a class on a specific music genre or artist. Applying these and similar questions in the classroom can help develop a more critical mindset at university, but also at school, and, thus, society. This implies that we, as academic teachers, have a major sociocultural and political responsibility.

NOTES

1. Civil Rights Trail Tours was managed by Leon Burnette (1951–2023). With thanks to tour director Steve Myers (tour logistics), Miles Tibbs-Burnette (tour manager), and Joshua Henley (transportation).

2. Cf. Michael Moore (director), *Bowling for Columbine* (2002).

3. For further meanings, cf. *Merriam Webster Dictionary* online, https://www.merriam-webster.com/dictionary/authentic (last accessed September 1, 2024). I elaborated this interrelation of authenticity, nostalgia, and utopia in more detail in the forthcoming chapter "Folk Revivalism" (Sweers forthcoming 2025; see also Cole 2021). This subchapter and the section on nostalgia are a condensed version of these reflections initially folk revival discourses.

4. In *Primitive Music* (1893), Austrian comparative musicologist Richard Wallaschek (1860–1917) had denied African American music an individual legacy by arguing that the spirituals were only arrangements of "national songs of all nations, from military signals, well-known marches, German student-songs, etc.," that is, they emerged by the means of copying white musical practices.

5. "Nostalgia." Merriam Webster Online Dictionary. https://www.merriam-webster.com/dictionary/nostalgia.

6. The Imagined Village, *The Imagined Village*. RealWorld Records (CDRW147), Virgin (50999-503867-2-7), 2007.

7. Yet human-made. While Mississippi floodings had always occurred, their devastating impact in the nineteenth century had also been the result of (white man-made) damming of the river. See Barry (1997) for a fascinating study on this subject.

REFERENCES

Barry, John M. 1997. *Rising Tide: The Great Mississippi Flood of 1927 and How It Changed America*. New York, London: Simon and Schuster.

Boym, Svetlana. 2001. *The Future of Nostalgia*. New York: Basic Books.

Claviez, Thomas, Kornelia Imesch, and Britta Sweers. 2020a. "Introduction." In Thomas Claviez, Kornelia Imesch, and Britta Sweers (eds.), *Critique of Authenticity*, viii–xix. Wilmington, DE: Vernon Press.

Claviez, Thomas. 2020b. "A critique of authenticity and recognition." In Thomas Claviez, Kornelia Imesch, and Britta Sweers (eds.), *Critique of Authenticity*, 43–58. Wilmington, DE: Vernon Press.

Cole, Ross. 2021. *The Folk: Music, Modernity, and the Political Imagination*. Oakland: University of California Press.

Dutton, Denis. 2003. "Authenticity in Art." In Jerrold Levinson (ed.), *The Oxford Handbook of Authenticity*, 258–74. New York, Oxford: Oxford University Press.

Harker, Dave. 1985. *Fakesong: The Manufacture of British "Folksong" 1799 to the Present Day*. Milton Keynes and Philadelphia: Open University.

Geeta, Chowdhry, and Sheila Nair (eds.). 2013. *Power, Postcolonialism and International Relations: Reading Race, Gender and Class*. London: Routledge.

Herder, Johann Gottfried. 1778/79. *Stimmen der Völker in Liedern. Volkslieder. Zwei Teile*. (Heinz Rölleke, ed.) Stuttgart: Reclam, 1975.

Hitchcock, H. Wiley. 2019 [1969]. *Music in the United States: A Historical Introduction* (with Kyle Gann). 4th ed. Upper Saddle River, NJ: Prentice Hall/ Pearson.

Hobsbawm, Eric. 1992. "Introduction: Inventing Traditions." In Eric Hobsbawm and Terence Ranger (eds.), *The Invention of Tradition*, 1–14. Cambridge: Cambridge University Press.

IFMC (International Folk Music Council). 1955. "Definition of Folk Music." In *Journal of the International Folk Music Council* 7: 9–29.

Korczynski, Marek, Michael Pickering, and Emma Robertson. 2013. *Rhythms of Labour: Music at Work in Britain*. Cambridge: Cambridge University Press.

Stokes, Martin. "Migration and Music." 2020. *Music Research Annual* I: 1–24.

Sweers, Britta. 2005a. *Electric Folk: The Changing Face of English Traditional Music*. New York, Oxford: Oxford University Press.

Sweers, Britta. 2005b. "The Power to Influence Minds: German Folk Music During the Nazi Era and After." In Annie J. Randall (ed.), *Music, Power, and Politics*, 65–86. New York and London: Routledge.

Sweers, Britta. 2023. "The Transforming Perception of German Folk Song: Some Case Studies." In Christine Guillebaud, Sibylle Emerit, and Julien Jugand (eds.), *Orchestrer le passé— Singing the Past*, 131–74. Nanterre: Presses universitaires de Paris Nanterre.

Sweers, Britta. 2025 (forthcoming). "Chapter 13: Folk Revivalism." In Ross Cole (ed.), *Cambridge Companion to Folk Music*. Cambridge: Cambridge University Press.

Wallaschek, Richard. 1893. *Primitive music: an inquiry into the origin and development of music, songs, instruments, dances, and pantomimes of savage races*. London and New York: Longmans, Green.

ABOUT THE CONTRIBUTORS

Franz Andres Morrissey is an adjunct researcher at the English Department of the University of Bern, Switzerland, and former lecturer in modern English linguistics. His publications include *Language, the Singer and the Song: The Sociolinguistics of Folk Performance* (Cambridge University Press) and various papers on the interface between language, discourse, and music. He is also an active musician with a focus on folk music from the British Isles and Americana.

Mat Callahan is a musician and author originally from San Francisco. Recent projects include the republication of *Songs of Freedom* by Irish revolutionary James Connolly; the recording and publication of *Working Class Heroes*; and the launch of *Songs of Slavery and Emancipation*, comprising a book, two CDs, and a film. He is the author of five books, including *The Explosion of Deferred Dreams* (PM Press) and *A Critical Guide to Intellectual Property* (Zed Books). For more information, visit: http://www.matcallahan.com. Callahan can be reached at: info@matcallahan.com

Suzanne G. Cusick is a professor of music at the Faculty of Arts and Science at New York University. Cusick has published extensively on gender and sexuality in relation to the musical cultures of early modern Italy and contemporary North America. Additionally, she has studied the use of sound and sexual shaming in the detention and interrogation of prisoners. She was one of the first scholars to write about the use of music torture during the twenty-first century's "global war on terror." She can be reached via the faculty page at NYU: https://as.nyu.edu/faculty/suzanne-cusick.html.

Lt. Col. (USAF, Ret.) James E. Dillard is a faculty member at the National Intelligence University in Washington, DC, where he teaches covert action and cultural intelligence analysis. His graduate work includes PhD studies in international security policy at the University of Maryland, a master's degree in international relations from Syracuse University, and a master's in history from Southern Illinois University. Named NIU's Faculty Member of the Year in 2009, Jim was also honored as the Outstanding Academy Educator at the US Air Force Academy in 1995.

Steven Garabedian is associate professor of history at Marist College in Poughkeepsie, New York. He is a historian of the twentieth-century United States, with a research specialization in race, music, and radicalism, and a teaching concentration in US public history and African American studies. He is the author of *A Sound History: Lawrence Gellert, Black Musical Protest, and White Denial* (University of Massachusetts Press, 2020). He lives in the Hudson Valley in New York.

Jim Rogers is associate professor of communications in the School of Communications, Dublin City University, where he has taught for the past twenty years. His research focuses on media and cultural production, especially popular music, with particular emphasis on the role of intellectual property in shaping the outcome of new technologies in the music industries, and the recent evolution of music industries per se. He is author of *The Death and Life of the Music Industry in the Digital Age* (2013), *A Critical Guide to Intellectual Property* (with Mat Callahan, 2017), and *Sounds Irish, Acts Global* (with Michael Murphy, 2023). He has also published widely in peer-reviewed journals and edited collections.

Elissa Stroman is an oral historian, archivist, and musicologist based in West Texas. She is the assistant archivist of the Oral History Program at the Southwest Collection/Special Collections Library at Texas Tech University (Lubbock). Prior to her appointment in March 2022, she was a unit manager in the archive's audiovisual department for twelve years. She holds a bachelor of art from McMurry University (Abilene, Texas), and her master's degree in musicology and PhD in fine arts from Texas Tech. She is a certified archivist and the editor of the *West Texas Historical Review*. Her research focuses on American musical women's work and reception history, and she is currently writing a book that traces the early activities of music clubwomen as seen in music periodicals (1890–1930).

Britta Sweers is professor of cultural anthropology of music at the Institute of Musicology (since 2009) and was director of the Center for Global Studies

(2016–2020) at the University of Bern (Switzerland). The transformation of traditional musics in a global context has been a central focus of her research, including *Electric Folk: The Changing Face of English Traditional Music* (2005). Sweers is coeditor of the *European Journal of Musicology* and of the Equinox book series *Transcultural Music Studies*.

Dick Weissman has pursued a long-term career as a musician and composer, with emphasis on recording. This includes playing banjo and guitar on dozens of recording sessions, producing records, writing songs and instrumental pieces, and touring. He has written or coauthored over twenty books on American roots music and/or the music, and is associate professor emeritus of music at the University of Colorado at Denver. Dick is a long-term musician's union activist, who has served on the executive boards of the Portland, Oregon, and Denver locals of the American Federation of Musicians.

INDEX

Illustrations are indicated by *italic* page numbers.

Abel, Ben, 219
AC/DC, 227
Acheson, Dean, 195
Adams, Judy, 188
Adorno, Theodor, 25, 337
African American music, 38–41, 43, 331
African Americans and US war, 306–8
Afro-American Folksongs: A Study in Racial and National Music (Krehbiel), 332
"After the Ball" (Harris), 125, 149, 153
Agawu, Kofi, 338–41
Aguilera, Christina, 220, 227
Ali, Muhammad, 308, 311
"Alice's Restaurant" (Guthrie), 289
Allen, William Francis, 331
Almanac Singers, 281
"Amazing Grace" (song), 51
American Anti-Slavery Songs (Eaklor), 50
American Federation of Musicians, 167–93;
  AI and, 190–91; Black musicians and, 174–76; bonus funds, 172; Broadway and, 172, 181; consolidation and, 179–81; decline of, 178; government legislation and, 174; ineffective advocacy by, 182–86, 192nn20–21; MPTF and, 168–69; new music styles and, 172–73, 176–78; opportunities for unionization by, 181–82, 192n19; recording musicians and, 170–71; roots of, 167–68; royalties/contract issues, 186–89; structure and representation in, 169; symphony musicians/orchestras, 170–72; UMAW and, 189–90
American folk music, 6–7, 110
American Folk Music and Left Wing Politics, 1927–1957 (R. and J. Reuss), 7, 55

American Folklore Society, 39
American Folksongs of Protest (Greenway), 85–86
American music, (mis)representation of, 322–43; alternative representation, 340–41; analysis of, 338–40; historical definitions, 325–26; histories of, 330–38; limitations/influences on, 326–27; overview, 322–25; Protestant music, 327–30
American Music Fairness Act (AMFA), 186–87
American Slave: A Composite Autobiography (Rawick), 44
American Society for Creators, Authors and Publishers (ASCAP), 157–60
American Technology Corporation, 218
America's Music: From the Pilgrims to the Present (Chase), 334, 336–37
And Quiet Flows the Don (Sholokhov), 282
Andres Morrissey, Franz, chapters by, 97, 265
Anschutz Entertainment Group (AEG), 254
Anthology of American Folk Music (Smith), 33n22, 54, 56, 333
Aptheker, Herbert, 16–17, 38
Arditi, David, 245
Armstrong, Louis (Satchmo), 198, 201, 203, 209–10, 212, 214
Art Music Activism (Fava), viii
artificial intelligence (AI), 190, 236–39
Astor, Nancy, 269–70
Atlantic Records, 187–88
"Auld Lang Syne" (Burns), 104–5
Autry, Gene, 275
Ayler, Albert, 3
Azoulay, Ellie Armon, 87–88, 90

"Babylon Is Fallen" (Work), 49, 51
"Backlash Blues" (Hughes), 315
Baker, Nancy Kovaleff, 65
Baldwin, James, 303–4, 307
Balin, Marty, 6
"Ballad of Ozzie Powell" (Hughes), 78
Baltzell, William, 121
"Band Played Waltzing Matilda, The" (Bogle), 289–90, 295
Baraka, Amiri (LeRoi Jones), 22, 335–36
Barney the purple dinosaur, "I Love You," 220, 222
Barnicle, Mary Elizabeth, 74
Barr, Alfred, 199
Bastiat, Frederic, 235
Bates, Isaacher, 328
Bauer, Emilie Frances, 127
Bay Psalm Book, 48, 327
Beatles, 10, 148, 177
bebop, 173, 201
Begle, Howell, 188
Belgian Congo, 210
Berlin, Irving, 157–59, 161
Bernstein, Leonard, 327, 334–35
Bernstein, Louis, 154
Berry, Mary Frances, 303–4
Bibliography of Early Secular American Music, A (Sonneck), 332
Billboard (magazine), 199, 233–34, 242
Billings, William, 328
Billington, Scott, 188
Black, Brown and Beige (Ellington), 201
"Black, Brown and White" (Broonzy), 304, 308, 318n19
Black Reconstruction (Du Bois), 13, 17
Black Song: The Forge and the Flame (Lovell), 336
Blackburn, Marsha, 187
blackface minstrelsy, 39, 43, 46, 50–52, 57n18
Blackface Nation (Roberts), 51
Blake, William, 11, 24
Blanco, Fern, 126, 128
Blassingame, John W., 303–4
Bloomfield Zeisler, Fannie, 124
blues and war protest, 300–321; African American war experience, 306–9; blues and African American protest, 303–6; denial of, 316–17; nuclear war, 311–12; overview, 300–302; post-WWII, 309–11;

Vietnam War, 312–15. *See also* Dixon, Willie; *and specific artists and songs*
Blues Legacies and Black Feminism (Davis), 303
Blues People (Jones), 22, 335–36
blues revival, 301, 316
Bogle, Eric, 289–90
Bomberger, Douglas, 120
"Bonnie Woodhaa" (song), 268
"Born in the USA" (Springsteen), 291–92, 295
Bourget, Ernest, 154
Bowers, William, 74, 77–78
British folk movement, 110, 113n14, 292–93
Britt, Elton, 277–78
Broadway, 172, 180–81
Bronson, B. H., 105, 107
Broonzy, William Lee Conley "Big Bill," 304, 308
"Brother in Korea, A" (Osborne), 277
Brough, Mr. (lecturer), 330
Brown, Cora Stanton, 127
Brown, Gabriel, 74, 76, *76*
Brown, Lawrence, 70, *70*
Brown, Ruth, 187–88
Brown, Sterling, 61, 69, 78–79, 82–83, 85–86, 88–89
Brown v. Board of Education (1954), 196
Brubeck, Dave, 198, 202–4, 206–7, 210
Burkart, Patrick, 243
Burns, Robert, 104–5
Byrd, Joseph, 57n18

Caesar, Irving, 150
Callahan, Mat: chapters by, 3, 35, 322; *James Connolly's Songs of Freedom*, 14–15, 35; *Songs of Slavery and Emancipation*, 14, 17, 35, 37, 112, 336; *Working Class Heroes*, 14–15, 35, 53
"Camouflage" (Ridgeway), 291
camp meetings, 48, 57n7, 328–29
Campaign for Nuclear Disarmament (CND), 110, 292–93
Campbell, Gavin James, 118, 122, 136n26
Campbell, Ian, 283, 293
Cantwell, Robert, 316
capitalism, 14, 23, 28, 47, 97, 143, 146, 333
Carson, Eddie, 311–12
Carter, Asa, 201
Caruso, Enrico, 54

Castro, Fidel, 208–9
Central Intelligence Agency (CIA), 195–97, 200, 203–4, 209–10, 213, 221–22
Chain Gang (White), 304
Chambers Brothers, 6, 8
Chappell Music, 161
Charles, Ray, 187, 311–12, 317
Charters, Samuel, 65–66, 316
Chartist Hymns, 112
Chase, Gilbert, 51, 334, 336–37
"Cheek to Cheek" (Berlin), 159
Child, Francis James, 7, 39, 106–7, 151
Chybowski, Julia, 118, 124, 132, 137n43, 138nn63–64
Cimbala, Paul A., 41–44
civil rights movement, 7, 12, 65
Clash (band), 56–57
Clef Club Orchestra, 175
"Clerk Saunders" (Scott), 106
Cohan, George M., 161
Cohen, Norm, 87
Cohen, Ronald, 52
Cold War: and civil rights, 195–96; cultural legacies of, 212–14; early years, 194–95; and international broadcasting, 207–9; and proxy wars, 271; songs of, 292–94
Collette, Buddy, 175–76
Collier, Jeremy, 3
Columbia Records, 6, 8
communism, 197, 271, 285, 292
community singing, 37, 48
"Compared to What?" (McDaniels), 322
Cone, Edward T., 223
Cone, James, 301
Conforth, Bruce, 66, 82
Connolly, James, 14–15, 35, 56
Connor, Bull, 211
Conover, Willis, 195–96, 198–200, 212
Conrad, Earl, 79, 83
Cooke, James Francis, 121, 130, 132, 139n88
Copland, Aaron, 49
Cotton, James, 310
Country Blues, The (Charters), 316
Courlander, Harold, 81–82
Cousin Joe, 309
Cove, Nellie, 128
Crite, Sylvia, 313
Crosby, Stills, Nash and Young, 291
Crudup, Arthur, 189, 309–10, 317

Cuba, 208–9, 311, 327
Cullen, Countee, 69
Culture Industry (Adorno), 337
Cunard, Nancy, 69, 78–79
Cusick, Suzanne G., chapter by, 217

Dalhart, Vernon, 54
"Danger Zone, The" (Mayfield), 311–12, 317
Dangerous Melodies (Rosenberg), viii
Darby, W. Dermot, 332
"Darling Nelly Gray" (Hanby), 51
Davis, Angela, 303–4
"D-Day Dodgers, The" (song), 269–70, 295, 297n3
De Francesco, Joey La Neve, 169, 191n4
Debord, Guy, 25, 337
Delmore Brothers, 277
Denning, Michael, viii, 20–21, 65
Densmore, Frances, 130
"Devastating Bombs, The" (Carson), 311–12
Dietrich, Marlene, 282
Dillard, James E., chapter by, 194
DiMaggio, Paul, 122–23
disco, 177–78
Dixon, Shirli, 305
Dixon, Willie: antiwar sentiments of, 306–7; career/blues philosophy of, 300–303, 305–6, 316–17; "Hoochie Coochie Man," 305; *I Am the Blues* (album/autobiography), 302; "It Don't Make Sense (You Can't Make Peace)," 300, 302, 306; "It's in the News," 302; mainstream recognition of, 316; *Mighty Earthquake and Hurricane* (album), 300; *Peace?* (album), 302; "Spoonful," 305; "Study War No More," 302–3. *See also* blues and war protest
Donaldson, Walter, 161
Dorson, Richard, 86
Douglas, Memphis Minnie, 167
Douglass, Ada B., 126
Douglass, Frederick, 50
Dowd, Tom, 187
Dr. Dre, 220
Dransfield, Robin, 292–93
Dresser, Paul, 161
Dreyfus, Max, 161
Du Bois, W. E. B., 13, 17, 69, 202, 307
Dulles, Allen, 210
Dulles, John Foster, 204, 206, 209–10

Dunaway, David, viii
Dunham, Katherine, 20, 200
Dupree, Champion Jack, 315
D'Urfey, Thomas, 104
Dylan, Bob, 6–7, 177, 237, 252, 283–84

Eaklor, Vicki Lynn, 50
Eanes, Jim, 280
Edward B. Marks (music publisher), 153
Edwards, David "Honeyboy," 309
Eisenhower, Dwight D., 196, 202, 204, 206–7, 209–11
Ellington, Duke, 173, 195, 198–99, 201, 204, 211–12
Ellis, Bill, 286
Elson, Louis C., 147, 332
Eminem, 220, 226–27
Encyclopaedia of Music, An (Moore), 331
English and Scottish Popular Ballads, The (Child), 106
Epstein, Dena J., 39–40, 57n7
Eras Tour (Swift), 233
Ertegun, Ahmet, 187–88
Ervin, Frankie, 309–10
Estes, Adam, 311
Etude, The (journal), 117–40, *118*, *122*, *129*, *133*; American musical culture and, 117, 121, 123, 131–32; canon formation and clubwomen, 125–30, 137n46, 138nn63–64; founding and growth of, 119–24, 135n15, 136n31, 136n33; impact of, 132–34; musical hierarchy and, 124–25, 127, 132, 137n50; overview, 117–19; popular music's encroachment into, 130–31, 139n83; Presser on the success of, 124; readership decline, 132; tastemakers and, 121–22; World War I and, 131–32, 139n87
Europe, James, 175
Evans, David, 87
"Everybody Is Crying About Vietnam" (Lenoir), 313

Falay, Muvaffak, 206
Fallujah, Iraq, 29, 219
Farrakhan, Louis, 303
Farrar and Rinehart (publisher), 72–74
Farwell, Arthur, 130, 332
Fava, Maria Cristina, viii
Feather, Leonard, 195

Feist, Leo, 146
Finck, Henry T., 119, 121
Fleischer, Rasmus, 240
Fletcher, Alice, 130
"Floo'ers o' the Forest" (song), 267, 295
Foley, Barbara, 69
folk music, 27, 98, 107
"Folk Music as a Source of Social History" (Seeger), 334
Folk Song of the American Negro (Work), 40, 332–33
Ford Foundation, 171
"Forgotten Men" (song), 280–81
French, Rochelle, *76*
French music, 326–27
Fugs (band), vii

Garabedian, Steven, chapters by, 61, 300
Garrison, Lucy McKim, 331
Gaughan, Dick, 293–94, 296
Gellert, Ernest, 82
Gellert, Hugo, 63, 68–73, 82
Gellert, James, 69, 90n2
Gellert, Lawrence, 61–96, *69*, *81*, *88*; African American peers and, 61, 71–77, 82; as ally in racial fight, 79; Black musical protest and, 62–66; disappearance/death of, 62, 90n2; early life, 68; FBI investigation of, 82; Folkway Records and, 81–82; Hughes encounter with, 83–84; *Me and My Captain: Chain Gang* (songbook), 68; "Negro Songs of Protest" (article series), 63–65, 69, 72, 86; newspaper work, 86; overview, 61–62; parallels to James's work, 87–90; Reuss interviews with, 81, 87; Rockefeller Foundation grant, 80; Silber's denial of, 66–67; travel with Brown and Cunard, 78–79; in Tryon, 68; uprooting from folklore, 85–90; "A West Point 'Sacred Tradition'" (article), 84–85; WWII service of, 80–81. See also *Negro Songs of Protest*
Gellert, Otto, 69
Gerald of Wales, 339
Gershwin, George, 130, 148, 158, 161
Getz, Stan, 198
Giddens, Rhiannon, 108
Gillespie, Dizzy, 195, 198, 201–7, 210, 212
Gilroy, Paul, 200

Ginsberg, Allen, vii
"Give Me a 32-20" (Crudup), 309
Glazier, Mitch, 242
Gleason, Ralph J., vii
"God, Please Protect America" (Osborne), 273
Gold, Michael, 69, 71
Goldberg, Isaac, 146, 152–53, 256, 333
Golden Trade (Jobson), 339
Goldmark, Daniel, 149–50
Goodman, Benny, 173, 202, 206–7, 210
"Got My Call Card" (Lawson), 310–11
Gould, Nathaniel D., 331
Grainger, Percy, 99, 107, 113n9
Grange, Lucien, 238
Grassmuck, Volker, 244
Great Awakenings, 329
Greenway, John, 85–86
Groom, Bob, 309, 311
"Grunt" (Ellis), 286
Guantanamo Bay, 220, 227–28
Guthrie, Arlo, 289
Guthrie, Woody, 6, 15–16, 35, 52, 65, 110, 185, 281–82, 297n9
Gutterson, John H., 123

Haggart, Blayne, 157
Hair, Ray, 169
Hamm, Charles, 148–49, 336
Hampton, Lionel, 198, 201, 203, 211
Hanby, Benjamin, 50–51
Handcox, John, 16, 18, 53
Hard Hitting Songs for Hard-Hit People (Lomax, Guthrie, Seeger), 15–16, 35, 52–53, 111
Hardcastle, Paul, 291
Harms, Witmark, and Remick (music publisher), 161
Harris, Charles K., 149, 152–53
Harvard University, 39
Hawaii and Hawaiian music, 323, 326
Hayes, Phillip, 328
"Heartsick Soldier on Heartbreak Ridge, A" (Tubb), 277, 279
heavy metal, 178, 227
Henrion, Paul, 154
Herbert, Victor, 157–58, 161
"Here's the Tender Coming" (song), 269, 295
Herman, Woody, 198
Herron, Isaac, 242

Hickerson, Joe, 283
Higginson, Thomas W., 331
Hill, Joe, 52, 110
Hill and Range (publisher), 189
hip-hop, 23, 38, 177–78
History of American Music, The (Elson), 147, 332
History of Church Music in America, A (Gould), 331
History of Music in America (Ritter), 331–32
Hobsbawm, Eric, 31n4
Holiday, Billie, 20–21, 65, 303
"Hoochie Coochie Man" (Dixon), 305
Hood, G., 330
Hooker, John Lee, 309, 313–15, 317
Hopkins, Sam "Lightnin'," 309–11
House Un-American Activities Committee (HUAC), 7, 82–83, 281, 283
Howard, John Tasker, 333–34
Hubbard, W. L., 332
Huber, Patrick, 52
Hughes, Langston, 61, 69–76, 78–79, 82–84, 307, 315
Huneker, James, 121, 124
Hungarian Revolution (1956), 207–8
Hurston, Zora Neale, 69, 74–76, 75, 79, 91n3
Hutchinson Family Singers, 38, 50–51

I Am the Blues (Dixon), 302
"I Don't Wanna Go to Vietnam" (Hooker), 315, 317
"I'd Leave My Happy Home for You" (Von Tilzer), 153–54
"I'd Rather Live Like a Hermit" (song), 309–10
"I-Feel-Like-I'm-Fixing-to-Die Rag" (McDonald), 288–89, 296
"I'll Be Waiting for You" (James), 280
"I'm Gonna Dig Myself a Hole" (Crudup), 309, 317
"I'm in Korea" (Lenoir), 279
"In the Shade of the Old Apple Tree" (Williams), 161
Inaba, Mitsutoshi, 305
India, 252–53
International Conference of Symphony and Opera Musicians (ICSOM), 169–70
International Federation of Phonographic Industries (IFPI), 235–36, 248, 250

International Folk Music Alliance, 185
Iran, 203–4, 207, 213
Iraq, 29, 204, 207, 213, 219–20
Irish rebel songs, 55–56
Issa, Darryl, 239
"It Don't Make Sense (You Can't Make Peace)" (Dixon), 300, 302, 306
"It's in the News" (Dixon), 302
I.W.W. Songs to fan the flames of discontent (songbook), 110

Jackie Doll and his Pickled Peppers, 274–75
Jackson, Matt, 156–57
Jagger, Mick, 316
James, Joni, 280
James, Willis Laurence, 87–90
James Connolly's Songs of Freedom (Callahan), 14–15, 35
jazz, vii–viii, 21, 29, 38, 130, 173, 176–77, 206, 212
jazz ambassadors, 194–216; Armstrong's African tour, 209–11; background, 194–95; cultural legacies of, 212–14; dual role of, 198–200; Ellington's influence as, 211–12; emergence of, 195–96; government's race narrative and, 201–5; modern jazz and, 200–201; success of, 205–7
Jean-Pierre, Karine, 238
Jerome H. Remick and Co. (music publisher), 161
Jim Crow America (Conrad), 79, 83
"Jim Crow Train" (song), 304
Jobson, Richard, 339
Johnson, Francis, 40–41
Johnson, Guy B., 75
Johnson, Hall, 61, 77, 77, 88–89
Johnson, James, 104–5
Johnson, Lyndon, 174, 312
Johnson, Plas, 176
Johnson, Sherman, 311
Johnston, Tom, 3
Jones, LeRoi (Amiri Baraka), 22, 335–36
Jones, Quincy, 205–6
Joplin, Scott, 54
Journal of American Folklore, 86–87
Jubilee Singers, 331

Karpeles, Maud, 107–8
Keating, Kenneth, 55
Kelley, Robin D. G., 70

Kellum, Kay, 279
Kennedy, John F., 208–9, 211–12, 311
Kern, Jerome, 148, 161
King, Martin Luther, Jr., 203, 291, 307
King, Sahpreem A., 241
"Kingdom's Coming" (Work), 51
"Koloda-Duda" (song), 282
Korall, Burt, 199
"Korea Blues" (Lenoir), 313
"Korean Mud" (Britt), 277–78
Korean War and music, 272–81; emotional distress, songs of, 279–81; historical background, 270–72; overview, 272; patriotic songs, 273–76; religious faith, songs of, 278–79; soldiers in battle, songs of, 276–78
Kovacs, Bela, 208
Krehbiel, Henry Edward, 332
Krueger, Alan, 252
Kuti, Fela, 3

La Vallee-Poussin, Etienne de, 208
labor movement, music of, 52–57
Landrum-Griffin Act (1959), 174
Lawson, L. B., 310–11
"Lay Down Late" (song), 70
Leavitt, Rod, 206
Lenoir, J. B., 279, 310, 312–13
Leo Feist Inc. (music publisher), 161
Leonard, Aaron, 82
Levine, Lawrence, 118
Lewis, George, 32n5
Library of Congress, 54
Lili'uokalanhi (Hawaiian queen), 326
Little Rock crisis (1957), 209–10
Live Nation Entertainment (LNE), 254
Lloyd, A. L., 110
Locke, Alain, 17, 69, 75
Lockwood, Robert, 309
Lomax, Alan, 7, 15–16, 35, 65–66, 74, 79, 80, 82, 281
Lomax, John, 79, 151, 333
Long, Worth, 305
Long Memory (Berry, Blassingame), 303
"Lost in Korea" (Johnson), 311
Louvin Brothers, 278–79
Lovell, John, Jr., 17, 33n26, 336
Luandrew, Albert "Sunnyland Slim," 309
Lumumba, Patrice, 210
Lynskey, Dorian, 233, 296

M. Witmark and Sons (music publisher), 160–61
MacArthur, Douglas, 274–75
MacColl, Ewan, 110, 283
MacDowell, Edward, 130
Maddox, Sylvia, 313
Making of a Counter Culture (Roszak), 5, 11
Makowicz, Adam, 199
Malone, Michael E., 32n5
"Mamma Talk to Your Daughter" (Lenoir), 313
"Man's a Man for A' That, A" (Burns), 104–5
"Marching Through Georgia" (Work), 51
Marcus, Greil, 56
Mardin, Arif, 206
Marks, Edward, 146
Marsh, J. B. T., 331
Marshall, Thurgood, 196
"Masters of War" (Dylan), 283–84, 295–96
Mathews, W. S. B., 121, 123
Maus, Fred, 223
Mayfield, Percy, 312
McCann, Les, 322
McCarthyism, 7, 20–21, 55, 281
McClary, Susan, 337
McClintock, Harry, 52
McCourt, Tom, 243
McCoy, Alfred W., 221
McDaniels, Gene, 322
McDonald, Country Joe, 288–89
McGill, P., 109
Me and My Captain: Chain Gang (Gellert), 68
Meeropol, Abel, 65
Memphis Slim, 315
Metallica, 219–20, 227
Mighty Earthquake and Hurricane (Dixon), 300
Miles, Luke "Long Gone," 311
Military Commissions Act (2006), 222
Miller, John, 180–81
Miller, Karl Hagstrom, 45
"Missing in Action" (Eanes), 280, 310
Mitchell, Billy, 206
Mitchell, Joni, 3
Mohammed, Benyan, 220
Moore, Frances, 235
Moore, John W., 331
Motown, 177
Mulder, Catherine, 181
Mules and Men (Hurston), 76, 91n3

Murrow, Edward R., 208
music, replacement of, 35–60; background, 35–36; blackface minstrelsy, 50–52, 57n18; criteria for, 36–37; labor movement, 52–57; music categorization, 38–39; music industry/academy, 39; popular music-making, 47–49; slave songs, 37–38, 40–47
music and the American state: ambassador's speech, 18–23; baby boom generation, 3–6; controversy of, vii–x; historical background, 12–18; music academy, 6–8; music industry, 8–9; music journalism, 9–11; music-state rivalry, 11–12, 24–26; Unholy Trinity, 6, 12, 14, 16. *See also specific topics*
Music and Some Highly Musical People (Trotter), 40–41, 331
music and war, 265–99; 1960–70s counterculture, 290–92; antihegemonic perspective, 281–84; Cold War, 292–94; conclusion, 294–96; historical antiwar songs, 267–70; introduction, 265–67. *See also* Korean War and music; Vietnam War and music; *and specific artists and songs*
music as torture/weapon, 217–32; acoustic weapons, 218–19; and the blogosphere, 224–28; detainee interrogations, 219–20; interrogation scene, 228–30; introduction, 217–18; music culture and, 222–24; no-touch torture, 220–22
music business, contemporary, 233–64; AI and, 235–39; author's reflections on, 254–56; digital developments, studies on, 243–45; early digital innovations, 239–42; expansion in, 252–54; features and characteristics of, 249–52; major labels, 245–49; wealth in, 233–35
Music Business Worldwide (website), 237
music curation, 97–116; conclusion, 111–13; historical perspective, 100–103; performance and perpetuation, 98–100; selection rationales and ideologies, 103–11; Unholy Trinity and, 97–98
music festivals, 4, 8, 184–85, 192n21
Music in America (Farwell, Darby, eds.), 332
Music in the New World (Hamm), 336
music industry, 141–66; alliances and market concentration, 160–62; ASCAP, 157–60; conclusion, 162–63; music copyright, 153–57; music entrepreneurs, 145–46;

music promotion, 152–53; origins of, 141–43; pianos, 146–47; popular songs, 143–45; popular songwriters, 147–51
Music Modernization Act (MMA, 2018), 239, 250
Musical Courier, The (journal), 123
Musical History of New England, A (Hood), 330
Musical Review, The (journal), 330
Musicians Guild, 170, 191n4
"Muskrat Ramble" (Ory), 289
Mutual Assured Destruction (MAD), 275, 292
"My Love Is Like a Red, Red Rose" (Burns), 104–5
"My Old New Hampshire Home" (Von Tilzer), 153–54
My People (Ellington), 211

Napster (P2P service), 241, 243–44
Nash, Michael, 236
Nasser, Gamal Abdel, 204–5
National Association for the Advancement of Colored People (NAACP), 201, 308
Native Americans, 130, 326
Negro: An Anthology (Cunard), 69, 78–79
Negro and His Songs, The (Odum, Johnson), 75
Negro Caravan, The (Brown, Davis, Lee, eds.), 79, 89
"Negro Folk Expression" (Brown), 79
Negro Folk Rhymes (Talley), 40, 44–46, 333
Negro Poetry and Drama (Brown), 78
Negro Slave Revolts in the United States 1526–1860 (Aptheker), 16–17, 38
"Negro Songs of Protest" (Gellert, article series), 63–65, 69, 72, 86
Negro Songs of Protest (Gellert, songbook): about, 69–70; Gellert on project origins, 72; Hughes's preface to, 71–74; performances/recordings of, 70, 74, 78; reviews of, 77–78, 86–87; "Sistren an' Brethren," 63–65; "Went to Atlanta," 62–63
Negro spirituals, 39–40, 329, 331
Negro Workaday Songs (Odum, Johnson), 75
Nettleingham, F. T., 109
New Jubilee Songs and Folk Songs of the American Negro (Work), 333
New Jubilee Songs as Sung by the Fisk Jubilee Singers (Work), 332–33

New Masses (magazine), 68–69, 71–72, 81, 86
New Song, A (Hughes), 71
New World Symphony, 171
Ngũgĩ Wa Thiong'o, 11–12, 18, 24–25
Niles, John Jacob, 67
"19" (Hardcastle), 291
Noise Uprising (Denning), viii
Nuzum, Eric, 32n6
Nye, Joseph, and "soft power," 18, 22, 98

"O Frankerych" (song), 267–68, 295
Ochs, Phil, 283, 287–88
Odum, Howard W., 75, 333
"Ohio" (Crosby, Stills, Nash and Young), 291
"Old Family Bible, The" (Osborne), 278
"Old soldiers never die" (song), 275
Old Town School of Folk Music, 182
"Old Weird America, The" (Marcus), 56
"On the Banks of the Wabash, Far Away" (Dresser), 161
On the Beach (Shute), 292
On the Trail of Negro Folk-Songs (Scarborough), 63–64
O'Neal, Jim, 316
Ory, Babette, 289
Ory, Kid, 289
Osborne, Jimmie, 273–76, 278
Osborne, Sonny, 277
Our American Music (Howard), 333–34
"Over There" (song), 288

Padmore, George, 69
Page, Will, 234, 249
Palmer, Earl, 176
Parizot, Victor, 154
Patterson, William L., 308
Peace? (Dixon), 302
Peer, Ralph, 54
peer-to-peer (P2P) file-sharing, 240, 243–44, 254–55
Penpoints, Gunpoints, and Dreams (Ngũgĩ Wa Thiong'o), 24–25
People Songs Bulletin (songbook), 282
Peterson, Oscar, 198
Petrillo, James, 168
Phillips, Kimberley, 307
Phillips, Sam, 311
pianos, 146–47
Piracy Crusade, The (Sinnreich), 248

"Plains of Waterloo, The" (song), 268, 295
Plato, *Republic*, vii–viii, 9, 24–25
"Please Send Me Someone to Love" (Mayfield), 312
"Poor Man's Blues" (Smith), 303–4, 308
popular songs: as a consumer commodity, 143–45; definition of, 49; film industry and, 162; form and structure, 148–49; genres, 149; pre-1880, 147–48; sentimental ballads, 149–50
popular songwriters, 147–50
Porter, Cole, 161
"Post-War Future Blues" (Cousin Joe), 309
Powell, Stewart, 276–77
"Practice of Refusal in Willis Laurence James's Song Collecting, The" (Azoulay), 87, 90
"Preacher and the Slave, The" (Hill), 52
Presser, Theodore, 119–21, 122, 132. See also *Etude, The*
Presser Publishers, 120–21
Priestley, J. B., 266
"Prisoner of War, A" (Eanes), 280
Proletarian Literature in the United States, 71
"Promises of Freedom" (song), 46
Propper, Irving, 159–60
Puerto Rico, 327
punk music, 178
Puritans, 47–48

Qahtani, Mohammed Al-, 220
Quakers, 48, 328
Queen (band), 252
Question of Torture, A (McCoy), 221
quills (musical instrument), 45

racism, 43–44, 50
Radio Free Europe (RFE), 196–97, 199
Radio Liberty (RL), 196–97
Radio Swan, 209
ragtime, 125–26, 131, 172–73
Rainey, Gertrude "Ma," 303
rap music, 38, 220, 226–27
Rawick, George, 44
Reagan, Ronald, 294, 300
Recording Industry Association of America (RIAA), 239, 250
Recording Musicians Association (RMA), 169–71

"Recruited Collier, The" (song), 269, 295
Reno, Don, 280–81
Representing African Music (Agawu), 338–41
Reuss, Joanne, 7, 55
Reuss, Richard, 7, 55, 70–71, 81, 87
rhythm and blues, 31n4, 38
Rhythm and Blues Foundation, 188
Ridgeway, Stan, 291
Riegger, Wallingford, 69
Ritter, Frederic Louis, 331–32
Road to Guantanamo, The (film), 229
Roberts, Brian, 51
Roberts, Michael James, 169, 176–77
Roberts, Myron, 32n5
Robertson, Sidney, 18
Robeson, Paul, 6, 20, 52, 61, 70, *70*, 74, 82–84, 85, 86, 195, 202
rock 'n' roll, vii–viii, 4–5, 10, 31n4, 32n6, 176–77, 315
Rogers, Jim, chapters by, 141, 233
Rogers, Jimmy, 309
Rolling Stone (magazine), 10, 237–38, 247
Rosenberg, Jonathan, viii
Roszak, Theodore, 5, 11
"Rotation Blues, The" (Powell), 276–77
Rubinson, David, 4, 8
Ruby, Harry, 147
"Run, N----r, Run" (song), 42
Rustin, Bayard, 304

Sacred Harp, The (songbook), 47
"Sad News from Korea" (Hopkins), 310
Sainte-Marie, Buffy, 287
Samuelson, Dave, 52
Scarborough, Dorothy, 63–64
Schneider, Cynthia, 18–22
Schomburg, Arthur, 69
Schuyler, George S., 69
Scott, Walter, 104–6
Seattle Symphony, 171
Seeger, Charles, viii–x, 7, 18, 25, 334, 336–37
Seeger, Peggy, 281
Seeger, Pete, 15–16, 35, 53, 65, 110, 112, 185, 281–83, 295
Segregating Sounds (Miller), 45
Selling Sounds (Suisman), 333
Shakers, 49, 328
shape-note singing, 47
Shapiro, Bernstein and Co., 145, 161–62

Shapiro, Maurice, 154
Sharp, Cecil, 7, 107–8
Shaw, Arnold, 163
Shaw, Artie, 173
Sherwood, William, 121
Sholokhov, Mikhail, 282
Shreffler, Anne, 137n46
Shute, Nevil, 292
Siegmeister, Elie, 69, 74
Silber, Irwin, 65–68
Simone, Nina, 315
Simpson, Joshua McCarter, 38, 50–51
Sinful Tunes and Spirituals (Epstein), 39–40, 57n7
Sinnreich, Aram, 247–48
"Sistren an' Brethren" (song), 63–65
slave revolts, 16, 38, 112
slave songs, 37–38, 40–47
Slave Songs of the United States (Allen, Garrison, Ware), 331
slaveowners, 42, 329
slavery, 38, 41, 44
Smiley, Red, 280–81
Smith, Bessie, 303–4, 308
Smith, Fanny Morris, 127
Smith, Harry, 33n22, 54, 56, 333
Smith, Mamie, 54
Smith, Margaret, 105
Snapes, Laura, 242
"Social Implications of the Negro Spiritual" (Lovell), 17, 336
Society of the Spectacle (Debord), 337
soft power, 18, 21–22, 32n20, 98, 196, 204–5
Soldier Songs (McGill), 109
Solomon, Mark, 70
Songs of Freedom (Connolly), 14–15, 35, 56
Songs of Slavery and Emancipation (Callahan), 14, 17, 35, 37, 112
Sonneck, Oscar, 332, 334
Sony Music Entertainment, 234, 248–53
Sousa, John Philip, 130, 157
Southern, Eileen, 40, 331
Southern Exposure (White), 304
Southland (Dunham), 200
Soviet Union (Union of Soviet Socialist Republics), 194, 197–98, 208–9
Spears, Britney, 227
Spencer, Herbert, 141
Spingarn, Arthur B., 79

Spirituals and the Blues, The (Cone), 301
Spivak, John, 69
"Spoonful" (Dixon), 305
Springsteen, Bruce, 252, 282, 291
Stars in de Elements (A Study of Negro Folk Music) (James), 88–90
"Star-Spangled Banner, The" (song), 337, 342n9
Stearns, Marshall, 206
"Steel Got to Be Drove" (song), 86
Steinbeck, John, 15, 65
Stern, Joseph, 145–46
Story of the Jubilee Singers, The (Marsh), 331
"Strange Fruit" (Meeropol), 65
Strayhorn, Billy, 198
streaming, of music, 237, 241–42, 244–45, 248, 252–53, 255
Stringer, Rob, 236
Stroman, Elissa, chapter by, 117
Stuckey, Sterling, 336
"Study War No More" (Dixon), 302–3
Suisman, David, 144–46, 149, 152, 333
"Sun Is Burning, The" (Campbell), 293, 295
Suno (AI music service), 239, 248
Sweers, Britta, chapters by, 265, 344
Swift, Taylor, 233–34, 238, 245, 253
Szwed, John, 64–65

T. B. Harms (music publisher), 161
Taft-Hartley Act (1947), 55, 174
"Take the A Train" (Strayhorn), 198–99
"Talking Vietnam Blues" (Ochs), 287–88
Talley, Thomas, 40, 44–46, 87–88, 333
Tams, John, 110
Tanous, Will, 235–36
Taylor, Herbert, 150
teenagers, vii, 32n5
Tell Tchaikovsky the News (Roberts), 176
"Thank God for the Victory in Korea" (Osborne), 274
Tharpe, Sister Rosetta, 46, 276
"That's All Right Mama" (Crudup), 189
"There Is Mean Things Happenin' in This Land" (Handcox), 18
"There Is Peace in Korea" (song), 276
"Think Again" (Gaughan), 293–94, 296
33 Revolutions per Minute (Lynskey), 296
"This Land Is Nobody's Land" (Hooker), 313–15

"This Land Is Your Land" (Guthrie), 282
Thomas, Leon, 315
Thomas, Theodore, 119, 130
Thompson, Stith, 86
Thomson, George, 104
"Through the Prism of Folklore" (Stuckey), 336
"Time Has Come Today" (Chambers Brothers), 8
Tin Pan Alley, 39, 45, 112, 144, 148–50, 161–63
Tin Pan Alley (Goldberg), 256, 333
Tortured Poets Department, The (Swift, album), 233
Trotter, James Monroe, 40–41, 56, 331
Truman, Harry S., 195–97, 275, 308, 310
Tubb, Ernest, 279

Udio (AI music service), 239, 248
UMusic Hotels, 247
Unholy Trinity, 6, 12, 14, 16, 97–98
Union of Musicians and Allied Workers (UMAW), 189–90
Union of Soviet Socialist Republics. *See* Soviet Union
Unions and Class Transformation (Mulder), 181
Universal Music Group (UMG), 233, 234, 237, 247–53
"Universal Soldier" (Sainte-Marie), 287, 295
US Congress, 174, 186–87, 239
US Information Agency (USIA), 207–8
US State Department: and CIA/VOA, 195–97; jazz tours, 200–207; and soft power, 18, 32–33n20, 194, 196, 204–5. *See also* jazz ambassadors

Van Cleve, J. S., 121
Van Rijn, Guido, 305, 309, 311
Van Ronk, Dave, 110
Vaughan Williams, Ralph, 107
"Viet Nam Blues" (Crite/Maddox), 313
"Vietnam" (Lenoir), 313
Vietnam War and music: antihegemonic perspective, 287–90; blues music, 312–14; cultural impact, 286–87; historical background, 284–86; overview, 284
Voice of America (VOA): criticism of, 200–201; expansion of, 208–9; jazz ambassadors and, 198–200; jazz diplomacy and, 196–97; State Department/CIA and, 195–96
"Voice of Free America, The" (Osborne), 275–76
Von Tilzer, Harry, 145–46, 150–51, 153–54, 161

Wagner Act (1935), 174
Walker, T-Bone, 315
War Heroes (graphic novel), 272
Ward, Brian, 301
Ware, Charles Pickard, 331
Warner Bros., 161–62
Warner Music Group, 234, 247–53
Waterman, Dick, 189
Watts, Isaac, 39, 49, 328
"We Shall Overcome" (Seeger), 8, 282
"Weapon of Prayer" (Louvin Brothers), 278–79
Weavers (band), 7
Weissman, Dick: chapter by, 167; *Which Side Are You On?*, 61
"Went to Atlanta" (song), 62–63
"West Point 'Sacred Tradition': Anti-Negro Violence, A" (Gellert, article), 84–85
West Side Story (Bernstein), 327
Westbrooks, Wesley, 167
Wexler, Jerry, 187
"What Is American Music?" (Bernstein), 334–35
"What's the Matter with the Mill?" (Douglas), 167
"When I Get Back" (Kellum), 279
"When the Mode of Music Changes" (song), vii
"When the Mode of the Music Changes, the Walls of the City Shake" (Ginsberg, essay), vii
"When They Drop the Atomic Bomb" (song), 274–75
"Where Have All the Flowers Gone" (Seeger), 282, 295
White, Josh, 79, 304
Whiteman, Paul, 173
"Why Am I Treated So Bad?" (Westbrooks), 167
Wickes, Edward Michael, 149–50
Wilgus, D. K., 86–87
Williams, Harry H., 161
Williams, Mary Lou, 20, 200

Williams, Robert Pete, 315
Willie Dixon: Preacher of the Blues (Inaba), 305
Wit and Mirth, or Pills to Purge Melancholy (D'Urfey), 104
"With God on Our Side" (Dylan), 283, 297n12
Witmark and Sons (music publisher), 145, 159–61
women and music, 27, 124, 126–29, 138n63
Work, Henry Clay, 38, 49–51
Work, John Wesley, 40, 48, 332–33
"Work All De Summer" (song), 70
Working Class Heroes (Callahan), 14, 15, 35, 53
World War I, 108–9, 111, 131–32, 265–66, 270, 276
World War II, 110, 281–82, 307–8, 314
Wrecking Crew (band), 176
Wright, Richard, 79
Wyatt, Marshall, 52

"Yankee Doodle" (song), 327
Young, Izzy, 81, 86
"Your King and Country Want You" (song), 265–66

www.ingramcontent.com/pod-product-compliance
Lightning Source LLC
Chambersburg PA
CBHW030603230426
43661CB00053B/1817